THE
BEST
BUSINESS
WRITING
2014

Columbia Journalism Review Books

COLUMBIA JOURNALISM REVIEW BOOKS
Series Editors: Victor Navasky, Evan Cornog, Elizabeth Spayd, and the editors of the *Columbia Journalism Review*

For more than fifty years, the *Columbia Journalism Review* has been the gold standard for media criticism, holding the profession to the highest standards and exploring where journalism is headed, for good and for ill.

Columbia Journalism Review Books expands upon this mission, seeking to publish titles that allow for greater depth in exploring key issues confronting journalism, both past and present, and pointing to new ways of thinking about the field's impact and potential.

Drawing on the expertise of the editorial staff at the *Columbia Journalism Review* as well as the Columbia Journalism School, the series of books will seek out innovative voices as well as reclaim important works, traditions, and standards. In doing this, the series will also incorporate new ways of publishing made available by the Web and e-books.

Second Read: Writers Look Back at Classic Works of Reportage, edited by James Marcus and the Staff of the *Columbia Journalism Review*

The Story So Far: What We Know About the Business of Digital Journalism, Bill Grueskin, Ava Seave, and Lucas Graves

The Best Business Writing 2012, edited by Dean Starkman, Martha M. Hamilton, Ryan Chittum, and Felix Salmon

The Art of Making Magazines: On Being an Editor and Other Views from the Industry, edited by Victor S. Navasky and Evan Cornog

The Best Business Writing 2013, edited by Dean Starkman, Martha M. Hamilton, Ryan Chittum, and Felix Salmon

The Watchdog That Didn't Bark: The Financial Crisis and the Disappearance of Investigative Journalism, Dean Starkman

Beyond News: The Future of Journalism, Mitchell Stephens

The New Censorship: Inside the Global Battle for Media Freedom, Joel Simon

THE BEST BUSINESS WRITING

2014

**Edited by
Dean Starkman,
Martha M. Hamilton,
and Ryan Chittum**

Columbia University Press   New York

Columbia University Press
Publishers Since 1893
New York   Chichester, West Sussex
cup.columbia.edu
Copyright © 2014 Columbia University Press
All rights reserved

ISBN 978-0-231-17015-4

Columbia University Press books are printed on permanent and durable
acid-free paper.
This book is printed on paper with recycled content.
Printed in the United States of America

p 10 9 8 7 6 5 4 3 2 1

Cover Design: Noan Arlow

Contents

Part IV. Unhealthy Business

Introduction
Dean Starkman

I t is a commonplace to observe that journalism is going to hell in a hand basket. Its business model collapsing thanks to the intertubes, the newspaper industry—the backbone of American journalism—is half the size it was a decade ago, with more than 15,000 reporters out on the street, in PR, or curating cat videos. The magazine business isn't doing much better. Yes, new digital-news organizations have arrived with different models, new forms, and fresh thinking. But these are, still, small players in the scheme of things—yes, even Buzzfeed—and the amount of labor-intensive fact gathering and painstaking writing they do is a drop in the bucket compared to what has been lost.

Business journalism, that distinctive subculture that deals with the world's money and other knotty issues, is just part of the great mudslide. *Fortune*, Henry R. Luce's brainchild launched on the eve of the Great Depression (1930), has cut back the number of its annual issues from twenty-five to eighteen. In 2014, the Forbes family sold control of the magazine it founded in 1917. The *Wall Street Journal*, swallowed by Rupert Murdoch's giant News Corp. in 2008, has been spun off with the company's other print operations into an uncertain future. *Businessweek*, bought by Bloomberg LP, is still hemorrhaging cash, according to published reports. And so on and so forth.

And yet. We've been doing this book for three years now, and I am here to testify: this is the best edition yet, by an order of magnitude, and the others were pretty darned good. I know I have an interest here, but just flip through the table of contents and see for yourself the extraordinary output from a brilliant array of writers. This book is called *The Best Business Writing* for a reason. There is some fabulous stuff from outlets that didn't exist a decade ago. Take, for instance, Jesse Eisinger's maddening piece in *ProPublica*, the digital nonprofit investigative site, on prosecutors' failure to hold Bank of America accountable for some of its myriad financial-crisis sins. And Steve LeVine writing for *Quartz*, the all-digital, all-business site, is brilliant in his meditative exposé of the collapse of a battery startup that promised GM the first electric car with a 200-mile range, And I defy you to predict where John Gravois is taking us in his exploration of California's artisanal toast craze (yes, you are reading that correctly) in *Pacific Standard*, relaunched in 2012 from the *Miller-McCune* magazine, itself of recent vintage.

Additionally, what we now call "legacy media," what used to be called "newspapers and magazines" (and "public radio"), continue to astonish with stories of depth and insight, compelling narrative, unforgettable characters, and surprises. *Vanity Fair*, first published in 1913 (its current incarnation began in 1983), uses the development of London's One Hyde Park—the world's most expensive apartment building—to explore the London that tourists never see: the London that has become a haven for hiding untold billions from tax and law-enforcement authorities. This is indeed a "Tale of Two Londons," and the epicenter is the City, a redoubt of financial power that is surprisingly insulated from the reach of regulation.

And the *Boston Globe*, founded by Yankee patricians in 1872, still uncorks scathing exposés like that of the "industry of distortion" in Washington. Its leading practitioner, the public-relations impresario Richard Berman, has mastered the art of half-truths and attack ads against popular nonprofits, activists, and consumer groups, on behalf of major industries that don't want to get their hands dirty. "Is Wayne Pacelle the Bernie Madoff of the Charity World?" one Berman-backed ad asks of the head of the Humane Society of the United States. The answer is, emphatically, *No!*, but as Michael Kranish explains, each charge Berman makes can be defended as accurate in the narrowest sense, while the overall picture is almost comically distorted. The *Wall Street Journal* (founded 1889), meanwhile, offers an epic look inside the empire of Bill Gross and his falling-out with his partner and presumed successor, Mohamed El-Erian, at the bond giant PIMCO. Looking for compelling anecdotes? Gregory Zuckerman and Kirsten Grind deliver, including this fight on the trading room floor: " 'I have a forty-one-year track record of investing excellence,' Mr. Gross told Mr. El-Erian, according to the two witnesses. 'What do you have?' 'I'm tired of cleaning up your s———,' Mr. El-Erian responded."

I can offer no sweeping insight into *why* this great journalism keeps happening, despite the wild upheaval in the media business and the vastly diminishing resources that underpin this kind of work. Maybe this rich output is the signal of a dramatic renaissance of business news. Perhaps it's a final flourish before the entire media world dissolves into a miasma of celebrity gossip and listicles. All I can say is that great business journalism *does* keep happening. It's almost like a boxer, having been battered for eight rounds, rallying with a flurry of roundhouse rights and stinging jabs to win back the championship belt.

And a word about business journalism: Leafing through this book, a reader will quickly grasp we define the term broadly. But we do so with a purpose. Business journalism began, historians believe, in the seventeenth century as shipping news and price lists for traders. It advanced with the creation of wire services, which employed messenger boys to ferry scraps of corporate news to and from stock markets. These were vital functions for the growth of commerce and the creation of the free enterprise system. But it was only in the postwar period, accelerating during the go-go 1980s, that business journalism truly moved into the pubic consciousness as great publications, such as the *Journal*, *Fortune*, *Businessweek*, and others, achieved some critical distance from the businesses they covered and broadened their focus to encompass business in all its manifestations and its effects on the wider economic, social, and political worlds. Thus was greatness born in a formerly obscure subculture, and this is the tradition *The Best Business Writing* series seeks to record, preserve, and perpetuate. There are few better commentaries on modern economic life at the bottom of the social scale, I would argue, than Andrea Elliot's gripping profile in the *New York Times* of Dasani, a twelve-year-old homeless girl adrift, with her fragile family, in the homeless-shelter archipelago of New York City. Similarly, it would be hard to find a more compelling look at the Internet economy's nether regions than David Kushner's harrowing profile of Ross Ulbricht, the notorious hacker and entrepreneur behind the twenty-first-century drug-and-gun bazaar known as Silk Road. Indeed, our collection of articles by Susan Faludi, Evgeny Morozov, and Rebecca Solnit offers a comprehensive and thoughtful critique of the technological culture now in ascendance over the American and global economies. And *Frontline*'s documentary "League of Denial" changed the way America talks about the big business known as pro football.

But business journalism's core constituency was and remains businesspeople, those actively engaged in the cut and thrust of corporate life, markets, and profit chasing, and here business journalism can be at its most useful. Henry R. Luce launched *Fortune* in 1930 as a bid to transcend the adversarial muckraking of an earlier era and the boosterism of business journalism in the 1920s to create a new, almost scientific business journalism, one capable of capturing the scale, grandeur, and vitality of business, what he called the "dominant institution of American civilization." "Both of ships and men," Luce wrote, "*Fortune* will attempt to write critically, appraisingly . . . with unbridled curiosity." That culture of arms-length, knowledgeable appraisal is very much represented by the several pieces here documenting how businesses and businesspeople continue to reinvent themselves in the struggle to maintain a competitive edge in a post-crisis age of slow growth and economic uncertainty. Danielle Sacks's look inside J.Crew is a case in point, as is Ashlee Vance's portrayal of the incredible comeback odyssey of the social network pioneer Ramona Pierson.

And make no mistake, the business news renaissance is important for much more than its own sake. Yes, of course, we enjoy these compelling stories for their craftsmanship, their reporting surprises, and their storytelling verve. But business journalism—today more than ever—serves an especially important role in holding a mirror up to a private sector that is playing an increasingly powerful, if not dominant role in shaping our society and our private lives. With government held in low esteem by a broad chunk of the political spectrum and once-powerful unions in eclipse, the power vacuum has been filled by the corporate world, for better and for worse. Whatever your view on this question of political power, never has the need been greater for journalism to step up to provide forthright and unsparing scrutiny of business—in all its intricacies—on behalf of a public that is increasingly confronted with complex problems. Because without public understanding, there is no hope of public input.

Acknowledgments

Dean Starkman thanks Alex, Julian, and his mom.

Ryan Chittum thanks his dad, Paul.

Martha Hamilton thanks Felix Burnett and her mom, Alec Hamilton.

THE
BEST
BUSINESS
WRITING

2014

Part I

Silicon Culture

Frakfurter Allgemeine Zeitung

For a long while, the technology industry evaded criticism even as it assumed an increasingly important and intrusive role in our lives. Now, though, some are waking up to the idea that maybe the tech business isn't as clean or benign as it seems. If they are, it's thanks in large part to Evgeny Morozov, our leading critic of Silicon Valley and its ascendant ideology. What if, he muses, the Post Office decided to send mail for free—on condition it be allowed to open letters, read them, and sell advertising based on their contents? Sounds crazy, doesn't it?

Evgeny Morozov

1. Why We Are Allowed to Hate Silicon Valley

I f Ronald Reagan was the first Teflon President, then Silicon Valley is the first Teflon Industry: no matter how much dirt one throws at it, nothing seems to stick. While "Big Pharma," "Big Food," and "Big Oil" are derogatory terms used to describe the greediness that reigns supreme in those industries, this is not the case with "Big Data." This innocent term is never used to refer to the shared agendas of technology companies. What shared agendas? Aren't these guys simply improving the world, one line of code at a time?

Something odd is going on here. While we understand that the interests of pharmaceutical, food, and oil companies naturally diverge from our own, we rarely approach Silicon Valley with the requisite suspicion. Instead, we continue to treat data as if it were a special, magical commodity that could single-handedly defend itself against any evil genius who dares to exploit it.

Earlier this year, a tiny scratch appeared on the rhetorical Teflon of Silicon Valley. The Snowden affair helped—but so did other events. The world seems to have finally realized that "disruption"—the favorite word of the digital elites—describes a rather ugly, painful phenomenon. Thus, university professors are finally complaining about the "disruption" brought on by the massive open online courses (MOOCs); taxi drivers are finally fighting services like Uber; residents of San Francisco are finally bemoaning the "disruption" of monthly rents in a city that has suddenly been invaded by millionaires. And then, of course, there are the crazy, despicable ideas coming from Silicon Valley itself: the latest proposal, floated by one tech executive at a recent conference, is that Silicon Valley should secede from the country and "build an opt-in society, ultimately outside the United States, run by technology." Let's share his pain: A country that needs a congressional hearing to fix a website is a disgrace to Silicon Valley.

This bubbling discontent is reassuring. It might even help bury some of the myths spun by Silicon Valley. Wouldn't it be nice if one day, told that Google's mission is to "organize the world's information and make it universally accessible and useful," we would finally read between the lines and discover its true meaning: "to monetize all of the world's information and make it universally inaccessible and profitable"? With this act of subversive interpretation, we might eventually hit upon the greatest emancipatory insight of all: Letting Google organize all of the world's information makes as much sense as letting Halliburton organize all of the world's oil.

But any jubilation is premature: Silicon Valley still holds a firm grip on the mechanics of the public debate. As long as our critique remains tied to the plane of technology and information—a plane that is often described by that dreadful, meaningless, overused word "digital"—Silicon Valley will continue to be seen as an exceptional and unique industry. When food activists go after Big Food and accuse those companies of adding too much salt and fat to their snacks to make us crave even more of them, no one dares accuse these activists of being antiscience. Yet a critique of Facebook or Twitter along similar lines—for example, that they have designed their services to play up our anxieties and force us to perpetually click the "refresh" button to get the latest update—almost immediately brings accusations of technophobia and Luddism.

The reason why the digital debate feels so empty and toothless is simple: framed as a debate over "the digital" rather than "the political" and "the economic," it's conducted on terms that are already beneficial to technology companies. Unbeknownst to most of us, the seemingly exceptional nature of commodities in question—from "information" to "networks" to "the Internet"—is coded into our language. It's this hidden exceptionalism that allows Silicon Valley to dismiss its critics as Luddites who, by opposing "technology," "information," or "the Internet"—they don't do plurals in Silicon Valley, for the nuance risks overwhelming their brains—must also be opposed to "progress."

How do you spot "the digital debate"? Look for arguments that appeal to the essences of things—of technology, information, knowledge, and, of course, the Internet itself. Thus, whenever you hear someone say "this law is bad because it will break the Internet" or "this new gadget is good because that's what technology wants," you know that you have left the realm of the political—where arguments are usually framed around the common good—and have entered the realm of bad metaphysics. In that realm, what you are being asked to defend is the well-being of phantom digital gods that function as convenient stand-ins for corporate interests. Why does anything that might "break the Internet" also risk breaking Google? This can't be a coincidence, can it?

Perhaps, we should ditch the technology/progress dialectic altogether. "Is it O.K. to be a Luddite?" ran the title of a fabulous 1984 essay by Thomas Pynchon—a question that he answered, by and large, in the affirmative. This question feels outdated today. "Is it okay not to be a Luddite but still hate Silicon Valley?" is a much better question, for the real enemy is not technology but the present political and economic regime—a wild combination of the military-industrial complex and the out-of-control banking and advertising—that deploys latest technologies to achieve its ugly (even if lucrative and occasionally pleasant) ends. Silicon Valley represents the most visible, the most discussed, and the most naive part of this assemblage. In short, it's okay to hate Silicon Valley—we just need to do it for the right reasons. Below are three of them—but this is hardly an exhaustive list.

The Rhetoric Is as Lofty as It Is Revolutionary

Reason number one: Silicon Valley firms are building what I call "invisible barbed wire" around our lives. We are promised more freedom, more openness, more mobility; we are told we can roam wherever and whenever we want. But the kind of emancipation that we actually get is fake emancipation; it's the emancipation of a just-released criminal wearing an ankle bracelet.

Yes, a self-driving car could make our commute less dreadful. But a self-driving car operated by Google would not just be a self-driving car: it would be a shrine to surveillance—on wheels! It would track everywhere we go. It might even prevent us from going to certain places if our mood—measured through facial expression analysis—suggests that we are too angry or tired or emotional. Yes, there are exceptions—at times, GPS does feel liberating—but the trend is clear: every new Google sensor in that car would introduce a new lever of control. That lever doesn't even have to be exercised to produce changes in our behavior— our knowledge of its presence will suffice.

Or take MOOCs. They would undoubtedly produce many shifts in power relations. We know of all the visible, positive shifts: students getting more, cheaper opportunities to learn; kids in Africa finally taking best courses on offer in America; and so on. But what about the invisible shifts? Take Coursera, a company that was started by a senior Google engineer and that has quickly become one of the leaders in the field. It now uses biometrics— facial recognition and typing speed analysis—to verify student identity. (This comes in handy when they issue diplomas!) How did we go from universities with open-door policies to universities that check their students with biometrics? As Gilles Deleuze put it in a 1990 conversation with Tony Negri, "compared with the approaching forms of ceaseless control in open sites, we may come to see the harshest confinement as part of a wonderful happy past." This connection between the seeming openness of our technological infrastructures and the intensifying degree of control remains poorly understood.

What does this invisible barbed wire mean in practice? Suppose you want to become a vegetarian. So you go to Facebook and use its Graph Search feature to search for the favorite vegetarian restaurants of all your friends who live nearby. Facebook understands that you are considering an important decision that will affect several industries: great news for the tofu industry but bad news for the meat section of your local supermarket.

Facebook would be silly not to profit from this knowledge—so it organizes a real-time ad auction to see whether the meat industry wants you more than the tofu industry. This is where your fate is no longer in your own hands. Sounds silly—until you enter your local supermarket and your smartphone shows that the meat section offers you a discount of 20 percent. The following day, as you pass by the local steak house, your phone buzzes again: you've got another discount offer. Come in—have some steak! After a week of deliberation—and lots of cheap meat—you decide that vegetarianism is not your thing. Case closed.

Of course, had the tofu industry won the ad auction, things might have gone in the opposite direction. But it doesn't matter who wins the auction. What matters is that a decision that seems fully autonomous is not autonomous at all. You feel liberated and empowered; you might even write a thank-you note to Mark Zuckerberg. But this is laughable: you are simply at the mercy of the highest bidder. And they are bidding to show you an ad that matters—an ad based on everything that Facebook knows about your anxieties and insecurities. It's not your bland, one-dimensional advertising anymore.

This example is hardly the product of my wild imagination: Last year, Facebook struck a deal with a company called Datalogix, which would allow it to tie what you buy at your local supermarket to ads that Facebook shows you. Google already has an app—Google Field—which constantly scans shops and restaurants in your area for latest deals. Nothing in this example hinges upon a hatred of technology or information: we are dealing here with political economy, advertising, autonomy. What does this have to do with the "digital debate"? Very little.

The data-centric model of Silicon Valley capitalism seeks to convert every aspect of our everyday existence—what used to be our only respite from the vagaries of work and the anxieties of the marketplace—into a productive asset. This is done not just by blurring the distinction between work and nonwork but also by making us tacitly accept the idea that our reputation is a work-in-progress—something that we could and should be honing 24/7. Therefore, everything is turned into a productive asset: our relationships, our family life, our vacations, our sleep (you are now invited to "hack" it so that you can get most of your sleep in the shortest amount of time).

The rhetoric attached to such "breakthroughs" is as lofty as it is revolutionary, especially when mixed with subjects like "the sharing economy." "This is the first stage of something more profound, which is the ability of people to structure their lives around doing multiple sharing economy activities as a choice in lieu of a nine-to-five, five-day-a-week job," said Arun Sundararajan, a professor at New York University and a big fan of "the sharing economy," in a recent interview. "This is technology-driven progress. This is what it's all about," he added. Oh yes, "progress" has never felt so good: who doesn't like working 24-7 instead of 9-5?

When Privacy Is Becoming Expensive

Reason number two: Silicon Valley has destroyed our ability to imagine other models for running and organizing our communication infrastructure. Forget about models that aren't based on advertising and that do not contribute to the centralization of data on private servers located in America. To suggest that we need to look into other—perhaps even publicly provided alternatives—is to risk being accused of wanting to "break the Internet." We have succumbed to what the Brazilian social theorist Roberto Unger calls "the dictatorship of no alternatives": we are asked to accept that Gmail is the best and only possible way to do e-mail, and that Facebook is the best and only possible way to do social networking.

But consider just how weird our current arrangement is. Imagine I told you that the post office could run on a different, innovation-friendly business model. Forget stamps. They cost money—and why pay money when there's a way to send letters for free? Just think about the world-changing potential: the poor kids in Africa can finally reach you with their pleas for more laptops! So, instead of stamps, we would switch to an advertising-backed system: we'd open every letter that you send, scan its contents, insert a relevant ad, seal it, and then forward it to the recipient.

Sounds crazy? It does. But this is how we have chosen to run our e-mail. In the wake of the NSA scandal and the debacle that is Healthcare.gov, trust in public institutions runs so low that any alternative arrangement—especially the one that would give public institutions a greater role—seems unthinkable. But this is only part of the problem. What would happen when some of our long cherished and privately run digital infrastructure begins to crumble as companies evolve and change their business models?

Five years ago, one could still publish silly little books with titles like *What Would Google Do?* on the assumption that the company had a coherent and mostly benevolent philosophy, eager to subsidize unprofitable services just because it could. After Google shut down Google Reader and many other popular services, this benevolence can no longer be taken for granted. In the next two-three years, there would come a day when Google would announce that it's shutting down Google Scholar—a free but completely unprofitable service—that abets millions of academics worldwide. Why aren't we preparing for this eventuality by building a robust publicly run infrastructure? Doesn't it sound ridiculous that Europe can produce a project like CERN but seems incapable of producing an online service to keep track of papers written about CERN? Could it be because Silicon Valley has convinced us that they are in the magic industry?

Now that our communication networks are in the hands of the private sector, we should avoid making the same mistake with privacy. We shouldn't reduce this complex problem to market-based solutions. Alas, thanks to Silicon Valley's entrepreneurial zeal, privatization is already creeping in. Privacy is becoming a commodity. How does one get privacy these days? Just ask any hacker: only by studying how the right tools work. Privacy is no longer something to be taken for granted or enjoyed for free: you have to expend some resources to master the tools. Those resources could be money, patience, attention—you might even hire a consultant to do all this for you—but the point is that privacy is becoming expensive.

And what of those who can't afford tools and consultants? How do their lives change? When the founder of a prominent lending start-up—the former CIO of Google, no less—proclaims that "all data is credit data, we just don't know how to use it yet," I can't help but fear the worst. If "all data is credit data" and poor people cannot afford privacy, they are in for some dark times. How can they not be anxious when their every move, their every click, their every phone call could be analyzed to predict if they deserve credit and at what rates? If the burden of debt wasn't agonizing enough, now we'll have to live with the fact that, for the poor people, anxiety begins well before they get the actual loan. Once again, one doesn't have to hate or fear technology to worry about the future of equality, mobility, and the quality of life. The "digital debate," with its inevitable detours into cultural pessimism, simply has no intellectual resources to tackle these issues.

Where Are the Apps to Fight Poverty or Racial Discrimination?

Reason number three: the simplistic epistemology of Silicon Valley has become a model that other institutions are beginning to emulate. The trouble with Silicon Valley is not just that it enables the NSA—it also encourages, even emboldens them. It inspires the NSA to keep searching for connections in a world of meaningless links, to record every click, to ensure that no interaction goes unnoticed, undocumented, and unanalyzed. Like Silicon Valley, the NSA assumes that everything is interconnected: if we can't yet link two pieces of data, it's because we haven't looked deep enough—or we need a third piece of data, to be collected in the future, to make sense of it all.

There's something delusional about this practice—and I don't use "delusional" metaphorically. For the Italian philosopher Remo Bodei, delusion does not stem from too little psychic activity, as some psychoanalytic theories would have it, but, rather, from too much of it. Delirium, he notes, is "the incapacity to filter an enormous quantity of data." While a sane, rational person "has learned that ignorance is vaster than knowledge and that one must resist the temptation to find more coherence than can currently be achieved," the man suffering from delusion cannot stop finding coherence among inherently incoherent phenomena. He generalizes too much, which results in what Bodei calls "hyper-inclusion."

"Hyper-inclusion" is exactly what plagues America's military-industrial complex today. And they don't even hide this: thus, Gus Hunt, the chief technology officer of the CIA, confesses that "since you can't connect dots you don't have . . . we fundamentally try to collect everything and hang on to it forever." Such hyper-inclusion, according to Bodei, is the prerogative of the deluded. For them, he writes, "the accidental, which most certainly exists in the external world, has no right of citizenship in the psychic one, where it is 'curved' to a certain explanation." For example, "a madman might find it significant that three people in a larger group are wearing a red tie, and might believe that this implies some form of persecution." Likewise, the delirious person believes that "the concept of St. Joseph includes not only the individual person but also a wooden table since St. Joseph was a carpenter." Well, it might be "delusion' for Bodei, but as far as Silicon Valley and Washington are concerned, we are talking bout "the semantic Web" and "Big Data"!

Silicon Valley doesn't care that some of these connections are spurious. When Google or Facebook messes up and shows us an irrelevant ad based on their misconceived view of who we are, it results in minor discomfort—and little else. When the NSA or CIA messes up, it results in a loud drone strike (if you are lucky, you might qualify for an all-expenses-paid, one-way trip to Guantánamo).

The other problem with Silicon Valley's epistemology is that its view of the world is heavily distorted by its business model. Silicon Valley has two responses to any problem: it can produce more "computation" (or code) or it can process more "information" (or data). Most likely, it will be a combination of the two, giving us yet another app to track calories, weather, and traffic. Such small successes allow Silicon Valley to redefine "progress" as something that naturally follows from their business plans. But while "more computation" or "more information" could be lucrative private responses to some problems, it doesn't follow that they are also most effective responses to the unwieldy, messy public problems have deep institutional and structural causes.

Much importance, at least in America, is attached to the immense potential of smartphones to solve a problem like obesity. How would this work? Well, the idea is that the smartphones already monitor how much we walk—they have sensors that do that—and they can tell us when we are walking less than the norm. They can also—perhaps, in some combination with Google Glass—monitor what we eat and keep track of our diet, telling us to refuse that tempting dessert. The assumption here, derived from behavioral economics, is that we make irrational decisions and that highly targeted information provided to us at the right time via this new digital infrastructure can finally conquer our irrationality.

But notice how, in this case, the very definition of a problem like obesity shrinks to the neoliberal and the banal: it's all our own fault! We are not really trying to solve the problem—only to deploy our tools—coding and information—to redefine the problem in the most convenient but also least ambitious way. It may be that if you are poor and you work several jobs and you don't have a car to go shopping at a farmer's market, then consuming junk food at a local McDonald's is a completely rational decision: you get the food you can afford. What's the point of telling you what you already know: that you are eating cheap and terrible food? The problem that needs addressing here is that of poverty— to be tackled through economic reforms—and not that of under-supply of information.

Sociologists have coined a term for this phenomenon: "prob-lem closure." To use one recent definition, it refers to "the situation when a specific definition of a problem is used to frame subse-quent study of the problem's causes and consequences in ways that preclude alternative conceptualizations of the problem." Once the causes and consequences have been narrowly defined, it's no wonder that particular solutions get most attention. This is where we are today: inspired by Silicon Valley, policy makers are beginning to redefine problems as essentially stemming from incomplete information while envisioning solutions that only do one thing: deliver more information through apps. But where are the apps to fight poverty or racial discrimination? We are build-ing apps to fix the problems that our apps can fix—instead of tackling problems that actually need fixing.

Let's Re-Inject Politics and Economics Into This Debate

Do people in Silicon Valley realize the mess that they are dragging us into? I doubt it. The "invisible barbed wire" remains invisible even to its builders. Whoever is building a tool to link MOOCs to biometric identification isn't much concerned with what this means for our freedoms: "freedom" is not their department, they are just building cool tools for spreading knowledge!

This is where the "digital debate" leads us astray: it knows how to talk about tools but is barely capable of talking about social, political, and economic systems that these tools enable and disable, amplify and pacify. When these systems are once again brought to the fore of our analysis, the "digital" aspect of such tool talk becomes extremely boring, for it explains nothing. Deleuze warned of such tool-centrism back in 1990:

> One can of course see how each kind of society corresponds to a particular kind of machine—with simple mechanical machines corresponding to sovereign societies, thermodynamic machines to disciplinary societies, cybernetic machines and computers to control societies. But the machines don't explain anything, you have to analyze the collective arrangements of which the machines are just one component.

In the last two decades, our ability to make such connections between machines and "collective arrangements" has all but atrophied. This happened, I suspect, because we've presumed that these machines come from "cyberspace," that they are of the "online" and "digital" world—in other words, that they were bestowed upon us by the gods of "the Internet." And "the Internet," as Silicon Valley keeps reminding us, is the future. So to oppose these machines was to oppose the future itself.

Well, this is all bunk: there's no "cyberspace," and "the digital debate" is just a bunch of sophistries concocted by Silicon Valley that allow its executives to sleep well at night. (It pays well, too!) Haven't we had enough? Our first step should be to rob them of their banal but highly effective language. Our second step should be to rob them of their flawed history. Our third step should be to re-inject politics and economics into this debate. Let's bury the "digital debate" for good—along with an oversupply of intellectual mediocrity it has produced in the meantime.

***London Review
of Books***

San Francisco has been transformed in recent years, and the tech boom down the peninsula is the reason. What had been a city friendly to outsiders—artists, gays, African Americans, Latinos, immigrants—is being overrun by a new class of techies who all come from essentially one demographic. The symbol of this transition is a sleek luxury bus bristling with technology. Every day, these swoop past mortal city residents and scoop up the chosen few. Rebecca Solnit's piece beautifully captures the fissures running through a boom city.

Rebecca Solnit

2. Diary: Google Invades

The buses roll up to San Francisco's bus stops in the morning and evening, but they are unmarked, or nearly so, and not for the public. They have no signs or have discreet acronyms on the front windshield, and because they also have no rear doors they ingest and disgorge their passengers slowly, while the brightly lit funky orange public buses wait behind them. The luxury-coach passengers ride for free and many take out their laptops and begin their work day on board; there is of course wifi. Most of them are gleaming white, with dark-tinted windows, like limousines, and some days I think of them as the spaceships on which our alien overlords have landed to rule over us.

Other days I think of them as the company buses by which the coal miners get deposited at the minehead, and the work schedule involved would make a pit owner feel at home. Silicon Valley has long been famous for its endless work hours, for sucking in the young for decades of sixty- or seventy-hour weeks, and the much celebrated perks on many jobsites—nap rooms, chefs, gyms, laundry—are meant to make spending most of your life at work less hideous. The biotech industry is following the same game plan. There are hundreds of luxury buses serving mega-corporations down the peninsula, but we refer to them in the singular, as the Google Bus, and we—by which I mean people I know, people who've lived here a while, and mostly people who don't work in the industry—talk about them a lot. Parisians probably talked about the Prussian army a lot too, in the day.

My brother says that the first time he saw one unload its riders he thought they were German tourists—neatly dressed, uncool, a little out of place, blinking in the light as they emerged from their pod. The tech workers, many of them new to the region, are mostly white or Asian male nerds in their twenties and thirties; you often hear that to be over fifty in that world is to be a fossil, and the two founders of Google (currently tied for thirteenth richest person on earth) are not yet forty.

Another friend of mine told me a story about the Apple bus from when he worked for Apple Inc. Once a driver went rogue, dropping off the majority of his passengers as intended at the main Apple campus, and then rolling on toward San Jose instead of stopping at the satellite location, but the passengers were tech people, so withdrawn from direct, abrupt, interventionary communications that they just sat there as he drove many miles past their worksite and eventually dumped them on the street in a slum south of the new power center of the world. At that point, I think, they called headquarters: another, more obedient bus driver was dispatched. I told the story to another friend, and we joked about whether they then texted headquarters to get the e-mail addresses of the people sitting next to them: this is a culture that has created many new ways for us to contact one another and atrophied most of the old ones, notably speaking to the people around you. All these youngish people are on the Google Bus because they want to live in San Francisco, city of promenading and mingling, but they seem as likely to rub these things out as to participate in them.

The Google Bus means so many things. It means that the minions of the non-petroleum company most bent on world domination can live in San Francisco but work in Silicon Valley without going through a hair-raising commute by car—I overheard someone note recently that the buses shortened her daily commute to 3.5 hours from 4.5. It means that unlike gigantic employers in other times and places, the corporations of Silicon Valley aren't much interested in improving public transport, and in fact the many corporations providing private transport are undermining the financial basis for the commuter train. It means that San Francisco, capital of the west from the Gold Rush to some point in the twentieth century when Los Angeles overshadowed it, is now a bedroom community for the tech capital of the world at the other end of the peninsula.

There are advantages to being an edge, as California long was, but Silicon Valley has made us the center. Five of the six most-visited websites in the world are here, in ranked order: Facebook, Google, YouTube (which Google owns), Yahoo!, and Wikipedia. (Number five is a Chinese-language site.) If corporations founded by Stanford alumni were to form an independent nation, it would be the tenth-largest economy in the world, with an annual revenue of $2.7 trillion, as some professors at that university recently calculated. Another new report says: "If the internet was a country, its gross domestic product would eclipse all others but four within four years."

That country has a capital that doesn't look like a capital. It looks like beautiful oak-studded hills and flatlands overrun by sprawl: suburban homes (the megamansions are more secluded) and malls and freeways often jammed with traffic and dotted with clunky campuses, as corporate headquarters of tech firms are always called. Fifty years ago, this was the "valley of heart's delight," one of the biggest orchard-growing regions in the world. It wasn't to everyone's delight: Cesar Chavez and the United Farmworkers movement started in San Jose because the people who actually picked all those plums and apricots worked long hours for abysmal wages, but the sight and smell of the 125,000 acres of orchard in bloom was supposed to be spectacular.

Where orchards grew Apple stands. The work hours are still extreme but now the wages are colossal—you hear tech workers complaining about not having time to spend their money. They eat out often, though, because their work schedules don't include a lot of time for shopping and cooking, and San Francisco's restaurants are booming. Cafés, which proliferated in the 1980s as places to mingle and idle, are now workstations for freelancers, and many of the sleeker locales are routinely populated by silent ranks staring at their Apple-product screens, as though an office had suddenly been stripped of its cubicles. The more than 1,700 tech firms in San Francisco officially employ 44,000 people, and a lot more are independent contractors doing piecework: not everyone rides the bus down south. Young people routinely make six-figure salaries, not necessarily beginning with a one, and they have enormous clout in the housing market (the drivers of the Google Bus, on the other hand, make between seventeen and thirty dollars an hour).

I weathered the dot-com boom of the late 1990s as an observer, but I sold my apartment to a Google engineer in 2011 and ventured out into both the rental market (for the short term) and home-buying market (for the long term) with confidence that my long standing in this city and respectable finances would open a path. That confidence got crushed fast. It turned out that the competition for any apartment in San Francisco was so intense that you had to respond to the listings—all on San Francisco–based Craigslist of course, the classifieds website that whittled away newspaper ad revenue nationally—within a few hours of their posting to receive a reply from the landlord or agency. The listings for both rentals and homes for sale often mentioned their proximity to the Google or Apple bus stops.

At the actual open houses, dozens of people who looked like students would show up with checkbooks and sheaves of résumés and other documents and pack the house, literally: it was like a cross between being at a rock concert without a band and the Hotel Rwanda. There were rumors that these young people were starting bidding wars, offering a year's rent in advance, offering far more than was being asked. These rumors were confirmed. Evictions went back up the way they did during the dot-com bubble. Most renters have considerable protection from both rent hikes and evictions in San Francisco, but there are ways around the latter, ways that often lead to pitched legal battles and sometimes illegal ones. Owners have the right to evict a tenant to occupy the apartment itself (a right often abused; an evicted friend of mine found a new home next door to his former landlord and is watching with an eagle eye to see if the guy really dwells there for the requisite three years). Statewide, the Ellis Act allows landlords to evict all tenants and remove the property from the rental market, a maneuver often deployed to convert a property to flats for sale. As for rent control, it makes many landlords restless with stable tenants, since you can charge anything you like on a vacant apartment—and they do.

A Latino who has been an important cultural figure for forty years is being evicted while his wife undergoes chemotherapy. One of San Francisco's most distinguished poets, a recent candidate for the city's poet laureate, is being evicted after thirty-five years in his apartment and his whole adult life here: whether he will claw his way onto a much humbler perch or be exiled to another town remains to be seen as does the fate of a city that poets can't afford. His building, full of renters for most or all of the past century, including a notable documentary filmmaker, will be turned into flats for sale. A few miles away, friends of friends were evicted after twenty years in their home by two Google attorneys, a gay couple who moved into two separate units in order to maximize their owner-move-in rights. Rental prices rose between 10 and 135 percent over the past year in San Francisco's various neighborhoods, though thanks to rent control a lot of San Franciscans were paying far below market rates even before the boom—which makes adjusting to the new market rate even harder. Two much-loved used bookstores are also being evicted by landlords looking for more money; sixteen restaurants opened last year in their vicinity. On the waterfront, Larry Ellison, the owner of Oracle and the world's sixth-richest man, has been allowed to take control of three city piers for seventy-five years in return for fixing them up in time for the 2013 America's Cup; he will evict dozens of small waterfront businesses as part of the deal.

All this is changing the character of what was once a great city of refuge for dissidents, queers, pacifists, and experimentalists. Like so many cities that flourished in the postindustrial era, it has become increasingly unaffordable over the past quarter-century but still has a host of writers, artists, activists, environmentalists, eccentrics, and others who don't work sixty-hour weeks for corporations—though we may be a relic population. Boomtowns also drive out people who perform essential services for relatively modest salaries, the teachers, firefighters, mechanics, and carpenters, along with people who might have time for civic engagement. I look in wonder at the store clerks and dishwashers, wondering how they hang on or how long their commute is. Sometimes the tech workers on their buses seem like bees who belong to a great hive, but the hive isn't civil society or a city; it's a corporation.

Last summer, I went to look at a house for sale whose listing hadn't mentioned that the house was inhabited. I looked in dismay at the pretty old house where a family's possessions had settled like silt over the decades: drum set, Bibles, faded framed portraits, furniture grimed with the years, cookware, toys. It was a display of what was about to be lost. The estate agent was on the front steps telling potential clients that they wouldn't even have to evict: just raise the rent far beyond what the residents can afford. Ye who seek homes, come destroy the homes of others more frail.

I saw the same thing happen in the building next door to the rental I eventually found through word of mouth after failing to compete in the open market. These families are not going to live like that again, in pleasant homes in the city center. Other buildings I visited had been emptied of all residents, and every unit was for sale, each furnished with brushed steel appliances, smooth surfaces and sleek neutral tones to appeal to the tastes of young technocrats.

In the poorer outskirts of the city, foreclosures and short sales (an alternative to foreclosure where the house is sold even though the sale won't cover the debts) go on as they have across much of the country since the crash in 2008, and a group called Occupy

Bernal Heights (a neighborhood spin-off of Occupy San Francisco, cofounded by the sex activist Annie Sprinkle) has shown up at the banks and at the houses to defend many owners, one home at a time. Poverty is cruel and destructive. Wealth is cruel and destructive, too, or at least booms are. The whole of the United States sometimes seems to be a checkerboard of these low-pressure zones with lots of time and space but no money, and the boomtowns with lots of money, a frenzied pace and chronic housing scarcity. Neither version is very livable.

San Francisco's tech boom has often been compared to the Gold Rush, but without much discussion about what the Gold Rush meant beyond the cute images of bearded men in plaid shirts with pickaxes looking a lot like gay men in the Castro in the 1970s. When gold was discovered in 1848, employees left their posts, sailors abandoned their ships, and San Francisco—then a tiny port town called Yerba Buena—was deserted. In the Mother Lode, some got rich; many died of contagious diseases, the lousy diet, rough life, and violence; some went broke and crawled back to the United States, as the settled eastern half of the country was called when the gold country was an outpost of newcomers mostly arriving by ship and the American West still largely belonged to the indigenous people.

Supplying the miners and giving them places to spend their money became as lucrative as mining and much more secure. Quite a lot of the early fortunes were made by shopkeepers: Levi Strauss got his start that way, and so did Leland Stanford, who founded the university that founded Silicon Valley. The Mexicans who had led a fairly gracious life on vast ranches before the Gold Rush were largely dispossessed, and the Native Californians were massacred, driven out of their homes; they watched their lands be destroyed by mining, starved, or died of disease: the Native population declined by about four-fifths during this jolly spree.

San Francisco exploded in the rush, growing by leaps and bounds, a freewheeling town made up almost exclusively of people from elsewhere, mostly male, often young. In 1850, California had a population of 120,000 according to one survey, 110,000 of them male. By 1852, women made up 10 percent of the population, by 1870, more than a quarter. During this era prostitution thrived, from the elegant courtesans who played a role in the city's political and cultural life to the Chinese children who were worked to death in cribs, as the cubicles in which they labored were called. Prices for everything skyrocketed: eggs were a dollar apiece in 1849, and a war broke out later over control of the stony Farallones islands rookery thirty miles west of San Francisco, where seabirds' eggs were gathered to augment what the chickens could produce. A good pair of boots was a hundred dollars. Land downtown was so valuable that people bought water lots—plots of land in the bay—and filled them in.

Wages were high too, until 1869, when the Central Pacific Railroad (built by Stanford and his three cronies) connected the Bay Area to the East Coast, and the newly unemployed railroad workers and the poor of the east poured in. *The Annals of San Francisco* describes the city twenty years earlier, in 1849:

> As we have said, there were no homes at this period in San Francisco, and time was too precious for anyone to stay within doors to cook victuals. Consequently an immense majority of the people took their meals at restaurants, boarding-houses and hotels—the number of which was naturally therefore very great; while many lodged as well as boarded at such places. Many of these were indeed miserable hovels, which showed only bad fare and worse attendance, dirt, discomfort and high prices. A few others again were of a superior class; but, of course, still higher charges had to be made for the better accommodation.

The oil and gas boomtowns of the present, in Wyoming, North Dakota, and Alberta, among other places, follow this model. Lots of money sloshes around boomtowns, but everyday life is shaped by scarcity, not abundance. The boom workers are newcomers. They work long hours, earn high wages, drive up the cost of housing for the locals, drive out some locals, eat out, drink a lot, brawl, overload local services, often get addicted or injured. In Wyoming last year I met a disability counselor who told me about the young men who go into the coal and gas mining business; make more money than they've ever seen; go into debt on a trailer home, a fancy truck, extravagant pleasures; and then get permanently disabled on the job and watch their lives fall apart. A journalist who'd been reporting on the boom in North Dakota told me about ranches ruined by toxins and a trailer park full of Native Americans who'd lived there for many decades evicted to make room for higher-paying miners with brand-new trailers. Like a virus, mining destroys its host and then moves on. There are ghost towns across the West full of dying businesses with the landscape around them ground into heaps leaching toxic residue.

There are ways in which Silicon Valley is nothing like this: it's clean, quiet work and here to stay in one form or another. But there are ways in which technology is just another boom and the Bay Area is once again a boomtown, with transient populations, escalating housing costs, mass displacements, and the casual erasure of what was here before. I think of it as frontierism, with all the frontier's attitude and operational style, where people without a lot of attachments come and do things without a lot of concern for their impact, where money moves around pretty casually, and people are ground underfoot equally casually. Sometimes the Google Bus just seems like one face of Janus-headed capitalism; it contains the people too valuable even to use public transport or drive themselves. In the same spaces wander homeless people undeserving of private space or the minimum comfort and security; right by the Google bus stop on Cesar Chavez Street immigrant men from Latin America stand waiting for employers in the building trade to scoop them up, or to be arrested and deported by the government. Both sides of the divide are bleak, and the middle way is hard to find.

The Baffler

Lean In, Sheryl Sandberg's manifesto for women, isn't just a phenomenally successful best-seller—or even just an organization of local women's clubs around the country seeking to emulate the Facebook CFO's success. It's closer to a cult, with a distinctive worldview and its special, corporatist-inflected twist on feminism. There is no writer more qualified to break down the contradictions of the *Lean In* phenomenon than Susan Faludi, one of our leading thinkers on gender, power, and matters economic.

3. Facebook Feminism, Like It or Not

The congregation swooned as she bounded on stage, the prophet sealskin sleek in her black skinny ankle pants and black ballet flats, a lavalier microphone clipped to the V-neck of her black button-down sweater. "All right!! Let's go!!" she exclaimed, throwing out her arms and pacing the platform before inspirational graphics of glossy young businesswomen in managerial action poses. "Super excited to have all of you here!!"

"Whoo!!" the young women in the audience replied. The camera, which was livestreaming the event in the Menlo Park, California, auditorium to college campuses worldwide, panned the rows of well-heeled Stanford University econ majors and MBA candidates. Some clutched copies of the day's hymnal: the speaker's new book, which promised to dismantle "internal obstacles" preventing them from "acquiring power." The atmosphere was TED-Talk-cum-tent-revival-cum-Mary-Kay-cosmetics-convention. The salvation these adherents sought on this April day in 2013 was admittance to the pearly gates of the corporate corner office.

"Stand up," the prophet instructed, "if you've ever said out loud, to another human being—and you have to have said it out loud—'I am going to be the number one person in my field. I will be the CEO of a major company. I will be governor. I will be the number one person in my field.'" A small, although not inconsiderable, percentage of the young women rose to their feet.

The speaker consoled those still seated; she, too, had once been one of them. When she was voted "most likely to succeed" in high school, she confided, she had begged a yearbook editor to delete that information, "because most likely to succeed doesn't get a date for the prom." Those days were long gone, ever since she'd had her conversion on the road to Davos: she'd "leaned in" to her ambitions and enhanced her "likeability"—and they could do the same. What's more, if they took the "lean in" pledge, they might free themselves from some of those other pesky problems that hold women back in the workplace. "If you lean forward," she said, "you will get yourself into a position where the organization you're with values you a lot and is therefore willing to be more flexible. Or you'll get promoted and then you'll get paid more and you'll be able to afford better child care." If you "believe you have the skills to do anything" and "have the ambition to lead," then you will "change the world" for women. "We get closer to the goal of true equality with every single one of you who leans in."

The pitch delivered, Lean In founder and Facebook chief operating officer Sheryl Sandberg summoned her deacon to close the deal. Rachel Thomas hustled onstage, a Sandberg Mini-Me in matching black ensemble (distinguished only by the color of her ballet flats and baubled necklace, both of which were gold). She's Lean In's president. (Before *Lean In* hit the bookstores, it was already a fully staffed operation, an organization purporting to be "a global community committed to encouraging and supporting women leaning in to their ambitions.") "I *really* want to invite you to join our community!" Thomas told the assembled. "You'll get daily inspiration and insights."

Joining "the community" was just a click away. In fact, the community was already uploaded and ready to receive them; all they had to do was hit the "Lean In Today" button on their computer screen . . . and, oh yeah, join Facebook. (There is no entry into Lean In's Emerald e-Kingdom except through the Facebook portal; Sandberg has kept her message of liberation confined within her own corporate brand.)

Thomas enumerated the "three things" that Lean In offered. (In the Lean In Community, there are invariably three things required to achieve your aims.) First, Thomas instructed, "Come like us on Facebook" (and, for extra credit, post your own inspirational graphic on Lean In's Facebook "photo gallery" and "tag your friends, tell them why you're leaning in!"). Second, watch Lean In's online "education" videos, twenty-minute lectures from "experts" (business school professors, management consultants, and a public speaking coach) with titles like "Power and Influence" and "Own the Room." Third, create a "Lean In Circle" with eight to ten similarly aspirational young women. The circles, Lean In literature stresses, are to promote "peer mentorship" only—*not* to deliver aid and counsel from experienced female elders who might actually help them advance. Thomas characterized the circle as "a book club with a purpose." All they had to do was click on the "Create a Circle" button on LeanIn.org and follow the "three easy steps." "We provide everything that you need to do it," Thomas assured. "All the materials, all the how-to information, and a very cool technology platform called Mightybell." Mightybell's CEO, it so happens, is Gina Bianchini, cofounder of Lean In. "So it's really easy to do, and don't wait!" Thomas said. "Go do it for yourself today!"

Since its unveiling this spring, the Lean In campaign has been reeling in a steadily expanding group of tens of thousands of followers with its tripartite E-Z plan for getting to the top. But the real foundation of the movement is, of course, Sheryl Sandberg's best-selling book, *Lean In: Women, Work, and the Will to Lead*, billed modestly by its author as "sort of a feminist manifesto." Sandberg's mantra has become the feminist rallying cry of the moment, praised by notable figures such as Gloria Steinem,

Jane Fonda, Marlo Thomas, and *Nation* columnist Katha Pollitt. A *Time* magazine cover story hails Sandberg for "embarking on the most ambitious mission to reboot feminism and reframe discussions of gender since the launch of *Ms.* magazine in 1971." Pretty good for somebody who, "as of two and a half years ago," as Sandberg confessed on her book tour, "had never said the word woman aloud. Because that's not how you get ahead in the world."

The lovefest continues on LeanIn.org's "Meet the Community" page, where tribute is paid by Sandberg's high-powered network of celebrities, corporate executives, and media moguls (*many* media moguls), among them Oprah Winfrey, *New York Times* executive editor Jill Abramson, *Newsweek* and *Daily Beast* editor in chief Tina Brown, *Huffington Post* founder Arianna Huffington, *Cosmopolitan* editor in chief Joanna Coles, former *Good Morning America* coanchor Willow Bay, former first lady Laura Bush (and both of her daughters), former California first lady and TV host Maria Shriver, U.S. senators Barbara Boxer and Elizabeth Warren, Harvard president Drew Gilpin Faust, Dun & Bradstreet CEO Sara Mathew, Yahoo CEO Marissa Mayer, Coca-Cola marketing executive Wendy Clark, fashion designer Diane von Furstenberg, supermodel Tyra Banks, and actor (and Avon "Global Ambassador") Reese Witherspoon.

Beneath highly manicured glam shots, each "member" or "partner" reveals her personal "Lean In moment." The accounts inevitably have happy finales—the Lean In guidelines instruct contributors to "share a positive ending." Tina Brown's Lean In moment: getting her parents to move from England to "the apartment across the corridor from us on East 57th Street in New York," so her mother could take care of the children while Brown took the helm at *The New Yorker.* If you were waiting for someone to lean in for child-care legislation, keep holding your breath. So far, there's no discernible groundswell.

When asked why she isn't pushing for structural social and economic change, Sandberg says she's all in favor of "public-policy reform," though she's vague about how exactly that would work, beyond generic tsk-tsking about the pay gap and lack of maternity leave. She says she supports reforming the workplace—but the particulars of comparable worth or subsidized child care are hardly prominent elements of her book or her many media appearances.

Sandberg began her TED Talk in December 2010, the trial balloon for the Lean In campaign, with a one-sentence nod to "flex time," training, and other "programs" that might advance working women, and then declared, "I want to talk about none of that today." What she wanted to talk about, she said, was "what we can do as individuals" to climb to the top of the command chain.

This clipped, jarring shift from the collective grievances of working women to the feel-good options open to credentialed, professional types is also a pronounced theme in *Lean In*, the book. In the opening pages, Sandberg acknowledges that "the vast majority of women are struggling to make ends meet" but goes on to stress that "each subsequent chapter focuses on an adjustment or difference that we can make ourselves." When asked in a radio interview in Boston about the external barriers women face, Sandberg agreed that women are held back "by discrimination and sexism and terrible public policy" and "we should reform all of that," but then immediately suggested that the concentration on such reforms has been disproportionate, arguing that "the conversation can't be only about that, and in a lot of ways the conversation on women is usually *only* about that." Toward the end of the Q&A period at the Menlo Park event, a student watching online asked, "What would you say to the critics who argue that lower socioeconomic status makes it difficult to lean in?" Sandberg replied that leaning in might be even "more important for women who are struggling to make ends meet," then offered this anecdote as evidence: She had received a fan e-mail from a reader who "never graduated from college" and had gone back to work in 1998 after her husband lost his job. "Until she read *Lean In*, she had never asked for a raise. And last week, she asked for a raise." Pause for the drum roll. "*And she got it*! That's what this is about."

Lean In's rank-and-file devotees don't get the marquee billing accorded the celebrity and executive set on the handpicked "Meet the Community" page. Nevertheless, they seem eager to "join the community": as of July 12, 2013, they "liked" Lean In 237,552 times. Their online participation on Lean In's Facebook page is limited to making comments—in response to the organization's announcements of the latest Lean In marketing triumphs. ("Very excited that Lean In is #1 on The New York Times Book Review—Six weeks in a row!"; "Very excited to see Sheryl Sandberg on the TIME 100 list of the most influential people in the world!"; "We're excited to watch Sheryl Sandberg Lean In with Oprah this weekend. Tune in to watch Oprah's Next Chapter on Sunday, March 24 at 9 p.m. ET/PT on OWN: Oprah Winfrey Network!")

Evidently the "likers" are excited, too: they cheer the media conquests of the Leaner-In-in-chief, whose success began at the top (thanks not to "peer mentoring" but to her powerful college adviser, former Harvard University president Larry Summers) and who has remained there ever since—a stratospheric hurtle from Harvard to the World Bank to the U.S. Treasury Department to Google to Facebook. The comments read like a Sandbergian amen corner: "Congratulations Sheryl! You diserve [*sic*] it!♥"; "This is such an awesome book! It has really energized me with refocusing on my career goals."; "am reading book on my kindle now, awesome so far!"; "Awesome talk!!!"; "God Bless! And lets [*sic*] continue to spread this message and lean in!"; "Sheryl is igniting the new feminine movement!"; "THANK YOU FOR LEADING THE REVOLUTION!!!!☺"; "sheryl is inspirational! I missed zumba for this and happy I did!"

The scene at the Menlo Park auditorium, and its conflation of "believe in yourself" faith and material rewards, will be familiar to anyone who's ever spent a Sunday inside a prosperity-gospel mega-church or watched Reverend Ike's vintage "You Deserve the Best!" sermon on YouTube. But why is that same message now ascendant among the American feminists of the new millennium?

Sandberg's admirers would say that Lean In is using free-market beliefs to advance the cause of women's equality. Her detractors would say (and have) that her organization is using the desire for women's equality to advance the cause of the free market. And they would both be right. In embodying that contradiction, Sheryl Sandberg would not be alone and isn't so new. For the last two centuries, feminism, like evangelicalism, has been in a dance with capitalism.

All as One

In 1834, America's first industrial wage earners, the "mill girls" of Lowell, Massachusetts, embarked on their own campaign for women's advancement in the workplace. They didn't "lean in," though. When their male overseers in the nation's first large-scale planned industrial city cut their already paltry wages by 15 to 20 percent, the textile workers declared a "turn-out," one of the nation's earliest industrial strikes. That first effort failed, but its participants did not concede defeat. The Lowell women would stage another turn-out two years later, create the first union of working women in American history, lead a fight for the ten-hour work day, and conceive of an increasingly radical vision that took aim both at corporate power and the patriarchal oppression of women. Their bruising early encounter with American industry fueled a nascent feminist outlook that would ultimately find full expression in the first wave of the American women's movement.

Capitalism, you could say, had midwifed feminism.

And capitalism, Sandberg would say, still sustains it. But what happened between 1834 and 2013—between "turn-out" and "lean in"—to make Lean In such an odd heir to the laurels of Lowell? An answer lies in the history of those early textile mills.

The Lowell factory owners had recruited "respectable" Yankee farmers' daughters from the New England countryside, figuring that respectable would translate into docile. They figured wrong. The forces of industrialization had propelled young women out of the home, breaking the fetters binding them to the patriarchal family, unleashing the women into urban areas with few social controls, and permitting them to begin thinking of themselves as public citizens. The combination of newly gained independence and increasingly penurious, exploitative conditions proved combustible—and the factory owners' reduction in pay turned out to be the match that lit the tinder. Soon after they heard the news, the "mill girls"—proclaiming that they "remain in possession of our unquestionable rights"—shut down their looms and walked out.

From the start, the female textile workers made the connection between labor and women's rights. Historian Thomas Dublin, in his book on the Lowell mill girls, *Women at Work*, cited an account in the Boston *Evening Transcript*. "One of the leaders mounted a pump," the article reported, "and made a flaming Mary Woolstonecroft [*sic*] speech on the rights of women and the iniquities of the '*monied* aristocracy.'" The speech "produced a powerful effect on her auditors, and they determined 'to have their own way if they died for it.'" In a statement the mill workers issued on the first day of the turn-out, titled "Union Is Power," they elaborated:

> The oppressing hand of avarice would enslave us, and to gain their object, they gravely tell us of the pressure of the times, this we are already sensible of, and deplore it. If any are in want, the Ladies will be compassionate and assist them; but we prefer to have the disposing of our charities in our own hands; and as we are free, we would remain in possession of what

kind Providence has bestowed upon us, and remain daughters of freemen still.

The mill proprietors looked on with unease at what they regarded
as an "amizonian [*sic*] display" and "a spirit of evil omen."

The Lowell turn-out was a communal endeavor, built on intense bonds of sisterhood forged around the clock: by day on the
factory floor, where the women worked in pairs, with the more
experienced female worker training and looking out for the newcomer, and by night in the company boarding houses, where
they shared cramped quarters, often two to a bed, and embroiled
themselves in late-night discussions about philosophy, music,
literature, and, increasingly, social and economic injustice. As
Dublin observed of the web of "mutual dependence" that prevailed in the Lowell mill workforce, the strike was "made possible
because women had come to form a 'community' of operatives in
the mill, rather than simply a group of individual workers." An
actual community, that is—not an online like-a-thon. Tellingly,
the strike began when a mill agent, hoping to nip agitation in the
bud, fired one of the more voluble factory workers whom he regarded as the ringleader. The other women immediately walked
out in protest over her expulsion. The petition they signed and
circulated concluded: "Resolved, That none of us will go back,
unless they receive us all as one."

In a matter of years, the Lowell women would become increasingly radical, as crusaders for both worker and gender equality.
They had originally been encouraged to write ladylike stories for
the mill girls' literary magazine, the *Lowell Offering*, which was
launched by a local minister and supported by the textile companies. By the 1840s, many young working women were filing copy
instead with the *Voice of Industry*, a labor newspaper published
by the Lowell Female Labor Reform Association. The paper's "Female Department," edited by the association's president, Sarah
Bagley, featured articles by and about women workers, with a

declared mission both to revamp "the system of labor" and "defend woman's rights." "You have been degraded long enough," an article in the *Voice* advised its female readers. "You have sufficiently long been considered 'the inferior'—a kind of 'upper servant,' to obey and reverence, and be in subjection to your equal." No more. "Enter at once upon your privileges," the article exhorted, calling on women to demand their equal rights to education, employment, and respect from men.

The mill workers went on to agitate against an unjust system in all its forms. When Lowell's state representative thwarted the women's statewide battle for the ten-hour day, they mobilized and succeeded in having him voted out of office—nearly eighty years before women had the vote. Mill women in Lowell and, in the decades to come, their counterparts throughout New England threw themselves into the abolitionist movement (drawing connections between the cotton picked by slaves and the fabric they wove in the mills); campaigned for better health care, safer schools, decent housing, and cleaner water and streets; and joined the fight for women's suffrage. Sarah Bagley went on to work for prison reform, women's rights, and education and decent jobs for poor women and prostitutes. After a stint as the first female telegrapher in the nation (where she pointed out that she was being paid two-thirds of a male telegrapher's salary), she taught herself homeopathic medicine and became a doctor, billing her patients according to her personal proviso, "To the rich, one dollar—to the poor gratis."

Increasingly, the mill girls were joined in these efforts by their middle-class sisters. Cross-class female solidarity surfaced early in Lawrence, Massachusetts, after the horrific building collapse of the Pemberton Mills factory in 1860, which killed 145 workers, most of them women and children. (The mills in Lawrence would later give rise to the famously militant "Bread and Roses" strike of 1912, in which female workers again played a leading role.) In the aftermath of the Pemberton disaster, middle-class women in the region flocked to provide emergency relief and, radicalized by what they witnessed, went on to establish day nurseries, medical clinics and hospitals, and cooperative housing to serve the needs of working women. By the postbellum years, with industrialization at full tide and economic polarization at record levels, a critical mass of middle-class female reformers had come to believe that the key to women's elevation was not, as they once thought, "moral uplift," but economic independence—and that cross-class struggle on behalf of female workers was the key to achieving it.

A host of organizations launched by professional women, like Sorosis and the Women's Educational and Industrial Union (WEIU), sprang up to campaign for the economic advancement of both middle- and working-class women. "From its first days," historian Mari Jo Buhle observed in *Women and American Socialism*, "Sorosis encompassed broader purposes than aid to a handful of aspiring women professionals. All workingwomen, the leaders believed, shared a common grievance and a common need for organization." The WEIU in Boston, like Lean In, held lectures to promote women in business—but it also sent investigative teams to expose poor conditions for women on the factory and retail floor, procured legal services for working women denied their rightful wages, offered job-referral services for women of all classes, and set up cooperative exchanges for homebound women to sell their handcrafts so that even they might achieve some measure of fiscal independence from their husbands. In Chicago, the Illinois Woman's Alliance launched a full-bore probe of abusive sweatshops that spawned a congressional investigation, successfully lobbied for a shorter workday for sweatshop workers, and even demanded legal rights for prostitutes, including the right to be free of police harassment.

From the sounds of recent pronouncements, it might seem that efforts to elevate the woman worker have finally paid off. With giddy triumphalism, books like Hanna Rosin's *The End of*

Men: And the Rise of Women and Liza Mundy's *The Richer Sex: How the New Majority of Female Breadwinners Is Transforming Sex, Love, and Family* (both published in 2012) celebrate the imminent emergence of a female supremacy. "For the first time in history, the global economy is becoming a place where women are finding more success than men," Rosin declared, noting that twelve of the fifteen jobs projected to grow the fastest in the United States in the next decade "are occupied primarily by women." The female worker, she wrote, is "becoming the standard by which success is measured." Mundy, who called this supremacy the "Big Flip," predicted that, thanks to the new economy, we would soon be living in a world "where women routinely support households and outearn the men they are married to," and men "will gladly hitch their wagon to a female star."

A star like Sheryl Sandberg, whose feminism seems a capstone of female ascendancy. Never mind that the "fastest-growing" future occupations for women—home health aide, child-care worker, customer-service representative, office clerk, food-service worker—are among the lowest paid, most with few to no benefits and little possibility for "advancement." Progress has stalled for many ordinary women—or gone into reverse. The poverty rate for women, according to the Census Bureau's latest statistics, is at its highest point since 1993, and the "extreme poverty rate" among women is at the highest point ever recorded.

But there seems to be little tangible cross-class solidarity coming from the triumphalists, despite their claims to be speaking for all womankind. "If we can succeed in adding more female voices at the highest levels," Sandberg writes in her book, "we will expand opportunities and extend fairer treatment to all." But which highest-level voices? When former British prime minister Margaret ("I hate feminism") Thatcher died, Lean In's Facebook page paid homage to the Iron Lady and invited its followers to post "which moments were most memorable to you" from Thatcher's tenure. That invitation inspired a rare outburst of *un-*"positive" remarks in the comment section, at least from some women in the U.K. "Really??" wrote one. "She was a tyrant. . . . Just because a woman is in a leadership position does not make her worthy of respect, especially if you were on the receiving end of what she did to lots of people." "So disappointing that Lean In endorses Thatcher as a positive female role model," wrote another. "She made history as a woman, but went on to use her power to work against the most vulnerable, including women and their children."

Even when celebrating more laudable examples of female leadership, Lean In's spotlight rarely roves beyond the uppermost echelon. One looks in vain through its website statements, literature, and declarations at its public events for evidence of concern about how the other half lives—or rather, the other 99 percent. As Linda Burnham observed in a perceptive essay on Portside.org, Lean In "has essentially produced a manifesto for corporatist feminism," a "1% feminism" that "is all about the glass ceiling, never about the floor." The movement originally forged to move the great mass of women has been hijacked to serve the individual (and privileged) girl.

As it turns out, it's a hijacking that's long been under way.

Dream On

The landmark year in the transition from common struggle to individual enhancement was 1920—ironically, the same year that women won the right to vote. In the course of the twenties, an ascendant consumer economy would do as much to derail feminist objectives as advance them. Capitalism, feminism's old midwife, had become its executioner. And a cleverly disguised one: this grim reaper donned a feminist-friendly face.

The rising new forces of consumer manipulation—mass media, mass entertainment, national advertising, the fashion and beauty industries, popular psychology—all seized upon women's yearnings for independence and equality and redirected them to the marketplace. Over and over, mass merchandisers promised women an ersatz version of emancipation, the fulfillment of individual, and aspirational, desire. Why mount a collective protest against the exploitations of the workplace when it was so much more gratifying—not to mention easier—to advance yourself (and only yourself) by shopping for "liberating" products that expressed your "individuality" and signaled your (seemingly) elevated class status?

The message was ubiquitous in 1920s advertising pitched to women. "An Ancient Prejudice Has Been Removed," decreed a Lucky Strike banner, above a picture of an unfettered flapper girl wreathed in cigarette smoke. Enjoy "positive agitation" at home, Hoover vacuum ads entreated, with the new machine's "revolutionary cleaning principle." "Woman suffrage made the American woman the political equal of her man," General Electric cheered. "The little switch which commands the great servant Electricity is making her workshop the equal of her man's." That "workshop," of course, was the domestic bower, to which privileged women were now expected to retire. In 1929, at the behest of the American Tobacco Company, Edward Bernays, the founding father of public relations, organized a procession of debutantes to troop down Fifth Avenue during the Easter Parade, asserting their "right" to smoke in public by puffing "torches of freedom." Women's quest for social and economic freedom had been reenacted as farce.

Where industrial capitalism had driven women as a group to mobilize to change society, its consumer variant induced individual women to submit, each seemingly of her own free will, to a mass-produced culture. They were then encouraged to call that submission liberation. This is the mode that much of American feminism has been stuck in ever since, despite attempts by late-1960s radical feminists to dismantle the female consumer armament of cosmetics, girdles, and hair spray. (The dismantling became quite literal in the 1968 demonstration against the Miss America Pageant, where young radicals hurled "instruments of female torture" into a "Freedom Trash Can.")

In the postindustrial economy, feminism has been retooled as a vehicle for expression of the self, a "self" as marketable consumer object, valued by how many times it's been bought—or, in our electronic age, how many times it's been clicked on. "Images of a certain kind of successful woman proliferate," British philosopher Nina Power observed of contemporary faux-feminism in her 2009 book, *One-Dimensional Woman.* "The city worker in heels, the flexible agency employee, the hard-working hedonist who can afford to spend her income on vibrators and wine—and would have us believe that—yes—capitalism is a girl's best friend."

In the 1920s, male capitalists invoked feminism to advance their brands of corporate products. Nearly a century later, female marketers are invoking capitalism to advance their corporate brand of feminism. Sandberg's "Lean In Community" is Exhibit A. What is she selling, after all, if not the product of the company she works for? Every time a woman signs up for Lean In, she's made another conquest for Facebook. Facebook conquers women in more than one way. Nearly 60 percent of the people who do the daily labor on Facebook—maintaining their pages, posting their images, tagging their friends, driving the traffic—are female, and, unlike the old days of industrial textile manufacturing, they don't even have to be paid or housed. "Facebook benefits every time a woman uploads her picture," Kate Losse, a former employee of Facebook and author of *The Boy Kings*, a keenly observed memoir of her time there, pointed out to me. "And what is she getting? Nothing, except a constant flow of 'likes.'"

When Losse came to Facebook in 2005, she was only the second woman hired in a company that then had fifty employees. Her job was to answer user-support e-mails. Low-wage customer-support work would soon become Facebook's pink ghetto. Losse recalled the decor that adorned the company walls in those years:

drawings of "stylized women with large breasts bursting from small tops." On Mark Zuckerberg's birthday, the women at the company were instructed to wear T-shirts displaying his photo, like groupies.

"It was like *Mad Men*," she wrote of the office environment in *Boy Kings*, "but real and happening in the current moment, as if in repudiation of fifty years of social progress." A few years into her tenure, Losse was promoted to oversee the translation of Facebook's site into other languages. The promotion didn't come with an increase in pay. When Losse, like the woman in Sandberg's anecdote, asked for a raise, she was refused. "You've already doubled your salary in a year," her manager told her, "and it wouldn't be fair to the engineers who haven't had that raise"—the engineers (virtually all male) who were already at the top of the pay scale, unlike her. Her final job at Facebook was to serve as Mark Zuckerberg's personal "writer and researcher." The job, or rather "the role," as Zuckerberg called it, required her to write "his" blog entries on Facebook and post "his" updates to the Zuckerberg fan page.

Losse quit in 2010 to become a writer—of her own words, not her boss's. Earlier this year, she wrote a thought-provoking piece about Lean In for *Dissent*, "Feminism's Tipping Point: Who Wins from Leaning In?" The winners, she noted, are not the women in tech, who "are much more likely to be hired in support functions where they are paid a bare minimum, given tiny equity grants compared to engineers and executives, and given raises on the order of fifty cents an hour rather than thousands of dollars." These are the fast-growth jobs for women in high technology, just as Menlo Park's postindustrial campuses are the modern equivalent of the Lowell company town. Sandberg's book proposed to remedy that system, Losse noted, not by changing it but simply by telling women to work harder:

> Life is a race, Sandberg is telling us, and the way to win is through the perpetual acceleration of one's own labor: moving

forward, faster. The real antagonist identified by Lean In then is not institutionalized discrimination against women, but women's reluctance to accept accelerating career demands.

For her candor, Losse came under instant attack from the Sandberg sisterhood. Brandee Barker, a Lean In publicist and former head of public relations for Facebook, sent Losse the following message: "There's a special place in hell for you." Losse defended herself the only way you can in the age of social media: she took a screenshot of Barker's nastygram and tweeted it. "Maybe sending Hellfire and Damnation messages is part of the Lean In PR strategy," Losse wrote in her tweet. "LEAN IN OR ELSE YOU'RE GOING TO HELL." Other Lean In naysayers have been similarly damned by Lean In devotees. When *New York Times* columnist Maureen Dowd wrote a measured critique of Lean In, Sandberg's fans promptly and widely denounced her. Losse said she's not surprised by the fire-and-brimstone ferocity of the response. "There's this cult-like religiosity to Facebook and Lean In," she told me. "If you're 'in,' you belong—and if you're not, you're going to hell."

That Lean In is making its demands of individual women, not the corporate workplace, is evident in the ease with which it has signed up more than two hundred corporate and organization "partners" to support its campaign. The roster includes some of the biggest American corporations: Chevron, General Electric, Procter & Gamble, Comcast, Bank of America and Citibank, Coca-Cola and Pepsico, AT&T and Verizon, Ford and GM, Pfizer and Merck & Co., Costco and Wal-Mart, and, of course, Google and Facebook. Never before have so many corporations joined a revolution. Virtually nothing is required of them—not even a financial contribution. "There are no costs associated with partnering with Lean In," the organization's manual assures. "We just ask that you publicly support our mission and actively promote our Community to your employees." All the companies have to do is post their logo on Lean In's "Platform Partners" page, along with a quote from one of their executives professing the company's commitment to advancing women. The testimonials are predictably platitudinous:

- Ed Gilligan, American Express president: "At American Express, we believe having more women in senior leadership is critical to fostering an environment that embraces diverse opinions and empowers all employees to reach their full potential. It's this spirit of inclusiveness that helps us make better decisions today to drive our growth for tomorrow."

- Paul Bulcke, Nestlé CEO: "At Nestlé we are committed to enhancing the career opportunities for both men and women, and the knowledge and expertise provided by Lean In will help accelerate our journey."

- Jeff Wilke, Amazon senior vice president, consumer business: "At Amazon, we lean in to challenge ourselves to develop as leaders by building things that matter. We solve problems in new ways and value calculated risk-taking; many decisions are reversible. Bold directions that inspire results help us to think differently and look around corners for ways to serve our customers."

That last statement manages to endorse Lean In without even bothering to mention women. Many of the high-level executives dispensing quotations are male—and a notable number of the female executives are in "communications," "human resources," or "diversity" posts. And funny—or not—how often professed "commitment" to women's advancement fails to bear up under inspection. Run some Platform Partner names through databases that track legal cases, and you will find a bumper crop of recent or pending EEOC grievances and state and federal court actions involving sex discrimination, sexual harassment, preg-

nancy discrimination, unfair promotion policies, wrongful termi-
nations, and gender-based retaliations against female employees.
Here are just a few:

- Lean In Platform Partner Citibank: In 2010, six current and
  former female employees sued Citibank's parent company,
  Citigroup, for discriminating against women at all levels,
  paying them less, overlooking them for promotions, and fir-
  ing them first in companywide layoffs. Their federal court
  complaint held that the company "turns a blind eye" to
  widespread discrimination against women and detailed the
  paltry numbers of women in upper management in every
  division—with the proportion of female managing directors
  in some divisions as low as 9 percent. All nineteen members
  of the bank's executive committee are male. "The outdated
  'boys club,'" the complaint concluded, "is alive and well at
  Citigroup."

- Lean In Platform Partner Booz Allen Hamilton: In 2011,
  Molly Finn, a former partner at the firm who had been fired
  after serving as its highest-ranking female employee and a
  star performer, sued for sex discrimination. She charged the
  company with creating an unwelcome environment for
  women and intentionally barring them from top leadership
  posts. During a review for a promotion (which she was subsequently denied), she was told to stop saying "pro-woman,
  feminist things," she recalled.

  Soon after Finn's suit, a second longtime partner and
  leading moneymaker, Margo Fitzpatrick, sued the company
  for sex discrimination and retaliatory termination. In court
  papers, she charged that the firm has "maintained a 'glass
  ceiling' that intentionally excludes highly-qualified women."
  The complaint went on to note, "Currently, The Firm has no
  female partners in the pipeline for Senior Partner." With the

termination of Fitzpatrick and Finn, "the number of females in the partnership has dwindled to 21—or only 18%."

- Lean In Platform Partner Wells Fargo: In 2011, the bank reached a class-action settlement with 1,200 female financial advisers for $32 million. The sex discrimination suit charged that the bank's brokerage business, Wells Fargo Advisors (originally Wachovia Securities), discriminated against women in compensation and signing bonuses, denied them promotions, and cheated them out of account distributions, investment partnerships, and mentoring and marketing opportunities.

- Goldman Sachs (whose philanthropic arm, the Goldman Sachs Foundation, is a Lean In Platform Partner): In 2010, former employees of Goldman Sachs filed a class-action suit against the company, accusing Wall Street's most profitable investment bank of "systematic and pervasive discrimination" against female employees, subjecting them to hostile working conditions and treating them "like disposable, second-class citizens."

- Lean In Platform Partners Mondelez and Nestlé: In 2013, an Oxfam investigation in four countries where the two companies outsourced their cocoa farms found that the women working in the cocoa fields and processing plants that the companies relied on "suffer substantial discrimination and inequality." When women at a cocoa-processing factory demanded equal treatment and pay, the investigation noted, all of the female workers were fired. The same companies that "put women first in their advertisements," Oxfam concluded, "are doing very little to address poor conditions faced by the women who grow cocoa."

- Lean In Platform Partner Costco: In 2012, a federal judge approved a huge class-action lawsuit that alleges Costco dis-

criminated against about 700 women and denied them promotions. The company, the suit charged, maintains a "glass
ceiling" that prevents women from advancing to assistant
manager and general manager positions. Costco's senior
management, the complaint observed, is virtually all male,
and less than 16 percent of general managers nationwide are
women. Costco cofounder and longtime CEO Jim Sinegal
(who retired in 2011), has argued that women don't want
warehouse-management posts because "women have a tendency to be the caretakers and have the responsibility for
the children and for the family."

And then there's Lean In Platform Partner Wal-Mart. In
2011, the world's largest retailer famously managed to dodge one
of the largest class-action sex-discrimination suits in U.S. history (involving 1.5 million women), after the U.S. Supreme
Court ruled on technical grounds that the case didn't constitute
a single class action. In preparation for a second round of individual and regional class-action proceedings, thousands of female
employees have already refiled sex-discrimination grievances in
forty-eight states.

Here's what Mike Duke, Wal-Mart CEO and president, had to
say in his statement on Lean In's Platform Partner page: "As we
lean in to empower women, it helps us to better serve our customers, develop the best talent, and strengthen our communities."

And what about Facebook? When asked about women's representation at the company during media appearances for her
book tour, Sandberg was vague. "We're ahead of the industry,"
she told one interviewer, noting that a woman heads Facebook's
"global sales" and another is "running design," before briskly
changing the subject.

I contacted Facebook's press office and submitted questions
about the numbers and percentage of women in management,
engineering, and so on. Ashley Zandy, media spokeswoman at
Facebook, e-mailed me back, thanking me "for reaching out"

and offering a "chat." The chat was off the record and, in any case, provided no additional information on women's representation at the company. Then she offered me an "off the record" conversation with Sandberg, which I declined: off the record meant I couldn't repeat what Sandberg told me—and, considering Sandberg's polish and power, I didn't understand her reticence. Zandy said she'd try to get the figures I'd requested and arrange interviews, including ones with Sandberg and Facebook's head of human resources.

Two days later, she sent me a second e-mail. "I appreciate you reaching out," she wrote. "Unfortunately, I won't be able to arrange any of the interviews you requested." Nor provide statistics. "Unfortunately, we don't share much of the detailed and quantitative data you have asked for." She was able to tell me the following:

- The names of Facebook's top executives (which the company, by law, has to disclose in its annual report). Except for Sandberg, they were all male.

- Names of "female leaders in operational roles." Of the nine, only one was on the engineering side of the aisle; the others were mostly in traditionally "female" roles like communications, consumer marketing, and human resources.

- Examples of Facebook's "incredible benefits" (a generous four-month paid parental leave and a $4,000 "baby cash" payment) and "strong resources for ALL employees—and for women" ("Women Leadership Day," "hosting speakers and mentoring student groups," etc.).

- And finally, "a FB statement in lieu of an interview": "Statement: Facebook supports the message of Lean In—that women should pursue their goals with gusto, no matter what they may be. We work hard to create a work environment that supports women and gives them the opportunities to have impact and lead. Our management and employees are incredibly passionate about not just recruiting and retaining women, but developing the right leadership, policies and support to create a culture and workplace where they can thrive."

I wrote back to say I appreciated the information and still wished to talk to Sandberg. "Though some of my questions are skeptical," I said, "I hoped that they might open an actual and meaningful dialogue on a subject both she and I care about." I presented four questions for Sandberg. Here are the first two:

1. A number of Lean In's corporate Platform Partners seem to have a woman problem—most notably (though not alone), the sex-discrimination legal actions against Wal-Mart and Costco. How do you ensure that corporate partners are not signing up as a way of whitewashing (agreeing publicly with the concept of women's advancement, and securing Lean In's imprimatur, to avoid addressing more systemic problems)? Is there an instance where you've said to such a company that you'd be glad to have it as a partner, but only after it cleans up its act? Wouldn't such a demand be an example of what you champion—that having women in power will benefit ordinary women?

2. Lean In Circles have been described as peer mentoring and as a sort of consciousness-raising for our times. If a Lean In Circle decides that members of its group have actual grievances with the companies they work for that require a political response, would Lean In be supportive of them taking political or legal action against those companies? Would you, for example, encourage a Lean In Circle to picket a discriminatory employer?

Zandy replied: "As I mentioned before, I do think an off the record conversation between you and Sheryl would be a great place to start the dialogue. Let me know if you would reconsider that." I again declined.

In the middle of the next week, I received an e-mail from another media spokesperson, this one with Lean In. Andrea Saul (formerly the press secretary for Mitt Romney's 2012 presidential campaign) informed me, "Unfortunately, an interview will not be possible." Instead, she sent me written answers to my questions, evidently drafted by Lean In's public relations apparatus (see below), and "a quote for your use":

> Lean In is a global community committed to encouraging and supporting women leaning in to their ambitions. We're incredibly grateful to our community and the individuals, and institutions, who have already made progress changing the conversation on gender. But we know there is so much more to do before we live in an equal world. That's why we're not just encouraging, but supporting, everyone and every company that wants to lean in. It's time to change the world, not just the conversation.

Upstairs, Downstairs

One Saturday several weeks into Sandberg's protracted multimedia tour, I drove to the mother root of American industry, the city that, as its historical literature puts it, "gave birth to the modern corporation." So many of New England's old textile factories have been gutted and converted into boutique and condo space. But in the 1970s, Lowell, Massachusetts, turned over millions of square feet of abandoned mills to the National Park Service. The 141 acres of factories, boardinghouses, and power canals are now the preserve of the Lowell National Historical Park.

Its centerpiece is the Boott Cotton Mills, "the cathedral of industry," a red brick behemoth that sits alongside the Merrimack River like a medieval fortress, ensconced within a rampart of thick red brick walls, accessible only by a single bridge spanning a deepwater canal. A huge bell tower presides over the courtyard: for decades, its 4:30 a.m. toll summoned a nearly all-female workforce to a fourteen-hour day. The Boott Mills is now a museum, its exhibition space a reminder of the vast divide between the men who owned it and the women who labored there.

Upstairs, a wing is adorned with large oil portraits of the gentlemen mill proprietors who formed the WASPy Boston Associates. Downstairs, the "weave room," a sprawling factory floor, has been restored to its early glory (minus the humid, lint-choked air that incubated spectacular rates of tuberculosis and other lung diseases, and minus the mass infestation of cockroaches that swarmed over employees' clothes and lunch pails). During visiting hours, museum staffers run a portion of the eighty-eight power looms to provide visitors with a modest sense of the earsplitting cacophony. (Even at reduced levels, the museum must dispense earplugs.) On the day I visited, two middle-aged women were operating the clanking looms. As I stood, half-hypnotized by a power shuttle flinging itself back and forth between the warp threads, they came over to ask if I had questions. Several minutes into our conversation, it was apparent that they were no ordinary docents. Francisca DeSousa and Cathy Randall were lifelong mill workers.

The textile factory where DeSousa had worked for more than a quarter century had hightailed it to Mexico, and she'd taken the job at the museum. Randall has continued to work in the few remaining mills, including for a time at one that has made certain adjustments to the times: it weaves carbon fiber for microchips. She was working, that is, at the industrial production end of the empire that Sheryl Sandberg presides over as chief operating officer.

DeSousa, like Randall, started at three dollars an hour. Later, she recalled, "they paid you four to five cents per piecework—to make you work faster." In the course of her employment, she and her husband, who also worked full time, had four children. After she gave birth, "I took one week off, unpaid," she said. "You didn't dare take more than that—you'd get fired."

"There was no vacation time," Randall recalled of her first job, "no health insurance, no benefits, and no sick days." After eleven years, she was making eleven dollars an hour. "Now they just don't give you the forty hours," she said, "so they don't have to pay you benefits."

DeSousa and Randall, like so many mill workers, saw many accidents: women who were mauled, women who lost body parts, women nearly scalped when the loom mechanism seized their hair. On the factory floor one day, Randall witnessed an "amputation": a young woman's arm was sucked into the machinery. The memory still haunts her. "She was one of the ones I trained," she said.

None of these jobs were unionized. At the first mill Randall worked for, she became involved in an organizing effort. The union campaign never came to a vote. "People were too afraid," she said, recalling how one of the women "came to me crying, 'Don't do this, I can't lose my job.'"

DeSousa led two ad hoc protest efforts of her own. The first was in response to a company announcement that the workers would no longer be given a lunch hour—which was actually a lunch *half* hour. "I told them we are going to sit down for half an hour, because we deserve it," she said. At first, her coworkers were leery of taking a stand. "It was hard keeping people together. I mean, I was scared, too—my God, what were they going to do to us?" But finally she convinced her colleagues. "I told them, 'Listen, if we stick together, they can't fire all of us.'" After two weeks of sit-downs, the company relented. Then the company announced that mill workers would be required to work overtime on Saturdays. While the women were glad for the extra money, many were single mothers with no weekend day care. "If you didn't show up on Saturday, they'd give you a yellow slip," DeSousa recalled, "and after you got several of them, they could fire you." DeSousa and another mill worker proposed a plan: "We stop all the looms—it's the only way to get their attention." The workers did, and a few minutes later, their overlords rushed in. "Even the big bosses from the main office came running." After a tense negotiation, the women won their fight. DeSousa's supervisor, though, let her know that she better not try for a third victory. "My boss came over," DeSousa recalled, "and he said to me, 'Some day, Norma Rae, I'm going to *get you.*'"

I asked the two women if they had heard of Lean In. Randall said she had seen a couple of Sandberg's TV appearances, but didn't quite understand the message. I told her that Lean In argues that women need to break down "internal obstacles" within themselves that are preventing them from moving up the work ladder. "There *are* a lot of barriers women face," Randall said. She ticked off a few: lousy pay, no benefits, no sick leave, no unions, sexism, and a still highly sex-segregated workforce. "There are lots of jobs that are still considered women's work," she said. "In one of the mills, I was actually referred to as 'the girl.'"

What Randall described is what most American working women face. And they are also the sort of problems that the advocates of Lean In and its sister impulses must address if they are not to be seen as individual women empowering themselves by deserting other women—if they are to be called, as Sheryl Sandberg calls herself, feminist.

What about "internal obstacles," I asked Randall—the sort of obstacles that cause women to curb their ambitions because they're afraid they won't be likeable? She pondered the question for a time. "I don't know," she said finally. "That's just not the world I came from."

My Questions for Sheryl Sandberg . . . and the Answers from Her PR Department

Q: A number of Lean In's corporate Platform Partners seem to have a woman problem—most notably (though not alone), the sex-discrimination legal actions against Wal-Mart and Costco. How do you ensure that corporate partners are not signing up as a way of whitewashing (agreeing publicly with the concept of women's advancement, and securing Lean's imprimatur, to avoid addressing more systemic problems)? Is there an instance where you've said to such a company that you'd be glad to have it as a partner, but only after it cleans up its act? Wouldn't such a demand be an example of what you champion—that having women in power will benefit ordinary women?

A: We reject this premise. There are over 200 companies who have joined as platform partners, and it seems early to judge their motivations. We are not setting up a watchdog organization or an audit function. Rather, we are providing high-quality educational materials and technology at scale that companies can use to improve their understanding of gender bias. We want to make these materials available to everyone—because every company can get better, and we want them to.

Q: Lean In Circles have been described as peer mentoring and as a sort of consciousness-raising for our times. If a Lean In Circle decides that members of its group have actual grievances with the companies they work for that require a political response, would Lean In be supportive of them taking political or legal action against those companies? Would you, for example, encourage a Lean In Circle to picket a discriminatory employer?

A: Lean In Circles are a starting point, not an endpoint. We are encouraging people to set up Circles and take them where they will through an open and constructive dialogue—and share their learnings with other Circles. Lean In provides a framework but we want each Circle to decide what it does or focuses on, because each Circle is different and has different needs.

Q: Lean In has described itself as a "movement." Social movements in my experience are all about solidarity and confrontation—that is, a collective response that confronts powerful institutions and people who are holding a group down. What is the confrontation here, and who or what is being confronted? Or does the sort of self-awareness endorsed by Lean In Circles stop when external confrontation begins? Put another way, is the confrontation all with one's self, to appeal to the corporation?

A: Again, we reject this premise. We are a community that seeks to promote awareness and empower individual, as well as collective, action. Lean In is made up of individuals and organizations coming together to further the common aim of understanding gender bias and helping other women achieve their goals.

Q: Lean In emphasizes individual solutions to problems of individual advancement. How do you keep this focus on individual initiative from undermining an alternative group awareness necessary to fuel an actual movement?

A: This is not a zero-sum solution. It takes both individual and collective initiative. In fact, Lean In makes clear that individuals can facilitate institutional reform. The more people are focused on issues for gender, the more of both there will be. We think Lean In is already demonstrating results—individuals taking action, women asking for and getting raises, companies changing policies. The questions we would ask back is: "Has overall group awareness of these important social issues increased since Lean In launched?" Our answer is that while there is so much more to do, changes have begun.

Rolling Stone

For many of us, the Internet—in its vastness, its potential for anonymity, its sense of limitless freedom combined equally with a sense of constant surveillance—is already a pretty uncanny place. David Kushner's riveting profile of Ross Ulbricht shows us just how creepy and bizarre it can get. Ulbricht, a.k.a. Dread Pirate Roberts, went from being an exceptionally smart but seemingly normal suburban slacker to a libertarian ideologue and the diabolically entrepreneurial creator of Silk Road, an anonymous online bazaar of drugs, firearms, and other contraband. It didn't end well.

David Kushner

4. Dead End on Silk Road

Internet Crime Kingpin Ross Ulbricht's Big Fail

On October 1, 2013, inside the science-fiction section of the Glen Park library in San Francisco, one of the Internet's most-wanted men sat typing quietly on his laptop. He'd allegedly assumed multiple identities and made nearly half a billion dollars in under three years. He was said to be as grandiose as he was cold-blooded, championing freedom while ordering hits on those who crossed him.

None of the geeks milling around the stacks that day, nor even those closest to Ross Ulbricht, suspected that the slight, pale twenty-nine-year-old was, according to prosecutors, the notorious hacker known as Dread Pirate Roberts. He was allegedly the founder of Silk Road, an online illegal-goods bazaar that had been dubbed the eBay of vice. A Texas native with a master's in materials science and engineering and a mop of brown hair, Ulbricht bore such a resemblance to Robert Pattinson that girls stopped him in the street to take their picture with him. The library was near where he had been living since moving to the city a year earlier. He liked to come here for the silence and the free wifi.

But at three-fifteen p.m., the quiet was broken when, out of nowhere, a young woman in street clothes charged toward Ulbricht yelling, "I'm so sick of you!" and grabbed his laptop. Ulbricht leapt from his seat to grab it back, when the half dozen other readers at nearby tables suddenly lunged for him, pushing him up against a window. Hearing the commotion, the librarian rushed over to assist Ulbricht. "Go back to your desk," the woman who had started it all told her. "We're making an arrest."

Stripping off their civilian shirts to reveal FBI vests, the agents told Ulbricht to turn around. He had no expression when they cuffed him. As they led him toward the door, the female agent turned to the mystified onlookers and said, "Surprise!"

.   .   .

Seven weeks later, during Ulbricht's bail hearing in a New York courtroom, few were more surprised to see him in prison khakis, sitting before a federal judge, than his family and friends, watching anxiously from a back row. They listened as federal prosecutors accused Ulbricht of running an elaborate illegal enterprise, "the most sophisticated and extensive criminal marketplace on the Internet today."

Named after the ancient Asian trade route that linked merchants from East to West, Silk Road was a dizzying illicit emporium, with neatly organized categories of drugs and weapons, complete with photos and descriptions. There were fake IDs, bogus passports, driver's licenses, social security cards. Hacking tools were on tap, including tutorials for robbing ATMs and software programs for taking control of someone's computer. There were hackers for hire too—even assassins for hire. "Hitmen," one post listed, "(10+ countries)."

Silk Road existed in the Deep Web, the vast ocean of hidden sites (roughly 500 times as many as the ones you surf) that Google and other search engines can't easily access. Much of the Deep Web is too dynamic to be indexed—such as library catalogs, job classifieds, medical databases—but it's also home to sites that don't want to be found because they're dealing in illegal goods.

Ironically, the federal government helped transform the Deep Web into a haven for outlaws. In the midnineties, scientists at the U.S. Naval Research Lab conceived of a way to surf the Net without being tracked or identified—a necessity for government communication and foreign dissidents. With federal funding, free software called Tor, which stands for The Onion Router, was developed and released in 2002 to bring this to life. When used with a Web browser, Tor functions like an invisibility cloak, encrypting your locations as well as the destinations you surf. It didn't take long for surfers trading in child porn, drugs, and other contraband to create sites that could only be accessed using Tor. And Silk Road was among them.

For even greater stealth, transactions on Silk Road used Bitcoin, the digital currency introduced in 2009. With its value set by supply and demand (currently trading at about $1,000 for one Bitcoin), it's being increasingly accepted by a variety of businesses, from the NBA's Sacramento Kings to Subway sandwich shops. But what made it perfect for Silk Road was its lack of government oversight and the ability to complete transactions without involving banks.

According to a recent study by *Addiction* journal, nearly 20 percent of drug consumers in the United States used narcotics bought on Silk Road. By facilitating more than a million transactions, the site generated the equivalent of more than $1.2 billion in revenues during its two-and-a-half-year run. With approximately $420 million in commissions, the feds allege, it made Ross Ulbricht one of the most successful entrepreneurs of the dot-com age.

It purportedly made him a deadly one, too. Assistant U.S. Attorney Serrin Turner claims Ulbricht spent $730,000 of his earnings on hiring hitmen to kill six of his enemies. "While portraying himself as a champion of 'freedom' on the Silk Road website, opposed to the use of any kind of 'force' against others, he was in fact a quite ruthless criminal," as Turner put it, "one who, with seeming ease and lack of conscience, nonchalantly ordered murders for hire amidst fixing server bugs and answering customer-support tickets."

Charged with narcotics trafficking, money laundering, computer hacking, and attempted murder, Ulbricht faces life in prison. When the New York judge denied bail, his family, who had raised $1 million in bail money pledged from Ulbricht's many supporters, gasped. It was impossible to believe that Dread Pirate Roberts could be him. "In his entire life, with all these people who know him, something would have been indicated that he was capable of this," his mother, Lyn, tells me, "and it never has."

.   .   .

Growing up in Austin, Ulbricht was, his father, Kirk, recalls, "a healthy, happy, unflappable Buddha of a kid." His parents built and rented bamboo solar-powered houses on the Costa Rican coast, and Ulbricht spent his summers running barefoot among the monkeys and learning from his dad how to be a big-wave rider. "He would go out surfing, and I'd be on binoculars and say, 'Get in here now,'" his mother recalls. "Because he's so enthusiastic, sometimes he's a little too fearless."

But Ulbricht had a geeky side as well. He later recalled feeling like "a dorky kid." An Eagle Scout like his dad and a comic-book fanatic, he won the third-grade math olympics in school. Ulbricht spent hours doodling monsters in notebooks and was more interested in painting miniatures for the fantasy board game Warhammer than playing video games. "We didn't want our kids on the computer," says Kirk. "We wanted them outside playing." Taking a cue from his parents, Ulbricht was an entrepreneurial kid, selling ice pops and magazine subscriptions door to door.

By high school, "Rossman," as he was known to his friends, had become an easygoing and fun-loving Austin hipster, skateboarding with friends, one of whom shaved Ulbricht's hair into a mohawk on a whim. On some weekends, his crew would pile into trucks and drive out to a hill-country ranch to party. Classmate Sean Gaulager recalls Ulbricht leaping over a bonfire and dabbling in hallucinogens. "Ross, to me, was always a fucking awesome dude," Gaulager says. When another friend, René Pinnell, told Ulbricht how he had merely "dipped a toe" in drinking and drugs during high school, Ulbricht told him that "I did, like, a cannonball . . . in that department."

But Ulbricht was always able to balance partying with grades. Graduating with a 1460 SAT score, he earned a full scholarship to the University of Texas at Dallas, where he became, as one friend puts it, a "physics hippie." Making a name for himself at the college's NanoTech Institute, where he published papers on solar-cell technology, Ulbricht strolled around campus shirtless and barefoot, ingested mind-spinning psychedelics, and spouted Eastern philosophy. He loved staying up late watching trippy movies like Richard Linklater's *Waking Life* and talking about the nature of reality. "My whole philosophy at the time," he later recalled, was "of being super-open and loving and connected to everything."

He graduated in 2006 and won another full scholarship to Penn State to pursue a master's in materials science and engineering. While researching thin-film crystals as a research scientist, Ulbricht grew a scraggly beard, practiced yoga, and took up conga drumming. He felt, as he posted on Facebook, "overwhelmed with the glory of being alive."

He was also evolving into a hardcore libertarian. In 2007, when Mitt Romney posed a question on YouTube, asking, "What do you believe is America's single greatest challenge?" Ulbricht sat in front of his webcam and said, "The most important thing is getting us out of the United Nations," which he saw as somehow impeding political freedom. He would eventually discover the work of Ludwig von Mises and the Austrian School of economics, which further crystallized his beliefs.

By the time he finished his master's in 2009, he had become disillusioned with being a scientist. "It wasn't for him," his mother says. "He wanted to be an entrepreneur." When family and friends questioned him about his change of course, Ulbricht remained adamant. "I remember him saying, 'I just don't want to do this,'" his lifelong friend Alden Schiller recalls. "He didn't like the idea of being an employee, or being in the lab setting." Moving back to Austin, he started his own used-book company, Good Wagon, donating a portion of the proceeds to an inner-city youth program and leftover books to a prison-literacy project. "We raised him to be empathetic," his mother says, proudly, "and to put yourself in others' shoes." One day, however, Ulbricht walked into his company warehouse to find that the shelves had collapsed. Thousands of books he'd spent weeks organizing were a mess, and it would take an ungodly amount of hours to put them back into place. Ulbricht seemed to see it as a sign and closed the business. As his mother says, "He thought, 'I've got to do something else.'"

•   •   •

Silk Road was rooted in its founder's frustration over, as he wrote, "what seemed to be insurmountable barriers between the world today and the world I wanted." He'd begun working on the idea in 2010, inspired by his libertarian beliefs. "All of the sudden, it was so clear," he went on. "Every action you take outside the scope of government control strengthens the market and weakens the state." And the action he decided to take was in creating a marketplace for personal liberties online.

According to prosecutors, a journal found by the FBI on Ulbricht's computer stated that he wanted "to create a website where people could buy anything anonymously, with no trail whatsoever that could lead back to them." At first, he thought to call it Underground Brokers, but then divined a better name, something that sounded more eternal. "Silk Road is going to become a phenomenon," he wrote, "and at least one person will tell me about it, unknowing that I was its creator."

In January 2011, an announcement appeared online for the launch of Silk Road, explaining how to use the Tor browser to connect to it. "Every precaution is made to ensure your anonymity and security," it read. The same month, a user named Altoid (prosecutors believe this to be an alias for Ulbricht himself) spread the word on online forums, comparing Silk Road to "an anonymous Amazon.com."

Silk Road wasn't just a place to buy dope; it was a well-designed and well-organized shop. There were rules. Child porn was not permitted, nor were stolen items. Drugs were broken down into discrete sections: cannabis, dissociatives, Ecstasy, psychedelics, opioids, stimulants.

Like eBay, Silk Road implemented seller ratings for quality control. For more assurance, industrious dealers offered samples of their products to prospective reviewers, who could then post accounts of their highs (or lows). Products would arrive by post, often with bogus return addresses. Drugs would be slipped inside DVD cases, lip-balm dispensers and other decoys.

It wasn't just the efficient shopping experience that customers liked, it was their fearless leader, too. The site's as-yet-unnamed founder was an active presence, attentively addressing his customers' concerns and rallying them around the brave new world they were creating. "There are heroes among us here at Silk Road," he wrote in one post. "Every day they risk their lives, fortunes and precious liberty for us."

At times, the founder sounded like he was giving a stump speech. "Silk Road is about something much bigger than thumbing your nose at the man and getting your drugs anyway," he wrote. "It's about taking back our liberty and our dignity and demanding justice." He seemed to have a politician's talent for creating a good-natured sense of false intimacy. When a customer asked for a virtual embrace, the benevolent leader replied, "Hugs not drugs. . . . No wait, hugs AND drugs!"

As traffic flooded the site, it wasn't only drug dealers and buyers who took notice. After a *Gawker* story ran about Silk Road in June 2011, New York Sen. Chuck Schumer demanded the site be shut down. "[It] represents the most brazen attempt to peddle drugs online that we have ever seen," he told the press.

The feds soon began to quietly monitor the site's activities. In January 2012, thirty-two-year-old Jacob Theodore George IV, a Maryland-based Silk Road dealer, was busted by federal agents. As part of his plea, which was only recently made public, he turned over his e-mails, financial records, and shipping details—a bounty of insight into Silk Road's underworld.

But the feds kept the bust quiet, building their case, and Silk Road's business continued unabated. As revenues increased, the site announced a change in the commission structure, shifting from a flat rate to a sliding scale based on the price of sales items (10 percent of the first $50 to 1.5 percent for sales more than $1,000). When the community balked, their leader didn't hesitate to remind them who was boss. "Whether you like it or not, I am the captain of this ship," he wrote. "If you don't like the rules of the game, or you don't trust the captain, you can get off the boat."

Soon, the site had taken on a life of its own, so much so that its elusive creator told his followers that it was time for a symbolic change. "Silk Road has matured, and I need an identity separate from the site," the administrator wrote. "I am Silk Road, the market, the person, the enterprise, everything. But I need a name."

He took one from a character in *The Princess Bride*: Dread Pirate Roberts, a fearsome pirate whose name was not just his own but one to be passed on to others who might succeed him. "Drumroll please . . . ," he wrote. "My new name is: Dread Pirate Roberts."

.   .   .

Throughout this time, Ulbricht seemed like the same old Ross, though his hippie persona had taken on an edge of grandiosity. "Who is the smartest, most talented programmer you know?" he posted on Facebook in October 2011. "Tell them your awesome Facebook friend Ross is recruiting for a seed-funded Bitcoin startup company. Thanks." When his friend Noah replied by asking what Ulbricht was doing, Ulbricht brushed it off. "Don't worry, Mr. Noah," he wrote. "Just find me some programmers! You can Google 'Bitcoin.' "

A posting on his LinkedIn page was similarly mysterious. "I want to use economic theory as a means to abolish the use of coercion and aggression amongst mankind," he wrote. "The most widespread and systemic use of force is amongst institutions and governments. The best way to change a government is to change the minds of the governed. To that end, I am creating an economic simulation to give people a firsthand experience of what it would be like to live in a world without the systemic use of force." Ulbricht spent hours alone, standing barefoot on a hard floor at a stand-up desk. In one apartment, he had his keyboard, monitor, and mouse stacked on wobbly piles of books; to his right was a thrift-store painting of a blue peacock. He worked for so long that he nibbled away his fingernails and his feet throbbed—until a friend suggested he wear sandals. When he wasn't working, he could be found playing poker on rooftops or frequenting local music haunts. He went to the Austin City Limits festival, lounging with buddies in the grass in an undershirt and gray fedora. He was dating an attractive photographer, Sarah Allen, whom he'd met at an African drumming club.

"He was so sweet and loving and so good-looking and intelligent," Allen tells me. They went swimming in Barton Springs, did yoga outside, and spent long nights partying with Allen's models at her studio. "I would start singing and dancing," model Samantha Schreibvogel recalls. "It wouldn't take him long before he'd be dancing with me."

Following a rocky patch with Allen, Ulbricht sold his black Ford F150 and, in November 2011, he moved to Australia, where his older sister, Cally, was living. The two had always been close and had even applied to go on the *Amazing Race* TV show together. "We were always a team," she tells me. Ulbricht still lived like a student. "He didn't buy much," Cally says with a laugh. "He's been wearing the same clothes for twenty years." Ulbricht spent months surfing the local beaches. "Forecast: warmth and smiles," he posted on Facebook. "It's sunny again!!!" But he was less forthcoming about how he was paying the bills. "I thought he was working with foreign currencies, but I don't really know what that means," Cally says. Their mother just knew that he was doing some kind of financial work on the computer. "When he would explain things, I was like, 'Oh, OK, whatever,'" Lyn says. "He doesn't tell his mother everything."

.   .   .

One of the few people whom Dread Pirate Roberts, or DPR, trusted was Curtis Clark Green, who lived with his wife in a comfortable house in Spanish Fork, Utah. Green claimed to be a former paramedic and started posting on Silk Road forums in June 2011 as the site's drug sage. Using the handles Chronicpain and Flush, he often alluded to his enjoyment of self-medicating with opioids and to having suffered an undisclosed "accident" that sidelined his plans to complete a nursing degree. Green doled out advice on how to get maximum highs with minimum overdose risk and the best places on the body to shoot up ("Don't use your feet. Blood clots can form very easily if it's done this way"). When he put pharmaceutical fentanyl up on Silk Road, he promised to "personally test each batch to make sure it's up to par."

In the summer of 2012, after news surfaced of the first public arrest of a Silk Road user—thirty-two-year-old Paul Leslie Howard, charged with trafficking coke and Ecstasy through the site—DPR appeared to realize that Silk Road was now on the feds' radar and that he needed someone to help run his operation. By the end of 2012, Green was on payroll. According to prosecutors, when DPR got a message that December from a new seller looking to unload large quantities of cocaine, he put Green on the job of brokering the deal. "We have a buyer for you," DPR wrote the seller. "One of my staff is sending the details."

Though DPR was careful to keep a distance from his customers, he occasionally lifted the veil slightly—after Green helped the seller unload a kilo of coke to a buyer for $27,000 worth of Bitcoins, DPR reached out to him. "Congrats on the sale," DPR wrote, initiating an exchange in which he later referenced his girlfriend. Curious about how DPR managed his double life, the seller asked, "Does she know who you are? . . . Dread, I mean."

"No way," DPR replied. "Maybe never."

"How can you hide that from her? I have to guess that [you are] spending at least 10 to 12 hours a day on SR."

"I've become good at hiding," DPR replied.

On January 17, 2013, a postal worker delivered Green his package, which he opened to find 1,092 grams of coke inside. But he never had the chance to pass it along to his buyer. The postal worker was, in fact, an undercover agent, and Green was immediately arrested. Though it's unclear how much DPR knew about the bust, he trusted the seller enough to confide in him about the arrest. He also claimed that Green had stolen $350,000 in Bitcoins from Silk Road vendors, whom DPR now had to pay back.

"I'd like him beat up, then forced to send the Bitcoins he stole back," DPR wrote. The seller agreed to send thugs to take care of this for DPR. As he explained to the seller the next day, DPR feared that Green "was on the inside for a while, and now that he's been arrested, I'm afraid he'll give up info." This called for heavier means. "Can you change the order to execute rather than torture?" DPR wrote. He had "never killed a man or had one killed before," he added, "but it is the right move in this case."

DPR agreed to pay the seller $80,000, promising half up front and half when the job was done. According to prosecutors, DPR arranged for $40,000 to be wired from Australia in early February, saying that before sending the rest, he needed "proof of death," as he put it. "Ask for a video, if they can't do that, then pictures. . . . I'm more concerned about silencing him than getting the money back. . . . I have to assume he will sing."

On February 12, DPR logged online and got the word. The plan was in action. Green "is still alive but being tortured," the seller wrote. The killers "are good; they should break him."

"Shouldn't be hard," DPR typed back.

But DPR's bluster seemed to waver when the seller sent him pictures of Green being tortured. He was "a little disturbed, but I'm OK," he wrote. "I'm new to this. . . . I don't think I've done the wrong thing. . . . I'm sure I will call on you again at some point, though I hope I won't have to." When the next photo came, on February 21, it showed Green, dead from asphyxiation, his pale, heavy body lifeless and inert. "I'm pissed I had to kill him, but what's done is done," the seller wrote. DPR replied, "I just can't believe he was so stupid. . . . I just wish more people had some integrity."

•　　　•　　　•

After spending several months in Australia and a short stint back in Austin, Ulbricht had moved to San Francisco on the suggestion of his childhood friend René Pinnell, who offered him a job and a place to stay. Ulbricht, still a seeker at heart, agreed. "It seemed cosmic," he later recalled, "and the thing to do."

Ulbricht quickly fell for the town. "The crazy thing about San Francisco," he told Pinnell in an interview the two recorded for StoryCorps, "is it feels like home already." In public, Ulbricht seemed like his old carefree self. He hit up the local parties, went camping in the mountains, and played Frisbee. "Paradise is here or nowhere," he posted on Facebook.

But around this time, Dread Pirate Roberts was posting on Silk Road that he felt lonely and isolated. "I have no one to share my thoughts with in physical space," he lamented. "Security does not permit it, so thanks for listening." The challenges to Ulbricht's alleged alter ego, DPR, were mounting, and the business was growing rougher. New black-market sites—such as Atlantis, Sheep Marketplace, and Black Market Reloaded—were moving in on his turf. When Silk Road went offline for nearly a week after a hacking attack in April 2013, concern rose that it had been the work of its competitors.

DPR had even more problems. According to messages seized by the FBI, a Silk Road user nicknamed FriendlyChemist was demanding $500,000, which he needed to pay off his drug suppliers, or he would divulge a trove of personal data hacked from the site's online community. To prove he wasn't bluffing, FriendlyChemist sent DPR some samples of the personal data he was prepared to leak.

"Have your suppliers contact me here, so I can work something out with them," DPR replied. A few days later, DPR heard from another Silk Road user, Redandwhite—the well-known alias for the Hells Angels. "We are the people FriendlyChemist owes money to . . .," Redandwhite messaged. "What do you want to talk to us about?" Apparently recognizing the value of Redandwhite's connections, DPR made a pitch. "FriendlyChemist aside," DPR wrote, "we have access to illicit substances in quantity and are having issues with bad distributors. If you don't already sell here on Silk Road, I'd like you to consider becoming a vendor."

"If you can get FriendlyChemist to meet up with us, or pay us his debt, then I'm sure I would be able to get people in our group to give this online side of the business a try," Redandwhite replied. DPR proposed a deal. FriendlyChemist, he wrote, "is a liability and I wouldn't mind if he was executed. . . . I have the following info and am waiting on getting his address."

After FriendlyChemist ramped up his threat two days later, demanding the $500,000 within seventy-two hours, DPR messaged Redandwhite, saying FriendlyChemist was "causing me problems. . . . I would like to put a bounty on his head, if it's not too much trouble for you." The next day, he wrote him again: "This kind of behavior is unforgivable to me. Especially here on Silk Road, anonymity is sacrosanct." The murder, he added, "doesn't have to be clean."

Redandwhite told him the killing would cost between $150,000 and $300,000, "depending on how you want it done." DPR balked. "Don't want to be a pain here, but the price seems high," he replied. "Not long ago, I had a clean hit done for $80K. Are the prices you quoted the best you can do?" They finally settled on 1,670 Bitcoins—roughly $150,000—which DPR promptly sent. "I received the payment," Redandwhite replied. DPR handed over the real name of FriendlyChemist and said he lived in White Rock, British Columbia, with his wife and three kids. "We know where he is," Redandwhite said. "He'll be grabbed tonight. I'll update you."

Twenty-four hours later, the job was done. "Your problem has been taken care of . . . ," Redandwhite messaged DPR. "Rest easy though, because he won't be blackmailing anyone again. Ever." He included a picture that showed the corpse, which had a piece of paper near it with a series of numbers that DPR had instructed him to write for added veracity. "I've received the picture and deleted it," DPR replied. "Thank you again for your swift action."

At this point, Redandwhite said that before killing Friendly-Chemist, the hitmen made sure "he spilled everything," including the location of another Silk Road user, Tony76, who lived in Surrey, British Columbia, and had been conspiring with him "on this scheme to blackmail you." Tony76 was a drug dealer who lived and worked with three others, Redandwhite had learned. After some more back-and-forth, DPR agreed to pay Redandwhite $500,000 to kill Tony76 and his three roommates. Then he transferred the Bitcoins to Redandwhite.

The next week, on April 15, 2013, Redandwhite sent DPR a message telling him "that problem was dealt with. I'll try to catch you online to give you details. Just wanted to let you know right away so you have one less thing to worry about."

"Thanks," DPR replied.

•   •   •

By summer 2013, the feds seemed to be closing in on Silk Road. In May, a fourteen-year-old boy was busted in Fishers, Indiana, for buying Ecstasy on the site. In June, news broke that the U.S. Drug Enforcement Administration had seized $814 in Bitcoins— the first such seizure of digital currency—from a thirty-one-year-old Charleston man for allegedly dealing on Silk Road under the name Casey Jones.

In late July, the FBI's cybercrime team had enough to access one of Silk Road's secret servers in an undisclosed country. They obtained data going back to 2011, including more than 1.2 million financial transactions. In the course of their investigation, they would also uncover an archive of DPR's e-mails, including his correspondence with Redandwhite and requests by DPR to buy fake IDs, which he said he needed to rent more servers under assumed names.

On July 26, there was a knock at Ulbricht's door. Ulbricht had recently moved to an apartment on Fifteenth Avenue in San Francisco. For $1,200 a month, the sublet, which he shared with two roommates, was a modest place on a picturesque street. If Ulbricht's roommates heard the men at the door ask for Ulbricht by name, however, they would have been surprised. They only knew him as Joshua Terrey. "Josh" had answered their Craigslist ad in June, describing himself in his e-mail as a "29 yo Texan man, good natured and clean/tidy." He said he was a currency trader who did freelance IT work and that he was new to the area and didn't have a cell phone yet. "Would you mind if I paid in cash?" he'd asked.

But it seemed that Josh wasn't Ulbricht's only alias. The men at the door were federal agents, and they had come to investigate a package of nine phony driver's licenses that had been intercepted at the Canadian border and sent to this address. One of the agents handed Ulbricht a California driver's license that bore his picture but a different name: Sean David Lake. Ulbricht showed them his Texas license but refused to entertain their questions, other than saying that "hypothetically," anyone could buy fake IDs on a site called Silk Road.

Though it's unclear why Ulbricht name-checked the site, the agents left without incident. But in an August 2013 interview with *Forbes* over an encrypted chat, DPR said he was feeling the heat. "The highest levels of government are hunting me," he typed from an undisclosed location. "I can't take any chances."

In early September, Ulbricht was with his family at a home they had rented in San Francisco's Noe Valley. His sister was in town for a wedding, so they had decided to make it a family get-together. Ulbricht's parents drove up from Austin. Ulbricht seemed in good spirits and made no mention of the visit by the federal agents. "It was just fun," his dad, Kirk, recalls, "and great to be all together again." His sister, Cally, says, "Ross seemed really relaxed and really comfortable."

Two weeks later, Lyn and Kirk were back in Austin when their phone rang. Lyn watched Kirk's face drop. "Oh, my God," he said. He turned to his wife and told her, "Ross has been arrested."

When Ulbricht was apprehended at the Glen Park library, the feds claimed to have caught him red-handed. Prosecutors say his laptop showed he was logged on to a Silk Road administration panel listing messages from customers needing his attention. He was also allegedly logged on to a Silk Road page titled "Mastermind."

The feds say that despite his tech savvy, Ulbricht had left loose ends, exposing, via an alias, his e-mail address when soliciting a developer to join a Bitcoin startup. Files allegedly found on Ulbricht's laptop were even more damning. There was the private log detailing DPR's murder-for-hire plots involving Redandwhite, who has not yet been publicly identified or charged. The Redandwhite hits remain a mystery; Canadian authorities found no reports of homicides in the area that matched the supposed victims, and the whole thing may well have been an elaborate con. As for the hit DPR ordered on Green, it was actually a sting operation involving an undercover agent, and the murder was staged with Green's cooperation. But whatever the outcomes, prosecutors say that "Ulbricht clearly intended for these killings to happen."

The feds also say they discovered research Ulbricht had conducted to flee the country and to obtain citizenship in the Caribbean. A file labeled "emergency" detailed his escape plan if caught: "Encrypt and backup important files on laptop to memory stick. Destroy laptop, destroy phone, hide memory stick, get new laptop, go to end of train, find place to live on Craigslist for cash, create new identity (name, backstory)." As the prosecutors put it, "He had contemplated and prepared for a life on the run." They also seized money from Ulbricht's computer—roughly $30 million in Bitcoins—with more, perhaps, out there to be found.

· · ·

Since his arrest, Ulbricht's loved ones have struggled to make sense of the allegations. "It's like hearing that your grandmother was accused of this stuff," says his friend Schiller. "It just doesn't add up." None are more flummoxed than Ulbricht's family. "I would stake my life that he's not a murderer," Lyn says. "This is way beyond something he could ever be capable of," says Kirk. "I believe they got the wrong guy."

Raising legal-defense money through their site, Freeross.org, the family has hired a high-powered lawyer to handle the case: Joshua Dratel, who, having defended al-Qaeda operatives and a Guantánamo Bay inmate, has experience with controversial clients. Though Ulbricht filed a claim requesting the return of the Bitcoins seized by the government from his computer, stating that he "has an interest as owner," Dratel has said that "the evidence will establish that he's not the person who the government says he is." As for the tens of millions on Silk Road's servers, a federal judge ordered it all to be forfeited in January.

As the federal case against him unfolds, Ulbricht is biding his time playing ping-pong, teaching yoga, and reading at the Metropolitan Detention Center in Brooklyn, where he is denied Internet access. But the Silk Road fallout continues. Dealers and buyers have been arrested around the world for using the site, and federal scrutiny into the online illegal-drug market has never been higher.

Still, other black-market sites have attempted to capitalize on Silk Road's abandoned community, among them a revamped version of Silk Road, whose administrator has adopted the moniker Dread Pirate Roberts and sounds a lot like his martyred predecessor. "You don't need drugs to care about privacy," he recently tweeted. "We are freedom fighters."

Ulbricht has been thinking about his own legacy. In the Story-Corps interview, Pinnell asked him where he saw himself in twenty years. "I want to have had a substantial positive impact on the future of humanity by that time," Ulbricht said. But it didn't end there. When Pinnell asked, "Do you think you're going to live forever?" a smile spread across Ulbricht's face. "I think there's a possibility," he replied.

Part II

Brave New Economic World

Vanity Fair

A giant modernist building of opaque glass in London's posh Knightsbridge section—said to house the world's most expensive apartments—provides just enough of an opening for Nicholas Shaxson to explore the flood of foreign money pouring into the City, London's deregulated financial enclave that, we learn, is surprisingly insulated from regulation or, indeed, law of any kind. Here, in a fascinating narrative, we learn exactly where and how the super-rich live and how they hide their assets.

Nicholas Shaxson

5. A Tale of
Two Londons

Up until the eighteenth century, Knightsbridge, which borders genteel Kensington, was a lawless zone roamed by predatory monks and assorted cutthroats. It didn't come of age until the Victorian building boom, which left a charming legacy of mostly large and beautiful Victorian houses, with their trademark white or cream paint, black iron railings, high ceilings, and short, elegant stone steps up to the front door.

This will not be the impression a visitor now gets as he emerges from the Knightsbridge subway station's south exit. He will be met by four hulking joined-up towers of glass, metal, and concrete, sandwiched between the Victorian splendors of the Mandarin Oriental Hotel, to the east, and a pretty five-story residential block, to the west. This is One Hyde Park, which its developers insist is the world's most exclusive address and the most expensive residential development ever built anywhere on earth. With apartments selling for up to $214 million, the building began to smash world per-square-foot price records when sales opened, in 2007. After quickly shrugging off the global financial crisis the complex has come to embody the central-London real-estate market, where, as high-end property consultant Charles McDowell put it, "prices have gone bonkers."

From the Hyde Park side, One Hyde Park protrudes aggressively into the skyline like a visiting spaceship, a head above its red-brick and gray-stone Victorian surroundings. Inside, on the ground floor, a large, glassy lobby offers what you'd expect from any luxury intercontinental hotel: gleaming steel statues, thick gray carpets, gray marble, and extravagant chandeliers with radiant sprays of glass. Not that the building's inhabitants need venture into any of these public spaces: they can drive their Maybachs into a glass-and-steel elevator that takes them down to the basement garage, from which they can zip up to their apartments.

The largest of the original eighty-six apartments (following some mergers, there are now around eighty) are pierced by 213-foot-long mirrored corridors of glass, anodized aluminum, and padded silk. The living spaces feature dark European-oak floors, Wenge furniture, bronze and steel statues, ebony, and plenty more marble. For added privacy, slanted vertical slats on the windows prevent outsiders from peering into the apartments.

In fact, the emphasis everywhere is on secrecy and security, provided by advanced-technology panic rooms, bulletproof glass, and bowler-hatted guards trained by British Special Forces. Inhabitants' mail is X-rayed before being delivered.

The secrecy extends to the media, many of whose members, including myself and the London *Sunday Times*'s and *Vanity Fair*'s A. A. Gill, have tried but failed to gain entry to the building. "The vibe is junior Arab dictator," says Peter York, coauthor of *The Official Sloane Ranger Handbook,* the riotous 1982 style guide documenting the shopping and mating rituals of a certain striving class of Brits, who claimed Knightsbridge's high-end shopping area, which stretches from Harrods to Sloane Square, as their urban heartland.

•   •   •

One Hyde Park was built by two British brothers, Nick and Christian Candy, together with Waterknights, the international property-development company owned by Qatar's prime minister, Sheikh Hamad bin Jassim al-Thani. Christian, thirty-eight, a lanky former commodities trader, is the duo's discreet number cruncher, while his stockier, tousled-haired brother, Nick, forty, is its flashy, name-dropping, celebrity-loving public face. The Candys don't go in for small gestures. In October, Nick married the Australian actress Holly Valance in Beverly Hills, after she had announced their engagement by tweeting a photo of Nick down on one knee proposing on a beach in the Maldives. In flaming torches behind the happy couple, *WILL YOU MARRY ME* was written, without the usual question mark.

Designed by the architect Lord Richard Rogers, who also designed London's iconic Lloyd's building, One Hyde Park has divided Britain. Gary Hersham, managing director of the high-end real-estate agency Beauchamp Estates, says it is "the finest building in England, whether you like the style or you don't," while investment banker David Charters, who works in Mayfair, says, "One Hyde Park is a symbol of the times, a symbol of the disconnect. There is almost a sense of 'the Martians have landed.' Who are they? Where are they from? What are they doing?" Professor Gavin Stamp, of Cambridge University, an architectural historian, called it "a vulgar symbol of the hegemony of excessive wealth, an oversized gated community for people with more money than sense, arrogantly plonked down in the heart of London."

The really curious aspect of One Hyde Park can be appreciated only at night. Walk past the complex then and you notice nearly every window is dark. As John Arlidge wrote in the *Sunday Times*, "It's dark. Not just a bit dark—darker, say, than the surrounding buildings—but black dark. Only the odd light is on. . . . Seems like nobody's home."

That's not because the apartments haven't sold. London land-registry records say that seventy-six had been by January 2013 for a total of $2.7 billion—but, of these, only twelve were registered in the names of warm-blooded humans, including Christian Candy, in a sixth-floor penthouse. The remaining sixty-four are held in the names of unfamiliar corporations: three based in London; one, called One Unique LLC, in California; and one, Smooth E Co., in Thailand. The other fifty-nine—with such names as Giant Bloom International Limited, Rose of Sharon 7 Limited, and Stag Holdings Limited—belong to corporations registered in well-known offshore tax havens, such as the Cayman Islands, the British Virgin Islands, Liechtenstein, and the Isle of Man.

From this we can conclude at least two things with certainty about the tenants of One Hyde Park: they are extremely wealthy, and most of them don't want you to know who they are and how they got their money.

London Calling

Trevor Abrahmsohn, a U.K. real-estate agent, remembers London before the modern property boom began. "London was as Paris is today: an interesting, quirky souvenir town. We had the Tower of London, the Queen, the palace, and the Changing of the Guard," he says, adding scotch whisky as an afterthought. "That is what we stood for. London was not a tax haven."

Starting in the 1960s, new buyers began to fire up the market: crises of the Greek monarchy brought a significant influx of Greeks, pockets of which endure today. Next came the first wave of Americans, a trickle of bankers lured by London's unregulated Euro-markets, and West Coast buyers, often from Hollywood. "They swarmed in," remembers veteran London real-estate agent Andrew Langton, of Aylesford International. "They turned Chester Square into Little LA and tidied up all these properties, at enormous expense, with American kitchens, bathrooms, and showers."

The OPEC oil crisis of the 1970s lit the big fire under this market. Arab money surged into the so-called golden triangle of Knightsbridge, Belgravia, and nearby Mayfair, to buy high-end properties. Real-estate agents remember it as a tidal wave: "They came as a force," says Hersham. "When they wanted to buy, there were no hysterics or reticence." The fall of the shah of Iran brought a surge of Iranian money, followed by buyers from the biggest African ex-colony, newly oil-rich Nigeria.

The market paused for breath in the 1980s, with Britain's economy in the doldrums and as sagging world oil prices sapped wealthy foreign buyers' demand. But Margaret Thatcher's financial reforms, notably her "Big Bang" of Wild West financial deregulation in 1986, caused the stream of bankers to turn into a river, then a deluge. "We would wait for those e-mails ending in 'gs.com' to come rolling in," remembers Jeremy Davidson, a Belgravia-based property consultant. "Goldman [Sachs] partners, Morgan [Stanley] partners: they were the top of the market, and we had lots of them."

The fall of the Soviet Union, in 1989, and the vast, corrupt post-Soviet privatizations brought the biggest, most reckless wave of foreign buyers London had ever seen, with often questionable money sluicing in via the secretive British-linked stepping-stone tax havens of Cyprus and Gibraltar. "There is no real accountability of these guys coming in—the cops don't really investigate them," says Mark Hollingsworth, co-author of *Londongrad*, a 2009 book about the Russian invasion. "They see the capital as the most secure, fairest, most honest place to park their cash, and the judges here would never extradite them."

Nick Candy himself summarized the attractions neatly: "This is the top city in the world, and the best tax haven in the world for some."

•   •   •

"It seems to be that every big trading disaster happens in London," U.S. congresswoman Carolyn Maloney observed last June. "And I would like to know why." The disasters she was referring to were the ones that bankrupted Lehman Brothers and nearly bankrupted some other American firms, such as AIG and MF Global, as well as causing JPMorgan Chase's $6 billion loss at the hands of the trader popularly known as "the London Whale"— all of these happened to a high degree in the London branches of those firms and have cost the American taxpayer billions of dollars.

To answer her question and to understand why so much of the world's money goes to London in the first place, you need to go back hundreds of years, to the emergence of what must be the most peculiar, the oldest, the least understood, and perhaps one of the most important institutions in the menagerie of global finance: the City of London Corporation. It is the local authority for "the Square Mile," the pocket of prime financial real estate centered on the Bank of England and located about three miles to the east of Knightsbridge, along the Thames River. But the corporation is also much more, its identity embedded in—and slightly apart from—the British nation-state. The corporation has its own constitution, "rooted in the ancient rights and privileges enjoyed by citizens before the Norman Conquest, in 1066," and its own lord mayor of London—not to be confused with the mayor of London, who runs the Greater London metropolis, with its eight million inhabitants. One sign of the City of London's distinct identity is the fact that the Queen, on official visits there, will stop at the boundary of the Square Mile, where she is met by the lord mayor, who engages her in a short, colorful ritual, before she may proceed. Most Brits see this merely as a relic from a bygone age, a show for the tourists. They are wrong.

•   •   •

The lord mayor's principal official role, his website says, is to be "ambassador for all UK-based financial and professional services." He lobbies far afield, with offices in Brussels, China, and India, among other places, the better to "expound the values of liberalization" far and wide. The City Corporation and closely linked think tanks issue streams of publications explaining why finance should be less tethered by taxes and regulation. The corporation also has its own official lobbyist, with the delightfully medieval-sounding name of the Remembrancer (currently one Paul Double), lodged permanently in Britain's Parliament. Local elections in the City are unlike any other in Britain: multinational corporations vote alongside and vastly outnumber the tiny borough's 7,400 human residents.

Over the centuries the City has thrived, thanks to a simple advantage: it has had money to lend when governments or monarchs needed it. So the City has been granted special privileges, allowing it to remain a political fortress withstanding the tides of history that have transformed the rest of the British nation-state. It has nurtured a British tradition of welcoming foreign money, with few questions asked, and so has for centuries attracted the world's wealthiest citizens. "There the Jew, the Mahometan, and the Christian transact together," Voltaire wrote in 1733, "as though they all professed the same religion, and give the name of infidel to none but bankrupts."

When the British Empire crumbled in the mid-1950s, London replaced the cozy embrace of gunboats and imperial trading preferences with a new model: tempting the world's hot money through lax regulation and lax enforcement. There was always a subtle balance, involving dependable British legal bedrock fiercely upholding U.K. domestic rules and laws while turning a blind eye to foreign law breaking. It was a classic offshore-tax-haven offering that tells foreign financiers, "We won't steal your money, but we won't make a fuss if you steal other people's."

The term "tax haven" is something of a misnomer because tax havens offer escape routes not just from taxes but potentially from any of the rules, laws, and responsibilities of other jurisdictions—whether those be taxes, criminal laws, disclosure rules, or financial regulation. Tax havens are usually about parking your money "elsewhere," in jurisdictions such as the Cayman Islands, beyond the reach of your home country's regulators and taxmen. Or you park it in London: which is why some investment bankers have called it the Guantánamo Bay of finance. "The British think they do finance well," says Lee Sheppard, a tax and banking specialist at the U.S. trade publication *TaxAnalysts*. "No. They do the legal stuff well. Most of the big investment banks there are branches of foreign operations. . . . They go there because there is no regulation whatsoever."

James Henry, a former McKinsey chief economist, watched at close quarters the recycling of petrodollar wealth into Third World loans via London's unregulated Euro-markets, which among other things enabled Wall Street to avoid New Deal–era banking regulations. Henry saw a global private-banking network emerge, following the money, "helping Third World elites abscond with hundreds of billions in diverted loans, illicit commissions, and corrupt privatizations, and park it in London and other tax havens."

•　　　•　　　•

It comes as a surprise to most people that the most important player in the global offshore system of tax havens is not Switzerland or the Cayman Islands but Britain, sitting at the center of a web of British-linked tax havens, the last remnants of empire. An inner ring consists of the British Crown Dependencies—Jersey, Guernsey, and the Isle of Man. Farther afield are Britain's fourteen Overseas Territories, half of them tax havens, including such offshore giants as the Caymans, the British Virgin Islands (BVI), and Bermuda. Still further out, numerous British Commonwealth countries and former colonies such as Hong Kong, with deep and old links to London, continue to feed vast financial flows—clean, questionable, and dirty—into the City. The half-in, half-out relationship provides the reassuring British legal bedrock while providing enough distance to let the U.K. say "There is nothing we can do" when scandal hits.

Data are scarce, but in the second quarter of 2009 the three Crown Dependencies alone provided $332.5 billion in net financing to the City of London, much of it from tax-evading foreign money. Matters are so out of hand that in 2001 Britain's own tax authorities sold off 600 buildings to a company, Mapeley Steps Ltd., registered in the tax haven of Bermuda to avoid tax.

Britain could close down this tax-haven secrecy overnight if it wanted, but the City of London won't let it. "We have, to put it provocatively, a second British empire, which is at the very core of global financial markets today," explains Ronen Palan, professor of international political economy at City University in London. "And Britain is very good at not advertising its position."

•   •   •

Despite the British passion for historic preservation, the recent huge influx of foreign money is changing the capital, both physically and socially. "Our Georgian and Victorian stock is so inflexible, frozen in time," said Ademir Volic, of Volume 3 Architects. "We're selling this city as a forward-looking metropolis, yet we can't change a single window in a conservation area. Everything has to be hidden underground."

That's just what the plutocrats are doing: digging down. Maggie Smith, of the London Basement company, which carries out basement renovations, dates the craze to the early to mid-1990s, when she noticed increasing numbers of people wanting to renovate their musty old basements. "It started quite small, with people doing thirty to forty square meters, generally under the front of a standard Victorian London house," she says. "Then they began digging out under parts of gardens, then entire gardens, installing light wells and glass bridges to bring in natural light."

Soon they built underground recreation centers, golf-simulation rooms, squash courts, bowling alleys, hair salons, ballrooms, and car elevators to the underground garages for their vintage Bentleys. The more adventurous installed climbing walls and indoor waterfalls.

"They would dig deep, have a media room and a funny sort of spring-loaded garage or a swimming pool," says Peter York. "And they would disturb the water table. You can imagine what old-fashioned British toffs thought of that." One Knightsbridge resident—and tension is such that he declines to identify himself or his street—says that on his short street of fifteen or twenty properties he has recently suffered through nine simultaneous renovations.

Cable-TV mogul David Graham outraged his neighbors, near Lennox Gardens Mews, south of One Hyde Park, by seeking planning permission to excavate deeper than the height of neighboring homes, extending all the way under his house and garden. The Duchess of St. Albans, a neighbor, calls the plans "absolutely monstrous and unnecessary." So far, permission has not been granted.

·　　·　　·

As the renovations grew, so did the conflicts. "It may look village-y, but we live like sardines in tins," says Terence Bendixson, of the Chelsea Society, a residents' association. "A lot of people have been here quite a long time, who aren't rich, who aren't bankers, who are solid middle-class and upper-class people." Stroll through Knightsbridge today (or check Google Street View) and you will see so many conveyor belts bringing up soil from under houses that you can be forgiven for thinking that a new mining boom is under way.

"Economically, culturally, and socially, London has now left Britain behind, blasting off from the rest of the nation like some vast UFO," says Neil O'Brien, director of the think tank Policy Exchange. "The politicians, civil servants, and journalists who make up Britain's governing class run one country, but effectively live in another." As Abrahmsohn sees it, London could "easily declare independence. A lot of these wealthy people don't even know these outlying regions exist. They don't care."

In fact, the chasm is sharpest inside London itself: a report for the British government in January 2010 estimated that the richest 10 percent of Londoners own well over 270 times the wealth of the poorest 10 percent.

"Knightsbridge is an un-English activity," says York. "The former *gratin* [upper crust], a combination of old toffs, Knightsbridge Americans who wanted to be old toffs, plutocrats who wanted to know the Form, people who weren't here for funny-money reasons: all those things have been completely obliterated by a mad kind of very, very gauche overseas money. It's absentee money: the kind of money that has bodyguards. It is the world of Maybachs and absurd-looking Ferraris in absurd colors, and kids who buy them straight out of the shop window. These people have no substantive relationship with anything British at all. It's everywhere: I can't emphasize enough how everywhere-ish it is."

Many in London are uncomfortable not just with the flagrant display of super-wealth but also with the rising number of absentee residents who are based in foreign countries. "Those people who do buy these houses, particularly the bigger ones, in many cases don't buy them to live in permanently: they are part of a portfolio," said Bendixson. "That doesn't add much jollity to your street: houses with the shutters down and nobody there."

Edward Davies-Gilbert, of the Knightsbridge Association, sees the area gaining the flavor of "a ghost town, peopled by ghost blocks."

Thus One Hyde Park, where only seventeen apartments of the seventy-six sold are registered as primary residences, has become a totem for the gaping chasm between the powerful rootless plutocrats in London and the rest.

The Candy Men Can

Nick and Christian Candy, the two British brothers who put together the One Hyde Park project, built their fortunes on the post-Soviet privatization real-estate boom in London. They started out with a $9,300 loan from their grandmother, buying a one-bedroom apartment in semi-fashionable Earl's Court for $190,000 in 1995, then renovating and selling it for a profit the following year. They repeated the trick and soon discovered a new niche at the very top of the market, above traditional luxury. In 1999 they set up Candy & Candy, an interior-design company, honing their skills on yachts, private aircraft, and private members' clubs, with walls in hand-painted silk and cushions that cost $3,200 apiece.

Thanks to an aggressive, hyperactive business strategy (not to mention a soaring market), the brothers climbed very high, very fast. "The Candy brothers are two young zealots who were quite fearless as to how they approached people and where they found money," says Andrew Langton. "They realized that the bling was what was wanted, whether it's a yacht or plane or an expensive apartment. There is a culture of decoration, a culture of security, of privacy, that they had understood."

Shabby English chic was out, and luxury concierge services, eel-skin walls, and bulletproof glass were in. It is a hard market to get right, and Abrahmsohn notes the huge diversity in taste it encompasses. "The Greeks are the most understated of all the buyers, including the British," he says. "The Nigerians are very flamboyant. They like lots of very bright colors, glitz and glitter. They are not shy. The Russians are fairly easygoing, but they do like their glitz." Indians decorate their houses in super-lavish style, he continues. "Lots of detail, lots of colors, extremely ornate, a lot of gilt: Louis XIV would be far too understated for them."

·　　·　　·

Somehow, the Candys found their way through this maze, and in 2001 they sold a $6.2 million apartment in Belgrave Square to the Russian oligarch Boris Berezovsky, who had fled to the refuge of London after being accused of fraud and embezzlement. As described in *Londongrad*, it had "bullet-proof CCTV cameras, a fingerprint entry system that can remember 100 fingerprints, remote-controlled cinema and television screens in the bathroom walls, laser-beam alarms, and smoke bombs. An electronic system recognized the residents' favorite music and TV programs and followed him or her from one room to another."

"The Russians are creatures of habit," explains Hollingsworth. "When Berezovsky bought in Belgrave Square, [Russian oligarch Roman] Abramovich bought around the corner in Lowndes Square, next to Harvey Nichols, and then Chester Square. They are like heads of gangs in a schoolyard and love to show off: 'My house is bigger than yours.'" In the wake of the Berezovsky sale, an aura developed around the brothers as Russian newcomers demanded to buy Candy & Candy properties.

In 2004, Christian Candy set up the CPC Group, registered in the tax haven of Guernsey, to tackle bigger projects, including, eventually, One Hyde Park. In a fast-rising market, as more and more buyers from more and more parts of the world crammed in, the Candys knew they could ask for the moon and get it. When they launched sales of apartments for One Hyde Park, in 2007, typical London prime prices were $2,900 per square foot, with peaks at $4,500. In One Hyde Park's first year, the rate was $8,800, and $10,900 the following year, ultimately rising last year to almost $12,000. Prices in New York have occasionally matched these levels: recently, a Russian oligarch bought Sanford I. Weill's penthouse at 15 Central Park West for just over $13,000 per square foot—but that was considered an anomaly. According to Susan Greenfield, senior VP at the real-estate brokers Brown Harris Stevens in New York, sales in that building in 2012 have averaged $6,100 per square foot. "One Hyde Park changed the map," says property consultant Davidson. "The prices were off the scale—I was astonished. It created a market of its own."

•　　　•　　　•

Living in an elite bubble, the brothers appear to have a tin ear for the public mood. In late 2010, amid national austerity, tax protests erupted in more than fifty towns and cities across Britain, led by a movement called Uncut. They were protesting against tax avoidance by large corporations and by prominent figures such as the British retail billionaire Philip Green. In December of that year, the Candy brothers played a game of the British version of Monopoly with a *Financial Times* reporter in Christian's apartment in One Hyde Park. Christian landed on the "super tax" square. "What!" he reportedly cried. "I don't pay tax. I am a tax exile." (A spokesperson for the Candys denied that Christian, who is a resident of Monaco and Guernsey, said this.)

Subsequent revelations by the London *Sunday Times* and others about the extent of offshore ownership of the apartments in

One Hyde Park stoked new outrage in Britain, and the government came under intense pressure to crack down. Chancellor George Osborne, noting that the zero-tax treatment on the sale of properties owned through offshore companies "rouses the anger of many of our citizens," introduced new legislative proposals, now coming into effect, to, among other things, levy a sales-transaction tax of up to 15 percent on properties bought through offshore companies and levy an annual charge of up to $221,000 on expensive properties owned offshore. Many austerity-parched Britons welcomed the moves. An outraged Nick Candy called them "absolutely disgraceful."

Home Away from Home

Who are the owners in One Hyde Park? One $39.5 million apartment is registered openly in the name of Anar Aitzhanova: this may be a Kazakh singer, who did not respond to *Vanity Fair*'s queries. Another two, for a combined $49.8 million, are held jointly by Irina Viktorovna Kharitonina and Viktor Kharitonin. The latter is likely to be a co-owner of Russia's largest domestic drug maker, though the couple's representatives also failed to reply. Another apartment is registered to Rory Carvill, a British insurance broker; another is held in the name of Bassim Haidar, who appears to be the founder and CEO for Channel IT, a Nigeria-based telecommunications company, and who also did not respond to queries. A $35.5 million apartment is registered in the name of Karmen Pretel-Martines, who could not be further identified, as is the case with a Beijing-registered buyer named Kin Hung Kei, who paid $11.6 million.

Nick Candy himself owns an eleventh-floor duplex penthouse, and seven other apartments are believed to be owned by members of the Project Grande consortium, which is behind One Hyde Park. (The Candys will not confirm or deny this.) The best apartment of all—a triplex on floors 11, 12, and 13 of Tower C—is owned (via a Cayman company) by Sheikh Hamad bin Jassim al-Thani, of Qatar, Project Grande's partner.

Another buyer, who bought and merged two apartments for a total of $215.9 million, is Rinat Akhmetov, the Ukraine's richest man, with an estimated personal net worth of $16 billion. He has interests in coal, mining, power generation, banking, insurance, telecoms, and media and has been a big beneficiary of privatization auctions in his native country. A spokeswoman for Akhmetov's holding company, System Capital Management, said last year that the purchase was a "portfolio investment"; U.K. land-registry documents say it is held through a BVI company, Water Property Holdings Ltd.

Another owner is Vladimir Kim, who chairs the London-listed Kazakh copper giant Kazakhmys PLC. Kim was once a top official in the political party behind Kazakh president Nursultan Nazarbayev, who has often been accused of sanctioning severe abuses of human rights and media freedom. Sheikh Mohammed Saud Sultan al-Qasimi, head of finance for the government of Sharjah, bought an $18.1 million apartment, while at least one more belongs to the Russian real-estate magnate Vladislav Doronin, who is dating model Naomi Campbell.

An $11.7 million second-floor apartment is owned by Galina Weber, a significant shareholder in the Russian gas giant Itera. Two apartments, worth a combined $43.7 million, are owned by Professor Wong Wen Young, with London and Taipei addresses. This is presumably the billionaire Taiwan-born entrepreneur Winston Wong Wen Young, who has enjoyed a close business relationship with Jiang Mianheng, the son of former Chinese president Jiang Zemin. A $12 million apartment is held jointly by Desmond Lim Siew Choon and Tan Kewi Yong, a billionaire Malaysian couple with a big property empire. Last September the real-estate company Jones Lang LaSalle estimated that nearly a sixth of all recent buyers of new central-London property were Malaysian—and only 19 percent British. Wealth is currently pouring out of Malaysia ahead of imminent elections, which could see the scandal-ridden ruling coalition ousted for the first time since independence.

·   ·   ·

Less is known about others, but clues can be found. Land-registry documents for four apartments provide contact details for Alastair Tulloch, a British lawyer who Hollingsworth said is known in Russian-oligarch circles as "the new Stephen Curtis"—a reference to the Russians' go-to London lawyer, who died in a mysterious helicopter crash in 2004. Tulloch has represented the interests of Alexander Lebedev, a banking oligarch who owns London's *Evening Standard* and a sizable piece of the Russian airline Aeroflot, among other holdings, and has worked closely with the jailed Russian oligarch Mikhail Khodorkovsky.

Apartments bought by corporations with particularly flamboyant names such as Shoolin Investments Ltd., Wondrous Holding and Finance Inc., and Smooth E Co. Ltd. hint at possible Asian ownership, the last registered in Bangkok, Thailand. Other corporate names are more impenetrable. One is the Caymans-based Knightsbridge Holdings Ltd., registered in Ugland House—a modest building where some 20,000 companies are registered and which President Obama in a 2009 speech said was "either the largest building in the world or the largest tax scam in the world." (What Obama was getting at was that no real economic activity happens there: it is merely an entry in accountants' workbooks.)

Trying to penetrate the corporate veils thrown over these apartments is a thankless task. Of the tax havens used, the Isle of Man is probably the most forthcoming: you can easily download company reports online for under two dollars apiece. But even here, you will not get far. Take Rose of Sharon 4, which owns a $10.2 million, fifth-floor apartment. Rose 4 was set up in 2010 with five company directors from the Isle of Man, and its shares were held by two almost identical-sounding entities: Barclaytrust International Nominees (Isle of Man) Ltd. and Barclaytrust (Nominees) Isle of Man Ltd. In April 2012, the shares were transferred to a BVI entity listed as "Prospect Nominees (BVI) Ltd," and the five Isle of Man directors were replaced by two new ones: Craig Williams, a BVI insolvency practitioner, and Kenneth Morgan, who works for HSBC in the BVI. Both declined requests for further information.

Such structures typically straddle several jurisdictions: an Isle of Man company may be owned by a BVI company, which could be held by a Bahamas trust, with trustees somewhere else; either structure might own a Swiss bank account; and so on. At each step of this global dance of ownership, fees are skimmed off, and the secrecy deepens.

In fact, land-registry documents show that five apartments, for a combined $123 million, are owned by companies under the Rose of Sharon name, all based in the Isle of Man. These have been widely reported to be owned by Folorunsho Alakija, a Nigerian billionaire who is a part owner of Famfa Oil Ltd. (Efforts to contact her were unsuccessful.) According to an industry risk profile of the company, Famfa received 600,000 barrels of oil per month from the giant Nigerian deepwater Agbami oil field in the first four months of 2010, in partnership with the U.S. oil company Chevron, in a longer-term agreement. The report cites a Nigerian Department for Petroleum Resources source as saying that Alakija was "one of the [Nigerian] First Lady's favorite dress designers" and that Alakija's stake in Famfa was "a reward to a loyal friend." *Forbes* ranked Alakija's net worth at $600 million, but last year *Ventures Africa*, a business magazine, recalculated it based on public information at $3.3 billion, making her richer than Oprah Winfrey.

· · ·

All of this raises the question of why so many of One Hyde Park's apartments are owned offshore.

In fact, this is not unusual in England. According to the *Guardian*, some 95,000 offshore entities have been set up in Britain (or the U.K.) since 1999 purely to hold U.K. property: a hefty portion of the national prime stock. These buyers use offshore companies for three big and related reasons: tax, secrecy, and "asset protection." A property owned outright becomes subject to various British taxes, particularly capital-gains and taxes on transfers of ownership. But properties held through offshore companies can often avoid these taxes. According to London lawyers, the big reason for using these structures has been to avoid inheritance taxes—something that the government's recent limited crackdown did not address. And of course City of London lawyers and accountants are currently scurrying to find ways around the new rules.

But secrecy, for many, is at least as important: once a foreign investor has avoided British taxes, then offshore secrecy gives him the opportunity to avoid scrutiny from his own country's tax—or criminal—authorities too. Others use offshore structures for "asset protection"—frequently, to avoid angry creditors. That seems to be the case with a company called Postlake Ltd.—registered on the Isle of Man—which owns a $5.6 million apartment on the fourth floor. Postlake is in turn registered as owned by Purcey Ltd., a BVI entity, which is registered as held on behalf of an Isle of Man trust set up by the bankrupt Irish property developer Ray Grehan, who has been pursued by Ireland's National Asset Management Agency to recover more than \$350 million it says it is owed. Grehan had argued that the apartment is not really his but belongs to a family trust. Martin Kenney, a BVI lawyer, says BVI companies are frequently owned by foreign trusts from more outlandish jurisdictions, such as Nevis or the Cook Islands, deepening the secrecy. These structures are "debtor-friendly and creditor-unfriendly," he says, so in cases of fraud it can be very hard to recover assets.

.   .   .

Perhaps the most striking fact about One Hyde Park and the London super-prime property market is what it tells us about who the world's richest people are. Many people think the greatest winners of globalization today are financiers. A decade or so ago, that may have been true. But today another class sits above even them—the global commodity plutocrats: owners of mineral rights or dominant players in mineral-rich countries in sectors such as construction and finance that benefit from commodity booms. Hollingsworth notes in *Londongrad* that the oligarchs he studies became rich "not by creating new wealth but rather by insider political intrigue and exploiting the weakness of the rule of law." Arkady Gaydamak, a Russian Israeli oilman and financier, explained his elite view of accumulating wealth to me in 2005. "With all the regulations, the taxation, the legislation about working conditions, there is no way to make money," he said. "It is only in countries like Russia, during the period of redistribution of wealth—and it is not yet finished—when you can get a result. . . . How can you make \$50 million in France today? How?"

Russia's former privatization czar Anatoly Chubais put it less delicately: "They steal and steal. They are stealing absolutely everything."

London real-estate agents confirm that these commodity plutocrats dethroned the financiers some time before the financial crisis hit. "I can't remember the last time I sold a property to a banker," says Stephen Lindsay, of the real-estate agency Savills. "It's been hard for anyone to compete with the Russians, the Kazakhs. They are all in oil, gas—that is what they do. Construction—all that kind of stuff."

Even the Arab money has taken a backseat to the new buyers, says Hersham. "The wealth of the ex-Soviets is incredible," he says. "Unless you are talking about [Goldman Sachs CEO Lloyd] Blankfein or [Stephen Schwarzman], the head of Blackstone, or the head of one of the very big banks, there is no driver from the City of London at these levels anymore."

New York Times

In what can be read as a companion to Shaxson's exploration of the money behind One Hyde Park, Ben Judah spells out in the most scathing terms the implications of Britain's turning into one of the world's leading centers for money laundering. It's not just a city's real estate that's up for sale. It's the integrity of an entire country's elites.

Ben Judah

6. London's Laundry Business

ondon—The city has changed. The buses are still dirty, the people are still passive-aggressive, but something about London has changed. You can see signs of it everywhere. The townhouses in the capital's poshest districts are empty; they have been sold to Russian oligarchs and Qatari princes.

England's establishment is not what it was; the old imperial elite has become crude and mercenary. On Monday, a British civil servant was photographed arriving in Downing Street for a national security council meeting with an open document in his hand. We could read for ourselves lines from a confidential report on how Prime Minister David Cameron's government should respond to the Crimea crisis. It recommended that Britain should "not support, for now, trade sanctions," nor should it "close London's financial center to Russians."

The White House has imposed visa restrictions on some Russian officials, and President Obama has issued an executive order enabling further sanctions. But Britain has already undermined any unified action by putting profit first.

It boils down to this: Britain is ready to betray the United States to protect the City of London's hold on dirty Russian money. And forget about Ukraine.

Britain, open for business, no longer has a "mission." Any moralizing remnant of the British Empire is gone; it has turned back to the pirate England of Sir Walter Raleigh. Britain's ruling class has decayed to the point where its first priority is protecting its cut of Russian money—even as Russian armored personnel carriers rumble around the streets of Sevastopol. But the establishment understands that, in the twenty-first century, what matters is banks, not tanks.

The Russians also understand this. They know that London is a center of Russian corruption, that their loot plunges into Britain's empire of tax havens—from Gibraltar to Jersey, from the Cayman Islands to the British Virgin Islands—on which the sun never sets.

British residency is up for sale. "Investor visas" can be purchased, starting at £1 million ($1.6 million). London lawyers in the Commercial Court now get 60 percent of their work from Russian and Eastern European clients. More than fifty Russia-based companies swell the trade at London's Stock Exchange. The planning regulations have been scrapped, and along the Thames, up go spires of steel and glass for the hedge-funding class.

Britain's bright young things now become consultants, art dealers, private bankers, and hedge funders. Or, to put it another way, the oligarchs' valets.

Russia's president, Vladimir V. Putin, gets it: you pay them, you own them. Mr. Putin was absolutely certain that Britain's managers—shuttling through the revolving door between cabinet posts and financial boards—would never give up their fees and commissions from the oligarchs' billions. He was right.

In the austerity years of zero growth that followed the 2008 financial crash, this new source of vast wealth could not be resisted. Tony Blair is the latter-day embodiment of pirate Britain's Sir Walter Raleigh. The former prime minister now advises the Kazakh ruler Nursultan Nazarbayev on his image in the West. Mr. Blair is handsomely paid to tutor his patron on how to be evasive about the crackdowns and the mine shootings that are facts of life in Kazakhstan.

This is Britain's growth business today: laundering oligarchs' dirty billions, laundering their dirty reputations.

It could be otherwise. Banking sanctions could turn off the financial pipelines through which corrupt officials channel Russian money. Visa restrictions could cut Kremlin ministers off from their mansions. The tax havens that rob the national budget of billions could be forced to be accountable. Britain has the power to bankrupt the Putin clique.

But London has changed. And the Shard—the Qatari-owned, seventy-two-floor skyscraper above the grotty Southwark riverside—is a symbol of that change.

The Shard encapsulates the new hierarchy of the city. On the top floors, "ultra-high-net-worth individuals" entertain escorts in luxury apartments. By day, on floors below, investment bankers trade incomprehensible derivatives.

Come nightfall, the elevators are full of African cleaners, paid next to nothing and treated as nonexistent. The acres of glass windows are scrubbed by Polish laborers, who sleep four to a room in bedsit slums. And near the Shard are the immigrants from Lithuania and Romania, who broke their backs on construction sites but are now destitute and whiling away their hours along the banks of the Thames.

The Shard is London, a symbol of a city where oligarchs are celebrated and migrants are exploited but that pretends to be a multicultural utopia. Here, in their capital city, the English are no longer calling the shots. They are hirelings.

All Things Considered

Somewhere in the middle of the chain of commerce that produces the T-shirt on your back are a couple of Bangladeshi sisters dreaming of a better life. "Planet Money," the production of National Public Radio with Chicago Public Media, has for more than six years produced probing meditations on matters financial and economic. Here, it takes on globalization, its economic underpinnings, its mechanics, and its meaning for both consumers and the people whose lives are caught up in it.

Robert Smith et al.

7. How Technology and Hefty Subsidies Make U.S. Cotton King

From NPR News, this is *All Things Considered*. I'm Robert Siegel.

I have before me right now a fairly ordinary-looking but, in fact, unique T-shirt. It's gray, and on the front of it there's a picture of a squirrel holding a martini glass. But where the olive should be inside the drink there is, in fact, an acorn. What makes this 100 percent cotton T-shirt unique is that we know everything about how it was made.

Our Planet Money team commissioned the shirt. Then they followed the manufacturing process around the globe. It was touched by people in rich countries with advanced degrees and by people working for some of the lowest wages on earth.

All this week, we're going to hear their stories and today we start with the raw material. NPR's Robert Smith went in search of the farmer who grew the cotton that Planet Money's shirt was made from. And it took some detective work.

ROBERT SMITH: Imagine going into a gas station where you've just filled up your car and asking the guy: Hey, where did this gasoline come from? I mean where exactly was the well that produced the oil that got refined into this particular gas? That's what it was like when we asked people: Where is our cotton farm?

RANDY SCHELLING: Oh, gosh. That's a tough one to answer.

SMITH: That's Randy Schelling from the underwear company Jockey International. Jockey guided us on the technical side of this project. They introduced us to suppliers and factories that they work with. But even Randy didn't know where our cotton came from. Cotton in a T-shirt gets blended from farms across the globe.

SCHELLING: Anywhere from one farm to a hundred farms, potentially.

SMITH: But the folks at Jockey did recommend one place that might be able to tell us where our cotton came from, the place where our cotton takes its first step to becoming fabric. It's a spinning plant called Indorama and, by the way, it's in Indonesia.

Anil Tibrewal, the chief sales guy, meets us at the factory gate.

There's this amazing smell here.

ANIL TIBREWAL: It's the cotton smell. This is natural. If you go to the cotton fields, pick up a boll, smell it, it's almost similar like this.

SMITH: A little bit like the earth where it came from.

TIBREWAL: Yes.

SMITH: Anil leads us back through the warehouse and it's amazing. Cotton bales stacked three stories high. There's the Brazilian cotton, there are the Greek bales. There's an entire section from Australia. But Anil says, knowing your T-shirt, your type of cotton is probably way in the back. My producer Jess Jiang spots it first.

JESS JIANG: Is this from Arkansas?

TIBREWAL: Memphis, this is Memphis.

JIANG: Oh, Memphis.

SMITH: This is Charlotte. Charlotte? This is all . . .

TIBREWAL: This one the same lot. We won't . . .

SMITH: Is this Charlotte all the way?

TIBREWAL: This whole lot of bales is American cotton.

SMITH: I spy: Marmaduke, Arkansas; Halls, Tennessee; Lyon, Mississippi. It's like a road trip through the Delta.

Now, on the face of it, this doesn't seem to make much economic sense. There are farms that are much closer to Indonesia, places where the land is cheap and the labor is cheaper. Why ship a bunch of raw cotton from the United States, the furthest place you can find? Why get it from someone like this guy?

BOWEN FLOWERS: My name is Bowen Flowers. We're standing on one of my farms we call Omega.

SMITH: Clarksdale, Mississippi, 10,000 miles from Indonesia. And as far as we can guess—we're estimating here—OK, we're going to call it: The birthplace of the Planet Money T-shirt.

On this fall day, the cotton looks like a snow drift all the way to the horizon. I actually brought back some of the T-shirt cotton from that warehouse in Indonesia and showed it to Bowen. Can you identify it? Is that yours?

FLOWERS: Don't know, but it looks like the same as all the cotton around this area. That's for sure.

SMITH: Bowen is a huge man, six-feet-seven. And as we wade into the field, the plants only come up to his belt buckle. He's going to send this crop around the world. Just like the Swiss make the best watches, the Germans perfected the sports car, Americans grow the most desired cotton in the world. And just like those watches and cars, American cotton does it by being high-tech.

This is the John Deere 7760; iconic green color, big as a houseboat. Bowen bought five of them last year. And they were not cheap.

FLOWERS: They're right at 600,000 a piece. So we got in a big investment. We got to make something to make the payments on them every year.

SMITH: You bought $3 million worth of equipment last year to pick cotton.

FLOWERS: It's crazy, isn't it? Real crazy. We might need to have our brain examined.

SMITH: But these machines give Bowen an edge over small farmers in the rest of the world. He can pick cotton faster with fewer workers. Bowen can watch the progress of the pickers from his iPad sitting at home. And as cushy as it is for him, the driver up on top of the John Deere has an even sweeter gig.

Hey, we wanted to see if we could go a row with you.

I climb up a ladder up into picker number three to hitch a ride with Martovia Latrell Jones.

MARTOVIA LATRELL JONES: Oh.

SMITH: Hey, how's it going?

JONES: Good.

SMITH: Everyone calls him Toto. He puts the machine into gear. Whoa.

And then he lets go.

You just took your hands off the wheel. You didn't even have to touch it.

JONES: Yeah. Pretty much, everything's driving itself.

SMITH: The picker feels the cotton plants. It makes all the adjustments itself. Toto just sits there, calls his wife on the cell phone, cranks up the blues station.

JONES: You all might not like my singing.

SMITH: Toto has a lot of time up here to sit and think. He was raised by his grandfather, George, who worked on a cotton farm before all this technology. Toto heard the stories.

JONES: Had to get down on their hands and knees and get some blisters and splinters in their fingernails and everything.

SMITH: You do realize that you probably harvest more in five minutes than he did all day long.

JONES: Ah, yeah. I can make a round and pick more than they picked in their whole lifetime.

SMITH: These machines are not only fast, but, by the end of the process, the cotton they produce is clean. It's pure. It's untouched by human hands. And this is a big deal to the complicated factories around the world that make our T-shirt. In Indonesia, Anil Tibrewal told us that the many countries still handpick cotton. And those countries end up with a lot of trash in their cotton bales.

TIBREWAL: The contamination comes from human being—plastic bags, chips bags. If there are, say, 5,000 people picking cotton in the field, they can throw any kind of things and that comes with the cotton.

SMITH: One more thing about American cotton: It's not actually that much more expensive. And this is the final reason why America exports more cotton than anyone else in the world. According to a lot of people—well, according to our competitors especially—we cheat. We stack the deck. The richest government in the world is helping Bowen out.

PIETRA RIVOLI: Well, you've got the simplest things, which are the subsidies. And this is cash into the grower's pocket. You know, everybody understands that.

SMITH: Pietra Rivoli is an economist at Georgetown University. She was a paid consultant on our project, and she wrote the book that inspired it, *The Travels of a T-shirt in the Global Economy.*

Subsidies get complicated, but for the 4,000 acres of cotton that Bowen and his family farm, the operation could be expected to get more than $100,000 in direct payments from the government. But perhaps the bigger benefit that the government provides is protecting farmers like Bowen from risks.

RIVOLI: There are bad things that can happen: prices can fall, there can be too much rain, it can be too hot, it can be too cold. A lot of those risks are protected against by government programs, particularly insurance subsidies.

SMITH: So basically they give them cheap insurance.

RIVOLI: They give them cheap insurance.

SMITH: And to be fair, other countries also support their agricultural products in various ways. But no one does it as effectively as the United States. U.S. farmers have big farms. They buy big machines. They take big risks. And the government has a big safety net for them.

SMITH: Back up on top of the cotton picker, Toto can watch the harvest go by on a computer screen. All the green lights mean that everything is going perfectly. He and the other drivers are on track to harvest six million pounds of cotton this fall; enough cotton, in other words, from this one farm in Mississippi to make a T-shirt for every person in New York City.

JONES: I would like to just see that one day. Just, you know, see where all of it happens after it leaves the cotton gin.

SMITH: I told Toto about the next steps for our T-shirt, about the factories in Indonesia and Bangladesh and all the container ships in between. And I promised to send him one of our shirts, so that he can wear it and say . . .

JONES: I made that shirt.

Planet Money Spins a Yarn and Makes a "Perfect" T-Shirt

ZOE CHACE: These are our T-shirts.

RENEE MONTAGNE But in between the U.S. and Bangladesh, the Planet Money cotton makes a detour, thousands of miles out of the way to Indonesia. Robert Smith reports on how Indonesia grabbed the most secret and obscure part of the T-shirt process.

ROBERT SMITH: We chased our bales of Mississippi cotton through the streets of Jakarta, through gridlocked traffic, and out into the Indonesian countryside. Now, this is a place where rice fields have been turned into Honda plants and satellite farms. This is a busy, crowded place, until we walk into the doors of the Indorama factory. This building is as big as a football field, and there is seemingly nobody working here. It's just row after row of shiny, metal robots.

These are beautiful machines. They are, like, immaculate.

ANIL TIBREWAL: And very expensive.

SMITH: Very expensive. Anil Tebrewal is the chief salesman here, and he says these machines are his greatest sales tool, because this step in the T-shirt process requires perfection.

TIBREWAL: You should have perfect machines and a perfect culture to produce perfect things.

SMITH: And let it be very clear: the perfect thing that Anil is talking about is yarn. Indorama spins raw cotton into yarn. Now, whatever image you have in your head of yarn—your grandma knitting a sweater—no, no, forget it. Yarn, in the textile business, is the stuff you and I might casually call thread. Those tiny little lines, if you look at your T-shirt, that's yarn, and it's very complicated stuff. Jockey International guided us on the technical side of this project, and Randy Schelling from the company told us that they spent years developing the yarn that goes into the Planet Money T-shirt. It had to have just the right qualities.

RANDY SCHELLING: You have the twist, the amount of twist, the direction of the twist.

SMITH: They specify fiber content, something called tenacity.

SCHELLING: Newtons per text on the yarn. That's a relationship to the size of the yarn and amount of strength.

SMITH: So, that's if you tug on it, if it's going to break.

SCHELLING: Right.

SMITH: Randy says there are basically an infinite number of different yarns you can create. So I asked him about the Planet Money yarn. Can we have a copy of the spec sheet? Because we want to show our listeners exactly the kind of that's in their T-shirt.

SCHELLING: No, I don't believe so.

MARION SMITH: That's our special sauce.

SMITH: That was Randy's boss, Marion Smith, at the end there. And that's how big a deal yarn is: It is a trade secret. It's like the recipe for Coke, except so much softer against the skin. The reason for all this obsession and secrecy about yarn is that yarn has to be flawless. There's six miles of it in a T-shirt. And if they get the recipe wrong—they pick the wrong cotton or the incorrect twist, if it's not uniform—your T-shirt could be itchy. It could fit funny. It could fall apart—which is why at the Indorama factory, they use robots, lots and lots of expensive robots.

I watched a machine suck up the cotton and pull it into a long, thick ponytail—an infinite ponytail sailing above my head, in and out. And, suddenly, these machines make it very thin, spinning at 22,000 rotations per minute.

So, I'm actually touching the yarn coming—oh, it vibrates. It's like a violin string.

Yeah. It turns out, this is a huge no-no at the factory. Nobody touches the yarn. My producer, Jess Jiang, and I got a little lecture.

TIBREWAL: No. There is no touching here. Why should you touch the product by hand? You are destroying the product.

JESS JIANG: But what's destroying it? My hands are clean. I washed them.

TIBREWAL: No, your hands are not clean. Dirty hands are bound to touch it, and then—look at this—the yarn is destroyed.

SMITH: They've got to be careful. Indorama puts out enough yarn to make a T-shirt every second. That's enough yarn in a day to circle the globe twenty-four times. It took a lot to do that math. It is an efficient plant, but it still does not explain the basic question about the Planet Money T-shirt, which is: Why does all of this happen in Indonesia? Why not in Bangladesh, where they actually use the yarn? Or why not in the United States, where the cotton is grown? Because, I learned,

Indonesia is in a sort of sweet spot right now in the middle of the global T-shirt trade.

ANUPAM AHGRAHWALL: I think Indonesia is lucky to be in the middle of the process, but . .

SMITH: Wait—luck? You think it's really luck?

AHGRAHWALL: Partly, partly.

SMITH: This is Anupam Ahgrahwall. He is the boss of all the spinning here at Indorama. And he explains Indonesia carved out a cozy little space between those advanced industrial countries and the developing ones. Places like the United States and Europe, they simply have to pay their workers more. Indorama can do it cheaper. Now, developing countries, like Bangladesh and Myanmar, they do have even lower wages than Indonesia, but those countries aren't ready to build a $35 million plant like this one. And they don't have a good supply of what robots need to survive.

AHGRAHWALL: Infrastructure, electricity.

SMITH: But staying in the sweet spot in a changing global economy is almost impossible. You know the drill: some poor country scrapes together the money to build one of these plants. Maybe they figure out how to keep the power on twenty-four hours a day. They have cheaper workers. Maybe they're closer to the cotton or to the clothing factories. And all of a sudden, Indorama is undercut. Anyone who could produce this kind of high-quality yarn for a few pennies cheaper will win. And so that's why the folks at Indorama are so obsessed about that strand of cotton. That's how they stay in the T-shirt chain, even if no consumer will ever notice the time and effort they put into the Planet Money T-shirt.

AHGRAHWALL: When I see people picking up a T-shirt, and then just putting it back on the shelf in a store, I'm like, hey, man, we work very hard to make that yarn, which has made that T-shirt. Like, come on, give it some respect.

Two Sisters, a Small Room and the World Behind a T-Shirt

MELISSA BLOCK: All this week, our Planet Money Team is following the creation of a T-shirt it commissioned, from cotton fields in the U.S. to yarn spinners in Indonesia. And today we go to Bangladesh. It's been in the news this year for its clothing industry. In April, a factory there collapsed killing more than 1,000 workers. Over the last few months, huge protests have engulfed the capital, workers on strike demanding higher wages.

More and more, American clothing is manufactured in Bangladesh, and that includes Planet Money's men's T-shirt. Caitlin Kenny and Zoe Chase traveled to the factory there where the shirt was put together. Their assignment: To find out what life is like for the workers who made it.

CAITLIN KENNEY: This is the story about how this one industry, the garment industry, is radically transforming things in Bangladesh. It's also the story of two sisters, Shumi and Minu, who worked on the Planet Money T-shirt.

ZOE CHACE: When we pull out the shirt, Minu, the older one, jumps and points, shows us exactly what they did using English words.

MINU: Side seam, [unintelligible].

CHACE: Minu is the older one. She's in her mid twenties. She's cynical, a fast talker, chews tobacco wrapped in betel leaf. She has a seven-year-old daughter who lives back in the village with her grandparents.

CHACE: They miss her, she says. If she were here now, I'd be putting little clips in her hair. But there's nobody to watch her daughter while she's at work here in the city.

KENNEY: Shumi, the younger sister, is nineteen years old. Where Minu is reserved, Shumi is bubbly. Where Minu is serious, Shumi is smiling. She loves her makeup, spends a lot of time doing her hair, and it's hard for her to get through any story without laughing.

KENNEY: Today at work, she says, she and her friends were throwing clothes at each other. It was so funny.

KENNEY: Shumi and Minu work six days a week at Deluxe Fashions Limited in Chittagong, Bangladesh. This is the factory where our T-shirt was made. They operate sewing machines. And this is one of the better factories here in Bangladesh. It's got fans and fire exits. They sisters feel safe here, they say. They don't worry about a factory collapse, like the one at Rana Plaza.

CHACE: They each make about eighty dollars a month—not bad for Bangladesh. Bangladesh's garment workers are the lowest paid in the world for this type of work. The sisters live in this little room. It's a concrete block—one window, tin roof. They share this room with Minu's husband. Minu and her husband usually sleep on the floor. Shumi, the younger sister, gets the bed. They pull a curtain between them for privacy.

KENNEY: Shumi bathes in a tiny stall in the hallway. She dumps buckets of cold water over herself.

CHACE: Minu cooks over two tiny gas burners . . .

CHACE: . . . shared with their neighbors, which serves as a kitchen.

CHACE: Ooh . . .

CHACE: . . . a bunch of vegetables bubbling up.

MINU: Yeah.

CHACE: Vegetables and rice, tonight's dinner, tomorrow's breakfast and lunch—one dish, three meals in a row for both of them.

KENNEY: This is the world behind our T-shirts, behind lots of our clothes; very low wages, a tiny concrete room shared by three people.

There are over four million Shumis and Minus in Bangladesh working in the garment industry. The majority are women. To understand what's driven them to move to crowded cities where they work long days for very little money, it helps to understand where Shumi and Minu and the millions like them came from.

CHACE: Back in the village where Shumi and Minu grew up, their mom cooks lunch in the backroom. The difference between her life and her daughters' lives is very clear. No gas burners here. It's a fire pit made from mud. There're holes underneath to stick branches into, the room fills with smoke when she cooks.

KENNEY: Lots of Bangladesh's garment workers grew up cooking like this, with sticks instead of gas. Outside Shumi and Minu's parents' house, there's this pond. It's the bathtub, the dishwasher, the laundromat.

KENNEY: You're the father of Shumi and Minu.

JABAR: Mm-hmm.

KENNEY: This is Shumi and Minu's father, Abdul Jabar. Their father used to be the only one in the family making any money. And he didn't make enough. The consequences were horrible.

KENNEY: Three of his daughters died before they reached age seven. They were eating dirt. They got sick and their father couldn't afford to take them to the doctor.

JABAR: (*Through translator*) Still remember them at times and feel bad because my daughters, my kids. It fills emptiness in our family.

KENNEY: What Shumi remembers about this time is not having enough to eat.

SHUMI: (*Through translator*) We eat three times. But sometimes, our parents are not eating because the lack of food. They just give their food to us because we are little.

KENNEY: If I ask you to close your eyes and picture what it was like when you were growing up, you know, what do you see? What do you feel?

SHUMI: (*Through translator*) Oh, yes.

KENNEY: I'm sorry. I didn't mean to make you cry.

CHACE: Now that the sisters work in the garment industry things have really changed for this family. Shumi and Minu send money back to the village, so does another sister who works at a different garment factory in the city. And you can see the impact right here in the kitchen.

    The stove is the same as what they had growing up. But what's inside the pot is different.

KENNEY: What is it?

SHUMI: Murgi.

CHACE: Murgi.

UNIDENTIFIED MAN: Chicken.

CHACE: Back before the sisters made money, their family rarely ate meat. Now their holiday bonuses pay for all the chicken and fish they want. Factory money has paid for a new house for Shumi and Minu's parents. It's brick instead of bamboo. This money keeps their younger brother in school.

KENNEY: And for millions of young women like Shumi and Minu, garment-industry jobs have transformed their lives in other ways as well. And this transformation has been so rapid you can see the difference even inside one generation of this family.

CHACE: For Minu, the older sister, her life looks much more like the lives of the women before her. When Minu became a teenager, her father began to worry about getting her married.

JABAR: *(Through translator)* In Bangladesh, it's a burden to have girls not get married. It's a big burden for me.

KENNEY: Why is it a burden to have daughters in the house?

JABAR: *(Through translator)* Because when they grow up, I have to spend money on their fooding, lodging. It becomes a big burden. So if they marry, she will go to another boy's house.

    For centuries, we are seeing this. Like my forefathers also got their daughters married. This is the rule of this country, Bangladeshi rule. They have to get married.

KENNEY: Marrying Minu off meant she became her husband's burden, not her father's. And Minu's family thought the man they chose for their daughter had money. He paid for the wedding—that was a huge relief. But Minu's parents were wrong. The man they chose didn't have much money.

CHACE: So Minu took a job in the garment industry. And when she thinks back on it, she says she was just a kid back then. If she knew then what she knows now, she would have fought this choice that her parents made for her.

MINU: *(Through translator)* If I had the mental situation that time, like now, then I'm not getting married with him.

CHACE: Minu and her husband, they fight a lot. He gets jealous. He goes through her phone, accusing her of cheating with the men she works with.

So are you mad that your parents forced you to do this?

MINU: I am not capable to forgive my parents because they just destroyed my life.

CHACE: Minu says that's why I never go home to visit—I can't forgive them. Her sister says Minu has a hard heart.

KENNEY: Minu had no choice. She had to marry a man chosen by her parents. But by the time her younger sister, Shumi, was marrying age the rules were changing in Bangladesh. When Shumi was fifteen, there was another path. Another way of bringing money into your family that didn't involve marrying a man you hardly knew.

By the time Shumi was in her early teens, there were over two and a half million people working in the garment industry; the majority of them women. So Shumi decided to dropped out of school after seventh grade to go work at her big sister's factory and make some money. The fact that Shumi's young, unmarried and with a garment worker's salary means that her personal life looks nothing like Minu's. Shumi has her own bank account. She's saving up for something special, something that shows the control that she now has over her own life.

SHUMI: I just save the money if I need it for my marriage and then I use the money for my marriage.

KENNEY: So I got to ask. Do you have a groom in mind? Yes?

SHUMI: Yes.

KENNEY: What's his name? Shumi is blushing and laughing. She won't tell me his name. They work together. Is it a secret? Is it a secret romance?

CHACE: He would die [unintelligible].

KENNEY: Oh. Forbidden romance, very intriguing. Did you talk to him tonight? It's secret because he's Hindu and Shumi is Muslim. Back in the village, her father would never let her talk to a body who wasn't a relative, let alone a Hindu. But here in the city, she and her boyfriend take rickshaw rides together. He buys her jewelry.

They hold hands. He tells her he loves her.

CHACE: Minu, her older sister, she does not approve of Shumi's relationship. He's Hindu. That's a big problem for her. But Minu says when her own daughter grows up, she should make her own choice about who to marry.

KENNEY: This is the world behind our T-shirt, two sisters in a little room dreaming of a better life. If not for themselves, then for their children. And this life, by most Western standards, seems pretty wretched.

CHACE: There is not much room here for something to go wrong. In this family, if one sister, for some reason, couldn't work, they could get close to being hungry again, like they were before the sisters went to work in the factory. But here in Bangladesh, for these sisters, their life in the city is a big step up.

CHACE: Back in the city, Minu gives us a tour of their room. I ask, what's your favorite thing in here.

SHUMI: [Unintelligible] is all of my favorites because all of things I buy with my salary.

CHACE: OK. There is this one thing, though, that is this daily reminder of how far she's come from life in the village, the TV. She's still got the box that it came in. It's displayed on the shelf.

SHUMI: I think two [unintelligible] now because this is—I bought this TV with my salary, and when I was free, I just watching TV and think too good, too good.

KENNEY: But for Minu and for Shumi, her younger sister, this little room with the TV, this may be as far as they get. There aren't many other jobs here in Bangladesh, especially for women like them who dropped out of school.

CHACE: Minu's dreams are now for her daughter. She's hopeful that her daughter can stay in school, have lots of choices that she didn't have. Minu dreams that when her daughter grows up, they'll be all kinds of jobs in Bangladesh. She could work in an office or a bank, but not one of the garment factories.

Next Stop Bangladesh as We Follow Planet Money's T-Shirt

RENEE MONTAGNE: Today, Bangladesh, where it was put together. Bangladesh makes a lot of the world's clothing. If you bought underwear from Target or, say, pants at JCPenney, they could have come from Bangladesh. And why has Bangladesh gotten so popular? Well, continuing on our T-shirt's trail, Planet Money's Caitlin Kenney and Zoe Chace have the answer.

ZOE CHACE: This is where it starts. Where are we?

JOHN MARTIN: New Jersey, right? I don't know which city, though. I know we're in Wal-Mart.

CHACE: That's right, the Wal-Mart in Secaucus, New Jersey. And why are you here?

MARTIN: Of course, to grab boxers, socks, T-shirts, whatever else catch my eyes. Save me from doing laundry, being too lazy.

CHACE: This is how cheap our clothes are, that John Martin would rather buy a new six-pack of T-shirts than wash the ones he currently owns.

CAITLIN KENNEY: What John Martin doesn't know—most people don't—is that there's a pretty equation that has to line up in order for us to get our clothes this cheap. Bangladesh is a big part of that equation.

KENNEY: So, these are the sleeves.

MOHIUDDIN CHOWDHURY: Yes, the sleeves, yeah. Sleeve hem.

KENNEY: Sleeve hems, yeah. I'm in the middle of a sewing floor on a busy factory on a busy street in Bangladesh. The room is big and bright and filled with women sewing clothes. Tables are piled high with boxer briefs for Tommy Hilfiger, Calvin Klein, and one assembly line in particular working on a very special T-shirt.

CHOWDHURY: Planet Money. Wow.

KENNEY: These are our T-shirts. Mohiuddin Chowdhury runs this company, Clifton Apparels, Ltd. They make T-shirts for Jockey, the underwear company that's helping us make our T-shirt.

KENNEY: It takes thirty-two people just to sew our shirt together— six on the sleeve, three on the neck. So many hands on just one shirt.

CHACE: We're economics reporters, so we really came over here to Bangladesh to find one thing: How much did it cost to make our shirt?

CHOWDHURY: It's about two dollars.

CHACE: The whole shirt.

CHOWDHURY: Whole shirt. One big shirt is two dollars.

KENNEY: Two dollars. That's the price that Jockey paid Clifton per shirt.

CHACE: We bought our shirts from Jockey. Jockey paid Clifton to make them.

KENNEY: And two dollars, that's an approximate price. Ashutosh Biswas, another manager here, he talks us through it.

CHACE: So, out of this two dollars, OK, what is the most expensive part?

ASHUTOSH BISWAS: Fabric.

CHACE: Fabric. How much?

BISWAS: Seventy-five percent of the commerce.

KENNEY: OK, people. Real slow—math on the radio. Here we go: The fabric to make the T-shirt is 75 percent of the price—so, about a dollar fifty.

CHACE: In that one-fifty is the cost of cotton, the cost of turning that cotton into fabric. A dollar-fifty, so that leaves fifty cents. What's in the fifty cents?

KENNEY: Ashu says that's everything else: overhead, profit for Clifton. But mainly, it's people: managers, supervisors, and the many, many workers, all crammed into just fifty cents.

CHACE: Fifty cents seems so cheap for the workers' part of it.

KENNEY: That's so many people we just saw in that room, like, and fifty cents seems too small to cover all those people.

CHACE: Is this the cheapest place in the world to make a T-shirt—two dollars a shirt?

BISWAS: Yeah. We can—yeah. Compared to the other countries.

CHACE: And there you have it, ladies and gentlemen, the cheapest place in the world to make a T-shirt. That's according to Jalal Chowdhury, who founded this company—which is another way of saying Bangladesh has the lowest-paid workers in the world for this kind of work.

KENNEY: A fact that is not lost on the workers in Bangladesh.

KENNEY: Over the last few months, there have been violent protests in Bangladesh, workers demanding a higher minimum wage. And during the time we were there, the question of what the workers should be paid dominated the conversation.

CHACE: And that question was just answered. A new wage is set to take effect this month. The official minimum wage in Bangladesh will jump almost 75 percent from thirty-nine dollars a month to sixty-eight dollars a month—way less than the workers were asking for, and way more than the factory owners wanted to pay. Sirajul Islam Rony, he was on the wage board representing the workers.

SIRAJUL ISLAM RONY: *(Through translator)* We are not overly happy about it, but we are fine with it. With this rise, maybe their situation will improve a little bit, but not much. It won't be a really meaningful improvement.

RUBANA HUQ: It's going to be good for the workers. It's going to be a little tough for the owners, but I think we shall survive.

KENNEY: Rubana Huq runs a group of garment factories in Bangladesh making dress shirts and blazers. She says, you know, Bangladesh has done so well, in large part by being the cheapest place in the world to make clothes. Now Bangladesh is way closer to the garment-making world, and her biggest fear is that her customers will go somewhere else. In fact, she had a customer recently say, you know, you're as expensive as Cambodia right now.

HUQ: Do you know you're as expensive as Cambodia right now? So, I might as well get it from there.

KENNEY: This is a fear that factory owners and workers both share, that Western buyers will leave and take the jobs with them.

CHACE: One of those Western buyers—that's us, Planet Money—and Jockey, the T-shirt maker that we're working with. So we went to Jockey to ask if wages rise too much, will you guys leave?

KENNEY: What we found out is there's not a make-or-break figure that would make Jockey pull out of Bangladesh.

MARION SMITH: It depends on relevance to the rest of the world, to be honest with you.

KENNEY: This is Marion Smith, international sourcing guy at Jockey. And that answer—it depends relative to the rest of the world—it's sort of subtle but essential for understanding how a company like his makes choices about where to operate. To illustrate, Marion Smith tells us one story. A couple of years ago, he says, the price of cotton spiked.

SMITH: When we had the cotton crisis, in particular, and when it zoomed up from, like, seventy cents a pound to two-ten.

CHACE: Now, think about that: The price of cotton just about tripled, and cotton is a much bigger portion of the total cost of a T-shirt than the labor is. If you're making cotton T-shirts and cotton goes up by that much, it's hard to not pass that cost on to the end customer.

SMITH: And we did, and our competition did. The real thing was who was going to do it first? Everybody ate it for a long time. It was who could hold out the longest.

CHACE: If there'd been a place to go to get cheaper cotton, they all would have gone there, but there wasn't. So the companies just paid more, and passed some of that cost on to us.

KENNEY: But for decades, labor has been different. There's always been a place you could get it cheaper. First, it was Japan, then it was Korea, China. Lately, it's been Bangladesh. But Marion Smith says we might be at the point where labor is becoming more like cotton. There's no place to get it cheaper.

SMITH: It's like Bangladesh is going to go up. And who's cheaper than Bangladesh?

CHACE: So you think we've hit sort of absolute zero, here. We've chased the cost as far as it goes, and it's going to start rising?

SMITH: Yeah, as a global economy, yes.

CHACE: So, our clothes are going to get more expensive. Our T-shirts are going to get more expensive.

SMITH: That will be my prediction.

CHACE: But because labor's part in that equation is so small, a rise in T-shirt prices could just be a few cents—perhaps not even enough to make us do our own laundry.

Nixon and Kimchi: How the Garment Industry Came to Bangladesh

STEVE INSKEEP: OK. We've been reporting this week about the Planet Money T-shirt and the global factory that created it. For example, much of the sewing work was done in Bangladesh. Bangladesh is one of the top five suppliers of clothing to the United States. And it got to that position because of some unlikely events, including an obscure trade deal from the 1970s. Zoe Chace of NPR's Planet Money team reports.

ZOE CHACE: This story begins in the early seventies. Bangladesh was one of the poorest places on Earth—a civil war, a cyclone, a refugee crisis. It was bad. And it sparked the first Live Aid–style benefit concert ever.

GEORGE HARRISON: *(Singing)* Bangladesh, Bangladesh . . .

CHACE: That's George Harrison, one of the Beatles. Now, inside Bangladesh, there was this other guy working on a plan to help, Abdul Majid Chowdhury. Chowdhury was a businessman. He and a couple of his friends were looking around for ways to help their country's desperate economy.

ABDUL MAJID CHOWDHURY: We need employment. We need dollar. And we ask ourselves what the hell we want.

CHACE: Back then, there was hardly any industry there. The country's main export was this plant, jute, the main ingredient in burlap sacks. Chowdhury saw an opportunity making clothes to sell to the world—relatively low-cost, relatively low-skill. Only one problem . . .

CHOWDHURY: I did not know how many buttons I had in my shirt. We did not know. I mean, that is the thing.

CHACE: There was a place that did know exactly: the country of Korea. Chowdhury saw Korea as a model for Bangladesh. Also devastated by a war and written off, but its economy had rebounded, in part because they'd learned to make clothes and sell them to the world. So Chowdhury went to South Korea and toured a massive garment factory there, and he saw the jobs he'd been looking for.

CHOWDHURY: What I saw that lot of girls, they were working. And when I saw those girls, I remembered my country, and I can see that my girls can replace these girls . . .

(Soundbite of fingers snapping)

CHOWDHURY: . . . like that. And that was the intention.

CHACE: Chowdhury set up a meeting with the head of the factory, the CEO of the company Daewoo. The meeting was scheduled for forty-five minutes. It went over.

CHOWDHURY: You will not believe it. I started the meeting after lunch. It was about four o'clock. And I finished at two o'clock in the morning.

CHACE: Chowdhury emerged in the dead of night with a deal. Korea would help set up the first export-oriented garment factory in Bangladesh. Chowdhury had help convincing the Daewoo chairman to invest in Bangladesh, help from an unlikely source: Richard Nixon.

PRESIDENT RICHARD NIXON: And so what we're fighting for is for the protection of our textiles and our textile markets. But let's do it . . .

CHACE: This is President Nixon talking in Asheville, North Carolina, in 1970, promising to do something about the cheap clothes and textiles that were flooding in from places like Korea and threatening jobs in textile towns like Asheville.

NIXON: You know, textiles are produced all over the United States of America, and we have the problem of imports, imports from abroad.

CHACE: So, Nixon helped create this massive piece of trade policy in 1974: the Multifiber Arrangement. Sounds boring, but you could say it reshaped the entire global economy. It set these firm limits for how much clothing and textiles each country could sell to the United States. And around the time that Mr. Chowdhury had made his trip to the Daewoo clothing factory, Korea had hit its limit, which gave the Koreans an incentive: open up a factory in another country, say, Bangladesh, get made-in-Bangladesh labels put on their Korean-made shirts and sell them to the West. So, the deal Chowdhury and the Daewoo CEO worked out in the late hours of their meeting was for Chowdhury to come back to Korea with a whole bunch of Bangladeshis. The Koreans would train them for six months, and then they'd all go back to Bangladesh together and open a factory. Eventually, 128 Bangladeshis fly off to Korea, a country most of them had certainly never seen, and the culture clash was instant. Muhammad Nuruddin was on that trip.

MUHAMMAD NURUDDIN: The problem we had—the stinky food, kimchi. We could not eat them. Some girls were vomiting. They could not exist.

CHACE: Did they really? They threw up?

NURUDDIN: Yeah.

CHACE: The Bangladeshis weirded out the Koreans, too, I discovered.

KIM EUN HEE: Yeah, yeah, yeah.

CHACE: I reached Kim Eun Hee. He was the Korean trainer at Daewoo in charge of the collar-and-cuff section. Korea was still pretty isolated back then. Kim Eun Hee had never met someone from that part of the world.

HEE: *(Through translator)* When they approached me to shake hands, their hands smelled. I mean, they had this smell on their hands that I was not used to. Just generally, when they were around, there were these different spices that I could smell from them. And so it was not too easy at first to approach them and to be near them.

CHACE: Neither side had been prepared for this aspect of the training, the smell of each other, but they worked through it. Kim Eun Hee even tried the Bangladeshi food himself at a special event the Bangladeshis threw for the Koreans.

HEE: *(Through translator)* And what happened was they served some of their food to us, and we couldn't eat it. It was just repelling. We kind of sat there not eating it, and our CEO actually called all of us out. And he brought us to the corner of a room, and he said: We're going to be living in an international society, and this is something that we're just going to have to endure. So suck it up and just eat it.

CHACE: That part about the international society turns out to be true, certainly immediately for Korea. After six months of training, Kim Eun Hee flew to Bangladesh to help them set up the very first export-oriented garment factory there: Desh Garments, in Chittagong. That was in 1980. In thirty years, a country that had only the material to make burlap sacks to sell to the world became one of the biggest clothing makers on Earth, now more than 4,000 factories. Anwal Chowdhury, another person from the original group who went to Korea, he says you can trace every one back to our trip.

ANWAL CHOWDHURY: Wherever you go, the origin is there. Maybe it is now fourth or fifth generation that I train person, he train another person, and then again he train another person.

CHACE: Now, the rapid spread of the garment industry in Bangladesh has brought problems. The government is weak, the infrastructure weaker. You've probably heard of Rana Plaza, the factory that collapsed, killing more than a thousand people. The country industrialized so quickly, that sometimes it's dangerous. Kim Eun Hee—in fact, Daewoo, the company— stopped making clothes, moved into high-end fabrics and electronics, but he still remembers a little Bengali from those days.

HEE: *(Bengali spoken)* I love you.

UNIDENTIFIED MAN #1: That means I love you.

CHACE: Oh. Is that what you guys said to each other at the end?

HEE: *(Through translator)* Yeah, we did.

CHACE: Passing the T-shirt baton from one country to the next, all because of a piece of trade policy that changed the world and certainly utterly changed Bangladesh.

The Giant Book That Creates and Destroys Entire Industries

STEVE INSKEEP: Our Planet Money team has been making a T-shirt and all this week, we've been following its journey around the world, including to Colombia, where they were made. This is an exploration that tells you a lot about the global economy. And today, Jacob Goldstein meets those shirts as they arrive in Miami—and encounters a 3,000-page book that shapes economies around the world.

JACOB GOLDSTEIN: I'm walking around the port of Miami with Officer Lisa Sacco. She's with U.S. Customs and Border Protection. We are, literally, waiting for our ship to come in.

LISA SACCO: There's our ship.

GOLDSTEIN: The ship is called the *Hansa Kirkenes*. It left Cartagena, Colombia, about a week ago, carrying all 6,078 of Planet Money women's T-shirts. A giant crane lifts the container carrying all those shirts off the ship, and drops it at my feet. Boom.

GOLDSTEIN: They made it. The Planet Money women's T-shirts are here.

The T-shirts are here, and yet they're not quite here yet. If you've ever waited at an airport to clear Customs, that's where our T-shirts are now, waiting for permission to enter the country. I ask Office Sacco: What could Customs be worried about, with a container coming from Colombia to Miami? Drugs? Guns?

SACCO: The only thing I could think of is maybe a trade violation. Trade is a huge issue. I mean, that's what we do, is we protect our trade.

GOLDSTEIN: Protecting U.S. trade means following an incredibly elaborate set of rules that are part of U.S. law. And they're all spelled out in a giant book more than 3,000 pages long.

MICHAEL CONE: It is the book of everything—at least for the importer.

GOLDSTEIN: This is Michael Cone, a customs and international trade attorney in New York. The book is called the *Harmonized Tariff Schedule of the United States*. And Cone says it lists the tax importers have to pay on approximately every single thing in the universe—including, of course, T-shirts.

CONE: And chapter 6109 covers, generally, T-shirts, singlets, tank tops, and similar garments knitted or crocheted.

GOLDSTEIN: That's us.

CONE: That's us.

GOLDSTEIN: That's the Planet Money T-shirt—6109.

CONE: That's where we're going to be.

GOLDSTEIN: Now, the average tax rate on stuff coming into this country is about 2 percent. In the book of everything, Cone points to the rate we're going to have to pay for the Planet Money T-shirt.

CONE: The tariff is 16.5 percent.

GOLDSTEIN: So, sixteen-and-a-half percent is a lot.

CONE: It's a lot.

GOLDSTEIN: The Planet Money men's T-shirt was made in Bangladesh, and we're going to pay the full sixteen-and-a-half percent on the men's shirts. But the women's shirts, the ones that just arrived in Miami, came from Colombia, and the book of everything says we get a special deal on those.

CONE: It says free. Now, when you see free . . .

GOLDSTEIN: Free? I like free.

CONE: We all like free, and if you jump through the right hoops and you follow the direction that Uncle Sam has provided, you can come in duty-free.

GOLDSTEIN: So, why are we paying a sixteen-and-a-half percent tax on our shirts coming from Bangladesh, and zero on the shirts coming from Colombia? Start with this: the United States has had a tax on textile imports since 1789, the year the

Constitution took effect. Douglas Irwin, an economist at Dartmouth, says it really got going after the War of 1812.

DOUGLAS IRWIN: Imports began flooding into the United States, hurting all of these small new producers of textiles. And they clamored and went to Washington and said our industry's going to be wiped out. We're going to throw out of work thousands of people. We need protection to save our mills.

GOLDSTEIN: So, Congress raised the tariff, which made textile imports more expensive, and that protected U.S. mills. We've had a tariff on textiles ever since. But recently, another side of the debate has gotten louder, more powerful. The companies that import clothes into the U.S. and the retail stores that sell those clothes, they say this tariff gets passed on to consumers. It makes clothes more expensive for everybody in this country.

Economists agree with this, and they say tariffs distort the economy, make it less efficient. So that tariff on clothes and fabric that's been in place for hundreds of years is going away one country at a time. In the past few decades, Mexico, Honduras, Israel, they've all signed free trade deals with the U.S. And a few years ago, the U.S. made a free trade deal with Colombia. Luis Restrepo is the CEO of the Colombia company that made our T-shirts. He says that if there were a tariff on Colombia shirts, his company couldn't export to the U.S. at all.

LUIS RESTREPO: No. To export into the United States, no, will make our garments very expensive.

GOLDSTEIN: In other words, without this free trade deal, the Planet Money women's T-shirts that are arriving in Miami today would not have been made at Colombia at all. They would have been made somewhere else, somewhere cheaper. This is how a tiny tweak in U.S. tariff rules in the book of everything can create or destroy whole industries in other countries. Back at the port, I head over to the shipping company office to find out one last thing: Have our shirts been released by Customs, or is Customs going to hold us up to make sure we followed all those trade rules?

UNIDENTIFIED WOMAN: What's the container number?

GOLDSTEIN: 782939.

To me, this is a big moment. It's the first time I've ever cleared 6,078 T-shirts through Customs. For the woman helping me, it's the most routine thing in the world.

UNIDENTIFIED WOMAN: Everything's fully released.

GOLDSTEIN: So, basically, we're good to go.

UNIDENTIFIED WOMAN: Yes.

GOLDSTEIN: Good to go, duty-free and bound, eventually, for you.

Planet Money T-Shirt Exposes Issues of Work, Trade and Clothes

MELISSA BLOCK: All this week we've been hearing about the making of the Planet Money T-shirt, a global journey that's taken us from the United States to Indonesia, Bangladesh, Colombia, and back to the States. The series raised big questions about the nature of the garment industry and the role the very clothes on our back play in the global economy. I'm joined now by Planet Money's Alex Blumberg to wrap up the project. And Alex, when you think about all these stories, is there one single biggest takeaway that you're left with?

ALEX BLUMBERG: Well, the biggest takeaway was that this story is way more complicated than I'd sort of realized and I think sometimes than it gets presented. So our T-shirts were manufactured in two different countries. The men's T-shirts were manufactured in Bangladesh. The women's T-shirts were manufactured in Colombia. And we talked to the CEO of the plant in Colombia that manufactured our women's shirts and he told us this about the garment industry.

UNIDENTIFIED MAN: Our industry follows poverty.

BLOCK: Our industry follows poverty.

UNIDENTIFIED MAN: Our industry is like on roller skates. First it was Latin America, then we moved to China. Now China's becoming more expensive, we moved to Bangladesh or moved to Vietnam. And it goes like this.

BLOCK: Alex, that image of the industry moving around on roller skates is a really powerful one.

BLUMBERG: Yeah, and it is absolutely true. The garment industry is heavily labor dependent, especially in this phase where they cut and sew the shirts together. And they're constantly looking for the lowest wage labor. And so you can look at that and say this is an industry that is exploiting people in desperate circumstances. And that is sometimes very true.

The other part of it though that we sort of discovered is that there is a reason people in Bangladesh, for example, want to work in a garment factory. We talked to several people who worked in the factory that made the men's shirt. And they described their lives before they came to the factory when they lived in the rural villages where they were born. And they were living very close to the edge. . . . They were eating dirt and the family wasn't able to send them to get proper medical care because they didn't have enough money. . . .

BLOCK: Alex, I do have to ask you about some criticism that's been directed toward the series because when you announced it and you launched this Kickstarter campaign that would fund the creation of these T-shirts, there were people who said, look, this is an industry that doesn't treat its workers responsibly. There's a lot of exploitation. There's a lot of death.

If you commission these T-shirts, despite your best intentions, aren't you contributing to a really big problem? What do you say to that?

BLUMBERG: This is something that we wrestled with quite a bit. You know, obviously, if we're making a T-shirt and we find out that the factory where our T-shirt is made is employing, you know, underage workers or is using coercive tactics, we didn't find that. I mean, we investigated our factory and tried to find any instance of that. We didn't.

But still, the issue is there and, you know, it gets to this idea that we are all part of this global system unless you work very, very hard and only buy a very select brand of clothing, you're generally interacting with this global supply chain. And it's something that we all have to wrestle with, really. What is our responsibility to the people who make our shirts?

What are their lives like? And to the extent that we were able to shed light on that, I feel good about that.

New York Times

An excerpt from Andrea Elliott's serialized masterpiece takes us inside the world of a twelve-year-old homeless girl and, in doing so, connects us to life at the low end of the economic spectrum in a postcrisis world, a time when previous gains in the fight against poverty have been reversed. The piece recalls the work of great journalists dating to Jacob Riis in the late nineteenth century and can fairly be compared to the work of another writer who worked in serial form: Charles Dickens. This story, however, is true.

Andrea Elliott

8. Invisible Child
Girl in the Shadows: Dasani's Homeless Life

She wakes to the sound of breathing. The smaller children lie tangled beside her, their chests rising and falling under winter coats and wool blankets. A few feet away, their mother and father sleep near the mop bucket they use as a toilet. Two other children share a mattress by the rotting wall where the mice live, opposite the baby, whose crib is warmed by a hair dryer perched on a milk crate.

Slipping out from her covers, the oldest girl sits at the window. On mornings like this, she can see all the way across Brooklyn to the Empire State Building, the first New York skyscraper to reach one hundred floors. Her gaze always stops at that iconic temple of stone, its tip pointed celestially, its facade lit with promise.

"It makes me feel like there's something going on out there," says the eleven-year-old girl, never one for patience. This child of New York is always running before she walks. She likes being first—the first to be born, the first to go to school, the first to make the honor roll.

Even her name, Dasani, speaks of a certain reach. The bottled water had come to Brooklyn's bodegas just before she was born, catching the fancy of her mother, who could not afford such indulgences. It hinted at a different, upwardly mobile clientele, a set of newcomers who over the next decade would transform the borough.

Dasani's own neighborhood, Fort Greene, is now one of gentrification's gems. Her family lives in the Auburn Family Residence, a decrepit city-run shelter for the homeless. It is a place where mold creeps up walls and roaches swarm, where feces and vomit plug communal toilets, where sexual predators have roamed and small children stand guard for their single mothers outside filthy showers.

It is no place for children. Yet Dasani is among 280 children at the shelter. Beyond its walls, she belongs to a vast and invisible tribe of more than 22,000 homeless children in New York, the highest number since the Great Depression, in the most unequal metropolis in America.

Nearly a quarter of Dasani's childhood has unfolded at Auburn, where she shares a 520-square-foot room with her parents and seven siblings. As they begin to stir on this frigid January day, Dasani sets about her chores.

Her mornings begin with Baby Lele, whom she changes, dresses, and feeds, checking that the formula distributed by the shelter is not, once again, expired. She then wipes down the family's small refrigerator, stuffed with lukewarm milk, Tropicana grape juice, and containers of leftover Chinese. After tidying the dresser drawers she shares with a sister, Dasani rushes her younger siblings onto the school bus.

"I have a lot on my plate," she says, taking inventory: The fork and spoon are her parents and the macaroni, her siblings—except for Baby Lele, who is a plump chicken breast.

"So that's a lot on my plate—with some corn bread," she says. "That's a lot on my plate."

Dasani guards her feelings closely, dispensing with anger through humor. Beneath it all is a child whose existence is defined by her siblings. Her small scrub-worn hands are always tying shoelaces or doling out peanut-butter sandwiches, taking the ends of the loaf for herself. The bond is inescapable. In the presence of her brothers and sisters, Dasani has no peace. Without them, she is incomplete.

Today, Dasani rides the creaky elevator to the lobby and walks past the guards, the metal detector, and the tall, iron fence that envelops what she calls "the jail." She steps into the light and is met by the worn brick facade of the Walt Whitman projects across the street.

She heads east along Myrtle Avenue and, three blocks later, has crossed into another New York: the shaded, graceful abode of Fort Greene's brownstones, which fetch millions of dollars.

"Black is beautiful, black is me," she sings under her breath as her mother trails behind.

Dasani suddenly stops, puzzling at the pavement. Its condition, she notes, is clearly superior on this side of Myrtle.

"Worlds change real fast, don't it?" her mother says.

In the short span of Dasani's life, her city has been reborn. The skyline soars with luxury towers, beacons of a new gilded age. More than 200 miles of fresh bike lanes connect commuters to high-tech jobs, passing through upgraded parks and avant-garde projects like the High Line and Jane's Carousel. Posh retail has spread from its Manhattan roots to the city's other boroughs. These are the crown jewels of Mayor Michael R. Bloomberg's long reign, which began just seven months after Dasani was born.

In the shadows of this renewal, it is Dasani's population that has been left behind. The ranks of the poor have risen, with almost half of New Yorkers living near or below the poverty line. Their traditional anchors—affordable housing and jobs that pay a living wage—have weakened as the city reorders itself around the whims of the wealthy.

Long before Mayor-Elect Bill de Blasio rose to power by denouncing the city's inequality, children like Dasani were being pushed further into the margins, and not just in New York. Cities across the nation have become flash points of polarization, as one population has bounced back from the recession while another continues to struggle. One in five American children is now living in poverty, giving the United States the highest child-poverty rate of any developed nation except for Romania.

This bodes poorly for the future. Decades of research have shown the staggering societal costs of children in poverty. They grow up with less education and lower earning power. They are more likely to have drug addiction, psychological trauma, and disease or to wind up in prison.

Dasani does not need the proof of abstract research. All of these plights run through her family. Her future is further threatened by the fact of her homelessness, which has been shown, even in short spells, to bring disastrous consequences.

Dasani's circumstances are largely the outcome of parental dysfunction. While nearly one-third of New York's homeless children are supported by a working adult, her mother and father are unemployed, have a history of arrests, and are battling drug addiction.

Yet Dasani's trials are not solely of her parents' making. They are also the result of decisions made a world away, in the marble confines of City Hall. With the economy growing in 2004, the Bloomberg administration adopted sweeping new policies intended to push the homeless to become more self-reliant. They would no longer get priority access to public housing and other programs but would receive short-term help with rent. Poor people would be empowered, the mayor argued, and homelessness would decline.

But the opposite happened. As rents steadily rose and low-income wages stagnated, chronically poor families like Dasani's found themselves stuck in a shelter system with fewer exits. Families are now languishing there longer than ever—a development that Mr. Bloomberg explained by saying shelters offered "a much more pleasurable experience than they ever had before."

Just three days before the mayor made that comment at a news conference in August 2012, an inspector at Auburn stopped by Dasani's crowded room, noting that a mouse was "running around and going into the walls," which had "many holes."

"Please assist," the inspector added. "There is infant in room."

Dasani was about to start sixth grade at a promising new school. This would be a pivotal year of her childhood—one already marked by more longing and loss than most adults ever see.

A tangle of three dramas had yet to unspool.

There was the question of whether Dasani's family would remain intact.

Her mother had just been reunited with the children on the condition that she and her husband stay off drugs. The city's Administration for Children's Services was watching closely. Any slips, and the siblings could wind up in foster care, losing their parents and, most likely, one another.

The family's need for a home was also growing desperate. The longer they stayed in that one room, the more they seemed to fall apart. Yet rents were impossibly high in the city, and a quarter-million people were waiting for the rare vacancy in public housing. Families like Dasani's had been leaving the state. This was the year, then, that her parents made a promise: to save enough money to go somewhere else, maybe as far as the Pocono Mountains, in Pennsylvania.

Dasani could close her eyes and see it. "It's quiet and it's a lot of grass."

In the absence of this long-awaited home, there was only school. But it remained to be seen whether Dasani's new middle school, straining under budget cuts, could do enough to fill the voids of her life.

For children like Dasani, school is not just a place to cultivate a hungry mind. It is a refuge. The right school can provide routine, nourishment, and the guiding hand of responsible adults.

But school also had its perils. Dasani was hitting the age when girls prove their worth through fighting. And she was her mother's daughter, a fearless fighter.

She was also on the cusp of becoming something more, something she could feel but not yet see, if only the right things happened and the right people came along.

.   .   .

Dasani is a short, wiry girl whose proud posture overwhelms her four-foot-eight frame. She has a delicate, oval face and luminous brown eyes that watch everything, owl-like. Her expression veers from wonder to mischief. Strangers often remark on her beauty—her high cheekbones and smooth skin—but the comments never seem to register.

What she knows is that she has been blessed with perfect teeth. In a family where braces are the stuff of fantasy, having good teeth is a lottery win.

On the subway, Dasani can blend in with children who are better off. It is an ironic fact of being poor in a rich city that the donated garments Dasani and her siblings wear lend them the veneer of affluence, at least from a distance. Used purple Uggs and Patagonia fleeces cover thinning socks and fraying jeans. A Phil & Teds rain cover, fished from a garbage bin, protects Baby Lele's rickety stroller. . . .

When strangers are near, Dasani refers to Auburn as "that place." It is separate from her, and distant. But in the company of her siblings, she calls it "the house," transforming a crowded room into an imaginary home.

In reality, Auburn is neither. The forbidding, ten-story brick building, which dates back almost a century, was formerly Cumberland Hospital, one of seven public hospitals that closed because of the city's 1970s fiscal crisis.

In 1985, the city repurposed the former hospital into a shelter for families. This was the dawn of the period known as "modern homelessness," driven by wage stagnation, Reagan-era cutbacks, and the rising cost of homes. By the time Mayor Bloomberg took office in 2002, New York's homeless population had reached 31,063—a record for the city, which is legally obligated to provide shelter.

Among the city's 152 family shelters, Auburn became known as a place of last resort, a dreaded destination for the chronically homeless.

City and state inspectors have repeatedly cited the shelter for deplorable conditions, including sexual misconduct by staff members, spoiled food, asbestos exposure, lead paint, and vermin. Auburn has no certificate of occupancy, as required by law, and lacks an operational plan that meets state regulations. Most of the shelter's smoke detectors and alarms have been found to be inoperable.

There are few signs that children live at Auburn. Locked gates prevent them from setting foot on the front lawn. In a city that has invested millions of dollars in new "green spaces," Auburn's is often overrun with weeds.

Inside, prepackaged meals are served in a cafeteria where Dasani and her siblings wait in one line for their food before heading to another line to heat it in one of two microwaves that hundreds of residents share. Tempers fly and fights explode. The routine can last more than an hour before the children take their first bite.

The family's room is the scene of debilitating chaos: stacks of dirty laundry, shoes stuffed under a mattress, bicycles and coats piled high.

To the left of the door, beneath a decrepit sink where Baby Lele is bathed, the wall has rotted through, leaving a long, dark gap where mice congregate.

A few feet away, Dasani's legally blind, ten-year-old sister, Nijai, sleeps on a mattress that has come apart at the seams, its rusted coils splayed.

Hand-washed clothes line the guards on the windows, which are shaded by gray wool blankets strung from the ceiling. A sticky fly catcher dangles overhead, dotted with dead insects.

There is no desk or chair in the room—just a maze of mattresses and dressers. A flat-screen television rests on two orange milk crates.

To eat, the children sit on the cracked linoleum floor, which never feels clean no matter how much they mop. Homework is a challenge. The shelter's one recreation room can hardly accommodate Auburn's hundreds of children, leaving Dasani and her siblings to study, hunched over, on their mattresses.

Sometimes it feels like too many bodies sharing the same air. "There's no space to breathe 'cause they breathe up all the oxygen," Dasani says.

She carves out small, sacred spaces: a portion of the floor at mealtime, an upturned crate by the window, a bathroom stall.

The children spend hours at the playgrounds of the surrounding housing projects, where a subtle hierarchy is at work. If they are seen enough times emerging from Auburn, they are pegged as the neighborhood's outliers, the so-called shelter boogies.

Nothing gnaws at Dasani more.

A mucus-stained nose suggests a certain degradation, not just the absence of tissues but of a parent willing to wipe or a home so unclean that a runny nose makes no difference. Dasani and her siblings can get hungry enough to lose their concentration in school, but they are forever wiping one another's noses.

When Dasani hears "shelter boogies," all she can think to say is what her mother always tells her—that Auburn is "just a pit stop."

"But you will live in the projects forever, as will your kids' kids, and your kids' kids' kids."

She knows the battle is asymmetrical.

The projects may represent all kinds of inertia. But to live at Auburn is to admit the ultimate failure: the inability of one's parents to meet that most basic need.

·   ·   ·

Dasani ticks through their faces, the girls from the projects who might turn up at this new school. Some are kind enough not to gossip about where she lives. The others might be distracted by the sheer noise of this first day—the start of sixth grade, the new uniform, the new faces. She will hopefully slip by those girls unseen.

She approaches the school's steps on a clear September morning. Fresh braids fall to one side of her face, clipped by bright yellow bows. Her required polo and khakis have been pressed with a hair straightener, since Auburn forbids irons.

Her heart is pounding. She will be sure to take a circuitous route home. She will focus in class and mind her manners in the schoolyard. She only has to climb those steps.

Minutes pass.

"Come on, there's nothing to be scared about," her thirty-four-year-old mother, Chanel, finally says, nudging Dasani up the stairs.

She passes through the metal detector, joining 507 other middle- and high-school students at the Susan S. McKinney Secondary School of the Arts.

Housed in a faded brick building two blocks from Auburn, McKinney is a poor-kids' version of LaGuardia Arts, the elite Manhattan public school that inspired the television series *Fame*. Threadbare curtains adorn its theater. Stage props are salvaged from a nearby trash bin. Dance class is so crowded that students practice in intervals.

An air of possibility permeates the school, named after the first African American woman to become a physician in New York State.

There is Officer Jamion Andrews, the security guard who moonlights as a rap lyricist, and Zakiya Harris, the dance teacher who runs a studio on the side. And there is Faith Hester, the comedic, eyelash-batting humanities teacher who wrote a self-help book titled *Create a Life You Love Living* and fancies her own reality show.

The children also strive. Among them is a voice that periodically lifts the school with a *Madama Butterfly* aria. When the students hear it, they know that Jasmine, a sublimely gifted junior, is singing in the office of the principal, Paula Holmes.

The school matriarch closes her eyes as she listens. It may be her only tranquil moment.

Miss Holmes is a towering woman, by turns steely and soft. She wears a Bluetooth like a permanent earring and tends toward power suits. She has been at McKinney's helm for fifteen years and runs the school like a naval ship, peering down its gleaming hallways as if searching the seas for enemy vessels.

Miss Holmes has no tolerance for sagging—sartorial, attitudinal, or otherwise. . . .

For all of McKinney's pluck, its burdens are great. In the last six years, the city has cut the school's budget by a quarter as its population declined. Fewer teachers share a greater load. After-school resources have thinned, but not the needs of students whose families are torn apart by gun violence and drug use. McKinney's staff psychologist shuttles between three schools like a firefighter.

And now, a charter school is angling to move in. If successful, it will eventually claim McKinney's treasured top floor, home to its theater class, dance studio, and art lab. Teachers and parents are bracing for battle, announced by fliers warning against the "apartheid" effects of a charter co-location.

Dasani knows about charter schools. Her former school, PS 67, shared space with one. She never spoke to those children, whose classrooms were stocked with new computers. Dasani's own school was failing by the time she left.

At McKinney, Dasani quickly draws the notice of the older students, and not because she is short, though the nickname "Shorty" sticks. It is her electricity. When they dote on her, she giggles. But say the wrong thing and she turns fierce, letting the four-letter words fly.

It is still September when Dasani's temper lands her in the principal's office.

"Please don't call my mother," Dasani whispers.

Miss Holmes is seated in a rolling pleather chair held together by duct tape. She stares at the anguished girl. She has been at McKinney long enough to know when a child's transgressions at school might bring a beating at home.

The principal slowly scoots her chair up to Dasani and leans within inches of her face.

"OK," she says softly. "Let's make a deal." . . .

●   ●   ●

Dasani possesses what adults at McKinney consider an intuitive approach to learning, the kind that comes when rare smarts combine with extreme life circumstances. Her intelligence is "uncanny" and "far surpasses peers her age," one counselor writes. "Student is continuously using critical analysis to reflect upon situations and interactions."

Principal Holmes is also taking note. She can already see in this "precocious little button" the kind of girl who could be anything—even a Supreme Court justice—if only she harnesses her gifts early enough. "Dasani has something that hasn't even been unleashed yet," Miss Holmes says. "It's still being cultivated."

For now, Dasani's most honed skill might be obfuscation. She works hard to hide her struggles, staying quiet as other children brag about their new cell phones or sleepovers with friends. . . .

You can be popular in one of three ways, Dasani's mother always says. Dress fly. Do good in school. Fight.

The first option is out of the question. While Dasani clings to her uniform, other students wear coveted Adidas hoodies and Doc Marten boots. In dance class, Dasani does not even have a leotard.

So she applies herself in school. "I have a lot of possibility," she says. "I do."

Her strongest subject is English, where a poem she writes is tacked to a teacher's wall.

By October, she is on the honor roll, just as her life at Auburn is coming apart. . . .

•   •   •

By late fall, Chanel and Supreme [Dasani's stepfather] are fighting daily about money.

It has been years since Supreme lost his job as a barber and Chanel stopped working as a janitor for the parks department. He cuts hair inside the shelter and sells pirated DVDs on the street while she hawks odds and ends from discount stores. In a good month, their combined efforts can bring in a few hundred dollars.

This is not one of those times. Supreme is keeping tight control of the family's welfare income—$1,285 in food stamps and $1,122 in survivor benefits for his first wife's death. He refuses to give Chanel cash for laundry.

Soon, all of Dasani's uniforms are stained. At school, she is now wearing donated clothes, and her hair is unkempt, inviting the dreaded designation of "nappy." Rumors are circulating about where she lives. Only 6 of the middle school's 157 students reside in shelters.

When the truth about Dasani emerges, she does nothing to contradict it. She is a proud girl. She must find a way to turn the truth, like other unforeseeable calamities, in her favor.

She begins calling herself "ghetto." She dares the girls to fight her and challenges the boys to arm-wrestle, flexing the biceps she has built doing pull-ups in Fort Greene Park. The boys watch slack-jawed as Dasani demonstrates the push-ups she has also mastered, earning her the nickname "muscle girl."

Her teachers are flummoxed. They assume that she has shed her uniform because she is trying to act tough. In fact, the reverse is true. . . .

Part Two

Gracie Mansion is something of an oddity. In a city with a 2 percent vacancy rate and a shortage of public housing, the mayoral residence sits uninhabited on 11 pristine acres of the Upper East Side. It has been more than a decade since Mayor Michael R. Bloomberg chose to remain in his opulent townhouse, consigning Gracie Mansion to the status of a museum and venue for civic events.

Dasani knows none of these particulars when she steps through Gracie's doors on a school trip in February. She is looking for the mayor. She wants to see him up close, this mysterious "Wizard of Oz" figure who makes decisions about her life from behind a curtain of political power.

It never occurs to Dasani that the mayor does not live there. Who could have a mansion and not live in it?

"Look at that fireplace!" she marvels as her classmates step into the parlor where Mr. Bloomberg has given news conferences. The tour guide, a woman wearing gold-clasp earrings and tangerine lipstick, moves the children along, reminding them not to touch.

They shuffle into the library. Still no mayor. Dasani scans for clues like the FBI agents of her favorite television show, *Criminal Minds*. She inspects a telephone. "His last call was at eleven-fifteen," she whispers.

The tour guide opens French doors onto the veranda where New York's mayors have entertained dignitaries from around the world. "It's a very gracious way of living," she says. "Very elegant."

What impresses Dasani most are not the architectural details or the gold-bound volumes of Chaucer and Tolstoy but the astonishing lack of dust. She runs her hand lightly over the top of a Steinway piano.

"I tell you," she says. "This house is clean."

Dasani was still an infant when Mr. Bloomberg took office in 2002. Declaring Gracie Mansion "the people's house," he gathered $7 million in private donations—much of it his own money—to rehabilitate the pale yellow eighteenth-century home, which overlooks the East River. In came new plumbing, floors, lighting, and ventilation, along with exquisite touches like an 1820s chandelier and a four-poster mahogany bed.

Facing that same river, six miles away on the opposite side, is the Auburn Family Residence, the squalid city-run homeless shelter where Dasani has lived for more than two years. . . .

Adults who are homeless often speak of feeling "stuck." For children, the experience is more like a free fall. With each passing month, they slip further back in every category known to predict long-term well-being. They are less likely to graduate from the schools that anchor them, and more likely to end up like their parents, their lives circumscribed by teenage pregnancy or shortened by crime and illness.

In the absence of a steady home or a reliable parent, public institutions have an outsize influence on the destiny of children like Dasani. Whether she can transcend her circumstances rests greatly on the role, however big or small, that society opts to play in her life.

The question of public responsibility has gained urgency in recent decades. By the time Mr. Bloomberg was elected, children made up 40 percent of shelter residents.

"We're not walking away from taking care of the homeless," the mayor said early on. "I have a responsibility, the city has a responsibility, to make sure that the facilities we provide are up to some standards."

The Bloomberg administration set out to revamp the shelter system, creating 7,500 units of temporary housing, a database to track the shelter population, and a program intended to prevent homelessness with counseling, job training, and short-term financial aid. The new system also made it harder for families to be found eligible for shelter.

For a time, the numbers went down. But in the wake of profound policy changes and a spiraling economy, more children wound up in shelters than at any time since the creation of the shelter system in the early 1980s.

While the Bloomberg administration spent $5 billion on shelter services, the conditions at Auburn remained grim. Dasani and her siblings have grown numb to life at the shelter, where knife fights break out and crack pipes are left on the bathroom floor. In the words of their mother, they have "become the place." She has a verb for it: shelternized.

For Dasani, school is everything—the provider of meals, on-the-spot nursing care, security, and substitute parenting. On the Gracie trip, Dasani wears the Nautica coat donated by a school security guard and matching white gloves bestowed to her that morning by the principal.

A school like McKinney can also provide a bridge to the wider world.

It does not matter that Dasani's entire sixth grade must walk a mile to the subway in icy winds, take two trains, then walk another ten minutes before arriving. This round-trip journey, which occupies much of the day, is a welcome escape.

As Dasani leaves Gracie that afternoon, she refastens her neon-pink snow hat. She has given up on the mayor.

"He lives somewhere else," she says, waving an arm along East End Avenue before heading back to the subway.

Guardian

Russell Brand has given some brilliant performances as a comedian and actor but perhaps none as unforgettable as his speech to the GQ Awards, a flattery festival held by the magazine to lavish praise on celebrities and the odd politician in order to generate buzz for itself. Brand had the temerity to mention the awkward fact that the event's main sponsor, Hugo Boss, had supplied uniforms to the Nazis (and in fact the company owed its early success to its founders' ties to the party). Mayhem ensued, captured here brilliantly by Brand's first-person account.

9. Russell Brand and the GQ Awards

"It's Amazing How Absurd It Seems"

I have had the privilege of scuba diving. I did it once on holiday, and I'm aware that it's one of those subjects that people can get pretty boring and sincere about, and sincerity, for we British, is no state in which to dwell, so I'll be brief. The scuba dive itself was nuministic enough, a drenched heaven; coastal shelves and their staggering, sub-aquatic architecture, like spilt cathedrals, gormless, ghostly fish gliding by like Jackson Pollock's pets. Silent miracles. What got me, though, was when I came up for air, at the end. As my head came above water after even a paltry fifteen minutes in Davy Jones's Locker, there was something absurd about the surface. How we, the creatures of the land, live our lives, obliviously trundling, flat feet slapping against the dust.

It must have been a while since I've attended a fancy, glitzy event because as soon as I got to the GQ awards I felt like something was up. The usual visual grammar was in place—a carpet in the street, people in paddocks awaiting a brush with something glamorous, blokes with earpieces, birds in frocks of colliding colors that if sighted in nature would indicate the presence of poison. I'm not trying to pass myself off as some kind of Francis of Assisi, Yusuf Islam, man of the people, but I just wasn't feeling it.

I ambled into the Opera House across yet more outdoor carpets, boards bearing branding, in this case Hugo Boss, past paparazzi, and began to queue up at the line of journalists and presenters, in a slightly nicer paddock, who offer up mics and say stuff like:

"Who are you wearing?"

"I'm not wearing anyone. I went with clobber, I'm not Buffalo Bill."

Noel Gallagher was immediately ahead of me in the press line, and he's actually a mate. I mean, I love him: sometimes I forget he wrote "Supersonic" and played to 400,000 people at Knebworth because he's such a laugh. He laid right into me, the usual gear: "What the fook you wearing? Does Rod Stewart know you're going through his jumble?" I try to remain composed and give as good as I get, even though the paddock-side banter is accompanied by looming foam-tipped eavesdroppers, hanging like insidious mistletoe.

In case you don't know, these parties aren't like real parties. It's fabricated fun, imposed from the outside. A vision of what squares imagine cool people might do set on a spaceship. Or in Moloko. As we come out of the lift there's a bloody great long corridor flanked by gorgeous birds in black dresses, paid to be there, motionless, left hand on hip, teeth tacked to lips with scarlet glue. The intention, I suppose, is to contrive some Ian Fleming super-uterus of well fit mannequins to midwife you into the shindig, but me and my mate Matt just felt self-conscious, jigging through Robert Palmer's estrogen passage like aspirational Morris dancers. Matt stared at their necks and I made small talk as I hot stepped towards the preshow drinks. Now, I'm not typically immune to the allure of objectified women, but I am presently beleaguered by a nerdish whirling dervish and am eschewing all others. Perhaps the clarity of this elation has awakened me. A friend of mine said: "Being in love is like discovering a concealed ballroom in a house you've long inhabited." I also don't drink, so these affairs where most people rinse away their Britishness and twitishness with booze are for me a face-first log flume of backslaps, chitchat, eyewash, and gak.

After a load of photos and whatnot, we descend the world's longest escalator, which are called that even as they de-escalate, and in we go to the main forum, a high-ceilinged hall, full of circular cloth-draped, numbered tables, a stage at the front, the letters GQ, twelve-foot high in neon at the back; this aside, though, neon forever the moniker of trash, this is a posh do, in an opera house full of folk in tuxes.

Everywhere you look there's someone off the telly; Stephen Fry, Pharrell, Sir Bobby Charlton, Samuel L. Jackson, Rio Ferdinand, Justin Timberlake, Foreign Secretary William Hague, and mayor of London Boris Johnson. My table is a sanctuary of sorts; Noel and his missus, Sara; John Bishop and his wife, Mel, my mates Matt Morgan, Mick, and Gee. Noel and I are both there to get awards and decide to use our speeches to dig each other out. This makes me feel a little grounded in the unreal glare, normal.

Noel's award is for being an "icon" and mine for being an "oracle." My knowledge of the classics is limited but includes awareness that an oracle is a spiritual medium through whom prophecies from the gods were sought in ancient Greece. Thankfully, I have a sense of humor that prevents me from taking accolades of that nature on face value, or I'd've been in the tricky position of receiving the GQ award for being "best portal to a mystical dimension," which is a lot of pressure. Me, Matt, and Noel conclude it's probably best to treat the whole event as a bit of a laugh, and, as if to confirm this as the correct attitude, Boris Johnson—a man perpetually in pyjamas regardless of what he's wearing—bounds to the stage to accept the award for "best politician." Yes, we agree: this is definitely a joke.

Boris, it seems, is taking it in this spirit, joshing beneath his ever-redeeming barnet that Labour's opposition to military action in Syria is a fey stance that he, as GQ politician of the year, would never be guilty of.

Matt is momentarily focused. "He's making light of gassed Syrian children," he says. We watch, slightly aghast, then return to goading Noel.

Before long, John Bishop is on stage giving me a lovely introduction, so I get up as Noel hurls down a few gauntlets, daring me to "do my worst."

I thanked John, said the "oracle award" sounds like a made-up prize you'd give a fat kid on sports day—I should know, I used to get them—then that it's barmy that Hugo Boss can trade under the same name they flogged uniforms to the Nazis under and the ludicrous necessity for an event such as this one to banish such a lurid piece of information from our collective consciousness.

I could see the room dividing as I spoke. I could hear the laughter of some and louder still silence of others. I realized that for some people this was regarded as an event with import. The magazine, the sponsors, and some of those in attendance saw it as a kind of ceremony that warranted respect. In effect, it is a corporate ritual, an alliance between a media organization, GQ, and a commercial entity, Hugo Boss. What dawned on me as the night went on is that even in apparently frivolous conditions the establishment asserts control and won't tolerate having that assertion challenged, even flippantly, by that most beautifully adept tool: comedy.

The jokes about Hugo Boss were not intended to herald a campaign to destroy them. They're not Monsanto or Halliburton, the contemporary corporate allies of modern-day fascism; they are, I thought, an irrelevant menswear supplier with a double-dodgy history. The evening, though, provided an interesting opportunity to see how power structures preserve their agenda, even in a chintzy microcosm.

Subsequent to my jokes, the evening took a peculiar turn. Like the illusion of sophistication had been inadvertently disrupted by the exposure. It had the vibe of a wedding dinner where the best man's speech had revealed the groom's infidelity. With Hitler.

Foreign Secretary William Hague gave an award to former *Telegraph* editor Charles Moore, for writing a hagiography of Margaret Thatcher, who used his acceptance speech to build a precarious connection between my comments about the sponsors, my foolish answerphone scandal at the BBC, and the Sachs family's flight, 70 years earlier, from Nazi-occupied Europe. It was a confusing tapestry that Moore spun but he seemed to be saying that (a) the calls were as bad as the Holocaust and (b) the Sachs family may not've sought refuge in Britain had they known what awaited them. Even for a man whose former job was editing the *Telegraph* this is an extraordinary way to manipulate information.

Noel, who is not one to sit quietly on his feelings, literally booed while Charles Moore was talking, and others joined in. Booing! When do you hear booing in this day and age other than pantomimes and Parliament? Hague and Johnson are equally at home in either (Widow Twanky and Buttons, obviously) so were not unduly ruffled, but I thought it was nuts. The room by now had a distinct feel of "us and them," and if there is a line drawn in the sand I don't ever want to find myself on the same side as Hague and Johnson. Up went Noel to garner his gong, and he did not disappoint: "Always nice to be invited to the Tory party conference," he began, "Good to see the foreign secretary present when there's shit kicking off in Syria."

Noel once expressed his disgust at seeing a politician at Glastonbury. "What are you doing here? This ain't for you," he'd said. He explained to me: "You used to know where you were with politicians in the seventies and eighties cos they all looked like nutters: Thatcher, Heseltine, Cyril Smith. Now they look normal, they're more dangerous." Then, with dreadful foreboding: "They move among us." I agree with Noel. What are politicians doing at Glastonbury and the GQ awards? I feel guilty going, and I'm a comedian. Why are public officials, paid by us, turning up at events for fashion magazines? Well, the reason I was there was because I have a tour on and I was advised it would be good publicity. What are the politicians selling? How are they managing our perception of them with their attendance of these sequin-encrusted corporate balls?

We witness that there is a relationship between government, media, and industry that is evident even at this most spurious and superficial level. These three institutions support one another. We know that however cool a media outlet may purport to be, their primary loyalty is to their corporate backers. We know also that you cannot criticize the corporate backers openly without censorship and subsequent manipulation of this information.

Now I'm aware that this was really no big deal; I'm not saying I'm an estuary Che Guevara. It was a daft joke by a daft comic at a daft event. It makes me wonder, though, how the relationships and power dynamics I witnessed on this relatively inconsequential context are replicated on a more significant scale.

For example, if you can't criticize Hugo Boss at the GQ awards because they own the event, do you think it is significant that energy companies donate to the Tory party? Will that affect government policy? Will the relationships that "politician of the year" Boris Johnson has with City bankers—he took many more meetings with them than public servants in his first term as mayor—influence the way he runs our capital?

Is it any wonder that Amazon, Vodafone, and Starbucks avoid paying tax when they enjoy such cozy relationships with members of our government?

Ought we be concerned that our rights to protest are being continually eroded under the guise of enhancing our safety? Is there a relationship between proposed fracking in the UK, new laws that prohibit protest, and the relationships between energy companies and our government?

I don't know. I do have some good principles picked up that night that are generally applicable: the glamour and the glitz isn't real, the party isn't real, you have a much better time mucking around trying to make your mates laugh. I suppose that's obvious. We all know it, we already know all the important stuff, like: don't trust politicians, don't trust big business, and don't trust the media. Trust your own heart and each other. When you take a breath and look away from the spectacle it's amazing how absurd it seems when you look back.

Washington Post

The idea that a corporate board's main—nay, sole—job in life is to maximize value for shareholders seems as natural as the sun coming up in the east. The fact is, though, it has had enormous and, in some cases, enormously destructive implications for the economy, and, surprisingly, its provenance is only a few decades old. Jia Lynn Yang looks at the case of IBM to explore how the idea and especially its focus on short-term results have not always helped companies in the long run and have disconnected companies from other important stakeholders, namely, employees and surrounding communities.

Jia Lynn Yang

10. Maximizing Shareholder Value

The Goal That Changed
Corporate America

E ndicott, N.Y.—This town in the hills of upstate New
York is best known as the birthplace of IBM, one of
the country's most iconic companies. But there remain
only hints of that storied past.

The main street, once swarming with International Business Machines employees in their signature white shirts and
dark suits, is dotted with empty storefronts. During the 1980s,
there were 10,000 IBM workers in Endicott. Now, after years
of layoffs and jobs shipped overseas, about 700 employees are
left.

Investors in IBM's shares, by contrast, have fared much better. IBM makes up the biggest portion of the benchmark Dow
Jones industrial average and has helped drive that index to record
highs. Someone who spent about $16,000 buying 1,000 shares of
IBM in 1980 would now be sitting on more than $400,000 worth
of stock, a twenty-five-fold return.

It used to be a given that the interests of corporations and
communities such as Endicott were closely aligned. But no more.
Across the United States, as companies continue posting record
profits, workers face high unemployment and stagnant wages.

Driving this change is a deep-seated belief that took hold in
corporate America a few decades ago and has come to define

today's economy—that a company's primary purpose is to maximize shareholder value.

The belief that shareholders come first is not codified by statute. Rather, it was introduced by a handful of free-market academics in the 1970s and then picked up by business leaders and the media until it became an oft-repeated mantra in the corporate world.

Together with new competition overseas, the pressure to respond to the short-term demands of Wall Street has paved the way for an economy in which companies are increasingly disconnected from the state of the nation, laying off workers in huge waves, keeping average wages low, and threatening to move operations abroad in the face of regulations and taxes.

This all presents a quandary for policy makers trying to combat joblessness and raise the fortunes of lower- and middle-class Americans. Proposals by President Obama and lawmakers on Capitol Hill to change corporate tax policy, for instance, are aimed at the margins of company behavior when compared with the overwhelming drive to maximize shareholder wealth.

"The shift in what employers think of as their role not just in the community but [relative] to their workforce is quite radical, and I think it has led to the last two jobless recoveries," said Ron Hira, an associate professor of public policy at the Rochester Institute of Technology.

The change can be seen in statements from IBM's leaders over the years. When he was IBM's president and chief executive, Thomas J. Watson Jr., son of the company's founder, spoke explicitly about balancing a company's interests with the country's. Current chief executive Virginia Rometty has pledged to follow a plan called the "2015 Road Map" in which the primary goal is to dramatically raise the company's earnings-per-share figure, a metric favored by Wall Street.

Job cuts have come this summer—the biggest wave in years at the company. In Essex Junction, Vt., about 450 workers were axed in June. In Dutchess County, N.Y., 700 jobs were lost. At Endicott, at least fifteen workers were told to leave.

Retired software developer Linda Guyer saw the change over her twenty-nine-year career. In the beginning, "it was a wonderful place to work—maybe the way Google is today, really innovative," said Guyer, fifty-nine, who used to work for IBM in Endicott. But after training her overseas replacements and then being pushed into early retirement, Guyer said, "you end up feeling really cynical."

In 2009, IBM stopped breaking out how many workers it has in the United States vs. other countries. The company, based in Armonk, N.Y., probably began employing more workers in India than in this country around the same time, according to an analysis by Dave Finegold, a professor at the Rutgers School of Management and Labor Relations.

Many things have changed over the years about IBM, which has one of the oldest continuous histories of any company in the world. The firm that pioneered the floppy disk, an early version of the ATM, and one of the earliest best-selling PCs now makes nearly as much money selling consulting services as it does software. Defenders argue that the company has had to reinvent itself so many times to stay alive that the values of Watson are no longer as easy to apply as they used to be.

Doug Shelton, a spokesman for IBM, said that globalization and increased competition make it hard to compare the company with its earlier days under Watson and that it still has the biggest and most talented technology workforce in the world. Shelton said that the company's head count has expanded every year since 2002 and that it is hiring for positions across the United States.

"Change is constant in the technology industry," Shelton said in a statement. "IBM is investing in growth areas for the future: big data, cloud computing, social business and the growing mobile computing opportunity. The company has always invested in transformational areas, and as a result, we must remix our skills so IBM can lead in these higher-value segments, in both emerging markets and in more mature economies."

The cultural shifts in corporate America have not changed only IBM. The company is merely a representative of what has happened at most large, globalized U.S. firms. But some experts wonder whether these companies have gone too far, leaving the rest of the country behind.

"We don't build companies to serve Wall Street," said Margaret Blair, a professor at Vanderbilt Law School. "We build corporations to provide goods and services to a society and jobs for people."

"Social Responsibility"

In the decades after World War II, as the U.S. economy boomed, the interests of companies, shareholders, society, and workers appeared to be in tune. Towns such as Endicott flourished.

Even until 1981, the Business Roundtable trade group understood the need to balance these different stakeholders.

"Corporations have a responsibility, first of all, to make available to the public quality goods and services at fair prices, thereby earning a profit that attracts investment to continue and enhance the enterprise, provide jobs, and build the economy," the group said at the time, in a document cited this year in an article in the publication *Daedalus*.

It continued: "The long-term viability of the corporation depends upon its responsibility to the society of which it is a part. And the well-being of society depends upon profitable and responsible business enterprises."

But changes were already afoot in the academic world that would reshape the fundamental relationship between this country and its companies.

Lynn Stout, a professor of corporate and business law at Cornell University Law School, traces the transformation to the rise of the "Chicago school" of free-market economists.

In 1970, Nobel Prize–winning economist Milton Friedman wrote an article in the *New York Times Magazine* in which he famously argued that the only "social responsibility of business is to increase its profits."

Then in 1976, economists Michael Jensen and William Meckling published a paper saying that shareholders were "principals" who hired executives and board members as "agents." In other words, when you are an executive or corporate director, you work for the shareholders.

Stout said these legal theories appealed to the media—the idea that shareholders were king simplified the confusing debate over the purpose of a corporation.

More powerfully, it helped spawn the rise of executive pay tied to share prices—and thus the huge rise in stock-option pay. As a result, average annual executive pay has quadrupled since the early 1970s.

Part of this was a backlash to the dismal performance of the stock market during the 1970s, a decade that brought negative returns for investors. There was also the perception that companies, including IBM, had become lax in their management. Pressing executives to boost their returns created a new kind of accountability, just as the economy was becoming more globalized and more competitive.

The shift was dramatic. by 1997, the Business Roundtable had a new statement, also unearthed in the Daedalus article. It stated that the principal objective of a business enterprise "is to generate economic returns to its owners" and that if "the CEO and the directors are not focused on shareholder value, it may be less likely the corporation will realize that value."

The mantra that executives and corporate board members have a duty to maximize shareholder value has become so ingrained that many people assume it must be codified somewhere.

But legal experts say there is no statute in state or federal law requiring corporations and executives to maximize shareholder value. Blair, the professor at Vanderbilt, said that courts in fact allow wide latitude for managers and directors when it comes to business decisions.

"Let me be clear that this pressure comes from the media, from shareholder advocates and financial institutions in whose direct interest it is for the company to get its share price to go up," Blair said in testimony before a House hearing in 2008, "and from the self-imposed pressure created by compensation packages that provide enormous potential rewards for directors and managers if stock prices go up."

Some who defend the use of shareholder value as a measuring stick for corporate success argue that with retirees depending on stocks, whether through pension funds or 401(k)s, rising share prices benefit more than just Wall Street.

"If you stick it to the equity holders, you're going to stick it to the retirees," said Charles Elson, director of the John L. Weinberg Center for Corporate Governance at the University of Delaware.

Philosophical Changes

Like the Business Roundtable statements that changed over time, the message from companies such as IBM shifted as well.

Watson published a seminal text in 1963 called "A Business and Its Beliefs: The Ideas that Helped Build IBM." In it, he wrote that IBM's philosophy could be contained in three beliefs: One, the most important, was respect for the individual employee; the second, a commitment to customer service; and third, achieving excellence.

He wrote that balancing profits between the well-being of employees and the nation's interest is a necessary duty for companies. Watson took pride in the fact that his father avoided layoffs, even through the Great Depression.

"We acknowledge our obligation as a business institution to help improve the quality of the society we are part of," read the text of IBM's corporate values.

Under Watson's watch, IBM introduced groundbreaking computers that shot his father's company to the top of the technology world. Even into the 1980s, there was a saying that IBM's products were so reliable, "nobody ever got fired for buying IBM."

But by the time Louis V. Gerstner Jr. took over IBM in the early 1990s, the company was in trouble. Its main advantage in the PC business was eroding, and expenses were high compared with those of competitors.

Months into his tenure, Gerstner cut about 60,000 workers, at the time one of the biggest layoffs at a U.S. corporation.

In 1994, Gerstner outlined his own set of eight principles, a clear break from the old document. Near the top was that the company's primary "measures of success" were shareholder value and customer satisfaction. The last one: "We are sensitive to the needs of all employees and to the communities in which we operate."

Gerstner pulled off a turnaround considered legendary by those who study business history.

The culture at IBM was irrevocably changed, too. The chief executives who followed Gerstner have pushed the company hard to hit ambitious financial targets designed to please analysts on Wall Street. In the process, the iconic IBM charted a path that other companies have followed.

One of the most influential changes took place in 1999, when IBM overhauled its pension plan under Gerstner to help cut costs, shocking longtime employees.

Guyer, the former IBM software developer, said she still remembers the surprise of getting a letter in the mail showing her cash balance for retirement after about two decades at the company: $30,000.

"It was like, 'Oh, my God, we've been totally ripped off,'" she said.

IBM employees later filed a class-action lawsuit over the pension changes. In 2004, the company agreed to pay $320 million to current and former employees in a settlement.

William Lazonick, an expert on industrial competitiveness at the University of Massachusetts at Lowell, said the pension-plan change was a watershed moment.

"IBM was a critical company, because everybody after that said, 'If IBM is going in that direction, we'll all go in that direction,'" Lazonick said. "By 2000, really the whole system had changed."

The company has continued tinkering with its retirement benefits. Late last year, it changed its 401(k) contribution policy so that IBM matches employee savings just once a year rather than throughout the year. The company said it was making the change to stay competitive, but the new plan also means that employees who lose their jobs before a set date in December do not see any of the matching funds.

Since Gerstner's time running the company, the pressure to please shareholders has only ratcheted up. Samuel J. Palmisano, chief executive from 2002 to 2011, charted new goals in 2010, calling the plan IBM's "2015 Road Map." The primary objective: nearly doubling earnings per share, to twenty dollars.

IBM's current chief executive, Rometty, has picked up where Palmisano left off. The company's 2012 annual report notes that the company's road map "delivers long-term value and performance for all key IBM stakeholders—investors, clients, employees and society."

But as sales flatten, questions have emerged about how the company will hit its ambitious target, aside from slashing jobs.

"This is a horrible business model," said Lee Conrad, a co-ordinator for Alliance@IBM, a group that advocates for company employees. "It's all about the EPS [earnings per share] and not about growing the business. The customers are being impacted by this when good employees are being cut. It's just a mess."

Guyer said everyone in the office used to have a copy of Watson's manifesto on IBM's principles, the one that says "respect for the individual" came first. The company had its own printing press, so it was easy to get the book.

By the time she left, she did not see the book around as much. She remembers rescuing one from a trash can once. And her copy? It is stored in her garage somewhere, a bittersweet souvenir from her corporate career.

Part III

Frenzied Finance

New York

Sexist, homophobic, and insensitive? It's just the ultra-wealthy having their fun when they think no one is watching. In 2012, Kevin Roose sneaked into the annual induction ceremony of Kappa Beta Phi, a secret society for elite Wall Street financiers.

Kevin Roose

11. One Percent Jokes and Plutocrats in Drag

What I Saw When I Crashed a Wall Street Secret Society

Recently, our nation's financial chieftains have been feeling a little unloved. Venture capitalists are comparing the persecution of the rich to the plight of Jews at Kristallnacht, Wall Street titans are saying that they're sick of being beaten up, and this week, a billionaire investor, Wilbur Ross, proclaimed that "the 1 percent is being picked on for political reasons."

Ross's statement seemed particularly odd, because two years ago, I met Ross at an event that might single-handedly explain why the rest of the country still hates financial tycoons—the annual black-tie induction ceremony of a secret Wall Street fraternity called Kappa Beta Phi.

"Good evening, Exalted High Council, former Grand Swipes, Grand Swipes-in-waiting, fellow Wall Street Kappas, Kappas from the Spring Street and Montgomery Street chapters, and worthless neophytes!"

It was January 2012, and Ross, wearing a tuxedo and purple velvet moccasins embroidered with the fraternity's Greek letters, was standing at the dais of the St. Regis Hotel ballroom, welcoming a crowd of two hundred wealthy and famous Wall Street figures to the Kappa Beta Phi dinner. Ross, the leader (or "Grand Swipe") of the fraternity, was preparing to invite twenty-one new members—"neophytes," as the group called them—to join its exclusive ranks.

Looking up at him from an elegant dinner of rack of lamb and foie gras were many of the most famous investors in the world, including executives from nearly every too-big-to-fail bank, private equity megafirm, and major hedge fund. AIG CEO Bob Benmosche was there, as were Wall Street superlawyer Marty Lipton and Alan "Ace" Greenberg, the former chairman of Bear Stearns. And those were just the returning members. Among the neophytes were hedge fund billionaire and major Obama donor Marc Lasry and Joe Reece, a high-ranking dealmaker at Credit Suisse. All told, enough wealth and power was concentrated in the St. Regis that night that if you had dropped a bomb on the roof, global finance as we know it might have ceased to exist.

During his introductory remarks, Ross spoke for several minutes about the legend of Kappa Beta Phi—how it had been started in 1929 by "four C+ William and Mary students"; how its crest, depicting a "macho right hand in a proper Savile Row suit and a Turnbull and Asser shirtsleeve," was superior to that of its namesake Phi Beta Kappa (Ross called Phi Beta Kappa's ruffled-sleeve logo a "tacit confession of homosexuality"); and how the fraternity's motto, *Dum vivamus edimus et biberimus,* was Latin for "While we live, we eat and drink."

On cue, the financiers shouted out in a thundering bellow: *"DUM VIVAMUS EDIMUS ET BIBERIMUS."*

The only person not saying the chant along with Ross was me—a journalist who had sneaked into the event, and who was hiding out at a table in the back corner in a rented tuxedo.

I'd heard whisperings about the existence of Kappa Beta Phi, whose members included both incredibly successful financiers (New York City's Mayor Michael Bloomberg, former Goldman Sachs chairman John Whitehead, hedge-fund billionaire Paul Tudor Jones) and incredibly unsuccessful ones (Lehman Brothers CEO Dick Fuld, Bear Stearns CEO Jimmy Cayne, former New

Jersey governor and MF Global flameout Jon Corzine). It was a secret fraternity, founded at the beginning of the Great Depression, that functioned as a sort of one-percenter's Friars Club. Each year, the group's dinner features comedy skits, musical acts in drag, and off-color jokes, and its group's privacy mantra is "What happens at the St. Regis stays at the St. Regis." For eight decades, it worked. No outsider in living memory had witnessed the entire proceedings firsthand.

I wanted to break the streak for several reasons. As part of my research for my book, *Young Money*, I'd been investigating the lives of young Wall Street bankers—the twenty-two-year-olds toiling at the bottom of the financial sector's food chain. I knew what made those people tick. But in my career as a financial journalist, one question that proved stubbornly elusive was what happened to Wall Streeters as they climbed the ladder to adulthood. Whenever I'd interviewed CEOs and chairmen at big Wall Street firms, they were always too guarded, too on-message and wrapped in media-relations armor to reveal anything interesting about the psychology of the ultra-wealthy. But if I could somehow see these barons in their natural environment, with their defenses down, I might be able to understand the world my young subjects were stepping into.

So when I learned when and where Kappa Beta Phi's annual dinner was being held, I knew I needed to try to go.

Getting in was shockingly easy—a brisk walk past the sign-in desk, and I was inside cocktail hour. Immediately, I saw faces I recognized from the papers. I picked up an event program and saw that there were other boldface names on the Kappa Beta Phi membership roll—among them, then-Citigroup CEO Vikram Pandit, BlackRock CEO Larry Fink, Home Depot billionaire Ken Langone, Morgan Stanley bigwig Greg Fleming, and JPMorgan Chase vice chairman Jimmy Lee. Any way you count, this was one of the most powerful groups of business executives in the world. (Since I was a good twenty years younger than any other attendee, I suspect that anyone taking note of my presence assumed I was a waiter.)

I hadn't counted on getting in to the Kappa Beta Phi dinner, and now that I had gotten past security, I wasn't sure quite what to do. I wanted to avoid rousing suspicion, and I knew that talking to people would get me outed in short order. So I did the next best thing—slouched against a far wall of the room, and pretended to tap out e-mails on my phone.

After cocktail hour, the new inductees—all of whom were required to dress in leotards and gold-sequined skirts, with costume wigs—began their variety-show acts. Among the night's lowlights:

- Paul Queally, a private-equity executive with Welsh, Carson, Anderson, & Stowe, told off-color jokes to Ted Virtue, another private-equity bigwig with MidOcean Partners. The jokes ranged from unfunny and sexist (Q: "What's the biggest difference between Hillary Clinton and a catfish?" A: "One has whiskers and stinks, and the other is a fish") to unfunny and homophobic (Q: "What's the biggest difference between Barney Frank and a Fenway Frank?" A: "Barney Frank comes in different-size buns").

- Bill Mulrow, a top executive at the Blackstone Group (who was later appointed chairman of the New York State Housing Finance Agency), and Emil Henry, a hedge-fund manager with Tiger Infrastructure Partners and former assistant secretary of the Treasury, performed a bizarre two-man comedy skit. Mulrow was dressed in raggedy, tie-dye clothes to play the part of a liberal radical, and Henry was playing the part of a wealthy baron. They exchanged lines as if staging a debate between the 99 percent and the 1 percent. ("Bill, look at you! You're pathetic, you liberal! You need a bath!" Henry shouted. "My God, you callow, insensitive Republican! Don't you know what we need to do? We need to create jobs," Mulrow shot back.)

- David Moore, Marc Lasry, and Keith Meister—respectively, a holding company CEO, a billionaire hedge-fund manager, and an activist investor—sang a few seconds of a finance-themed parody of "YMCA" before getting the hook.

- Warren Stephens, an investment banking CEO, took the stage in a Confederate flag hat and sang a song about the financial crisis, set to the tune of "Dixie." (*"In Wall Street land we'll take our stand, said Morgan and Goldman. But first we better get some loans, so quick, get to the Fed, man."*)

A few more acts followed, during which the veteran Kappas continued to gorge themselves on racks of lamb, throw petits fours at the stage, and laugh uproariously. Michael Novogratz, a former army helicopter pilot with a shaved head and a stocky build whose firm, Fortress Investment Group, had made him a billionaire, was sitting next to me, drinking liberally and anno-tating each performance with jokes and insults.

"Can you fuckin' believe Lasry up there?" Novogratz asked me. I nodded. He added, "He just gave me a ride in his jet a month ago."

The neophytes—who had changed from their drag outfits into Mormon missionary costumes—broke into their musical finale: a parody version of "I Believe," the hit ballad from *The Book of Mormon*, with customized lyrics like "I believe that God has a plan for all of us. I believe my plan involves a seven-figure bonus." Amused, I pulled out my phone, and began recording the proceedings on video. Wrong move.

"Who the hell are you?" Novogratz demanded.

I felt my pulse spike. I was tempted to make a run for it, but—due to the ethics code of the *New York Times,* my then-em-ployer—I had no choice but to out myself.

"I'm a reporter," I said.

Novogratz stood up from the table.

"You're not allowed to be here," he said.

I, too, stood, and tried to excuse myself, but he grabbed my arm and wouldn't let go.

"Give me that or I'll fucking break it!" Novogratz yelled, grabbing for my phone, which was filled with damning evidence. His eyes were bloodshot, and his neck veins were bulging. The song onstage was now over, and a number of prominent Kappas had rushed over to our table. Before the situation could escalate dangerously, a bond investor and former Grand Swipe named Alexandra Lebenthal stepped in between us. Wilbur Ross quickly followed, and the two of them led me out into the lobby, past a throng of Wall Street tycoons, some of whom seemed to be hyperventilating.

Once we made it to the lobby, Ross and Lebenthal reassured me that what I'd just seen wasn't *really* a group of wealthy and powerful financiers making homophobic jokes, making light of the financial crisis, and bragging about their business conquests at Main Street's expense. No, it was just a group of friends who came together to roast each other in a benign and self-deprecating manner. Nothing to see here.

But the extent of their worry wasn't made clear until Ross offered himself up as a source for future stories in exchange for my cooperation.

"I'll pick up the phone anytime, get you any help you need," he said.

"Yeah, the people in this group could be very helpful," Lebenthal chimed in. "If you could just keep their privacy in mind."

I wasn't going to be bribed off my story, but I understood their panic. Here, after all, was a group that included many of the executives whose firms had collectively wrecked the global economy in 2008 and 2009. And they were laughing off the entire disaster in private, as if it were a long-forgotten lark. (Or worse, sing about it—one of the last skits of the night was a self-congratulatory parody of ABBA's "Dancing Queen," called "Bailout King.") These were activities that amounted to a gigantic middle finger to Main Street and that, if made public, could end careers and damage very public reputations.

After several more minutes spent trying to do damage control, Ross and Lebenthal escorted me out of the St. Regis.

As I walked through the streets of midtown in my ill-fitting tuxedo, I thought about the implications of what I'd just seen.

The first and most obvious conclusion was that the upper ranks of finance are composed of people who have completely divorced themselves from reality. No self-aware and socially conscious Wall Street executive would have agreed to be part of a group whose tacit mission is to make light of the financial sector's foibles. Not when those foibles had resulted in real harm to millions of people in the form of foreclosures, wrecked 401(k)s, and a devastating unemployment crisis.

The second thing I realized was that Kappa Beta Phi was, in large part, a fear-based organization. Here were executives who had strong ideas about politics, society, and the work of their colleagues but who would never have the courage to voice those opinions in a public setting. Their cowardice had reduced them to sniping at their perceived enemies in the form of satirical songs and sketches, among only those people who had been handpicked to share their view of the world. And the idea of a reporter making those views public had caused them to throw a mass temper tantrum.

The last thought I had, and the saddest, was that many of these self-righteous Kappa Beta Phi members had surely been first-year bankers once. And in the twenty, thirty, or forty years since, something fundamental about them had changed. Their pursuit of money and power had removed them from the larger world to the sad extent that, now, in the primes of their careers, the only people with whom they could be truly themselves were a handful of other prominent financiers.

Perhaps, I realized, this social isolation is why despite extraordinary evidence to the contrary, one-percenters like Ross keep saying how badly persecuted they are. When you're a member of the fraternity of money, it can be hard to see past the foie gras to the real world.

Guardian

Chris Arnade left his lucrative Wall Street career after twenty years to photograph drug addicts in the Bronx. In finance, he writes, incentives encourage unethical behavior, insane risk taking, and deliberately complex products. Someone occasionally gets nailed by regulators but never anyone in charge. Meanwhile, his subjects in Hunts Point, fourteen miles uptown from Wall Street, are in and out of the criminal-justice system. "When you're wealthy you make mistakes. When you are poor you go to jail."

Chris Arnade

12. Here's Why Wall Street Has a Hard Time Being Ethical

My first year on Wall Street, 1993, I was paid fourteen times more than I earned the prior year and three times more than my father's best year. For that money, I helped my company create financial products that were disguised to look simple, but which required complex math to properly understand. That first year I was roundly applauded by my bosses, who told me I was clever, and to my surprise they gave me $20,000 bonus beyond my salary.

The products were sold to many investors, many who didn't fully understand what they were buying, most of them what we called "clueless Japanese." The profits to my company were huge—hundreds of millions of dollars huge. The main product that made my firm great money for close to five years was called, in typically dense finance jargon, a YIF, or a Yield Indexed Forward.

Eventually, investors got wise, realizing what they had bought was complex, loaded with hidden leverage, and became most dangerous during moments of distress.

I never did meet the buyers; that was someone else's job. I stayed behind the spreadsheets. My job was to try to extract as much value as possible through math and clever trading. Japan would send us faxes of documents from our competitors. Many were selling far weirder products and doing it in far larger volume than we were. The conversation with our Japanese customers would end with them urging us on: "We can't fall behind."

When I did ask, rather naively, if this was all kosher, I would be assured multiple times that multiple lawyers and multiple managers had approved the sales.

One senior trader, consoling me late at night, reminded me, "You are playing in the big leagues now. If a customer wants a red suit, you sell them a red suit. If that customer is Japanese, you charge him twice what it costs."

I rationalized that our group was careful by Wall Street standards, trying to stay close to the letter of the law. We tried to abide by an unwritten "five-point rule": never intentionally make more than five percentage points of profit from a customer.

Some competitors didn't care about the rule. They were making 7 percent or 10 percent profit per trade from clients, selling exotic products loaded with hidden traps. I assumed they would eventually face legal charges, or at least public embarrassment, for pushing so clearly away from the spirit of the law.

They didn't. Rather, they got paid better, were lauded as true risk takers, and offered big pay packages to manage similar businesses.

Being paid very well also helped ease any of my concerns. Feeling guilty, kid? Here take a big check. I was, for the first time in my life, feeling valued for my math skills—the ones I had to hide throughout my childhood so as not be labeled a nerd or egghead. Ego and money are nice salves for any potential feeling of guilt.

After a few years on Wall Street it was clear to me: you could make money by gaming anyone and everything. The more clever you were, the more ingenious your ability to exploit a flaw in a law or regulation, the more lauded and celebrated you became.

Nobody seemed to be getting called out. No move was too audacious. It was like driving past the speed limit at 79 MPH and watching others pass by at 100, or 110, and never seeing anyone pulled over.

Wall Street did nod and wave politely to regulators' attempts to slow things down. Every employee had to complete a yearly compliance training, where he was updated on things like money laundering, collusion, insider trading, and selling our customers only financial products that were suitable to them.

By the early 2000s that compliance training had descended into a once-a-year farce, designed to literally just check a box. It became a one-hour lecture held in a massive hall. Everyone had to go once, listen to the rushed presentation, and then sign a form. You could look down at the audience and see row after row of blue buttoned shirts playing on their Blackberries. I reached new highs on Brick Breaker one year during compliance training. My compliance education that year was still complete.

By 2007 the idea of ethics education fell even further. You didn't even need to show up to a lecture hall; you just had to log on to an online course. It was one hour of slides that you worked through, blindly pushing the "forward" button while your attention was somewhere else. Some managers, too busy for such nonsense, even paid younger employees to sit at their computers and do it for them.

As Wall Street grew, fueled by that unchecked culture of risk taking, traders got more and more audacious, and corruption became more and more diffused through the system. By 2006 you could open up almost any major business, look at its inside workings, and find some wrongdoing.

After the crash of 2008, regulators finally did exactly that. What has resulted is a wave of scandals with odd names: LIBOR fixing, FX collusion, ISDA Fix.

To outsiders they sound like complex acronyms that occupy the darkest corners of Wall Street, easily dismissed as anomalies. They are not. LIBOR, FX, ISDA Fix are at the very center of finance, part of the daily flow of trillions of dollars. The scandals are scarily close to what some on Wall Street believe is standard business practice, a matter of shades of grey.

I imagine the people who are named in the scandals are genuinely confused as to why they are being singled out. They were just doing what almost everyone else was, maybe just more aggressive, more reckless. They were doing what they had been trained to do: bending the rules, pushing as far as they could to beat competitors. They had been applauded in the past for their aggressive risk taking, no doubt. Now they are just whipping boys.

That's the paradox at the core of the settlements we're seeing: where is the real responsibility? Others were doing it, yes. Banks should be fined, yes. But somebody should be charged. Yet the people who really should be held accountable have not. They are the bosses, the managers and CEOs of the businesses. They set the standard, they shaped the culture. The Chuck Princes, Dick Fulds, and Fred Goodwins of the world. They happily shepherded and profited from a Wall Street that spun out of control.

A precedent needs to be set to slow down Wall Street's wild behavior. A reminder that rules are there to be followed, not exploited. The managers knew what was going on. Ask anyone who works at a bank and they will tell you that.

The excuse we have long accepted is ignorance: that these leaders couldn't have known what was happening. That doesn't suffice. If they didn't know, it's an even larger sin.

The Atlantic

It kept its focus on inflation, not the possibility of a crash—sort of like a ship's captain worrying about the tide going out when a huge wave is curling overhead. As Matthew O'Brien details, the numbers from the transcripts of meetings before and during the 2008 crash tell the story. June 24–25, 2008: 468 mentions of inflation, 44 of unemployment, and 35 of systemic risks/crises. August 5, 2008: 322 mentions of inflation, 28 of unemployment, and 19 of systemic risks/crises. September 16, 2008: 129 mentions of inflation, 26 of unemployment, and 4 of systemic risks/crises.

Matthew O'Brien

13. How the Fed Let the World Blow Up in 2008

I t was the day after Lehman failed, and the Federal Reserve was trying to decide what to do.

It had been fighting a credit crunch for over a year, and now the worst-case scenario was playing out. A too-big-to-fail bank had just failed, and the rest of the financial system was ready to get knocked over like dominoes. The Fed didn't have much room left to cut interest rates, but it still should have. The risk was just too great. That risk was what Fed chair Ben Bernanke calls the "financial accelerator" and what everyone else calls a depression: a weak economy and weak financial system making each other weaker in a never-ending doom loop.

But the Fed was blinded. It had been all summer. That's when high oil prices started distracting it from the slow-burning financial crisis. They kept distracting it in September, even though oil had fallen far below its July highs. And they're the reason that the Fed decided to do nothing on September 16. It kept interest rates at 2 percent and intoned that "the downside risks to growth and the upside risks to inflation are both significant concerns."

In other words, the Fed was just as worried about an inflation scare that was already passing as it was about a once-in-three-generations crisis.

It brought to mind what economist R. G. Hawtrey had said about the Great Depression. Back then, central bankers had worried more about the *possibility* of inflation than the grim reality of deflation. It was, Hawtrey said, like "crying Fire! Fire! in Noah's flood."

• • •

The world changed on August 9, 2007. That's when French bank BNP Paribas announced that it wouldn't let investors withdraw money from its subprime funds anymore. It couldn't value them because nobody wanted to buy them. The effect was immediate. Banks stopped trusting, and lending to, each other. They all had their own subprime problems, but none of them knew whose was the worst—*or who had insured whom.*

Now, the Fed actually did a good job in this first part of the crisis. It aggressively cut interest rates from 5.25 percent in September 2007 to 2 percent in April 2008. And it midwifed a deal for Bear Stearns—taking on $30 billion of its crappiest assets—to prevent an all-out panic. By April, Bernanke was justified in saying that "we ought to at least modestly congratulate ourselves." The TED spread had come down from end-of-the-world-terrible to merely terrible levels. And though unemployment had risen to 5.4 percent, that wasn't too bad when you considered that housing had already fallen 20 percent from its 2006 peak.

It looked like we might muddle through with something like the 1990 recession: a shallow, but long, slump, with a weak financial system, but no panic. This is the three-chapter story of why that didn't happen, the story of the three Fed meetings that took place during the summer of 2008, whose much-anticipated transcripts were finally released last week.

1. June 24–25, 2008

468 mentions of inflation, 44 of unemployment, and 35 of systemic risks/crises

It was, Fed governor Frederic Mishkin said, "a perfect storm of shocks."

The economy was still teetering, the financial system was still paralyzed, and oil prices were still skyrocketing. The question was whether the Fed should be more concerned about markets melting down or prices melting up.

Boston Fed president Eric Rosengren, for one, wasn't ready to worry about inflation—not with the banking system so shaky. He'd done research that showed that Japan's credit crunch in the 1990s had even hurt *U.S.* businesses, so he wasn't going to underestimate our own. "The recent flurry of articles on Lehman before their announcement of their capital infusion," he said, "highlights the continued concerns about investment banks." His concerns extended to their counterparts—money market funds—which he pointed out would have broken the buck if Bear Stearns had gone into bankruptcy.

Rosengren wasn't nearly as concerned with 5 percent headline inflation—and with good reason. He reminded his colleagues that "monetary policy is unlikely to have much effect on food and energy prices," that "total [inflation] has tended to converge to core, and not the opposite," and that there was a "lack of an upward trend of wages and salaries."

In short, inflation was high today, but it wouldn't be tomorrow. They should ignore it. A few agreed. Most didn't.

Mishkin, Fed governor Donald Kohn, and then–San Francisco Fed chief Janet Yellen comprised Team: Ignore Inflation. They pointed out that core inflation hadn't actually risen, and that "inflation expectations remain reasonably well-anchored." The rest of the Fed, though, was eager to raise rates soon, if not right away. Philadelphia Fed president Charles Plosser recognized that core inflation was flat, but still thought they needed to get ready to tighten "or our credibility could soon vanish." Fed governor Kevin Warsh said that "inflation risks, in my view, continue to predominate as the greater risk to the economy" because he thought headline would get passed into core inflation.

And then there was Dallas Fed chief Richard Fisher, who had a singular talent for seeing inflation that nobody else could—a sixth sense, if you will. He was allergic to data. He preferred talking to CEOs instead. But, in Fisher's case, the plural of anecdote wasn't data. It was nonsense. He was worried about Frito-Lay's increasing prices 9 percent, Budweiser's increasing them 3.5 percent, and a small dry-cleaning chain in Dallas increasing them, well, an undisclosed amount. He even half-joked that the Fed was giving out smaller bottles of water, presumably to hide creeping inflation? "By the way, I notice that these little bottles of water have gotten smaller—this will be a Visine bottle at the next meeting [laughter]."

In the end, the Fed left rates unchanged at 2 percent but did change its policy statement to say more about inflation. Bernanke thought that the new "inflation paragraph is a little more hawkish"—and markets agreed.

Higher oil prices, and the Fed's hawkish words about them, convinced markets that rates would rise further and faster than they had thought before. It was effectively a 30 basis point tightening, just when the economy could least afford it.

And the economy *really* couldn't afford it if they decided, like Richmond Fed president Jeffrey Lacker suggested, that "at some point we're going to have to choose to let something disruptive happen." That is, let a too-big-to-fail bank fail.

2. August 5, 2008

322 mentions of inflation, 28 of unemployment, and 19 of systemic risks/crises

The economy was getting weaker, and the hawks were getting bolder.

Losses were piling up at the investment banks and Fannie and Freddie. Consumers were cutting back, especially on big-ticket items like cars, because they couldn't get credit. And oil prices were falling fast from their July highs. Now, headline inflation was still around 5 percent, but it was drifting down, and the Fed's economists expected it to keep doing so: they cut their second-half forecast for it by almost a full percentage point in August.

But even though inflation was falling, it was a lonesome time to be a dove. As the Fed's resident Cassandra, Rosengren tried to convince his colleagues that high headline inflation numbers "appear to be transitory responses to supply shocks that are not flowing through to labor markets." In other words, inflation would come down on its own, and the Fed should focus on the credit crunch instead. Mishkin worried that "really bad things could happen" if "a shoe drops" and there was a "nasty, vicious spiral" between weak banks and a weak economy. Given this, he wanted to wait to tighten until inflation expectations "actually indicate there is a problem," and not before.

The hawks didn't want to wait. Lacker admitted that wages hadn't gone up, but thought that "if we wait until wage rates accelerate or TIPS measures spike, we will have waited too long." He wanted the Fed to "be prepared to raise rates even if growth is not back to potential, and even if financial markets are not yet tranquil." In other words, to fight nonexistent wage inflation today to prevent possible wage inflation tomorrow, never mind the crumbling economy. Warsh, for his part, kept insisting that "inflation risks are very real, and I believe that these are higher than growth risks." And Fisher had more "chilling anecdotes"—as Bernanke jokingly called them—about inflation. This time, the culprit was Disney World and its 5 percent price increase for single-day tickets. (What were they doing, opening a park in Zimbabwe?).

The Fed was stuck in the same place in August that it'd been in June, even though the commodity spike was already fading.

Hawks were scared of inflation, doves were scared of a depression, and everyone else wasn't sure which to be more scared of. So, once again, the Fed left rates unchanged at 2 percent but did change its policy statement to say even more about inflation than the last time. Bernanke said that it was his "intention for [the statement] to be slightly hawkish—to indicate a slight uplift in policy."

It was a mistake, but it was nothing like the one that was to come. Hawks had convinced themselves that the financial crisis had been going on for so long that it wasn't one anymore. That banks had had more than enough time to cut their exposure to troubled firms. That one bankruptcy, say Lehman's, wouldn't cause a cascade of others. Or, as St. Louis Fed president James Bullard put it, that "the level of systemic risk has dropped dramatically, and possibly to zero."

This was Mishkin's last Fed meeting before he returned to Columbia, and what he was hearing scared the bejeezus out of him. He made sure his soon-to-be-ex-colleagues remembered that a crash could, in fact, come long after a crisis started—with a historical comparison to make a central banker blanche: "Remember that in the Great Depression, when—I can't use the expression because it would be in the transcripts, but you know what I'm thinking—something hit the fan, [laughter] it actually occurred close to a year after the initial negative shock."

Then he left the Fed with one last lesson, what he drolly called his "valedictory remarks." Actually, it was Milton Friedman's lesson, but Mishkin wanted to make sure they didn't forget it. That was "the danger of focusing too much on the federal funds rate as reflecting the stance of monetary policy." In other words, just because interest rates were low didn't *necessarily* mean that policy was easy—and vice versa. You could only tell by either looking at other interest rates, or inflation, or nominal GDP.

This was textbook economics—in fact, Mishkin had a whole chapter on it in *his* textbook—but the hawks kept getting it wrong. Lacker and Kansas City Fed chief Thomas Hoenig insisted that the Fed's 2 percent rates meant money was easy. But, as Bernanke explained, the facts disagreed. Mortgage rates had gone up even as the Fed had cut so that the gap between the them had increased from 120 basis points in 2007 to 260 basis points in 2008. Money was getting tighter, not easier, for households.

This had enormous implications for policy. If the Fed realized that money was tight despite low rates, then it would try to do more. But if the Fed assumed that money was loose, *because* rates were low, then it'd say there wasn't any reason to try to do more, it was already doing a lot! It'd sit by and watch a slump go on and on and on, like the Fed in the 1930s or the Bank of Japan in the 1990s. This was the history that Mishkin hoped the Fed wouldn't, but feared would, repeat—and not only because he'd recently bought a second house: "I just very much hope that this Committee does not make this mistake because I have to tell you that the situation is scary to me. I'm holding two houses right now. I'm very nervous."

3. September 16, 2008

129 mentions of inflation, 26 of unemployment, and 4 of systemic risks/crises

"We have a lot to talk about," Bernanke said. That they did. Lehman had failed the day before, and markets were trying to figure out what it meant. After some consideration, they decided it was the end of the world.

It was easy to see why. Markets had expected Lehman to be bailed out. *Lehman* had expected Lehman to be bailed out. So when it wasn't, nobody was prepared. It wasn't clear who had lost what and who had claims on what. But what was clear was that the insurance giant AIG was going to need a bailout. That money market funds were, as Rosengren had warned, about to break the buck. And that there was a run on every financial asset that wasn't guaranteed by the government.

The Fed, though, was surprisingly upbeat. Lacker had gotten the "disruptive" event he had wanted, and he was pretty pleased about it. "What we did with Lehman I obviously think was good," he said, because it would "enhance the credibility of any commitment that we make in the future to be willing to let an institution fail." Hoenig concurred that it was the "right thing" because it would suck moral hazard out of the market.

That doesn't mean the Fed wasn't worried. It *was* worried. About inflation.

The hawks were monomaniacally focused on headline inflation that hadn't yet fallen all the way from its summer peak. Even though commodity prices and inflation expectations were both falling fast, Hoenig wanted the Fed to "look beyond the immediate crisis," and recognize that "we also have an inflation issue." Bullard thought that "an inflation problem is brewing." Plosser was heartened by falling commodity prices but said, "I remain concerned about the inflation outlook going forward" because "I do not see the ongoing slowdown in economic activity is entirely demand driven." And Fisher half-jokingly complained that the bakery he'd been going to for thirty years—"the best maker of not only bagels, but anything with Crisco in it"— had just increased prices. All of them wanted to leave rates unchanged at 2 percent.

But it wasn't just the hawks who wanted to leave rates unchanged. It was *everybody* at the Fed, except for Rosengren. He was afraid that exactly what did end up happening would happen. That all the financial chaos "would have a significant impact on the real economy," that "individuals and firms will be become risk averse, with reluctance to consume or invest," that "credit spreads are rising, and the cost and availability of financing is becoming more difficult," and that "deleveraging is likely to occur with a vengeance." More than that, he thought that the "calculated bet" they took in letting Lehman fail would look particularly bad "if we have a run on the money market funds or if the nongovernment tri-party repo market shuts down." He wanted to cut rates immediately to do what they could to offset the worsening credit crunch. Nobody else did.

Even the day after Lehman, the Fed wasn't sure whether inflation or the financial crisis was the bigger risk to the economy. They wanted to wait and see what the data said. But if they had looked at what the markets were telling them, they wouldn't have had to. Five-year TIPS spreads had been falling fast, and, by September 16, showed that markets only expected 1.23 percent inflation. Some of that was because TIPS are illiquid, but not all of it. The fall in commodities and the rise in unemployment— which Fed economists saw "no reason to discount"—also said that demand was disappearing slowly, then all at once.

But the Fed didn't see it that way. It thought housing was going to stabilize, the financial crisis was going to abate, and oil prices were going to keep coming down so that GDP growth would *pick up* in 2009. Bernanke thought that the Fed's 2 percent interest rate was "the policy path consistent with achieving our objectives" and that a rate cut was premature:

> Overall I believe that our current funds rate setting is appropriate, and I don't really see any reason to change. . . . Cutting rates would be a very big step that would send a very strong signal about our views on the economy and about our intentions going forward, and I think we should view that step as a very discrete thing rather than as a 25 basis point kind of thing. We should be very certain about that change before we undertake it because I would be concerned, for example, about the implications for the dollar, commodity prices, and the like.

And so the Fed kept the firehoses ready while the economy drowned.

What Was to Be Done?

None of this was inevitable. The Fed could have ignored oil prices that summer and told us it was ignoring them. And it could have saved Lehman that fall. It wouldn't have been easy—or popular—but it wouldn't have been impossible, either. That's clear if you look at what Rosengren was saying in real-time. With that in mind, here's a look at what the Fed could have and didn't do to make the Great Recession a little less so.

1. Oil shock. Graded on a curve, the Fed did okay. At least it didn't raise rates that summer like the ECB did. But on an absolute scale, the Fed could have done better. It could have done in 2008 what it did in 2011, when another oil spike came along: say that the increase in inflation was transitory, and they were focused on long-term inflation expectations instead.

    Now, more dovish language that summer wouldn't have saved the world. But it would've kept money a little looser. And that could've given the financial system a little more breathing room to keep raising capital, like the Fed had been doing before.

2. Lehman. There are three magic words in central banking: whatever it takes. The Fed did that with Bear. It didn't do that with Lehman. It could have let Lehman become a bank holding company, which is what Lehman wanted, and what the Fed ended up doing for Goldman Sachs and Morgan Stanley a few weeks later. Or it could have given Lehman bridge financing to try to finish a deal after everything fell through on September 14. None of these would have been popular decisions, but what's the point of an independent central bank if it won't do unpopular things to save the economy?

After the fact, the Fed has said that it couldn't do these things, that it had no choice. But the transcripts show that it was a choice, and they knew it. Some of them thought nothing bad would happen. And they were happy about it in September—well, all but Rosengren—until they realized what a world-historical error it was.

Wall Street Journal

He wanted to spend more time with his family, or so the story went. Mohamed El-Erian, heir apparent to behemoth bond fund Pimco, left after a public confrontation with Bill Gross, the man he would have succeeded. Behind the scenes, Gregory Zuckerman and Kirsten Grind discover a different story: a tense workplace environment, a deteriorating relationship, and questions about business decisions led to the split.

Gregory Zuckerman
and Kirsten Grind

14. Gross vs. El-Erian

Inside the Showdown Atop the World's Biggest Bond Firm

Newport Beach, Calif.—Tension increased at Pacific Investment Management Co.'s headquarters here last summer. The bond market was under pressure, losses grew, and clients pulled billions of dollars from the firm.

Bill Gross, who cofounded Pimco in 1971 and is largely responsible for building it into a behemoth overseeing almost $2 trillion in assets, struck some of his colleagues as testier than usual. He argued openly with Mohamed El-Erian, Pimco's chief executive—something employees say they rarely had seen.

Mr. Gross—by his own admission, a demanding boss—had long showed respect for Mr. El-Erian and indicated that the younger man eventually would take over the world's biggest bond firm. But one day last June, the two men squared off in front of more than a dozen colleagues amid disagreements about Mr. Gross's conduct, according to two people who were there.

"I have a forty-one-year track record of investing excellence," Mr. Gross told Mr. El-Erian, according to the two witnesses. "What do you have?"

"I'm tired of cleaning up your s———," Mr. El-Erian responded, referring to conduct by Mr. Gross that he felt was hurting Pimco, these two people recall.

Later, after Mr. El-Erian told Mr. Gross he needed to change the way he interacted with employees, Mr. Gross, sixty-nine years old, agreed to make adjustments, several Pimco employees say. But last month, Pimco announced that Mr. El-Erian, fifty-five, would leave the firm—a surprise to both employees and investors.

In a note to clients, Pimco said Mr. El-Erian will leave in March but will remain on the management committee of Pimco's parent company, German insurer Allianz SE. Mr. Gross later said Mr. El-Erian wanted to write a second book and spend more time with his family.

Interviews with nearly two dozen individuals close to both men and to the firm suggest more-important factors in the departure: a high-pressure work environment that turned less collegial over the past year, a deteriorating relationship between the two senior executives, and certain decisions by Mr. Gross that confused some employees.

In a prepared statement, Mr. Gross said: "For more than forty years, Pimco has delivered superior results for our clients, consistently and during periods of extraordinary market volatility. We hold ourselves to the highest standards of excellence and performance, and I ask of others only what I demand of myself: hard work, dedication and intense focus on putting our clients first."

In an earlier interview with the *Wall Street Journal* in January, Mr. Gross denied tension with Mr. El-Erian was a factor in his departure. "It had nothing to do with friction," he said, although he acknowledged he can be difficult to work with. "Sometimes people will say 'Gross is too challenging,' and maybe so. I would say if you think I'm challenging now, you should have seen me twenty years ago."

Mr. El-Erian's abrupt departure raises questions about the leadership-succession plan at Pimco, a largely autonomous unit of Allianz. In late January, Pimco designated a new chief executive, Douglas Hodge, a new president and six deputy investment officers. The firm has yet to choose a new heir apparent for Mr. Gross.

"Pimco needs to avoid becoming an upside-down pyramid balanced only on Bill Gross," says Alex Friedman, global chief investment officer of UBS Wealth Management. "We're hoping others emerge to replace Mohamed."

Mr. Gross said in a recent interview that he would be stepping back from some investment duties, but others at the firm are skeptical he will give up any control.

"I'm ready to go for another 40 years!" Mr. Gross posted on Twitter after Mr. El-Erian's departure.

Messrs. Gross and El-Erian, fixtures on business television and in the press for their views on global markets, were always something of an odd couple. Mr. Gross is a former blackjack player and a trader at heart. Mr. El-Erian is an economist with a more methodical approach.

Mr. Gross's management style has produced stellar results. His Total Return Fund now manages $237 billion. In 2010 he was named the fixed-income manager of the decade by Morningstar Inc. In recent years, Mr. Gross was paid more than $200 million annually, according to employees.

"The culture is intense" because the firm manages the retirement savings for millions of people, says Neel Kashkari, who ran Pimco's equity business from late 2009 until departing in early 2013 to run for governor of California. "People work hard, and expectations are high. I had a terrific experience there."

The Pimco complex, located about a mile from the Pacific Ocean, is called "the Beach" on Wall Street trading desks. Mr. Gross has talked about how he has taken time off during the day to do yoga. But employees say the work environment is charged.

Most Pimco investment professionals arrive at the office around 4:30 a.m.—well before trading opens on Wall Street—and stay until five p.m. or later. The firm encourages internal competition, current and former employees say.

On the trading floor, Mr. Gross doesn't like employees speaking with him or making eye contact, especially in the morning, current and former employees say. He prefers silence and at times reprimands those who break it, even if they're discussing investments, these people say.

Mr. Gross, who served as a naval officer during the Vietnam War, has strict requirements for presentations to Pimco's investment committee. He has scolded employees for forgetting to number the pages in their presentations and has given them "communication demerits" that an assistant to Mr. Gross tracks to help determine year-end bonuses, according to people who have worked at Pimco.

Some at Pimco have been told to leave the firm but stuck around instead, waiting for Mr. Gross's anger to ebb and for him to change his mind, according to these people.

Bill Powers, a former Pimco senior executive who left in 2010, says Mr. Gross "routinely grew tired and wary of those closest to him who had assumed significant responsibility, power, and compensation. After a four to five-year honeymoon period, the chosen one's halo would turn into a crown of thorns where interactions with Bill would turn adversarial, short, and unpleasant."

When Mr. Gross establishes an investment thesis, he usually doesn't appreciate dissenting views, employees and former Pimco traders say. Once, when a senior investment manager said a bond in Mr. Gross's fund appeared to be expensive, Mr. Gross responded: "OK, buy me more of it," according to a Pimco executive. The purchase was made.

In 2005, Eric Flamholtz, a consultant and then a professor at the UCLA Anderson School of Management, was hired to advise the firm, he says. Mr. Flamholtz says he spent three years with Pimco employees and shared his results with the firm in 2008.

"You had a lot of very talented people who were, in effect, nervous about their positions," Mr. Flamholtz says. "It was an unhealthy atmosphere for Pimco in the long run, and they needed to address the issues."

Mr. Flamholtz says he doesn't know whether the firm took any steps in response. "The feedback did not make me very popular at Pimco," he says.

One day about ten years ago, recalls John Brynjolfsson, at the time a Pimco portfolio manager, Mr. Gross criticized him for not standing when a visiting client toured the trading floor. He recalls Mr. Gross telling him there would be "consequences."

Mr. Brynjolfsson says Mr. Gross suggested that he write a $10,000 check to Pimco's charitable foundation. Mr. Brynjolfsson, who says he considered the situation a misunderstanding, made the donation. Less than a year later, Mr. Brynjolfsson was named a Pimco partner.

"I knew he wouldn't have tested me if I couldn't handle it," says Mr. Brynjolfsson, who now runs a hedge fund. "He's a great motivator of top talent."

The prestige of working at Pimco has long attracted talented traders. The company pays among the highest compensation in the investment world. Mr. El-Erian earned more than $100 million each year in recent years, according to several current and former employees, while other senior executives made $20 million or more annually.

Mr. El-Erian, the son of an Egyptian diplomat, worked at the International Monetary Fund before joining Pimco in 1999 and rising to managing director. In 2006, he left Pimco to become the chief executive and president of Harvard Management Co., which manages Harvard University's endowment. He returned to Pimco in late 2007 to become the firm's co–chief executive officer and co–chief investment officer, along with Mr. Gross.

Colleagues say Mr. El-Erian traveled the world meeting Pimco clients while also helping to run the firm and manage some money. He hardly took a vacation and flourished in the firm's demanding environment, they say.

Mr. El-Erian favored a more structured approach to management than Mr. Gross's informal style, but the men rarely clashed in front of the staff, employees say.

Last summer, bonds came under pressure because investors were worried the Federal Reserve would reduce its bond purchases. In June, investors withdrew $9.6 billion from Mr. Gross's fund. "Don't jump ship now," Mr. Gross wrote clients that month.

But more investors cashed out, adding to the stress. Disagreements between Mr. Gross and Mr. El-Erian became common over trading strategy, personnel decisions, new products and more, employees say.

Some of Mr. Gross's decisions struck some employees as unusual. Last summer, during a rough time in the market, Mr. Gross limited the firm's trading, restricting it mostly to sales aimed at raising cash to meet client withdrawals, according to three Pimco employees. Some employees complained to Mr. Gross and Mr. El-Erian that they couldn't buy inexpensive investments and that Mr. Gross didn't seem to trust their abilities. Mr. Gross didn't budge. He had restricted trading during rough patches before. These restrictions were longer, lasting for several weeks, according to the three employees.

A Pimco spokesman said the firm's investment committee told employees to limit "nonessential" trading—as it sometimes does during market stress—and that overall trading volume didn't decline during those weeks.

Mr. El-Erian told Mr. Gross to be less combative with employees and to give others more leeway in investment decisions. In the late summer, Mr. Gross agreed to be less confrontational, but the change didn't last, according to senior Pimco executives.

During investment committee meetings, when Mr. El-Erian or others discussed stocks or other topics not related to bonds, Mr. Gross often looked bored, say people who attended the meetings. Sometimes he walked out of the room, effectively ending the discussions, they say, and he became more dismissive of Mr. El-Erian's views.

Late last year, in front of a number of traders, Mr. Gross said, "if only Mohamed would let me, I could run all the $2 trillion myself . . . I'm Secretariat," referring to the famed thoroughbred. "Why would you bet on anyone other than Secretariat?"

Pimco's performance added to strains. Mr. Gross's $237 billion Pimco Total Return fund lost 1.9 percent in 2013, the first year the fund posted a negative return since 1999, although it narrowly beat the benchmark Barclays U.S. Aggregate Bond Index, which fell 2.02 percent. Investors yanked a net $41.1 billion from Mr. Gross's fund—more withdrawals in a year, in dollar terms, than any fund in history, according to Morningstar, although it remained the world's largest bond fund.

Mr. El-Erian saw his own efforts to help build a stock-fund business falter and two funds he helped manage weaken.

In November, Pimco's executive committee tried to address the growing discord, establishing a task force to meet with both men, according to two Pimco executives. A month later, Mr. El-Erian was offered more power. Instead, he told Mr. Gross he was leaving.

"You can't resign," a Pimco executive recalls Mr. Gross telling Mr. El-Erian. "We need you."

Colleagues figured the men would find a way to patch up their relationship. Early this year, Mr. El-Erian agreed to work with a mediator to find a new way to operate the firm. Mr. Gross rejected the concept of bringing in a mediator, according to a Pimco executive.

Later in January, Mr. El-Erian told Mr. Gross he had made up his mind: He was leaving.

Since the announcement, Mr. Gross has expressed disappointment and bewilderment over Mr. El-Erian's departure, telling colleagues that Mr. El-Erian was offered whatever he wanted to entice him to stay.

Earlier this month, the firm began removing Mr. El-Erian's pictures from Pimco's walls and placing copies of a book he wrote in boxes for storage. They also moved Mr. El-Erian's office to a building far from Pimco's trading floor.

Last Tuesday, Pimco posted a question-and-answer session on the company website in which Mr. Gross extolled the new leadership structure, which he said "gives others the opportunity to lead . . . it will be great!"

Bloomberg

Were they fixing the "fix"? Reporting by Bloomberg's Liam Vaughan, Gavin Finch, and Bob Ivry sparked international investigations into spot currency trading, specifically whether senior traders, using instant message groups with names like "The Cartel" and "The Bandits' Club," were sharing client information to manipulate prices used by corporations and investors for 160 currencies worldwide.

Liam Vaughan, Gavin
Finch, and Bob Ivry

15. Secret Currency Traders' Club Devised Biggest Market's Rates

It's twenty minutes before four p.m. in London, and currency traders' screens are blinking red and green. Some dealers have as many as fifty chat rooms crowded onto four monitors arrayed in front of them like shields. Messages from salespeople and clients appear, get pushed up by new ones, and vanish from view. Orders are barked through squawk boxes.

This is the closing "fix," the thin slice of the day when foreign-exchange traders buy and sell billions of dollars of currency in the largely unregulated $5.3-trillion-a-day foreign-exchange market, the biggest in the world by volume, according to the Bank for International Settlements. Their trades help set the benchmark WM/Reuters rates used to value more than $3.6 trillion of index funds held by pension holders, savers, and money managers around the world.

Now regulators from Bern to Washington are examining evidence first reported by Bloomberg News in June that a small group of senior traders at big banks had something else on their screens: details of each other's client orders. Sharing that information may have helped dealers at firms, including JPMorgan Chase & Co., Citigroup Inc., UBS AG, and Barclays Plc, manipulate prices to maximize their own profits, according to five people with knowledge of the probes.

"This is a market where there is no law and people have turned a blind eye," said former senator Ted Kaufman, a Delaware Democrat who sponsored legislation in 2010 to shrink the largest U.S. banks. "We've been talking about banks being too big to fail. What's almost as big a problem is banks too big to manage."

"Bandits' Club"

At the center of the inquiries are instant-message groups with names such as "The Cartel," "The Bandits' Club," "One Team, One Dream," and "The Mafia," in which dealers exchanged information on client orders and agreed how to trade at the fix, according to the people with knowledge of the investigations who asked not to be identified because the matter is pending. Some traders took part in multiple chat rooms, one of them said.

The allegations of collusion undermine one of society's fundamental principles—how money is valued. The possibility that a handful of traders clustered in a closed electronic network could skew the worth of global currencies for their own gain without detection points to a lack of oversight by employers and regulators. Since funds buy and sell billions of dollars of currency each month at the four p.m. WM/Reuters rates, which are determined by calculating the median of trades during a sixty-second period, that means less money in the pension and savings accounts of investors around the world.

"Collusive Practices"

At stake is the integrity of a market that affects the daily valuations of private and public money alike, from the $261 billion

Sacramento-based California Public Employees' Retirement System to the $237 billion Scottish Widows Investment Partnership in Edinburgh, from the $4.1 trillion BlackRock Inc. in Manhattan, the world's largest asset manager, to the $1.2 trillion Tokyo-based Government Pension Investment Fund, the biggest pension.

"This is a market that is far more amenable to collusive practices than it is to competitive practices," said Andre Spicer, a professor at the Cass Business School in London, who is researching the behavior of traders.

"Big Profits"

Unlike sales of stocks and bonds, which are regulated by government agencies, spot foreign exchange—the buying and selling for immediate delivery as opposed to some future date—isn't considered an investment product and isn't subject to specific rules.

While firms are required by the Dodd-Frank Act in the United States to report trading in foreign-exchange swaps and forwards, spot dealing is exempt. The U.S. Treasury exempted foreign-exchange swaps and forwards from Dodd-Frank's requirement to back up trades with a clearinghouse. In the European Union, banks will have to report foreign-exchange derivatives transactions under the European Market Infrastructure Regulation.

A lack of regulation has left the foreign-exchange market vulnerable to abuse, said Rosa Abrantes-Metz, a professor at New York University's Stern School of Business in Manhattan.

"If nobody is monitoring these benchmarks, and since the gains from moving the benchmark are possibly very large, it is very tempting to engage in such a behavior," said Abrantes-Metz, whose 2008 paper "Libor Manipulation" helped spark a global probe of interbank borrowing rates. "Even a little bit of difference in price can add up to big profits."

Culture "Wrong"

The currency investigations are taking place as authorities grapple with a widening list of scandals involving the manipulation by banks of benchmark financial rates, including the London interbank offered rate, or Libor, and ISDAfix, used to determine the value of interest-rate derivatives. The U.K. regulator also is reviewing how prices are set in the $20 trillion gold market, according to a person with knowledge of the matter.

"Some of these problems developed over many years without anybody speaking up," said Andrew Tyrie, chairman of Britain's Commission on Banking Standards and Parliament's Treasury Select Committee. "This is remarkable. It suggests something very wrong with the culture at these institutions."

The story published by Bloomberg News in June, based on interviews with current and former traders, triggered internal probes as banks began reviewing millions of instant messages, e-mails, and transcripts of phone calls to see whether employees attempted to rig rates. The U.K.'s Financial Conduct Authority, the European Union, the Swiss Competition Commission, and the U.S. Department of Justice are all now investigating.

Deutsche Bank

In addition to seeking evidence of collusion, the FCA is looking into whether traders cut deals for personal profit before completing customers' orders, according to a person with knowledge of the probe. Bloomberg News reported in November, based on the accounts of two people who witnessed the transactions, that some dealers placed side bets for personal accounts or through friends in exchange for cash payments.

At least twelve currency traders have been suspended or put on leave by banks as a result of internal probes, and eleven firms have said they were contacted by authorities. Government-controlled Royal Bank of Scotland Group Plc turned over transcripts of instant messages. Deutsche Bank AG, Germany's largest lender, said it's cooperating with regulators and Zurich-based UBS, the world's fourth-biggest currency dealer, said it's taking unspecified disciplinary measures against employees.

Justice Department

Britain's FCA, which has about sixty people working on benchmark investigations, has asked foreign-exchange traders to come in for voluntary interviews, according to the people with knowledge of the probe. The individuals are among at least forty traders whose communications are being reviewed, one of them said. The conversations being examined date back to 2004, another said. Chris Hamilton, a spokesman for the FCA, declined to comment.

The Justice Department has issued subpoenas to banks, according to three people with knowledge of the probe who asked not to be identified because the investigation is confidential.

"The criminal and antitrust divisions have an active, ongoing investigation into possible manipulation of foreign-exchange rates," Peter Carr, a department spokesman, said in an e-mail. He declined to name any specific institutions.

EU competition commissioner Joaquin Almunia said in October the Brussels regulator's probe into currency markets was at a "very preliminary" stage. Several banks have come forward with information on possible rigging in the hope of winning leniency, Almunia's spokesman Antoine Colombani said in November.

"The Cartel"

None of the traders or the banks they work for has been accused of wrongdoing.

The investigations have had repercussions across the industry. UBS, RBS, Citigroup, Deutsche Bank, JPMorgan and Lloyds

Banking Group Plc are banning traders from using multibank chat rooms, people at the firms said. Investors are breaking their orders into smaller units and using more banks to reduce the opportunity for front-running, one of Europe's largest money managers said.

One focus of the investigation is the relationship of three senior dealers who participated in "The Cartel"—JPMorgan's Richard Usher, Citigroup's Rohan Ramchandani, and Matt Gardiner, who worked at Barclays and UBS—according to the people with knowledge of the probe. Their banks controlled more than 40 percent of the world's currency trading last year, according to a May survey by Euromoney Institutional Investor Plc.

Entry into the chat room was coveted by nonmembers interviewed by Bloomberg News, who said they saw it as a golden ticket because of the influence it exerted.

Minimizing Losses

Regulators are examining whether discussions among the traders amounted to collusion—if, with a few keystrokes, they were able to push around rates to boost bank profits and their own bonuses. Traders on the chat deny that, saying they were merely matching buyers and sellers ahead of the fix. That way they could minimize losses by avoiding trades at a time of day when prices typically fluctuate the most, they said.

The men communicated via Instant Bloomberg, a messaging system available on terminals that Bloomberg LP, the parent of Bloomberg News, leases to financial firms, people with knowledge of the conversations said.

The traders used jargon, cracked jokes, and exchanged information in the chat rooms as if they didn't imagine anyone outside their circle would read what they wrote, according to two people who have seen transcripts of the discussions.

Usher, Ramchandani, and Gardiner, along with at least two other dealers over the years, would discuss their customers' trades and agree on exactly when they planned to execute them to maximize their chances of moving the four p.m. fix, two of the people said. When exchange rates moved their way, they would send written slaps on the back for a job well done.

Bollinger Champagne

The conversations echo those uncovered by regulators about Libor, in which bankers promised bottles of Bollinger champagne or cash to counterparts at firms willing to help them rig the benchmark interest rates used to price $300 trillion of contracts from student loans to mortgages. More than six banks have been fined about $6 billion since June 2012, and regulators are investigating traders at half a dozen more firms.

The currency discussions were even more calculating, one of the people who reviewed the transcripts said.

Usher was the moderator of "The Cartel," people with knowledge of the matter said. He worked at RBS and represented the Edinburgh-based bank when he accepted a 2004 award from the publication *FX Week*. When he quit RBS in 2010, the chat room died, the people said. He revived the group with the same participants when he joined JPMorgan the same year as chief currency dealer in London.

Standard Chartered

Ramchandani is head of European spot trading at New York–based Citigroup. Born in India, and said by people who know him to be studious and polite, he joined the bank's trading desk after graduating from the University of Pennsylvania with a degree in economics, according to a spokesman for the school and a recruiter who has a copy of his résumé. He relocated to London from New York in 2004.

Both Ramchandani and Usher were part of the Bank of England's twenty-seven-member London Foreign Exchange Joint

Standing Committee subgroup of chief dealers as of the end of 2012, according to the central bank's bulletin. The group met three times last year to discuss matters including regulatory developments, the bulletin reported.

Gardiner joined Standard Chartered Plc in London in September as assistant chief currency dealer. He previously worked at UBS in Zurich and was co–chief dealer with Chris Ashton at Barclays in London.

FCA Inquiry

Usher, Ramchandani, and Gardiner were put on leave by their employers after the FCA opened its inquiry, according to people with knowledge of the matter. Ashton, now global head of spot trading at Barclays, was suspended along with five other spot traders at the bank in London and New York.

Ashton and Ramchandani declined to comment when contacted by telephone. Gardiner didn't return messages left on his mobile phone. JPMorgan declined to provide contact details for Usher, who couldn't be located through Internet searches or directory assistance. The bank also declined to comment about the probes, as did spokesmen for RBS, Standard Chartered, Citigroup, Barclays, and UBS. Deutsche Bank said in an e-mail that it's cooperating with investigations and "will take disciplinary action with regards to individuals if merited."

London is the world's biggest hub for currency trading, accounting for about 41 percent of all transactions, compared with 19 percent for New York and 6 percent for Singapore, according to a Bank for International Settlements survey published in September. About $5.3 trillion changes hands every day, BIS data show, as companies convert earnings into dollars, euros, or yen and managers overseeing pensions and savings buy and sell shares around the world.

Essex Countryside

Spot currency trading is conducted in a small and close-knit community. Many of the more than a dozen traders and brokers interviewed for this story live near each other in villages dotting the Essex countryside, a short train ride from London's financial district, and stay in touch over dinner, on weekend excursions, or with regular rounds of golf at local clubs.

Spot traders simply deal with buy and sell orders and don't need the complex math skills their counterparts on derivatives desks use to extrapolate prices. Developing and maintaining relationships are more important, the traders say.

"The foreign-exchange market has a very strong culture, in which practitioners feel more attached to each other than they do their banks," said Spicer, the Cass School of Business professor. "It is also dominated by an extremely small group of individuals, often with strong social ties formed by working with each other at some point in the past."

Golf Club

On one excursion to a private golf club in the so-called stockbroker belt beyond London's M25 motorway, a dozen currency dealers from the biggest banks and several day traders, who bet on currency moves for their personal accounts, drained beers in a bar after a warm September day on the fairway. One of the day traders handed a white envelope stuffed with cash to a bank dealer in recognition of the information he had received, according to a person who witnessed the exchange.

Such transactions were common and also took place in tavern parking lots in Essex, the person said.

Personal relationships often determine how well currency traders treat their customers, said a hedge-fund manager who asked not to be identified. That's because there's no exchange where trades take place and no legal requirement that traders ensure customers receive the best deals available, he said.

Eaton Vance

Hedge-fund managers get the best prices because they trade frequently and are the most sophisticated, according to a former U.S. currency dealer. Next in line are institutional funds—insurance companies and pension plans that get less-beneficial prices. At the bottom are firms from automakers to smartphone manufacturers that need to swap currencies to purchase materials abroad and repatriate earnings. Traders at banks take advantage of them because they know the least about the market, he said.

Eaton Vance Corp., a mutual-fund company that manages $281 billion, uses the WM/Reuters rate to value its portfolio, so the credibility of the rate as a result of rigging allegations is potentially worrisome and the firm is continuing to monitor its reliability, said Michael O'Brien, director of global trading.

While the Boston-based company has its own trading desk to make sure investors get the best prices, it uses bank traders for certain currencies, O'Brien said, adding that most customers have little choice.

Market Share

"Banks are market-makers in foreign exchange, and to a large degree you can't avoid them," O'Brien said. "People have to trust the pricing."

Four banks control more than half the foreign-exchange market, according to Euromoney's survey. Deutsche Bank, based in Frankfurt, was no. 1, with a 15.2 percent share, followed by Citigroup with 14.9 percent, Barclays with 10.2 percent, and UBS, Switzerland's biggest lender, with 10.1 percent.

The WM/Reuters rates for 160 currencies, used as a benchmark by companies and investors around the world, are determined by trades executed in a minute-long period called "the fix," starting thirty seconds before four p.m. in London.

The data are collected and distributed by World Markets Co., a unit of Boston-based State Street Corp., and Thomson Reuters Corp. Bloomberg LP competes with Thomson Reuters in providing news and information, as well as currency-trading systems and pricing data. Bloomberg LP also distributes the WM/Reuters rates on Bloomberg terminals.

State Street

Thomson Reuters said it "would lend its expertise to support any authorities' investigation into alleged disruptive behavior on benchmarks." The company doesn't administer the WM/Reuters rates, it added in an e-mailed statement.

"The WM/Reuters benchmark service is committed to reliability and robust operational standards," State Street said in an e-mail. "WM continually reviews recommended methodology and policies in order to ensure that industry best practices are considered."

Aside from trading after economic events such as interest-rate cuts, four p.m. is the busiest time for currency dealers as customers place orders to be transacted at the fix price.

Things are even more hectic on the last working day of the month, when tracker funds buy and sell currencies with their banks. The funds say they have to trade at the fix because the global indexes they track, such as the MSCI World Index, are calculated once a day using the four p.m. WM/Reuters rates.

The frenzy begins an hour earlier on trading floors as dealers jockey for advantage. Bids and offers are exchanged. Slang is common. Mio means million. A yard is a billion.

Loss-Leader

Because traders promise clients they'll get the fix price, it leaves banks open to losses if the market moves against them, one London-based dealer said. He described trading at the fix as a loss-leader that helped his firm win client business.

To make money, traders interviewed by Bloomberg News said they would share information with counterparts at other firms and trade ahead of large client orders. Most tracker funds place their orders as much as an hour before the fix, giving dealers a glimpse of possible future price movements, which they can use to take positions. Traders on instant-message groups increased their chances of predicting market moves by pooling details of their order books and agreeing to align positions at the fix, according to three people with knowledge of the practice.

Dealers can buy or sell the bulk of their client orders during the sixty-second window to exert the most pressure on the published rate, a practice known as banging the close. Because the benchmark is based on the median value of transactions during the period, breaking up orders into a number of smaller trades could have a greater impact than executing one big deal.

Market Movements

Some dealers said the tactic is legitimate and necessary for banks to protect themselves from losses. Traders who agree to buy or sell at the close need to push through the bulk of their orders during the window to minimize the risk of losses from market movements, the traders said.

One large transaction can be enough to move the market. A former bank trader said that if he received an order from a customer at three-thirty p.m. to sell 1 billion euros ($1.37 billion) in exchange for Swiss francs at the four p.m. fix, he would have two objectives: to sell his bank's own euros at the highest price and also to move the rate lower so that at four p.m. he could buy the currency from his client at a lower price.

While foreign exchange is unregulated, dealers are prohibited by market-abuse laws from trading on inside information and sharing confidential data about client orders with third parties. In recent years, banks have tightened rules on employees' trading for their own accounts. Many require staff to hold investments for at least thirty days and obtain written clearance from compliance officials for personal dealings.

Currency Futures

The U.S. Commodity Futures Trading Commission, which has no oversight of the spot market, does regulate foreign-exchange futures, contracts that allow companies or investors to speculate on or hedge against the price movements of currencies. Some of those contracts, such as cash-settled forwards traded on the Chicago Mercantile Exchange, use WM/Reuters rates to determine who owes what at settlement. The agency has been reviewing potential violations of the law, according to a person with knowledge of the matter.

Its chairman, Gary Gensler, who declined to comment about any investigation the agency might be conducting, said the CFTC is understaffed, with 670 employees, when more than 1,000 would better fulfill its mission.

"We need to make sure reference rates are not based on a closing price that's manipulated," Gensler said in an interview. "The CFTC does not have enough people, period."

U.K. Rules

In the U.K., the government is introducing laws designed to curtail market manipulation and punish traders found guilty of wrongdoing. In April, it became a criminal offense for anyone to knowingly make false or misleading statements relating to the setting of benchmarks. Other proposals include deferring bonuses for as long as ten years and guaranteeing rights for whistle-blowers. They stop short of recommending specific regulations of the spot foreign-exchange market.

Even if regulators were watching the currency market, there would be a question of what they'd see and whether they'd be able to identify wrongdoing, said Felix Shipkevich of Shipkevich PLLC, a derivatives law firm in New York.

"Who has the expertise to determine if there's any potential unlawful activity going on?" he said. "There are very few people who understand the over-the-counter market."

Financial Times

The famous and notorious Wall Street analyst Meredith Whitney is alternately seductive and self-righteously immune to criticism as she lunches with Lucy Kellaway of the *Financial Times*. Whitney became famous for calling it right in 2007 when she predicted that Citibank would cut its dividend and infamous in 2010 for predicting wrongly that fifty to one hundred municipal bonds would default—something she says is still possible. She picks at her food but projects a strong sense of herself.

16. Lunch with the FT: Meredith Whitney

Meredith Whitney arrived early for lunch at the Wolseley, and so, alas, I didn't see Wall Street's most notorious analyst making her entrance. I bet the other diners stared, though. They may not have known that this was the woman who predicted the U.S. banking crisis, but they couldn't have failed to clock her fishnet-clad legs, one ending in a patent leather high-heeled shoe with a diamante buckle, the other in a blue-and-pink trainer.

When I get there, the portion of Whitney visible above the starched white tablecloth looks exactly as a woman known as the "dollar dominatrix" ought to. A long position in gold is festooned around her neck and clamped to her ears; her hair is big and blonde; and her sweater, black and expensive.

Yet the smile is warm and girly. Please like me, it begs. "This is so nice of you. I'm so excited about this!" she says in a voice so low that I can barely hear it above the din of the restaurant.

Whitney can afford to whisper: people go to great lengths to listen to what she has to say, even if they sometimes regret it afterwards. In 2007 she predicted that Citibank would cut its dividend—and it did. But then in 2010 she predicted that fifty to one hundred municipal bonds would default—and they didn't. Call no. 1 had Michael Lewis saying she was "the closest thing Wall Street has to an oracle." Call no. 2 had Fox TV commentator

Charlie Gasparino saying she "didn't possess a single brain cell."

Oracle or lobotomy victim, Whitney does her homework. She has been studying the data on Lunch with the FT, reading past examples, and has worked out the importance of getting the restaurant right. She explains her thinking behind the choice of one of London's swankiest places to eat.

"I didn't want to pick anywhere too grand."

Pouring coffee from the silver jug she has already ordered, she tells me she's in town for a couple of meetings; that London gets "a lot more high-end" every time she comes—and that she has hurt her foot.

"I ran yesterday and was trying to keep up with my girlfriend and completely ate dirt." Completely did what? It's not just the low volume that's a problem: the forty-three-year-old Whitney talks as if she were back in her dorm at Brown.

"I was so klutzy," she explains. "I tripped and now one foot looks like an American football." She pokes a swollen ankle out from under the tablecloth and the waiter advancing to take our orders almost trips over it.

"What's the biggest crowd pleaser: the sole or the halibut?" she asks him, conscientiously collecting more data before she makes her menu call. He duly recommends halibut—the more expensive dish—so she orders that. I say I'll have the fish of the day, trout.

•　　　•　　　•

It is odd how cross people are with Whitney about that municipal bond call she made two and a half years ago. Her initial bearish view was shared by such financial luminaries as Bill Gross and Nouriel Roubini; she only departed from them by being specific and saying defaults would run into hundreds of billions dollars within a year. When the defaults didn't happen, she made everyone even crosser by declining to say sorry.

Now she has written a book justifying her position. In it she argues that the coastal states that were hardest hit by property collapse will suffer a mass exodus as people flee from regulation, debt, and punitive taxation, moving to the "flyover" states in the middle where taxes are lower.

I protest that I'd rather endure any amount of tax and red tape in New York than live in South Dakota. Whitney stops smiling and leans across the table, big brown eyes narrowing.

"That's interesting," she snaps, "because Julian Robertson [the former hedge-fund manager] certainly can afford to live in New York City but he chose to live outside. Ron Burkle [the private-equity magnate] can afford to live in California but isn't it interesting that he lives there fewer than half the days in the year?"

So is she herself quitting New York? Um, no. She'd love to move to Bermuda, where she owns a weekend house with John "Bradshaw" Layfield, the wrestler turned financial adviser whom she met on live TV and subsequently married. But, unfortunately, her clients need her in NYC.

The waiter places a big chunk of white fish in front of her. "Oh, my goodness! That looks great!" she says, putting a speck of Béarnaise on a tiny flake of fish: "Hundreds of billions [of defaults] is still absolutely possible," she goes on. "You hope it's not—but Detroit is a matchstick away from going bankrupt."

Meanwhile, any apparent improvement in California's finances is an illusion. She rehearses again her central argument with an intensity that is slightly scary: taxpayers are getting fed up with footing the bill while bondholders get paid in full. Something's got to give.

I want to know if she feels bad about the people who followed her and lost money. She shakes her head and insists it wasn't like that. It was year-end, and there were technical factors behind the fall in bond prices.

Then, without warning, she changes the subject. "It feels good to me to be nice. It's a return-on-investment deal. I get so much more out of the day when I'm nice to people. You get paid off in spades that way, it's incredible."

I'm slightly nonplussed by this. Is she suggesting I try the same return-on-investment deal myself? Or is she helping me out with my analysis of her? Whatever the reason, I say this niceness isn't what one expects from someone famous for bearish calls.

"It was math, it wasn't personal. Some people make all this stuff personal and it's not."

And yet the way people have gone for her has been very personal indeed. They've made death threats. They call out mockingly in the street.

"It's nasty. If someone does that to me, I have the ability of never knowing their name again, I don't care about them, and they're still walking around in their shoes."

As the waiter removes the halibut into which she's made the feeblest of inroads, I put my theory to her that the market is as bad at valuing analysts as it is at valuing stocks. Whitney looks blank. So I say she has been a victim of this: the "oracle" and the "lobotomy" ratings are equally daft.

"I'm not a victim," she replies. "I'm grateful that I've got name recognition—not since then has there been anyone with name recognition. Analysts are not really a sexy community."

Indeed she tells me that they're the dullest, geekiest people on Wall Street, either wonks or resembling a "high-price concierge." Her first boss was so gauche "he was looking for the restroom and he walked into a closet and stayed there for 120 seconds."

I'm rather enjoying listening to her traduce her entire industry and briefly fancy that I'd like to be her friend. But then she reverts to self-promotion. "I'm known for the Citi call but I'm not a one-hit wonder at all. I was loaded for bear that entire time."

Loaded for what?

"Meaning I didn't miss a beat the entire financial crisis, and so it wasn't one call, it was all of the calls. So, two weeks after the

Citi call I wrote a piece describing how the rating agencies were so central to the capital needs of banks. It was pitch-perfect."

That was in 2008 when she was still working for Oppenheimer, a minor Wall Street outfit, and Whitney was flying around the world, hired out by the hour to talk to clients. When I ask what her hourly rate was, she doesn't blink: "A hundred thousand dollars."

This time I've heard, but I get her to repeat it anyway: $100,000 an hour? Could anyone be worth such an insane amount?

"I was," she says solemnly. "If I wasn't, people wouldn't pay it, right? The market's fair that way." What she thought less fair was that Oppenheimer pocketed most of the cash. "So I'm, like, if I'm so smart, how come I'm not making the money? In August I was on the cover of Fortune magazine. There was not so much as a firm-wide e-mail, not so much as a pizza party . . ."

Were they jealous? "I don't know. Jealousy's not even on the radar screen for me. But it really hurt my feelings and I decided to throw everything in—as girly as that sounds . . ."

What she did wasn't girly at all. In 2009 she set up Meredith Whitney Advisory Group and with a team of ten puts out 500-page research documents, which clients pay for but which she suspects they don't read. So now she's decided to go further and start investing her own money and other people's in "the whole investment super-cycle." I ask whether it's the idea of being even richer that motivates her.

"The thing for me is being right," she says, brown eyes darkening to black, taking on that frightening look again. Has she ever been wrong? She thinks for a bit, and dredges up a few minor calls, all made some time ago.

The waiter comes for orders, and she declares herself full but orders a plate of cheese anyway. I order a lemon tart. The conversation shifts to bankers, and I ask how well she gets on with them. "I got an e-mail from Mike O'Neill at Citi, saying thanks so much for the kind words about how dull I am. Because I'd said dull was the new black." Running banks these days is a boring job, she says, best done by boring people. Brian Moynihan at Bank of America is the sort of solid chap she rates, James Gorman at Morgan Stanley, not so much. "He's a consultant," she says crisply. "I think that's all you need to say."

When I ask why she thinks there are still so few women on Wall Street, her first response is that women are too smart for it. Then she says women aren't interested in finance. But then she adds that men aren't either. So why is she? The answer seems to be because it's hard. "I got better grades in school with harder classes. If a class was supposed to be an easy A, I usually didn't get an A. I would just get distracted."

.   .   .

A few weeks before we meet, the hedge-fund boss Paul Tudor Jones caused a storm by saying that breastfeeding mothers couldn't make decent investment decisions. I wonder if Whitney, who is childless, agrees. "I don't know. He's a really great guy, probably quoted out of context." She pauses, and then goes on: "But I've thought about it more recently because my friend's kids are so cute and so much fun. I wish I'd had kids. And if I had had them . . . my priorities would definitely have been different."

She produces this private regret as she produces everything, as simple fact. Her main sadness is that her husband would have made a great father. She pushes away her almost untouched cheese plate and says, "John is nearly a saint. If he was a cartoon character, he'd have two birds on his shoulders."

But as it is, he isn't a cartoon character. He's several hundred pounds of muscle, with careers as wrestling commentator, philanthropist, author, financial adviser, and entrepreneur. One business, Mamajuana Energy, launched in 2008 and financially backed by his wife, was a soft drink that claimed it would improve your sex life. Has it done well? "No," she says, shutting the conversation down.

The waiter comes bearing another jug of coffee for her and mint tea for me. Whitney suddenly points to a nearby table: "Look at those skinny, beautiful girls drinking champagne!"

I think it's odd that this successful professional woman is wistful at the sight of a couple of bimbos. I start to say that she's not exactly ugly herself. I expect her to cringe, but she beams, "Oh, thank you!"

But then isn't being gorgeous part of the job spec if you are a woman on Wall Street and want anyone to listen to what you have to say about interest rates—especially on TV?

"In finance, maybe. But not in business in general—I don't want to get myself in trouble but those CEOs . . ." She rolls her eyes. "They're proud of their St John knitwear."

While I'm trying to unpack this reference to what I subsequently discover is a frumpy U.S. clothing brand, she says, "You get the face you earn."

Rubbish, I say. Whitney shakes her beautifully highlighted blonde hair at me and says, "You've one major choice in life; be happy or be unhappy—simple choice."

This is too big a topic for the remains of lunch—it is the essence of the different worldviews of Americans and Brits. What is true, I say, is that you get the face you pay for.

Whitney then declares that she's not a natural blonde and has had her frown lines done. I praise the smoothness of her forehead and in return she looks at me as if in search of something to admire.

"You've got a great neck!" she says.

Although I'm enjoying the turn the conversation has taken, I'm worrying about how it will look on the page: take a serious woman out to lunch and discuss knitwear and Botox. So I ask if she found being female tough on Wall Street.

Yup, she says. Good-looking women aren't taken seriously. I point out that in her case this is nonsense. She has moved the market, so how much more seriously does she want to be taken?

The bill is brought, and Whitney offers to split it, just as if we had been two ladies who lunched. I tell her it's against the rules, pay, and we get up to go. She shows me again her comically asymmetrical legs, and on a whim I ask to see her fingers. She extends her hand, her fingers adorned with gold rings and the nails painted baby blue. It's just as I expected: the ring finger is longer than the index finger. I explain about the research showing that testosterone can be measured by the ratio between the two; her fingers suggest she has as much testosterone as a man.

"Right!" she exclaims, giving her broadest smile. "I like that!"

ProPublica

Did the punishment fit? It wasn't prosecuted as a crime, but Jesse Eisinger recounts the wrist-slapping denouement of the Bank of America's spectacularly disastrous 2008 acquisition of Merrill Lynch. The bank won approval of the takeover by lying to shareholders about Merrill's losses and not disclosing huge bonuses to executives, the combination of which would help trigger federal bailouts.

Jesse Eisinger

17. How the Case Against Bank of America CEO Fizzled

The regulatory cloud has lifted for Kenneth D. Lewis. Last week, the former head of Bank of America received a modest penalty, paid for by his former employer, and a temporary ban from an industry he is no longer a part of.

In this seminal financial crisis investigation, regulators put on a master class in how to take a strong case and render it weak.

It's worth recounting the story from its beginning.

Bank of America was an unwieldy agglomeration of dozens of banks tacked together with spit and Excel spreadsheets. As the world economy imploded in the middle of September 2008, the bank rushed into yet another acquisition, taking over Merrill Lynch. Merrill was failing, facing the same short-term funding run that would have collapsed all the investment banks had it not been for the government's intervention.

In what now reads as unintended comedy, Mr. Lewis called it the "strategic opportunity of a lifetime." Oh, and he said there had been "absolutely no pressure" from the Federal Reserve to take Merrill over. He would later acknowledge this was untrue.

We now know, of course, that Bank of America's acquisition of Merrill was one of the worst deals in corporate history. As the two banks moved to consummate the merger in the fourth quarter of 2008, Merrill bled billions while paying huge bonuses to its executives. Bank of America ended up needing two bailouts from the Treasury Department, as well as extraordinary lending from the Federal Reserve.

On February 4, 2010, Andrew M. Cuomo, then New York State's attorney general, accused Bank of America of misleading its shareholders and the public about the losses and the bonuses by failing to disclose them before shareholders voted on the merger on December 5, 2008.

According to the complaint, Bank of America executives wrestled over whether to tell investors about the mounting Merrill losses. On November 13, 2008, Bank of America's general counsel, Timothy J. Mayopoulos, and the bank's outside lawyers from Wachtell, Lipton, Rosen & Katz decided that the numbers would have to be disclosed in a Securities and Exchange Commission filing, according to the complaint. Then they consulted with Joe Price, the bank's chief financial officer, and decided to reverse their decision.

On December 4, the complaint alleges, Mr. Price knew that the losses had breached the threshold that Mr. Mayopoulos had laid out as the benchmark for requiring disclosure. The shareholder vote went ahead without any filing.

On December 9, according to Mr. Cuomo's complaint, Mr. Mayopoulos listened while Mr. Price told the board that Merrill was going to lose $9 billion in the fourth quarter. This was not accurate. In truth, Merrill had already lost $9 billion and expected to lose billions more before the quarter was over. After the board meeting, Mr. Mayopoulos tried to discuss the losses with Mr. Price, who was unavailable.

The next morning, Mr. Mayopoulos was fired and frog-marched out of the building, according to people briefed on the matter.

Bank of America installed Brian T. Moynihan as general counsel of one of the nation's largest banks. Mr. Moynihan hadn't practiced law in fifteen years. His legal career was such an afterthought that he had let his bar membership lapse. He would go on to become the chief executive of the bank.

Mr. Mayopoulos wasn't alone in his concerns. Merrill's auditors, Deloitte & Touche, told Bank of America that it "might want to consider" informing shareholders of the losses, according to the complaint. Bank of America's corporate treasurer, urging the bank to disclose, said in a conversation with Mr. Price that he did not want to be talking about Merrill's losses "through a glass wall over a telephone."

Merrill's fourth-quarter loss would eventually be more than $15.8 billion, and Merrill paid more than $3.6 billion in bonuses.

It is a crime to knowingly deceive shareholders about the financial condition of your company. Top officers of Bank of America knew about giant, surprising Merrill losses but did not disclose them promptly or precisely to the board or shareholders. They took steps to cut out people who advocated disclosing the information. That sure seems like a lot of smoke.

At least one regulator thought it merited a criminal investigation. The Office of the Special Inspector General for the Troubled Asset Relief Program referred the case for criminal investigation to the United States attorney's office in Manhattan.

Raymond J. Lohier, who was the chief of the securities and commodities fraud task force at the office, took charge of the investigation. But he seemed to view it with skepticism, according to a person close to the investigation. The Federal Reserve, both a regulator and one of the potential victims because it was lending to Bank of America, contended that it did not consider the losses material. The investigation didn't go anywhere.

Mr. Lohier, the Fed, and the United States attorney's office declined to comment.

White-collar criminal cases are always difficult, and this one would have been especially hard. One big problem: Mr. Mayopoulos, the general counsel who was summarily fired, never flipped against his former bosses.

Moreover, the government's role in the transaction may have been ultimately absolving. Though his bank hadn't disclosed the Merrill losses publicly, Mr. Lewis used them as a cudgel to push for a second round of bailout money from the Treasury. Through the course of the various investigations, Bank of America executives cited the government's involvement in defending their actions.

The Justice Department, of course, isn't the only securities law enforcer out there. The Securities and Exchange Commission brought its own case. Internally, however, the SEC felt that New York State complaint overreached, unconvinced, for instance, that Mr. Mayopoulos was fired over the issue of whether to disclose the losses. The agency eventually settled with the bank in August 2009 for a paltry $33 million.

Judge Jed S. Rakoff of the United States District Court in Manhattan found that amount ludicrously low. Several months later, the agency bumped it up to $150 million, and Judge Rakoff reluctantly signed off, writing with obvious fury that this was "half-baked justice at best."

The New York case was settled last week. Mr. Lewis agreed to pay $10 million, which was provided by Bank of America, which also reached a settlement with the state for $15 million. He did not admit or deny any of the charges. He is barred from being an executive or director of a public company. I don't consider that entirely toothless; it damages his standing in society. But it's not exactly severe.

On Friday, the office of the New York attorney general, Eric T. Schneiderman, intends to seek to permanently bar Mr. Price, who did not settle, from serving as a director, officer, or in any capacity in the securities industry, according to a person close to the investigation. If it happens, it would be a serious accomplishment.

Mr. Price's lawyer did not respond to a request for comment.

Mr. Schneiderman moved so slowly that a class-action lawsuit, relying on the facts laid out in the original complaint, settled for

$2.4 billion in September 2012. A quirky New York legal decision precluded the state from getting greater restitution for taxpayers because the class-action suit had already been settled. With that opportunity blown, the attorney general went for a fine from Mr. Lewis.

Here's a "Where Are They Now?" roster. Mr. Lohier was appointed by President Obama to be a judge on the United States Court of Appeals for the Second Circuit. Mr. Mayopoulos became the chief executive of Fannie Mae. Mr. Cuomo became governor of New York.

Then there is Mr. Lewis's high-priced lawyer. The lawyer issued a scathing assessment of the case initially. Mr. Cuomo's decision to sue was "a badly misguided decision without support in the facts or the law," this lawyer said. There is "not a shred of objective evidence" to support the case.

Who was this zealous advocate? One Mary Jo White. You may recall her from such roles as the current chairwoman of the Securities and Exchange Commission.

And the public? We got as much justice as we have come to expect.

Part IV

Unhealthy
Business

ProPublica

It seems like a harmless painkiller, but the data show that acetaminophen, the active ingredient in Tylenol, is linked to more deaths than any other over-the-counter pain medication. McNeil Consumer Healthcare, a unit of Johnson & Johnson, has helped fund the development of an antidote to acetaminophen poisoning that has saved many lives. But at the same time, McNeil has quietly fought against proposals by the U.S. Food and Drug Administration to safeguard consumers.

Jeff Gerth and
T. Christian Miller

18. Use Only as Directed

During the last decade, more than 1,500 Americans died after accidentally taking too much of a drug renowned for its safety: acetaminophen, one of the nation's most popular pain relievers.

Acetaminophen—the active ingredient in Tylenol—is considered safe when taken at recommended doses. Tens of millions of people use it weekly with no ill effect. But in larger amounts, especially in combination with alcohol, the drug can damage or even destroy the liver.

Davy Baumle, a slender twelve-year-old who loved to ride his dirt bike through the woods of southern Illinois, died from acetaminophen poisoning. So did tiny five-month-old Brianna Hutto. So did Marcus Trunk, a strapping twenty-three-year-old construction worker from Philadelphia.

The toll does not have to be so high.

The U.S. Food and Drug Administration has long been aware of studies showing the risks of acetaminophen—in particular, that the margin between the amount that helps and the amount that can cause serious harm is smaller than for other pain relievers. So, too, has McNeil Consumer Healthcare, the unit of Johnson & Johnson that has built Tylenol into a billion-dollar brand and the leader in acetaminophen sales.

Yet federal regulators have delayed or failed to adopt measures designed to reduce deaths and injuries from acetaminophen overdose, which the agency calls a "persistent, important public health problem."

The FDA has repeatedly deferred decisions on consumer protections even when they were endorsed by the agency's own advisory committees, records show.

In 1977, an expert panel convened by the FDA issued urgently worded advice, saying it was "obligatory" to put a warning on the drug's label that it could cause "severe liver damage." After much debate, the FDA added the warning thirty-two years later. The panel's recommendation was part of a broader review to set safety rules for acetaminophen, which is still not finished.

Four years ago, another FDA panel backed a sweeping new set of proposals to bolster the safety of over-the-counter acetaminophen. The agency hasn't implemented them. Just last month, the FDA blew through another deadline.

Regulators in other developed countries, from Great Britain to Switzerland to New Zealand, have limited how much acetaminophen consumers can buy at one time or required it to be sold only by pharmacies. The FDA has placed no such limits on the drug in the U.S. Instead, it has continued to debate basic safety questions, such as what the maximum recommended daily dose should be.

For its part, McNeil has taken steps to protect consumers, most notably by helping to fund the development of an antidote to acetaminophen poisoning that has saved many lives.

But over more than three decades, the company repeatedly fought against safety warnings, dosage restrictions, and other measures meant to safeguard users of the drug, according to company memos, court records, documents obtained under the Freedom of Information Act, and interviews with hundreds of regulatory, corporate, and medical officials.

In the 1990s, McNeil tried to create a safer version of acetaminophen, an effort dubbed Project Protect. But after the initiative failed, the company kept its experiments confidential, even when the FDA inquired about the feasibility of developing such a drug.

Later, McNeil opposed even a modest government campaign to educate the public about acetaminophen's risks, in part because it would harm Tylenol sales.

All the while, it has marketed Tylenol's safety. Tylenol was the pain reliever "hospitals use most," one iconic ad said. The one "recommended by pediatricians," said another. "Safe, fast pain relief," its packages promised.

In written responses to questions for this story, as well as a prerecorded statement by its vice president for medical affairs, McNeil said it has always acted to ensure its products were used safely.

"McNeil takes acetaminophen overdose very seriously, which is why we have taken significant steps over the years to mitigate the risk," the company wrote. McNeil has engineered safety packaging and spent millions on research, education, and poison control centers that advise people who have overdosed.

The company said that science on acetaminophen had evolved over time and that it had implemented safety measures accordingly. Most recently, it announced it will soon add red lettering to the caps of medicine bottles saying they contain acetaminophen and that users should read the label.

In several cases, after FDA advisors recommended the agency enact safety measures over McNeil's objections, the company adopted them before the agency forced it to do so. The company then said it was taking such steps voluntarily. McNeil also stressed that it has always followed FDA regulations.

McNeil objected to the thrust of questions from *ProPublica* and *This American Life*, saying they indicated "a clear bias" in favor of plaintiff's lawyers who are suing the company.

The company declined to answer questions about individual cases of death or injury. "Our hearts go out to those who have suffered harm from acetaminophen overdose, and to the families of those who lost their lives as a result," McNeil wrote in its statement.

FDA officials said the agency saw the benefits of keeping acetaminophen widely available as outweighing the "relatively rare" risk of liver damage or death. Some patients cannot tolerate drugs such as ibuprofen, and for them acetaminophen may be the best option, said one agency official.

The FDA has bolstered acetaminophen warnings as new science about the drug emerged, the agency said in a statement.

But FDA officials acknowledged the agency had moved sluggishly to address the mounting toll of liver damage caused by acetaminophen. They blamed changing research, small budgets, an overworked staff, and a cumbersome process for changing rules for older drugs such as Tylenol slowing them down.

The agency has greater authority over prescription drugs, and it has already slapped medications containing acetaminophen with a "black box warning" that says overdosing can lead to "liver transplant and death." Paradoxically, the same medicine sold over the counter does not tell patients that death is a possible side effect.

"Among over-the-counter medicines, it's among our top priorities," said Dr. Sandy Kweder, one of the FDA's top experts on acetaminophen. "It just takes time."

Many doctors believe in acetaminophen, and some medical associations advise patients to take it for mild to moderate pain or reducing fever. "Given the number of doses given annually, the track record is incredibly safe," said Dr. Bill Banner, a pediatrician and the medical director of the Oklahoma Poison Control Center.

Every over-the-counter pain reliever can cause harm. Even without overdosing, aspirin and ibuprofen can lead to stomach bleeding. In extremely rare cases, according to the FDA, recommended doses of ibuprofen and acetaminophen can provoke a skin reaction that can kill.

But the FDA says acetaminophen carries a special risk. About a quarter of Americans routinely take more over-the-counter pain relief pills of all kinds than they are supposed to, surveys show. That behavior is "particularly troublesome" for acetaminophen, an FDA report said, because the drug's narrow safety margin places "a large fraction of users close to a toxic dose in the ordinary course of use."

The FDA sets the maximum recommended daily dose of acetaminophen at four grams, or eight extra strength acetaminophen tablets. That maximum applies to both over-the-counter and prescription drugs with acetaminophen.

Taken over several days, as little as 25 percent above the maximum daily dose—or just two additional extra strength pills a day—has been reported to cause liver damage, according to the agency. Taken all at once, a little less than four times the maximum daily dose can cause death. A comparable figure doesn't exist for ibuprofen because so few people have died from overdosing on that drug.

About as many Americans take ibuprofen as take acetaminophen, according to consumer surveys from the mid-2000s.

The U.S. Centers for Disease Control and Prevention and the American Association of Poison Control Centers collect data on the number of deaths associated with each drug, but the figures are incomplete, making comparisons subject to question. McNeil contends the databases do not contain the information needed to draw conclusions about the relative risks of different medicines. The company and some epidemiologists maintain that these data sets undercount deaths resulting from chronic use of naproxen, ibuprofen, and similar pain relievers.

Still, the data show that acetaminophen is linked to more deaths than any other over-the-counter pain reliever.

From 2001 to 2010, annual acetaminophen-related deaths amounted to about twice the number attributed to all other over-the-counter pain relievers combined, according to the poison control data.

In 2010, only fifteen deaths were reported for the entire class of pain relievers, both prescription and over-the-counter, that includes ibuprofen, data from the CDC show.

That same year, 321 people died from acetaminophen toxicity, according to CDC data. More than half—166—died from accidental overdoses. The rest overdosed deliberately or their intent was unclear. For the decade 2001 through 2010, the data show, 1,567 people died from inadvertently taking too much of the drug.

Acetaminophen overdose sends as many as 78,000 Americans to the emergency room annually and results in 33,000 hospitalizations a year, federal data show. Acetaminophen is also the nation's leading cause of acute liver failure, according to data from an ongoing study funded by the National Institutes for Health.

Behind these statistics are families upended and traumatized and, in the worst cases, shattered by loss.

•　　•　　•

Just before Christmas 1999, twelve-year-old Davy Baumle came down with a sore throat. For a week, his parents, David and Udosha Baumle, gave him Maximum Strength Tylenol Sore Throat, measuring out doses of the thick syrup.

But instead of getting better, Davy became listless. On Christmas Day, he threw up blood. His father took him to a local emergency room wrapped in a fuzzy brown blanket. A few days later, the boy was declared brain dead.

The Baumles later sued McNeil, claiming the company had failed to warn consumers of its product's lethal danger. At trial, they testified they never gave Davy more than the recommended dose, four grams per day, or eight tablespoons. An expert for the company testified that lab work suggested the boy had ingested more, six to ten grams, over several days.

The difference amounted to as little as four tablespoons a day, but the company prevailed, persuading the jury that the Baumles had not used Tylenol precisely as specified.

David Baumle said he would never have given his son the drug if he knew it was potentially lethal. At the time, the label simply warned of "serious health consequences" in case of overdose.

"They tell you it's medicine," he said. "They don't tell you it can kill you."

·   ·   ·

Tylenol was born in 1955, when the family-owned McNeil Laboratories introduced a liquid for children called Tylenol Elixir.

The drug's key ingredient, acetaminophen, was developed in the late 1800s in Germany's coal tar industry. McNeil seized on the drug's potential after American research suggested that the medication does not cause stomach bleeding, as aspirin can. McNeil named the product based on letters in the chemical term for acetaminophen, N-ace*tyl*-p-aminoph*enol*.

Johnson & Johnson acquired McNeil in 1959, the same year that Tylenol was approved for over-the-counter sales. Soon thereafter, the first adult version of Tylenol rolled off the company's production line in Fort Washington, Pa., the site of McNeil's current headquarters.

Unlike companies that develop prescription drugs, McNeil has no patent on acetaminophen and so no right to sell it exclusively. Virtually every drug store stocks generic acetaminophen, usually on the same shelf as Tylenol. To sell Tylenol at a premium, the company had to persuade customers they were getting extra value.

Tylenol has had "generic competition for forty years," said Ashley McEvoy, then the president of McNeil, in a webcast interview posted in 2008. "If I look back at what's garnered success for McNeil, it's the enduring value of brands."

The company aimed its early sales pitches at doctors, according to a company history, working to persuade them to recommend Tylenol as a safer alternative to aspirin. To this day, the company's formula for success hinges on positioning Tylenol as safer than other painkillers and more trustworthy than generics.

Perhaps the most famous chapter in McNeil's corporate history is its response when several people in the Chicago area died in 1982 after taking Tylenol laced with cyanide.

The mysterious deaths terrorized the country—and raised questions about the safety of the company's products. But in what later became a business-school case study, McNeil removed Tylenol from the market, offered refunds, and eventually developed tamper-resistant pills. By the end, it had transformed a disaster into a public relations coup.

McNeil's marketing campaigns for its master brand were also skillful, burnishing Tylenol's image while usually avoiding claims of absolute safety or zero side effects. One slogan: "The brand of pain reliever that doctors recommend more than any other." Another: "Trust TYLENOL. Hospitals do."

"We never use the word 'safe' in our advertising," said Anthony Temple, McNeil's longtime medical director, in a legal case in 1993. "We will say 'a superior safety profile' or some language to suggest its relative safety to other" over-the-counter pain relievers.

McNeil's advertising budget for Tylenol has frequently exceeded $100 million per year: $115 million in 2003, according to *Brandweek*; $138 million in 2005, according to *Advertising Age*; and $162 million in 2008, according to *Adweek*. In 2004, marketing was the largest department in the company, employing about 150 professionals, McEvoy said in a court deposition.

McNeil's recent chief executives have often come from marketing backgrounds. Johnson & Johnson, a conglomerate of more than 250 companies, does not even place McNeil into its pharmaceutical division, which is responsible for prescription drug products. Instead, the company is part of the consumer division, along with shampoo, mouthwash, and skin-care products.

Johnson & Johnson does not release sales figures for individual products, but Tylenol is the dominant acetaminophen brand in the United States. Although the drug is available in cheaper generic forms, McNeil accounted for nearly half of all over-the-counter sales of acetaminophen, according to a 2010 McNeil presentation.

Sales of acetaminophen by all companies have also grown. It became the nation's most-used drug in the mid-2000s, according to surveys. In 2009, more than 27 billion doses of acetaminophen were sold in the United States, most over the counter.

One way McNeil has reached ever-more households is through a marketing strategy known as line extension: targeting market niches by adding products, all under the halo of the Tylenol brand. Between 1988 and 2002, the company notified the FDA of plans to introduce fifty-four different kinds of packages, ranging from chewable tablets to coated pills, packed into bottles, pouches, cartons, and blister packs.

In the webcast interview, McEvoy, a marketing expert who rose into Johnson & Johnson's corporate ranks, called Tylenol "a billion-dollar brand."

Internally, company officials refer to it simply as "the Brand."

⋅　　　⋅　　　⋅

The first reports of deaths from acetaminophen emerged in the late 1960s.

Researchers subsequently learned that when the drug is broken down in the liver, it produces a potentially toxic byproduct. In an overdose, the liver can no longer safely dispose of the byproduct and can fail in a matter of days, shriveling like a deflated balloon.

The concerns with acetaminophen emerged at a time when the American system for drug oversight was undergoing a sea change. Congress had passed a law in 1962 requiring the FDA to institute more rigorous testing for new drugs and to review the safety and efficacy of those already on the market.

In 1972, as part of the review of existing drugs, the FDA assembled a group of doctors and scientists to assess painkillers, including acetaminophen. Over five years, the panel held fifty meetings, heard from scores of witnesses, and scoured thousands of pages of research—much of it submitted by drug makers themselves.

As the panel's work was going on, one of the world's most prestigious medical journals weighed in on acetaminophen. The London-based *Lancet* declared in a 1975 editorial that if the drug "were discovered today it would not be approved" by British regulators. "It would certainly never be freely available without prescription."

The journal's editorial board called the drug's apparent safety "deceptive." They pointed out that "not much more than the recommended maximum daily dosage" could cause liver damage and that acetaminophen poisoning was already "one of the commonest causes" of liver failure in Britain. (The drug is known there and in many countries as paracetamol.)

Relatively few cases of acetaminophen poisoning had been documented in the United States. But an American study published in 1975 identified four acetaminophen-related deaths in one year in one city, Denver. The article suggested a reason why so few cases had previously been found: "If you do not look for something you will not diagnose it."

McNeil dispatched a top official to meet with one of the study's authors. The company then gave him funding to help develop the acetaminophen antidote.

Two years later, in 1977, the FDA's expert panel delivered its 1,200-page report on pain relievers.

While the committee found that acetaminophen was generally safe when used as directed, it warned that "some advertising for acetaminophen gives the impression that it is much safer than aspirin." So the panelists urged the FDA to add a clear, specific warning to the acetaminophen label.

The language the panel suggested: "Do not exceed recommended dosage because severe liver damage may occur." The panel had only advisory power, but it felt so strongly that it told the FDA the warning was "obligatory."

Committee members wanted to drive home the potentially devastating consequences of taking too much acetaminophen, said Ninfa Redmond, a toxicologist who served on the panel.

"We felt very strongly the evidence was conclusive," Redmond said.

•   •   •

For McNeil, the proposed liver warning put a lot at stake. Just the year before, Tylenol had become the no. 1 brand in the over-the-counter pain medication market, according to a company history.

As McNeil prepared its response to the advisory panel's recommendation, new reports of harm from the drug emerged.

In September 1977, the *Annals of Internal Medicine* published articles about patients who suffered liver damage after taking acetaminophen for an extended period of time at or slightly above therapeutic doses, underscoring what the *Lancet* had said about the drug's narrow margin for error.

That December, McNeil filed a voluminous response to the FDA opposing the recommendation for a liver warning. It's not known if the individuals who drafted the company's filing were aware of the journal articles, but the company asserted that people who overdosed were "almost invariably" trying to kill themselves. Indeed, McNeil maintained it had never seen a "documented case" of a person harmed while taking the drug for medical reasons.

A liver warning "is unnecessary and serves only to confuse and frighten the vast majority of consumers who use acetaminophen in a rational and appropriate fashion," the company concluded. It also wouldn't help consumers, the company said, because signs of liver damage often don't emerge until it's too late to get help.

McNeil raised another objection: The warning would put it at a competitive disadvantage.

Bayer, one of the world's largest aspirin makers, had started running advertisements citing acetaminophen's potential to harm the liver, based on the advisory panel's recommendation. "Losses are already in the millions of dollars," McNeil stated in its submission to the FDA.

Almost a decade would pass without the FDA coming to any decision. While the label advised consumers to seek medical assistance if they overdosed, McNeil was able to sell its drug without warning that it could harm the liver. The agency's decision was delayed, at least in part, because regulators extended deadlines to review new research.

Redmond called such additional review unnecessary because the basic facts about the drug were well established. She said she was mystified by regulators' failure to act on the panel's recommendation. "It's very surprising, and it's sad," she said. "How many people might have died because of that?"

Finally, in 1988, the FDA announced a "tentative" ruling. The agency agreed a warning was necessary but said there was no need to specify that the drug could injure the liver.

The agency explained that it didn't want people who were considering suicide to know what an overdose could do. And, it said, liver damage didn't produce telltale symptoms for several days, when it was often too late for doctors to intervene.

So it mandated a catchall warning: In case of overdose, consumers should seek prompt medical attention "even if you do not notice any signs or symptoms."

McNeil had won a reprieve from having to put a phrase on its bottles that company officials believed scared off buyers: "severe liver damage." And the FDA would not return to the issue until many, many years later.

As the FDA's deliberations over the label crawled on, research began to emerge about the risks of drinking alcohol and taking acetaminophen—and McNeil took steps to counter the research.

As early as the 1970s, an FDA panel had examined whether to put an alcohol warning on the acetaminophen label. In 1978, according to an internal McNeil memo, the company had been "successful in convincing" FDA officials "that such a warning was not indicated." But the issue had not gone away.

According to a corporate memo from February 1986, McNeil had test-marketed how consumers would interpret different versions of an alcohol warning. No matter how the warning was phrased, consumers reacted negatively: Most respondents concluded that drinkers should reduce or discontinue using Tylenol, even at recommended levels.

The following month, the *Annals of Internal Medicine* published a study describing alcoholics who developed liver damage after taking "apparently moderate" amounts of acetaminophen.

Two weeks after the article's publication, a McNeil official issued a memo to Tylenol's sales force warning representatives to "not initiate discussions with your physicians" about the danger of mixing alcohol and acetaminophen. A senior McNeil official would later testify in a deposition that the issue was controversial and complex. Sales reps, he said, were "not equipped" to discuss it.

Then, in August 1987, a relatively obscure Swedish journal published a study on the dangers of drinking and taking acetaminophen.

Thomas Gates, then McNeil's medical director, shot off a memo to the chief executive of Johnson & Johnson, the president of McNeil and other top officials, laying out a detailed "plan of action" for "diffusing media interest" in the research and "limiting the extent and duration of the coverage."

Gates envisioned two possibilities: "Low Level of Publicity (most probable scenario)" and "High Level of Publicity (worst case scenario)." For the latter, Gates suggested a series of responses: a letter-writing campaign to medical societies, doctors, pharmacists, and academics; a coordinated public relations response with the FDA; even placing on retainer scientists whose research the company favored.

"If there is another wave of publicity," Gates warned, "the FDA might be compelled to reconsider the matter and require a specific warning regarding a possible risk of toxicity in chronic alcohol abusers."

Gates, long retired from McNeil, was too ill to respond to questions, his wife said.

Ultimately, the Swedish study received little attention.

Gates' memo summarized cases in the scientific literature over the previous decade that documented acetaminophen's risk for drinkers. He wrote that thirty-eight "chronic alcoholics" had reportedly suffered liver and/or kidney damage while taking acetaminophen. In just over half the cases, users substantially exceeded dosing limits.

However, there were eighteen instances in which they took less than 6/2/2014 grams a day, not much more than the four grams considered safe, Gates noted.

He stressed that "the amount of acetaminophen ingested is open to question since alcoholics are notoriously unreliable informants."

But "if accurate," he wrote, the amount of acetaminophen that harmed those eighteen patients "bring us uncomfortably close" to the maximum recommended daily dose.

Although McNeil had been preparing for the possibility that the FDA would require an alcohol warning, it took years before the agency publicly grappled with the issue.

In 1993, the FDA convened an advisory panel to look at the risk of mixing alcohol and acetaminophen. Such panels are made up of outside experts. While the FDA does not have to follow their recommendations, it usually does.

McNeil argued against the warning, saying the scientific evidence did not justify it and that it would frighten customers into taking other pain relievers that the company claimed were riskier.

But the panel found that an alcohol warning was warranted. The chairman called the science behind it "unusually strong and well-supported."

At the same time, McNeil was seeking FDA approval for a new product, extended release Tylenol. Because it was a post-1962 drug, the agency could push for a warning with less red tape. It moved to do so on the new product, raising the possibility that regular Tylenol would have no alcohol warning but that the time-release product would have one.

After the FDA approved extended release Tylenol with an alcohol alert in 1994, McNeil voluntarily added the warning to all Tylenol products.

"After careful deliberation and discussion with the FDA, McNeil has made several label changes to Tylenol over the years—all for the purpose of eliminating potential confusion by consumers and protecting consumer safety," the company wrote in response to questions. "A label change does not mean that a prior label was inadequate, and in fact label changes are an indication that our medical understanding is evolving."

Four years after McNeil acted, the FDA required all acetaminophen manufacturers to add an alcohol alert to their products.

People who drank three or more alcoholic drinks every day were advised to consult their doctors and were warned that liver damage could occur.

•   •   •

The warning label came too late for Antonio Benedi.

Benedi, who worked as a special assistant to President George H. W. Bush, often drank two or three glasses of wine with dinner. On a Friday in February 1993, just weeks after Bush left office, Benedi came down with the flu. Over the next several days, he said, he took Tylenol, never exceeding the maximum dose.

Benedi said he was careful to read labels. At the time, nothing on his box of Extra Strength Tylenol warned about the risk of drinking or liver damage.

Several nights later, he woke up, confused and incoherent. His wife called an ambulance to rush him to a hospital near their home in the Virginia suburbs of Washington, D.C.

By the time he arrived, Benedi had slipped into a coma. Tests showed his liver enzyme levels were high, a sign of organ damage. He had brain swelling, so doctors drilled a hole in his skull to relieve the pressure.

After his third day in a coma, Benedi got a second chance at life. Doctors declared a young man taken to Benedi's hospital after a motorcycle accident to be brain dead, and Benedi received the man's liver.

Benedi spent two months in the hospital, more than 200 surgical staples holding his abdomen together in a raw wound that looked like the Mercedes-Benz symbol.

Almost two decades later, he still suffers from those few days of taking Tylenol. To keep his body from rejecting his transplanted liver, he had to take powerful medications that eventually destroyed his kidneys, requiring a kidney transplant.

He sued McNeil. In court, the company argued that a virus had destroyed his liver and that the warnings on Tylenol's label were adequate. The jury found for Benedi, awarding him an $8.5 million judgment in 1994. To this day, he will have nothing to do with Tylenol—he always tells doctors and nurses not to give him any.

"I have nothing against corporations. They do a lot of good, employ a lot of people," said Benedi. But "when a company omits a known danger to them that could hurt people, they're lying to us. I think that is outrageous."

•   •   •

As Benedi's case unfolded, McNeil was pressing ahead with a program dubbed Project Protect to create a safer version of acetaminophen.

But the company kept the program, which has never been reported, confidential. Even when the government specifically asked for scientific information on developing a safer acetaminophen, the company didn't mention its own research.

The concept of such a drug was not new. The 1975 *Lancet* editorial had called for the development of a version of acetaminophen that wouldn't harm the liver. In the United Kingdom, companies had developed drugs combining acetaminophen with one of its antidotes. But sales never took off—the drugs were too expensive, the pills were too large, and there were questions about the drugs' safety.

In the early 1990s, McNeil embarked on a series of experiments to combine acetaminophen with various protective agents. The effort involved almost twenty different lab and animal studies lasting several years, according to internal company documents and court records.

As the experiments progressed, however, one official worried that the research could be a double-edged sword.

A Johnson & Johnson manager based in Europe wrote to Ralph Levi, the head of Project Protect for McNeil, according to court documents. In his June 1994 note, the manager cautioned that a new, improved product touched on "a sensitive point," because the company would be acknowledging that its existing product "isn't so safe as we've always said before." Levi has since died, and the court documents identified the manager only by his first name, Geert.

To help keep Project Protect hidden, the company signed a confidentiality agreement with Rutgers University, where some of the research was conducted. A key clause: The publicly funded university agreed not to publicize "the identity or interest of McNeil in this area of technology." Rutgers said such agreements were standard when researchers worked with companies.

At least one line of research showed early promise, according to Rutgers documents, but there's no public evidence that it or any Project Protect compound made it beyond laboratory or animal studies.

McNeil's work remained confidential even after the FDA became interested in that field of research. In 2006, as part of a larger review of acetaminophen, the agency solicited information about combining the drug with antidotes.

In response, McNeil submitted a lengthy report citing fifty-one studies to document the drawbacks of such combinations. But the company did not mention that it had extensively researched the topic.

FDA officials said McNeil wasn't required to disclose its research in that response. Asked if the company had ever told the agency of its project, the FDA did not answer. "Those are the kind of things that we are always interested in knowing about," said Kweder, the FDA's acetaminophen expert. She added that even "if they didn't show anything, it'd be useful to us to know if didn't work scientifically."

In response to questions about Project Protect, McNeil acknowledged "research into acetaminophen overdose antidotes" but did not provide details. The company noted that confidentiality clauses are standard industry practice. It also said that the firm had complied fully with FDA reporting requirements.

The company said it halted the research after discovering that the most promising agent "posed a cardiovascular risk for individuals with a particular genetic defect." The company did not disclose the name of the agent.

"Had the research yielded a viable discovery, our intention was to launch a product," the company statement said. It continued: "Despite the outcome, we consider this type of research a responsible action on our part, and are proud of the many scientists who worked on it."

·   ·   ·

As McNeil quietly pursued a safer acetaminophen, a bespectacled, bow-tied Dallas doctor named Will Lee was pursuing research that would change the debate about the drug.

In 1997, Lee published a groundbreaking paper in the *New England Journal of Medicine* showing that acetaminophen was the leading cause of acute liver failure at Parkland Memorial hospital in Dallas, despite the drug's "apparent overall safety."

Not to be confused with chronic liver failure, such as that caused by alcoholism, acute liver failure is a sudden, often fatal condition that affects about 2,000 Americans each year.

Among twenty-one patients who had overdosed on acetaminophen accidentally, Lee found, three reported that they had not exceeded the maximum recommended dose of four grams per day. Only seven said they had taken more than ten grams.

Following the article, the National Institutes of Health funded a larger study involving many of the country's busiest liver transplant centers. Over the next fifteen years, Lee, who is currently a professor of internal medicine at the University of

Texas Southwestern Medical Center, confirmed that what he had documented in Dallas was true nationwide: Acetaminophen was the no. 1 cause of acute liver failure.

Over the years, almost half of the people in the study had overdosed by accident, Lee found, not by trying to kill themselves. Many of those patients had other risk factors; about one-fifth drank alcohol frequently.

One finding was downright counterintuitive: People trying to kill themselves with massive, one-time overdoses were more likely to survive than those who accidentally took too much.

The reason? The chemical antidote to acetaminophen poisoning that McNeil helped to develop has a high success rate if administered within eight hours of an overdose. Those who attempted suicide and later regretted their action often made it to a hospital in time.

Those who overdosed by accident were often unaware they had been poisoned. Their symptoms took several days to develop and resembled those of the flu, for which many of them had taken the drug in the first place. They were more likely to miss the window for the antidote.

Acetaminophen has "not been recognized as a poison—that's been part of the challenge," Lee said. "It's just like candy. If four is good, eight must be better."

McNeil disputed Lee's findings, saying they had "serious methodological weaknesses," such as relying upon patients to recall the amount of acetaminophen consumed.

But other researchers came to similar findings. At the Hospital of the University of Pennsylvania, Dr. Sarah Erush and a colleague found that half of forty-six patients treated for acetaminophen-related liver damage over four years had overdosed accidentally, not intentionally.

The amount of acetaminophen these patients had ingested was close to the recommended daily dose of four grams. The median was six grams per day—a surprise because the toxic dose was thought to be between ten and fifteen grams, Erush said. She also found that most of these patients had other risk factors, such as chronic alcohol use.

Although she didn't publish her research in a peer-reviewed journal, she presented it to the FDA.

"For almost every patient with accidental exposure, we said, 'Why did you take more than the recommended dose?'" Erush said in an interview. "They said two things: One, the label wasn't clear, and, two, they always thought it was a perfectly safe drug."

McNeil said that it had asked Lee and Erush for patient information in order to examine their conclusions. Both researchers said they had not provided McNeil such records, citing patient privacy issues.

.   .   .

Lee's research spurred the FDA to reexamine if the label on over-the-counter acetaminophen should explicitly warn about the risk of liver damage.

The agency invited a grieving mother to tell her story at a public hearing.

Kate Trunk's twenty-three-year-old son Marcus had hurt his wrist in 1995 while working on a construction job in Pennsylvania. Over the next two weeks, he took Tylenol with Codeine and Extra Strength Tylenol. He started to feel sick and started on Theraflu—apparently not realizing that it, too, contained acetaminophen.

Soon, Marcus felt bad enough to check himself into a hospital, where he lapsed into a coma. Eight days after Marcus entered the hospital, Kate and her husband decided to end life support.

"We stayed with him and held him and talked to him and kissed him and petted him," Trunk said. "He finally just went. It was total shock, walking around in a daze, not knowing, angry at God, angry at everything."

The mystified family did not find out the cause of Marcus' death until the autopsy came back: liver failure caused by acetaminophen. The Trunks sued McNeil and settled for an undisclosed amount. McNeil did not respond to questions about the case.

When the Trunks took their concerns to the FDA hearing, Kate was so nervous that her husband kept checking her blood pressure. But she delivered a call to action: She wanted acetaminophen clearly labeled to warn that the drug could poison and even kill.

"If our son or my husband and I even had an inkling that acetaminophen toxicity existed, I feel that the outcome of our story would be totally different," she said. She ended her testimony by saying that "death is not an acceptable side effect."

The committee recommended adding a warning aimed at all users, not just drinkers, that overdosing can damage the liver.

This time, McNeil gave ground, agreeing with the need for a liver warning. "We believe with you that the American consumer is smart, responsible, and can self-manage medications," Dr. Debra Bowen, McNeil's vice president of research and development, told the panel.

By 2005, McNeil began placing labels on Tylenol warning that taking too much could result in "liver damage" for anyone, not just people who drank alcohol.

In 2009, the FDA imposed stronger language, requiring all over-the-counter acetaminophen products to warn that overdosing may cause "severe liver damage."

The FDA's wording was nearly identical to what its expert panel had recommended thirty-two years earlier.

Asked about this time lag, the agency replied, "While we acknowledge that there has been some delay between available scientific information and the translation to labeling instructions for consumers, FDA has strengthened warnings on the acet-aminophen label accordingly as science has evolved."

•   •   •

While McNeil agreed on the need to warn consumers of acet-aminophen's potential to harm the liver, it vigorously ob-jected to the FDA's plans to raise public awareness of that very risk.

In 2004, the agency launched a modest public service adver-tisement initiative. The slogan: "Why is it important to know that all these medicines contain acetaminophen? Because too much can damage your liver."

A key problem the campaign hoped to address: double dip-ping, or overdosing by inadvertently taking more than one med-ication that contains acetaminophen.

That risk had grown as McNeil and its competitors expanded the number of acetaminophen products on drugstore shelves. The drug was in medications targeted at consumers suffering all manner of ills, from colds to arthritis aches to insomnia caused by pain.

The FDA didn't have a lot of money for the 2004 campaign, just $20,000, according to an Associated Press story from the time.

During this period, McNeil was spending more than $100 million a year to advertise Tylenol, trade publications reported.

Nevertheless, McNeil launched an intense and lengthy effort to overhaul the campaign.

The company sent a seventy-nine-page complaint demanding that, if left unchanged, the FDA's educational campaign would "negatively affect McNeil, the world's largest marketer of OTC acetaminophen products."

Indeed, the complaint said, the FDA should speed up its re-view "in order to limit the damage that is being done" by the nascent campaign.

McNeil wanted the FDA to include warnings about other over-the-counter pain relievers, arguing that they posed risks at least as serious as acetaminophen. The FDA's initiative, the company contended, created the false impression that "acetaminophen products are less safe" than other over-the-counter pain-killers and could spur consumers to switch to other pain medicines, resulting in more injuries and deaths—a frequent McNeil argument.

The FDA's Steven Galson, then the acting director of the agency's Center for Drug Evaluation and Research, disagreed.

Doubling the maximum daily dose of over-the-counter pain killers such as aspirin or ibuprofen "may slightly increase a person's risk for bleeding," in the stomach and gastrointestinal tract, he wrote, but "it is not even close to the seriousness presented by doubling the dose of acetaminophen," which can lead to liver failure.

McNeil took its case all the way to the FDA commissioner, who turned down the company's final appeal, saying the agency had "refuted each example to respond to your allegation."

McNeil did not respond directly to questions about its opposition to the campaign. But it stressed that it had launched numerous acetaminophen safety education efforts, both on its own and with industry and government partners. Altogether, McNeil said, these "acetaminophen awareness messages have been seen over one billion times."

Although the agency had prevailed, its safety initiative fizzled. Major media outlets were reluctant to run the public health announcements. Magazine publishers told agency officials that they "did not want to antagonize potential advertisers," according to an FDA report.

The FDA concluded that its campaign "did not appear to have a significant impact on the problem."

Indeed, a nationwide poll this year shows that many Americans don't recognize the risk of double dipping.

Thirty-five percent of respondents said it was safe to take the maximum recommended dose of Extra Strength Tylenol with NyQuil, a cold remedy that also contains acetaminophen. The margin of error was 3.5 percentage points.

Among parents, 35 percent thought it was safe to give a child the maximum dose of Children's Tylenol with Children's Tylenol Plus Multi-Symptom Cold, both of which contain acetaminophen. The margin of error for the parents' subgroup was 6.7 percentage points.

In both these examples, mixing the two medicines would not be safe, according to the FDA.

(The survey of 1,003 respondents—conducted by Princeton Survey Research Associates International and commissioned by *ProPublica* and *This American Life*—was completed in March.)

With the public education campaign faltering, the FDA regrouped in 2006 and convened a team to examine the agency's handling of acetaminophen—including what a former top official described as "the interactions between the FDA and McNeil over this thirty-year history."

Officials reviewed the science, the reports of deaths and side effects, and the long history of regulatory delays. The 265-page report that emerged was both a blunt assessment of the drug's dangers and a plan for mitigating them.

Officials concluded that deaths from acetaminophen poisoning had risen dramatically over the decade between 1995 and 2005. They zeroed in on how the drug differed from other over-the-counter pain relievers.

"The 4 gram per day recommended dose is also the maximum safe dose, one that must not be exceeded, an unusual situation for any drug, particularly an OTC drug, one placing a large fraction of users close to a toxic dose in the ordinary course of use," the report said.

Officials proposed more than a dozen solutions, including several aimed at widening the drug's safety margin, such as lowering the maximum recommended daily dose and reducing the amount of the drug in each pill. The report also suggested removing an entire class of pediatric products to reduce the potential for dosing mix-ups.

Taken together, the proposals constituted a blueprint for sweeping safety reforms.

At the same time, the FDA officials who wrote the report gave a candid assessment of the fierce resistance they expected from drug makers to certain proposals.

To the notion of lowering the recommended daily dose, the agency expected a "possible industry challenge."

To the proposal to decrease the amount of acetaminophen per pill, the report anticipated "possible industry resistance to costs related to reformulation" and to "possible loss of revenue from elimination of 500 mg products."

In June 2009, the agency gathered nearly forty experts in a Maryland Marriott to weigh in on its recommendations. Everyone in the room, including executives from McNeil and other companies, knew the stakes.

Edwin Kuffner, McNeil's medical director, had prepared for the meeting by attending some one hundred practice sessions with a consulting company that specialized in readying corporate clients to speak before the FDA, according to a court deposition.

Kuffner objected to dropping the daily recommended dose below four grams. For decades, the company's labels had advised users to take no more than one gram, or the equivalent of two Extra Strength Tylenol pills, at a time. He suggested directing consumers to take one pill at a time until they felt pain relief, gradually easing up to a maximum of four grams a day only as necessary. Even though a company document calls this practice "good medicine," McNeil has not added this instruction to Tylenol labels.

When it came time to vote, Judith Kramer, a physician and professor of medicine at Duke University, reminded her fellow panelists of the opportunity before them, noting that attempts to make acetaminophen safer had foundered for decades.

"There is an elephant in the room that we really should talk about explicitly," she said. "There are tremendous cost and commercial implications to some of the recommended changes. These conditions frequently can overshadow the public health considerations. And I think that we can't let that happen."

The panel handed McNeil a defeat, endorsing most of the FDA's proposals.

But then, the agency's momentum stalled.

·   ·   ·

Four years later, the agency has not enacted any of its own suggestions for over-the-counter acetaminophen.

In fact, the FDA has still not completed the review of the drug that began back in the 1970s, as part of the agency's larger mandate to assess the safety and efficacy of older medicines.

In interviews, FDA officials acknowledged that it has taken longer than it should. They blamed a combination of science and bureaucracy.

Despite fifty years of sales and more than 30,000 published papers, there remain unknowns about acetaminophen. In a little-publicized 2011 announcement, the FDA acknowledged it was still unable "to identify precise toxic thresholds and/or specific populations for whom currently recommended dosages are not safe."

A Canadian government study found six people had suffered serious liver damage after taking less than the maximum recommended dose. By contrast, a case report described a man who survived after ingesting as much as sixty grams all at once. In response to questions, McNeil first wrote in an e-mail that eight grams, or double the maximum daily dose, over several days can damage the liver. Later, when asked to confirm this figure, the company declined to do so. It pointed to data showing that at least ten grams a day for at least two to three days can threaten the liver.

Setting the right dose "has been one of the big challenges for us," the FDA's Kweder said. "There is so much disagreement among experts who are well respected and can present data on where they'd draw that line."

Agency officials also said that McNeil has often resisted changes.

McNeil was "more aggressive than most," a former top FDA official said. "It's a company that feels very strongly about the competitive nature of the marketplace."

McNeil countered: "Our marketing practices are appropriate and align with the regulatory standards for our industry."

It also added that the company had a "deep respect for the Food and Drug Administration (FDA) and its role in establishing and enforcing regulations" and noted that it has voluntarily implemented some safety measures before the agency required it to do so.

The FDA delays are, at least in part, self-inflicted.

The agency said that the procedure it set back in the 1970s for revising rules for older drugs "was not rapid, but there were many fewer steps to the process that today is long." Indeed, actions that were supposed to take months have dragged on for years or even decades.

For prescription drugs, the FDA can act more swiftly, and it has limited the amount of acetaminophen in such medicines.

In 2011, the FDA limited the amount of acetaminophen that can be put in prescription drugs to 325 milligrams per pill, and gave companies until January 2014 to implement the change.

Yet the agency continues to allow the sale of over-the-counter pills that contain up to 650 milligrams of acetaminophen—twice as much.

Asked why it permits such potent pills to be sold directly to consumers, an FDA official said the agency "believes there is a benefit to having acetaminophen available."

In addition to lowering the dose per pill, the FDA slapped prescription acetaminophen with a so-called black box warning, the agency's most serious. It states that "acetaminophen has been associated with cases of acute liver failure, at times resulting in liver transplant and death."

The label for the over-the-counter version of the drug, taken by far more Americans, mentions neither of those potential consequences.

The agency's disparate actions on prescription and over-the-counter acetaminophen have given rise to glaring inconsistencies.

Tylenol with Codeine No. 3, made by a Johnson & Johnson company, combines acetaminophen with codeine, which can be bought only with a prescription. Tylenol 3, as it is commonly known, carries a black box warning about acetaminophen, and each pill contains 300 milligrams, less than the new limit of 325 milligrams.

By contrast, a single pill of Extra Strength Tylenol—sold at newsstands, gas stations, and big-box retailers across the land—delivers 500 milligrams of acetaminophen. The bottle carries no black box warning.

Two pills, containing the same medication, made by the same corporation, carrying the same brand name, regulated by the same agency—but subject to different standards.

• • •

While the FDA remains stuck on rules for over-the-counter acetaminophen, McNeil has reversed course on one major proposal.

Just a month after adamantly opposing dosing reductions at the 2009 advisory committee meeting, McNeil wrote top FDA officials, offering a plan that recognized the will of the advisory committee.

Although the company had insisted for half a century that four grams of medicine per day was the most appropriate dose for pain relief, the company said it was ready to recommend taking no more than three grams a day (or six pills) of its flagship product, Extra Strength Tylenol. The company implemented the change in 2011.

The move echoed other instances, such as the alcohol warning, in which the company opposed safety proposals until the FDA signaled its intent. Then the company adopted measures voluntarily as the agency plodded toward final rules.

Kuffner, McNeil's vice president for medical affairs, said in an interview that the company changed its dosing instructions "after hearing the discussion" at the 2009 advisory committee. The lower dose is "intended to increase the margin of safety," he said.

McNeil hasn't standardized the new daily dose across all its products, however. For Tylenol Arthritis Pain, the company's label puts the daily limit at 3.9 grams. And the company didn't change the dose for customers worldwide. In Canada and other countries, the company still instructs users of Extra Strength Tylenol that they can take up to four grams a day—eight pills.

Kuffner said the "root causes" of acetaminophen overdose differ from region to region.

"The safety of consumers in every region is important to us. When you really go back and look at root causes, some of the root causes weren't as prevalent as in other regions," he said. "There are differences in the prevalence of acetaminophen overdose and liver injury."

"At the end of the day, when people take four grams or three grams, both of them are safe doses," Kuffner said.

The FDA had said it would issue proposed rules for over-the-counter acetaminophen by the end of August. But the agency missed that deadline, pushing it back to December.

Dr. Thomas Garvey, a former FDA official and drug industry consultant who has testified against McNeil in trials, called the amount of time the FDA had taken to reach a final ruling "remarkable and unusual."

"There are still many questions about this drug," Garvey said. "It's still killing people."

Mother Jones

Nowadays, it's easy to cook up some crystal meth at home, outdoors, or in the trunk of a car. Two states returned pseudoephedrine, a decongestant found in cold and allergy medicines like Claritin D and Sudafed and the key ingredient in methamphetamine, to prescription drug status. And it worked—the number of meth labs in Oregon dropped 96 percent since its passage of the law. That's why, as Jonah Engle shows, the pharmaceutical industry has pulled out all the stops to make sure no other state follows suit.

19. Merchants of Meth

How Big Pharma Keeps the Cooks in Business

The first time she saw her mother passed out on the living room floor, Amanda thought she was dead. There were muddy tracks on the carpet and the room looked like it had been ransacked. Mary wouldn't wake up. When she finally came to, she insisted nothing was wrong. But as the weeks passed, her fifteen-year-old daughter's sense of foreboding grew. Amanda's parents stopped sleeping and eating. Her once heavy mother turned gaunt, and her father, Barry, stopped going to work. She was embarrassed to go into town with him; he was covered in open sores. A musty stink gripped their increasingly chaotic trailer. The driveway filled up with cars as strangers came to the house and partied all night.

Her parents' repeated assurances failed to assuage Amanda's mounting worry. She would later tell her mother it felt "like I saw an airplane coming in toward our house in slow motion and it was crashing." Finally, she went sleuthing online. The empty packages of cold medicine, the canisters of Coleman fuel, the smell, her parents' strange behavior all pointed to one thing. They were meth cooks. Amanda (last name withheld to protect her privacy) told her grandparents, who lived next door. Eventually, they called police.

Within minutes, agents burst into the trailer. They slammed Barry up against the wall, put a gun to his head, and hauled him and Mary off in handcuffs. It would be two and a half years before Amanda and her ten-year-old sister, Chrissie, would see their father again.

The year was 2005, and what happened to Amanda's family was the result of a revolution in methamphetamine production that was just beginning to make its way into Kentucky. Meth users called it the "shake-and-bake" or "one-pot" method, and its key feature was to greatly simplify the way meth is synthesized from pseudoephedrine, a decongestant found in cold and allergy medicines like Claritin D and Sudafed.

Shake and bake did two things. It took a toxic and volatile process that had once been the province of people with *Breaking Bad*–style knowledge of chemistry and put it in the bedrooms and kitchens of meth users in rural America. It also produced the most potent methamphetamine anywhere.

If anyone wondered what would happen if heroin or cocaine addicts suddenly discovered how to make their own supply with a handful of cheap ingredients readily available over the counter, methamphetamine's recent history provides an answer. Since 2007, the number of clandestine meth sites discovered by police has increased 63 percent nationwide. In Kentucky, the number of labs has more than tripled. The Bluegrass State regularly joins its neighbors Missouri, Tennessee, and Indiana as the top four states for annual meth-lab discoveries.

As law-enforcement agencies scramble to clean up and dispose of toxic labs, prosecute cooks, and find foster homes for their children, they are waging two battles: one against destitute, strung-out addicts, the other against some of the world's wealthiest and most politically connected drug manufacturers. In the past several years, lawmakers in twenty-five states have sought to make pseudoephedrine—the one irreplaceable ingredient in a shake-and-bake lab—a prescription drug. In all but two—Oregon and Mississippi—they have failed as the industry, which sells an estimated $605 million worth of pseudoephedrine-based drugs a year, has deployed all-star lobbying teams and campaign-trail tactics such as robocalls and advertising blitzes.

Perhaps nowhere has the battle been harder fought than in Kentucky, where Big Pharma's trade group has broken lobbying spending records in 2010 and 2012, beating back cops, doctors, teachers, drug experts, and lawmakers from both sides of the aisle. "It frustrates me to see how an industry and corporate dollars affect commonsense legislation," says Jackie Steele, a commonwealth's attorney whose district in southeastern Kentucky has been overwhelmed by meth labs in recent years.

•　　　•　　　•

Before it migrated east to struggling Midwestern farm towns and the hollers of Appalachia, methamphetamine was a West Coast drug, produced by cooks working for Mexican drug-trafficking organizations and distributed by biker gangs. Oregon was particularly hard hit, with meth labs growing ninefold from 1995 to 2001. Even then, before shake and bake, police had their hands full decontaminating toxic labs that were often set up in private homes. Social workers warned of an epidemic of child abuse and neglect as hundreds of kids were being removed from meth houses.

In despair, the Oregon Narcotics Enforcement Association turned to Rob Bovett. As the lawyer for the drug task force of Lincoln County—a strip of the state's central coast known for its fishing industry, paper mills, and beaches—he was all too aware of the scourge of meth labs. Having worked for the Oregon Legislature and lobbied on behalf of the State Sheriffs' Association, he also knew his way around capitol procedure.

Bovett knew that law enforcement couldn't arrest its way out of the meth-lab problem. They needed to choke off the cooks' supply lines.

Bovett first approached the legislature about regulating pseudoephedrine in 2000. "The legislative response was to stick me in a room with a dozen pharmaceutical lobbyists to work it out," he recalls. He suggested putting the drugs behind the counter (without requiring a prescription) to discourage mass buying, but the lobbyists refused. They did eventually agree to a limit on the amount of pseudoephedrine any one person could buy, but the number of meth labs remained high, so in 2003 Bovett tried once again to get pseudoephedrine moved behind the counter. "We got our asses kicked," he admits.

Then, in Oklahoma, state trooper Nikky Joe Green came upon a meth lab in the trunk of a car. The cook overpowered Green and shot him with his own gun. The murder, recorded on the patrol car's camera, galvanized the state's legislature into placing pseudoephedrine behind the counter and limiting sales in 2004.

The pharmaceutical industry fought the bill, saying it was unlikely to curb meth labs. But Oklahoma saw an immediate drop in the number of labs its officers busted, and Oregon followed suit later that year.

But the meth cooks soon came up with a work-around: They organized groups of people to make the rounds of pharmacies, each buying the maximum amount allowed—a practice known as smurfing. How to stop these sales? Bovett remembered that until 1976, pseudoephedrine had been a prescription drug. He asked lawmakers to return it to that status.

Pharma companies and big retailers "flooded our capitol building with lobbyists from out of state," he says. On the eve of the House vote, with the count too close to call, four legislators went out and bought twenty-two boxes of Sudafed and Tylenol Cold. They brought their loot back to the legislature, where Bovett walked lawmakers through the process of turning the medicine into meth with a handful of household products. Without exceeding the legal sales limit, they had all the ingredients needed to make about 180 hits. The bill passed overwhelmingly.

Since the bill became law in 2006, the number of meth labs found in Oregon has fallen 96 percent. Children are no longer being pulled from homes with meth labs, and police officers have been freed up to pursue leads instead of cleaning up labs and chasing smurfers. In 2008, Oregon experienced the largest drop in violent-crime rates in the country. By 2009, property crime rates fell to their lowest in forty-three years. That year, overall crime in Oregon reached a forty-year low. The state's Criminal Justice Commission credited the pseudoephedrine prescription bill, along with declining meth use, as key factors.

For Big Pharma, however, Oregon's measure was a major defeat—and the industry was not about to let it happen again. "They've learned from their mistakes in Oregon, they've learned from their mistakes in Mississippi," says Marshall Fisher, who runs the Bureau of Narcotics in Mississippi. "They know if another state falls, and has the results that we've had, the chances of national legislation are that much closer. Every year they can fight this off is another year of those profits."

•　　•　　•

On a sunny winter afternoon, narcotics detective Chris Lyon turns off a country lane outside the town of Monticello in southeastern Kentucky, the part of the state hardest hit by the meth-lab boom. In a case that shocked the state in 2009, a twenty-month-old boy in a dilapidated trailer nearby drank a cup of Liquid Fire drain cleaner that was being used to make meth. The solution burned Kayden Branham from inside for fifty-four minutes until he died.

This afternoon, Lyon is following up on a call from a sheriff's deputy about several meth labs in the woods. His Ford F-150 clambers up a steep muddy slope turned vivid ochre by the night's rain. In the back are a gas mask, oxygen tanks, safety gloves, and hazmat suits, plus a bucket of white powder called Ampho-Mag that's used to neutralize toxic meth waste. Cleaning up labs is hazardous work: In the last two years, more than 180 officers have been injured in the process. The witches' brew that turns pseudoephedrine into meth includes ammonium nitrate (from fertilizer or heat packs), starter fluid, lithium (from batteries), drain cleaner, and camping fuel. It can explode or catch fire, and it produces copious amounts of toxic gases and hazardous waste even when all goes well.

Halfway up Edwards Mountain, Lyon pulls over in a clearing along the forested trail. Scattered over fifty yards are a half-dozen soda bottles, some containing a grayish, granular residue, others sprouting the plastic tubes cooks use to vent gas. Lyon snaps on black safety gloves, pulls a gas mask over his face, and carefully places each bottle in its own plastic bucket. Further up the mountain he finds more outdoor labs and repeats the procedure.

Lyon will drive his haul back to the Monticello Police Department, where a trailer is jam-packed with buckets he's filled in the past few days. "No suspects, no way of making an arrest—it's pretty much a glorified garbage pickup," he says with an air of dejection. "We have all kinds of information of people selling drugs," but there's no time for investigations. "About the time that we get started on something, the phone rings and it's another meth lab to go clean up."

It's a problem Lieutenant Eddie Hawkins, methamphetamine coordinator for the Mississippi Bureau of Narcotics, was all too familiar with before his state passed its prescription bill in 2010. Since then the number of meth labs found in the state has fallen 74 percent. "We still have a meth problem," Hawkins says, "but it has given us more time to concentrate on the traffickers that are bringing meth into the state instead of working meth labs every night." Now, he says, they go after international criminal networks rather than locking up small-time cooks.

The spread of meth labs has tracked the hollowing out of rural economies. Labs are concentrated in struggling towns where people do hard, physical work for low wages, notes Nick Reding, whose book *Methland* charts the drug's rise in the Midwest: "Meth makes people feel good. Even as it helps people work hard, whether that means driving a truck or vacuuming the floor, meth contributes to a feeling that all will be okay." But the highly addictive drug can also wreak havoc on users, ravaging everything from teeth and skin to hearts and lungs. And the mushrooming of shake-and-bake labs has left its own trail of devastation: hospitals swamped with injured meth cooks, wrecked and toxic homes, police departments consumed with cleaning up messes rather than fighting crime.

Meth-related cleanup and law enforcement cost the state of Kentucky about $30 million in 2009, the latest year for which the state police have produced an estimate. That doesn't include the cost of crimes addicts commit to support their habit, of putting out meth fires, of decontaminating meth homes, of responding to domestic-abuse calls or placing neglected, abused, or injured kids in foster care. Dr. Glen Franklin, who oversees the burn unit at the University of Louisville Hospital, says his unit alone sees fifteen to twenty meth-lab burn patients each year, up from two or three a decade ago. They are some of his most difficult cases, often involving both thermal and chemical burns to the face and upper body from a bottle that burst into flames. Many, he notes, have also been abusing OxyContin or other prescription opiates, "so it makes their pain control that much more difficult." According to a study coauthored by Franklin in 2005, it costs an average of nearly $230,000 to treat a meth-lab victim—three times more than other burn patients—and that cost is most often borne by taxpayers. Meth use as a whole, according to a 2009 RAND Corporation study, costs the nation anywhere between $16 billion and $48 billion each year.

. . .

With silver hair, glasses, and a gentle manner, Linda Belcher looks like the retired grade school teacher she is. Though her district, just south of Louisville, has a meth lab problem, she didn't know much about the issue until Joe Williams, the head of narcotics enforcement at the Kentucky State Police, invited her and a few other lawmakers to state police headquarters. After a dinner of barbecue, coleslaw, and pork and beans, the guests descended to the basement to be briefed about key public safety issues. One was meth labs, whose effects and increasing numbers were depicted in a series of huge charts. One of Williams' officers laid out the startling facts. Meth labs were up for the second year in a row in Kentucky, and they were spreading eastward across the state. They were turning up in cars, motel rooms, and apartment buildings, putting unsuspecting neighbors at risk. Police had pulled hundreds of children from meth-lab locations. Prisons were filling up with cooks, and officers were being tied up in cleanup operations.

Belcher had been aware of methamphetamine, but she'd had no idea how bad things were getting. She set about learning more. "I went to a meeting, and there was a young lady there who had been on meth," Belcher recalls. "During the time she was on it, she didn't care about anything—not her daughter, not her parents. All she wanted was to get money and get meth. That convinced me."

Belcher asked Williams and other law enforcement officials what they thought should be done. They told her about what had happened in Oregon. It could work in Kentucky, they said. In February 2010, Belcher filed a bill to require a prescription for pseudoephedrine.

Soon her phone started ringing off the hook. The callers were angry. If her bill passed, they said, they would have to go to the doctor each time they were congested. It wasn't true—more than one hundred cold and allergy drugs made without pseudoephedrine, such as Sudafed PE, would have remained over the counter. And for those who didn't like those alternatives, doctors could renew prescriptions by phone.

Members of the House Health and Welfare Committee, the key panel Belcher's bill had to clear, were also getting calls. Tom Burch, the committee's chairman, says the prescription measure garnered more calls and letters than any he's dealt with in his nearly forty years at the capitol, except for abortion bills. "I had enough constituent input on it to know that the bill was not going to go anywhere."

Yet the legislation had gotten hardly any media coverage. How had Kentuckians become so outraged?

In April of that year, Donnita Crittenden was processing monthly lobbying reports at the Kentucky Legislative Ethics Commission when a figure stopped her in her tracks. A group called the Consumer Healthcare Products Association reported having spent more than $303,000 in three weeks. No organization had spent nearly that much on lobbying in the entire previous year.

Curious, Crittenden called CHPA. It was, she learned, a Washington-based industry association representing the makers and distributors of over-the-counter medicines and dietary supplements—multinational behemoths like Pfizer and Johnson & Johnson. CHPA had registered to lobby in Kentucky just weeks before, right after Belcher filed her bill. But it had already retained M. Patrick Jennings, a well-connected lobbyist who'd earned his stripes working for Senate Minority Leader Mitch McConnell (R-Ky.) and GOP Rep. Ed Whitfield.

The bulk of CHPA's record spending, though, was not for lobbyists. It was for a tool more commonly used in hard-fought political campaigns: robocalls, thousands of them, with scripts crafted and delivered by out-of-state PR experts to target legislators on the key committees that would decide the bill's fate.

CHPA's Kentucky filings don't show which firm made the robocalls, but the association's 2010 and 2011 tax returns show more than $1 million worth of payments to Winning Connections, a robocall company that typically represents Democratic politicians and liberal causes such as the Sierra Club's campaign against the Keystone XL pipeline. On its website, the company boasts of its role in West Virginia, where it helped defeat a pseudoephedrine bill that had "strong backing among special interests groups and many in the State Capitol" via focused calls in key legislative districts. CHPA's former VP for legal and government affairs, Andrew C. Fish, is quoted as saying that Winning Connections helped "capture the voice of consumers, which made the critical difference in persuading legislators to change course on an important issue to our member companies." Nowhere does Winning Connections' site mention the intent of the bill or the word "methamphetamine." CHPA spokeswoman Elizabeth Funderburk says the association used the calls, which allowed people to be patched through directly to their legislators, to provide a platform for real consumers to get their voices heard.

Belcher's bill never came up for a vote. Over the ensuing months, the number of meth labs found in Kentucky would grow by 45 percent, surpassing 1,000.

Belcher had learned a lesson. When she reintroduced the prescription bill in 2011, it had support from a string of groups with serious pull at the capitol—the teachers' union, the Kentucky Medical Association, four statewide law-enforcement organizations, and Kentucky's most senior congressman, Hal Rogers. Belcher also had bipartisan leadership support in the legislature, and the Republican chairman of the judiciary committee, Tom Jensen—whose district included the county with the second-highest number of meth labs—introduced a companion bill in the state Senate.

But the pharmaceutical industry came prepared, too. Its team of lobbyists included some of the best-connected political operatives in Kentucky, from former state GOP chairman John T. McCarthy III to Andrew "Skipper" Martin, the chief of staff to former Democratic governor Paul Patton. In addition to a new round of robocalls, CHPA now deployed an ad blitz, spending some $93,000 to blanket the state with sixty-second radio spots on at least 178 stations. The bill made it out of committee, but with the outcome doubtful, Jensen never brought it up for a vote on the Senate floor.

John Schaaf, the Kentucky Legislative Ethics Commission's counsel, describes CHPA's strategy as a game changer. "They have completely turned the traditional approach to lobbying around," he says. "For the most part, businesses and organizations that lobby, if they have important issues going on, they'll add lobbyists to their list. They'll employ more people to go out there and talk to legislators. CHPA employs very few lobbyists, and they spend 99 percent of their lobbying expenditures on this sort of grassroots outreach on phone banking and advertising. As far as I know, nothing's ever produced the number of calls or the visibility of this particular effort."

In other words: Rather than relying on political professionals to deliver their message, CHPA got voters to do it—and politicians listened, in Kentucky and beyond. There has been no major federal legislation to address meth labs since 2005, when pseudoephedrine was put behind the counter and sales limits were imposed. Lawmakers in twenty-four states have tried to pass prescription bills since 2009. In twenty-three of them, they failed.

The single exception was Mississippi, where a prescription measure supported by Republican governor Haley Barbour passed in 2010. The head of the state Bureau of Narcotics, Marshall Fisher, says one key to the bill's passage was making sure it was not referred to the legislature's health committee, where members tend to develop close relationships with pharma lobbyists. Fisher has testified about prescription bills before health committees in several other states. "It seems like every time we've done that, the deck is stacked against us," he says. "You can't fight that." Following the bill's passage, the number of meth labs busted in Mississippi fell more than 70 percent. The state narcotics bureau, which tracks the number of drug-endangered children, reported the number of such cases fell 81 percent in the first year the law was in effect.

Everywhere else, industry has prevailed. Many states have very limited laws on what lobbyists must report, and they don't monitor spending on robocalls or ads. But news reports and my interviews with legislators in Southeastern and Midwestern states where meth labs are most concentrated—and where CHPA had the biggest fight on its hands—show that the pharmaceutical industry deployed a mix of robocalls, print and radio ads, as well as a Facebook page and a website, stopmethnotmeds.com. These states include Alabama, Kansas, Missouri, North Carolina, Oklahoma, and Tennessee. The media campaign was backed up by each state's top lobbyists and PR firms.

"They'll outspend us one hundred to one," says Alabama state senator Roger Bedford, whose prescription bill has failed twice. In Indiana, which consistently ranks among the top states for meth labs, prescription bills have been defeated five years running. "I met a lot of resistance by the over-the-counter drug manufacturers," says former Indiana state representative Trent Van Haaften. "They were concerned about market share." In West Virginia, a prescription bill almost made it to the governor's desk in 2011, when it passed the House but ended up with a tie in the Senate.

In North Carolina, CHPA bought newspaper ads in Raleigh and Charlotte to defeat a 2011 prescription bill. Its sponsor, Craig Horn, was taken aback by the vitriolic calls he got. "Big Pharma has a lot of influence," he says. "They suggested that making pseudoephedrine-containing medication prescription-only would create a hardship on consumers, [and] that it would cost the state millions of dollars in Medicaid money." North Carolina saw dramatic increases in meth-lab discoveries in 2011 and 2012.

In Oklahoma, state Rep. Ben Sherrer sponsored prescription bills in 2011 and 2012. The first bill got out of committee but never came up for a vote on the floor. "I was told by the pharmaceutical industry it was going to be killed," Sherrer says. "They had a very brisk media campaign—radio, some large ads in the two major newspapers." He likens CHPA's messaging on pseudoephedrine to the tactics of the gun lobby: "The 'stop meth, not meds' campaign—it's sexy in the same way that we see a passionate plea to people who own weapons that they are coming for your guns."

· · ·

Detective Jason Back is one of two full-time narcotics officers in Laurel County, a stretch of hills and farms that boasts the site of

Colonel Sanders's original Kentucky Fried Chicken. With his tight black "I ♥ LA" shirt, Back stands out from his colleagues in their beige uniforms. Below a well-worn ball cap, he's got several days of stubble. A camouflage pistol grip sticks out of his jeans.

In Back's cramped office, a big flat-screen TV is perched incongruously in a corner. It was confiscated from a drug dealer, just like the truck Back drives for work. On his desk are two piles of paper with scribbled notes. One contains tips about meth labs, the second about prescription pills.

Like Detective Chris Lyon, Back returned to his hometown after a stint in the military. Both now spend their days putting away men and women they grew up with. "It happens all the time," Back says. A typical arrest will start with: "Hey, what's up, how's your family? Good. How's yours? All right." He's learned to shrug it off. "The people that burn out in law enforcement, that's a big thing—they take it too personal." Former senator Tom Jensen, the Republican sponsor of the prescription bill, is an attorney who recently represented a family friend's daughter, arrested for smurfing. Jackie Steele, the commonwealth's attorney in the county and one of the bill's major law-enforcement backers, has a family member who was sent to jail for having meth precursors.

Back's boss, Sheriff John Root, beat a crowded field for the Republican nomination by promising to go to war on meth. "When I came into office," Root says, "about every complaint that we had was meth-related. If we went on a domestic, if we went on a burglary, a theft, if we went to check on a welfare check, you would normally find the meth labs there."

Busting smurfers is grunt work. At the Walgreens off Highway 192 in London, which until recently sold more pseudoephedrine than any pharmacy in the state, it's like fishing in a well-stocked pond. "People drive up in a piece of shit car in trashy outfits and they are looking around," says Back. "One goes in, one goes out, another one comes in and another comes out. Tail 'em, traffic stop 'em—'cause they can't drive, half of 'em ain't got licenses, ain't got insurance, got dead tags." Faced with a one-to-five-year sentence for buying pseudoephedrine with intent to make meth, some will turn evidence against the cooks and dealers. In the meantime, they often end up in the county jail, an octagonal fortress just a few yards from Back's office. Unable to make bail—meth tends to rob addicts of everything they have, including the support of loved ones—some remain there, waiting for trial, for as long as a year.

That's what happened to a man I'll call Jeff. In 2010, Back arrested him after spotting him driving down Main Street in a car with no windshield. The car was so filthy, searching it left Back with a staph infection. Inside, the officer found Sudafed and ammonium nitrate. Jeff pleaded guilty to possession of drug paraphernalia and served four months in the Laurel County Jail. Six days after his release, Back arrested him again for making meth while raiding a trailer on Love Road, just outside London.

Just three years earlier, Jeff had a good job working construction, which allowed him to pay off his house and spoil his four children. He was married to his middle-school sweetheart. She drove a BMW; he had a Chevy truck. His parents had been addicted to cocaine, and he was raised by the state, shuttling from boys' camps to boys' homes. Now, the twenty-eight-year-old was giving his children the life he never had. Jeff was a fiercely independent, hardworking guy. "I don't have no family to get me nothing," he told me. "We worked for everything we had."

Meth, which makes users feel strong and invincible, fit in perfectly with that ethos. "Everybody around me was using it," Jeff says. "Friends, people I worked with doing construction work." So one day he smoked some. He liked it. "It don't cost much money, and I can work all day long, feel good, come home, mow the grass, play with the kids," he says. "As you get to like it more and more, you do it more."

Soon Jeff's life narrowed down to a single all-consuming quest: getting and staying high. He lost his wife, his kids, his job, his house, his tools, and his truck. He was shot in the face at point-blank range and stabbed while driving, both times by other addicts. By the time Back arrested him, he was drifting from trailer to trailer in Laurel County, welcomed for his skills as a cook. Jeff's wife found other ways to stay high. "She's got every guy in town that's more than willing to give her as much drugs as she wants," he says. She, too, ended up in the Laurel County Jail. But Jeff has no contact with the woman he calls the love of his life. His greatest wish, he told me, was to be released, get his kids back from his mother-in-law, and be the father he once hoped he could be.

County jailer Jamie Mosley says around 100 of his jail's approximately 350 inmates are there for meth offenses, and many others are in for crimes committed to support their habit. Prison is not a deterrent for these folks, says commonwealth's attorney Steele. "You are looking at putting somebody in jail for twenty to fifty years or life, and they are still out cooking."

.   .   .

One January night in 2012, some one hundred people sat around large round tables at the fire hall in London, eating battered fish and fries prepared by the county judge. After dinner, a chaplain in cowboy boots offered a prayer to open the town hall part of the evening. Sheriff Root had invited residents in to vent their concerns. Most wanted to talk about meth and pain pills.

Dwight Larkey, who installs heating and air conditioning systems, asked what was being done about thieves ripping out brand-new $1,500 units for $40 worth of copper. Jim Dorn, a semiretired official at the local credit union, was upset about news that seven churches had been burglarized in one night the week before. Another man worried about thieves who prey on old people, often going straight for their medicine cabinets in hopes of finding cold meds or Oxy.

Then Steele took the stage. Laurel County led the state in meth labs, he said. "Not coincidentally, we are also no. 1 for the sale of pseudoephedrine." Make your voices heard in Frankfort, he urged the audience.

A lanky man with spiky hair and glasses, Steele is part of a group of public officials who have taken the lead in pushing for a prescription bill. They couldn't afford robocalls or big ad buys—last year they raised about $10,000, enough to put ads on a dozen radio stations and set up a website. Still, they had hopes that Belcher and Jensen's third run at legislation would be the charm.

But CHPA was ready for them. The group began running ads two and a half weeks before the legislature reconvened, up to twelve times a day in the state's major markets. The association also hired two Kentucky PR firms, Peritus and BK Public Affairs; Peritus handed the job to Karl Rove's former deputy, Scott Jennings. CHPA would end up setting a new Kentucky lobbying record that session, spending almost a half million dollars, three and a half times more than the next biggest spender. Most of the money went to robocalls.

In public, the task of defending CHPA's argument against prescription bills falls to Carlos Gutierrez. A slight man with graying temples, the Texas native joined CHPA in 2010 as its head of state government affairs and since then has crisscrossed the nation putting out fires for the industry.

Gutierrez disputes the effectiveness of the prescription approach. He points out that meth labs began to drop in Oregon even before that state's law took effect. He notes that states bordering Oregon and some of Mississippi's neighbors have also seen large declines in meth labs. (A U.S. Government Accountability Office study released in February found that those declines were due in part to cuts in federal meth-lab cleanup funds. It said the drop in labs in Oregon was strongly correlated to the prescription bill's passage.)

Gutierrez also notes that having to get a prescription makes pseudoephedrine drugs more expensive to consumers, and that most meth in the United States still comes from Mexico. (Drug enforcement officials confirmed this, though none could give me an estimate of how much meth is domestically produced; some noted that locally cooked meth is often dominant in rural areas.)

When testifying before lawmakers, Gutierrez says the industry is committed to preventing medicines from being diverted into the drug trade: "We've invested, frankly, millions of dollars into systems to prevent diversion," he said during a hearing in Kentucky. He was referring to a tracking system the industry underwrites, the National Precursor Log Exchange, which logs pseudoephedrine sales in twenty-five states (some retailers, including Rite Aid and CVS, have also installed it in stores nationwide). The system, known as NPLEx, blocks customers from buying pseudoephedrine once they reach the limit set by each state's laws. Police can also access sales information to look for suspicious purchases. Gutierrez touts NPLEx as an alternative to prescription bills, though the GAO report found the system has not reduced labs because cooks are still finding ways to smurf.

What Gutierrez doesn't tell legislators is that CHPA vigorously fought the federal law NPLEx is designed to enforce, the 2005 Combat Methamphetamine Epidemic Act, just as it has regularly fought attempts to control the chemicals used to make meth since the 1980s. In 2004, CHPA's then-president, Linda Suydam— a twenty-one-year Food and Drug Administration veteran— personally argued against the 2005 bill, saying it would "have a greater impact on sick kids, caregivers, and flu sufferers than on criminals."

Today, though, pharmaceutical companies use the NPLEx system as one of their top arguments in fighting new regulation— including in Washington, where they have managed to keep a lid on any discussion of a federal prescription bill. "Honestly, because industry's pull in Congress is so strong," one Hill aide told me, "every time we would schedule a meeting or do anything, anybody who got wind of it would have a meeting with someone from the pharmaceutical industry. They got scared of it."

When I called CHPA spokeswoman Emily Skor, she said: "It really comes down to balancing what is the best way to stop criminal activity while enabling consumers to buy the medicines when and where they need them. That sums up our overall approach through time."

Kentucky was the first state to adopt the NPLEx system—it was piloted in Laurel County. "We wanted it to work," says Dan Smoot, the vice president of a drug enforcement and prevention organization called Operation UNITE who helped implement NPLEx in southeastern Kentucky. But the number of meth labs has tripled in Kentucky since NPLEx went into effect across the state in 2008. Nationwide, many states that adopted NPLEx have also seen their meth-lab numbers increase. (Advocates for NPLEx say this is because the tracking system is helping police find more of them.) Today Smoot is one of the major law-enforcement backers of prescription legislation.

Rob Bovett has a lot of sympathy for Kentucky. "They are in that same position" Oregon law enforcement was in a decade ago, he says: "They are frustrated. They want real solutions. They've tried things that haven't worked; they've bought the industry's line. They are done with that."

In 2012, Belcher introduced her bill once again. When it went before the House Judiciary Committee, chairman John Tilley estimates he received more than 1,000 calls, e-mails, and letters. Most came from the major media markets of Louisville and Lexington, not his constituents.

In the end, the legislature passed an industry-approved measure that barred people with prior drug offenses from buying pseudoephedrine for five years. Despite stiff opposition from CHPA, lawmakers also included reductions in the maximum amount of pseudoephedrine Kentuckians can purchase—limits that law enforcement says have halted the three-year run of record-breaking meth-lab numbers in the state. Kentucky finished 2012 with 1,060 meth labs, the fourth most in the nation.

·   ·   ·

Amanda's teen years were upended by her parents' meth arrest. Her father was sent to a federal prison in northern West Virginia for two and a half years. Her mother spent six months in jail on a lesser charge. At school ugly rumors spread, and soon Amanda dropped out. She and her sister stayed with their ailing grandparents, who died while the girls' father was still in jail.

After being released from jail, Mary went to rehab, and eventually Barry came home and found work at a car wash. Today, Amanda is back in the family home. When I visited, her mother cooed over Amanda's new baby, Logan, while at the front of the trailer, Amanda and her husband, Joey, showed off their new bedroom—teal walls, a queen bed, a crib in the corner. You wouldn't know it, but this was where Amanda's parents cooked meth. Barry still has a hard time talking about the events that tore his family apart. "It usually ends up with Dad about to cry," says Amanda.

But the pain of separation has brought the family closer. That's why Barry and Joey spent two weeks fixing up that bedroom, once corroded and filled with junk. They tore the walls down to the studs and put in all new carpet and drywall. "They don't want me to leave," Amanda says.

New York Times Magazine

One in three adults and one in five kids are considered clinically obese, and 24 million Americans are afflicted by type-two diabetes, often caused by poor diet. This situation did not arise by accident. It happened by the design of the processed-food industry, which has "optimized" its brands for addiction with sugar, salt, and fat, always seeking "the bliss point."

Michael Moss

20. The Extraordinary Science of Addictive Junk Food

On the evening of April 8, 1999, a long line of Town Cars and taxis pulled up to the Minneapolis headquarters of Pillsbury and discharged eleven men who controlled America's largest food companies. Nestlé was in attendance, as were Kraft and Nabisco, General Mills and Procter & Gamble, Coca-Cola and Mars. Rivals any other day, the CEOs and company presidents had come together for a rare, private meeting. On the agenda was one item: the emerging obesity epidemic and how to deal with it. While the atmosphere was cordial, the men assembled were hardly friends. Their stature was defined by their skill in fighting one another for what they called "stomach share"—the amount of digestive space that any one company's brand can grab from the competition.

James Behnke, a fifty-five-year-old executive at Pillsbury, greeted the men as they arrived. He was anxious but also hopeful about the plan that he and a few other food-company executives had devised to engage the CEOs on America's growing weight problem. "We were very concerned, and rightfully so, that obesity was becoming a major issue," Behnke recalled. "People were starting to talk about sugar taxes, and there was a lot of pressure on food companies." Getting the company chiefs in the same room to talk about anything, much less a sensitive issue like this, was a tricky business, so Behnke and his fellow organizers had scripted the meeting carefully, honing the message to its barest essentials. "CEOs in the food industry are typically not technical guys, and they're uncomfortable going to meetings where technical people talk in technical terms about technical things," Behnke said. "They don't want to be embarrassed. They don't want to make commitments. They want to maintain their aloofness and autonomy."

A chemist by training with a doctoral degree in food science, Behnke became Pillsbury's chief technical officer in 1979 and was instrumental in creating a long line of hit products, including microwaveable popcorn. He deeply admired Pillsbury but in recent years had grown troubled by pictures of obese children suffering from diabetes and the earliest signs of hypertension and heart disease. In the months leading up to the CEO meeting, he was engaged in conversation with a group of food-science experts who were painting an increasingly grim picture of the public's ability to cope with the industry's formulations—from the body's fragile controls on overeating to the hidden power of some processed foods to make people feel hungrier still. It was time, he and a handful of others felt, to warn the CEOs that their companies may have gone too far in creating and marketing products that posed the greatest health concerns.

The discussion took place in Pillsbury's auditorium. The first speaker was a vice president of Kraft named Michael Mudd. "I very much appreciate this opportunity to talk to you about childhood obesity and the growing challenge it presents for us all," Mudd began. "Let me say right at the start, this is not an easy subject. There are no easy answers—for what the public-health community must do to bring this problem under control or for what the industry should do as others seek to hold it accountable for what has happened. But this much is clear: For those of us who've looked hard at this issue, whether they're public-health professionals or staff specialists in your own companies, we feel sure that the one thing we shouldn't do is nothing."

As he spoke, Mudd clicked through a deck of slides—114 in all—projected on a large screen behind him. The figures were staggering. More than half of American adults were now considered overweight, with nearly one-quarter of the adult population—40 million people—clinically defined as obese. Among children, the rates had more than doubled since 1980, and the number of kids considered obese had shot past 12 million. (This was still only 1999; the nation's obesity rates would climb much higher.) Food manufacturers were now being blamed for the problem from all sides—academia, the Centers for Disease Control and Prevention, the American Heart Association, and the American Cancer Society. The secretary of agriculture, over whom the industry had long held sway, had recently called obesity a "national epidemic."

Mudd then did the unthinkable. He drew a connection to the last thing in the world the CEOs wanted linked to their products: cigarettes. First came a quote from a Yale University professor of psychology and public health, Kelly Brownell, who was an especially vocal proponent of the view that the processed-food industry should be seen as a public-health menace: "As a culture, we've become upset by the tobacco companies advertising to children, but we sit idly by while the food companies do the very same thing. And we could make a claim that the toll taken on the public health by a poor diet rivals that taken by tobacco."

"If anyone in the food industry ever doubted there was a slippery slope out there," Mudd said, "I imagine they are beginning to experience a distinct sliding sensation right about now."

Mudd then presented the plan he and others had devised to address the obesity problem. Merely getting the executives to acknowledge some culpability was an important first step, he knew, so his plan would start off with a small but crucial move: the industry should use the expertise of scientists—its own and others—to gain a deeper understanding of what was driving

Americans to overeat. Once this was achieved, the effort could unfold on several fronts. To be sure, there would be no getting around the role that packaged foods and drinks play in over-consumption. They would have to pull back on their use of salt, sugar, and fat, perhaps by imposing industrywide limits. But it wasn't just a matter of these three ingredients; the schemes they used to advertise and market their products were critical, too. Mudd proposed creating a "code to guide the nutritional aspects of food marketing, especially to children."

"We are saying that the industry should make a sincere effort to be part of the solution," Mudd concluded. "And that by doing so, we can help to defuse the criticism that's building against us."

What happened next was not written down. But according to three participants, when Mudd stopped talking, the one CEO whose recent exploits in the grocery store had awed the rest of the industry stood up to speak. His name was Stephen Sanger, and he was also the person—as head of General Mills—who had the most to lose when it came to dealing with obesity. Under his leadership, General Mills had overtaken not just the cereal aisle but other sections of the grocery store. The company's Yoplait brand had transformed traditional unsweetened breakfast yogurt into a veritable dessert. It now had twice as much sugar per serving as General Mills' marshmallow cereal Lucky Charms. And yet, because of yogurt's well-tended image as a wholesome snack, sales of Yoplait were soaring, with annual revenue topping $500 million. Emboldened by the success, the company's development wing pushed even harder, inventing a Yoplait variation that came in a squeezable tube—perfect for kids. They called it Go-Gurt and rolled it out nationally in the weeks before the CEO meeting. (By year's end, it would hit $100 million in sales.)

According to the sources I spoke with, Sanger began by re-minding the group that consumers were "fickle." (Sanger de-clined to be interviewed.) Sometimes they worried about sugar, other times fat. General Mills, he said, acted responsibly to both the public and shareholders by offering products to satisfy dieters and other concerned shoppers, from low sugar to added whole grains. But most often, he said, people bought what they liked, and they liked what tasted good. "Don't talk to me about nutrition," he reportedly said, taking on the voice of the typical consumer. "Talk to me about taste, and if this stuff tastes better, don't run around trying to sell stuff that doesn't taste good."

To react to the critics, Sanger said, would jeopardize the sanctity of the recipes that had made his products so successful. General Mills would not pull back. He would push his people onward, and he urged his peers to do the same. Sanger's response effectively ended the meeting.

"What can I say?" James Behnke told me years later. "It didn't work. These guys weren't as receptive as we thought they would be." Behnke chose his words deliberately. He wanted to be fair. "Sanger was trying to say, 'Look, we're not going to screw around with the company jewels here and change the formulations because a bunch of guys in white coats are worried about obesity.'"

The meeting was remarkable, first, for the insider admissions of guilt. But I was also struck by how prescient the organizers of the sit-down had been. Today, one in three adults is considered clinically obese, along with one in five kids, and 24 million Americans are afflicted by type-two diabetes, often caused by poor diet, with another 79 million people having pre-diabetes. Even gout, a painful form of arthritis once known as "the rich man's disease" for its associations with gluttony, now afflicts eight million Americans.

The public and the food companies have known for decades now—or at the very least since this meeting—that sugary, salty, fatty foods are not good for us in the quantities that we consume them. So why are the diabetes and obesity and hypertension numbers still spiraling out of control? It's not just a matter of poor willpower on the part of the consumer and a give-the-people-what-they-want attitude on the part of the food manufacturers. What I found, over four years of research and reporting, was a conscious effort—taking place in labs and marketing meetings and grocery-store aisles—to get people hooked on foods that are convenient and inexpensive. I talked to more than 300 people in or formerly employed by the processed-food industry, from scientists to marketers to CEOs. Some were willing whistle-blowers, while others spoke reluctantly when presented with some of the thousands of pages of secret memos that I obtained from inside the food industry's operations. What follows is a series of small case studies of a handful of characters whose work then, and perspective now, sheds light on how the foods are created and sold to people who, while not powerless, are extremely vulnerable to the intensity of these companies' industrial formulations and selling campaigns.

I. "In This Field, I'm a Game Changer"

John Lennon couldn't find it in England, so he had cases of it shipped from New York to fuel the "Imagine" sessions. The Beach Boys, ZZ Top, and Cher all stipulated in their contract riders that it be put in their dressing rooms when they toured. Hillary Clinton asked for it when she traveled as first lady, and ever after her hotel suites were dutifully stocked.

What they all wanted was Dr Pepper, which until 2001 occupied a comfortable third-place spot in the soda aisle behind Coca-Cola and Pepsi. But then a flood of spinoffs from the two soda giants showed up on the shelves—lemons and limes, vanillas and coffees, raspberries and oranges, whites and blues and clears—what in food-industry lingo are known as "line extensions," and Dr Pepper started to lose its market share.

Responding to this pressure, Cadbury Schweppes created its first spinoff, other than a diet version, in the soda's 115-year history, a bright red soda with a very un–Dr Pepper name: Red Fusion. "If we are to reestablish Dr Pepper back to its historic growth rates, we have to add more excitement," the company's president, Jack Kilduff, said. One particularly promising market, Kilduff pointed out, was the "rapidly growing Hispanic and African American communities."

But consumers hated Red Fusion. "Dr Pepper is my all-time favorite drink, so I was curious about the Red Fusion," a California mother of three wrote on a blog to warn other Peppers away. "It's disgusting. Gagging. Never again."

Stung by the rejection, Cadbury Schweppes in 2004 turned to a food-industry legend named Howard Moskowitz. Moskowitz, who studied mathematics and holds a Ph.D. in experimental psychology from Harvard, runs a consulting firm in White Plains, where for more than three decades he has "optimized" a variety of products for Campbell Soup, General Foods, Kraft, and PepsiCo. "I've optimized soups," Moskowitz told me. "I've optimized pizzas. I've optimized salad dressings and pickles. In this field, I'm a game changer."

In the process of product optimization, food engineers alter a litany of variables with the sole intent of finding the most perfect version (or versions) of a product. Ordinary consumers are paid to spend hours sitting in rooms where they touch, feel, sip, smell, swirl, and taste whatever product is in question. Their opinions are dumped into a computer, and the data are sifted and sorted through a statistical method called conjoint analysis, which determines what features will be most attractive to consumers. Moskowitz likes to imagine that his computer is divided into silos, in which each of the attributes is stacked. But it's not simply a matter of comparing Color 23 with Color 24. In the most complicated projects, Color 23 must be combined with Syrup 11 and Packaging 6, and on and on, in seemingly infinite combinations. Even for jobs in which the only concern is taste and the variables are limited to the ingredients, endless charts and graphs will come spewing out of Moskowitz's computer. "The mathematical model maps out the ingredients to the sensory perceptions these ingredients create," he told me, "so I can just dial a new product. This is the engineering approach."

Moskowitz's work on Prego spaghetti sauce was memorialized in a 2004 presentation by the author Malcolm Gladwell at the TED conference in Monterey, Calif.:

> After . . . months and months, he had a mountain of data about how the American people feel about spaghetti sauce. . . . And sure enough, if you sit down and you analyze all this data on spaghetti sauce, you realize that all Americans fall into one of three groups. There are people who like their spaghetti sauce plain. There are people who like their spaghetti sauce spicy. And there are people who like it extra-chunky. And of those three facts, the third one was the most significant, because at the time, in the early 1980s, if you went to a supermarket, you would not find extra-chunky spaghetti sauce. And Prego turned to Howard, and they said, "Are you telling me that one-third of Americans crave extra-chunky spaghetti sauce, and yet no one is servicing their needs?" And he said, "Yes." And Prego then went back and completely re-formulated their spaghetti sauce and came out with a line of extra-chunky that immediately and completely took over the spaghetti-sauce business in this country. . . . That is Howard's gift to the American people. . . . He fundamentally changed the way the food industry thinks about making you happy.

Well, yes and no. One thing Gladwell didn't mention is that the food industry already knew some things about making people happy—and it started with sugar. Many of the Prego sauces—whether cheesy, chunky, or light—have one feature in common: The largest ingredient, after tomatoes, is sugar. A mere half-cup of Prego Traditional, for instance, has the equivalent of more than two teaspoons of sugar, as much as two-plus Oreo cookies. It also delivers one-third of the sodium recommended for a majority of American adults for an entire day. In making these sauces, Campbell supplied the ingredients, including the salt, sugar, and, for some versions, fat, while Moskowitz supplied the optimization. "More is not necessarily better," Moskowitz wrote in his own account of the Prego project. "As the sensory intensity (say, of sweetness) increases, consumers first say that they like the product more, but eventually, with a middle level of sweetness, consumers like the product the most (this is their optimum, or 'bliss,' point)."

．　　　．　　　．

I first met Moskowitz on a crisp day in the spring of 2010 at the Harvard Club in Midtown Manhattan. As we talked, he made clear that while he has worked on numerous projects aimed at creating more healthful foods and insists the industry could be doing far more to curb obesity, he had no qualms about his own pioneering work on discovering what industry insiders now regularly refer to as "the bliss point" or any of the other systems that helped food companies create the greatest amount of crave. "There's no moral issue for me," he said. "I did the best science I could. I was struggling to survive and didn't have the luxury of being a moral creature. As a researcher, I was ahead of my time."

Moskowitz's path to mastering the bliss point began in earnest not at Harvard but a few months after graduation, sixteen miles from Cambridge, in the town of Natick, where the U.S. Army hired him to work in its research labs. The military has long been in a peculiar bind when it comes to food: how to get soldiers to eat more rations when they are in the field. They know that over time, soldiers would gradually find their meals-ready-to-eat so boring that they would toss them away, half-eaten, and not get all the calories they needed. But what was causing this MRE fatigue was a mystery. "So I started asking soldiers how frequently they would like to eat this or that, trying to figure out which products they would find boring," Moskowitz said. The answers he got were inconsistent. "They liked flavorful foods like turkey tetrazzini, but only at first; they quickly grew tired of them. On the other hand, mundane foods like white bread would never get them too excited, but they could eat lots and lots of it without feeling they'd had enough."

This contradiction is known as "sensory-specific satiety." In lay terms, it is the tendency for big, distinct flavors to overwhelm the brain, which responds by depressing your desire to have more. Sensory-specific satiety also became a guiding principle for the processed-food industry. The biggest hits—be they Coca-Cola or Doritos—owe their success to complex formulas that pique the taste buds enough to be alluring but don't have a distinct, overriding single flavor that tells the brain to stop eating.

Thirty-two years after he began experimenting with the bliss point, Moskowitz got the call from Cadbury Schweppes asking him to create a good line extension for Dr Pepper. I spent an afternoon in his White Plains offices as he and his vice president for research, Michele Reisner, walked me through the Dr Pepper campaign. Cadbury wanted its new flavor to have cherry and vanilla on top of the basic Dr Pepper taste. Thus, there were three main components to play with. A sweet cherry flavoring, a sweet vanilla flavoring and a sweet syrup known as "Dr Pepper flavoring."

Finding the bliss point required the preparation of sixty-one subtly distinct formulas—thirty-one for the regular version and thirty for diet. The formulas were then subjected to 3,904 tastings organized in Los Angeles, Dallas, Chicago, and Philadelphia. The Dr Pepper tasters began working through their samples, resting five minutes between each sip to restore their taste buds. After each sample, they gave numerically ranked answers to a set of questions: How much did they like it overall? How strong is the taste? How do they feel about the taste? How would they describe the quality of this product? How likely would they be to purchase this product?

Moskowitz's data—compiled in a 135-page report for the soda maker—are tremendously fine-grained, showing how different people and groups of people feel about a strong vanilla taste versus weak, various aspects of aroma and the powerful sensory force that food scientists call "mouth feel." This is the way a product interacts with the mouth, as defined more specifically by a host of related sensations, from dryness to gumminess to moisture release. These are terms more familiar to sommeliers, but the mouth feel of soda and many other food items, especially those high in fat, is second only to the bliss point in its ability to predict how much craving a product will induce.

In addition to taste, the consumers were also tested on their response to color, which proved to be highly sensitive. "When we increased the level of the Dr Pepper flavoring, it gets darker and liking goes off," Reisner said. These preferences can also be cross-referenced by age, sex, and race.

On page 83 of the report, a thin blue line represents the amount of Dr Pepper flavoring needed to generate maximum appeal. The line is shaped like an upside-down U, just like the bliss-point curve that Moskowitz studied thirty years earlier in his army lab. And at the top of the arc, there is not a single sweet spot but instead a sweet range, within which "bliss" was achievable. This meant that Cadbury could edge back on its key ingredient, the sugary Dr Pepper syrup, without falling out of the range and losing the bliss. Instead of using 2 milliliters of the flavoring, for instance, they could use 1.69 milliliters and achieve the same effect. The potential savings is merely a few percentage points, and it won't mean much to individual consumers who are counting calories or grams of sugar. But for Dr Pepper, it adds up to colossal savings. "That looks like nothing," Reisner said. "But it's a lot of money. A lot of money. Millions."

The soda that emerged from all of Moskowitz's variations became known as Cherry Vanilla Dr Pepper, and it proved successful beyond anything Cadbury imagined. In 2008, Cadbury split off its soft-drinks business, which included Snapple and 7-Up. The Dr Pepper Snapple Group has since been valued in excess of $11 billion.

II. "Lunchtime Is All Yours"

Sometimes innovations within the food industry happen in the lab, with scientists dialing in specific ingredients to achieve the greatest allure. And sometimes, as in the case of Oscar Mayer's bologna crisis, the innovation involves putting old products in new packages.

The 1980s were tough times for Oscar Mayer. Red-meat consumption fell more than 10 percent as fat became synonymous with cholesterol, clogged arteries, heart attacks, and strokes. Anxiety set in at the company's headquarters in Madison, Wis., where executives worried about their future and the pressure they faced from their new bosses at Philip Morris.

Bob Drane was the company's vice president for new business strategy and development when Oscar Mayer tapped him to try to find some way to reposition bologna and other troubled meats that were declining in popularity and sales. I met Drane at his home in Madison and went through the records he had kept on the birth of what would become much more than his solution to the company's meat problem. In 1985, when Drane began working on the project, his orders were to "figure out how to contemporize what we've got."

Drane's first move was to try to zero in not on what Americans felt about processed meat but on what Americans felt about lunch. He organized focus-group sessions with the people most responsible for buying bologna—mothers—and as they talked, he realized the most pressing issue for them was time. Working moms strove to provide healthful food, of course, but they spoke with real passion and at length about the morning crush, that nightmarish dash to get breakfast on the table and lunch packed and kids out the door. He summed up their remarks for me like this: "It's awful. I am scrambling around. My kids are asking me for stuff. I'm trying to get myself ready to go to the office. I go to pack these lunches, and I don't know what I've got." What the moms revealed to him, Drane said, was "a gold mine of disappointments and problems."

He assembled a team of about fifteen people with varied skills, from design to food science to advertising, to create something completely new—a convenient prepackaged lunch that would have as its main building block the company's sliced bologna and ham. They wanted to add bread, naturally, because who ate bologna without it? But this presented a problem: There was no way bread could stay fresh for the two months their product needed to sit in warehouses or in grocery coolers. Crackers, however, could—so they added a handful of cracker rounds to the package. Using cheese was the next obvious move, given its increased presence in processed foods. But what kind of cheese would work? Natural cheddar, which they started off with, crumbled and didn't slice very well, so they moved on to processed varieties, which could bend and be sliced and would last forever, or they could knock another two cents off per unit by using an even lesser product called "cheese food," which had lower scores than processed cheese in taste tests. The cost dilemma was solved when Oscar Mayer merged with Kraft in 1989 and the company didn't have to shop for cheese anymore; it got all the processed cheese it wanted from its new sister company, and at cost.

Drane's team moved into a nearby hotel, where they set out to find the right mix of components and container. They gathered around tables where bagfuls of meat, cheese, crackers, and all sorts of wrapping material had been dumped, and they let their imaginations run. After snipping and taping their way through a host of failures, the model they fell back on was the American TV dinner—and after some brainstorming about names (Lunch Kits? Go-Packs? Fun Mealz?), Lunchables were born.

The trays flew off the grocery-store shelves. Sales hit a phenomenal $218 million in the first twelve months, more than anyone was prepared for. This only brought Drane his next crisis. The production costs were so high that they were losing money with each tray they produced. So Drane flew to New York, where he met with Philip Morris officials who promised to give him the money he needed to keep it going. "The hard thing is to figure out something that will sell," he was told. "You'll figure out how to get the cost right." Projected to lose $6 million in 1991, the trays instead broke even; the next year, they earned $8 million.

With production costs trimmed and profits coming in, the next question was how to expand the franchise, which they did by turning to one of the cardinal rules in processed food: When in doubt, add sugar. "Lunchables With Dessert is a logical extension," an Oscar Mayer official reported to Philip Morris executives in early 1991. The "target" remained the same as it was for regular Lunchables—"busy mothers" and "working women," ages twenty-five to forty-nine—and the "enhanced taste" would attract shoppers who had grown bored with the current trays. A year later, the dessert Lunchable morphed into the Fun Pack, which would come with a Snickers bar, a package of M&Ms, or a Reese's Peanut Butter Cup, as well as a sugary drink. The Lunchables team started by using Kool-Aid and cola and then Capri Sun after Philip Morris added that drink to its stable of brands.

Eventually, a line of the trays, appropriately called Maxed Out, was released that had as many as nine grams of saturated fat, or nearly an entire day's recommended maximum for kids, with up to two-thirds of the max for sodium and thirteen teaspoons of sugar.

When I asked Geoffrey Bible, former CEO of Philip Morris, about this shift toward more salt, sugar, and fat in meals for kids, he smiled and noted that even in its earliest incarnation, Lunchables was held up for criticism. "One article said something like, 'If you take Lunchables apart, the most healthy item in it is the napkin.'"

Well, they did have a good bit of fat, I offered. "You bet," he said. "Plus cookies."

The prevailing attitude among the company's food managers—through the 1990s, at least, before obesity became a more pressing concern—was one of supply and demand. "People could point to these things and say, 'They've got too much sugar, they've got too much salt,'" Bible said. "Well, that's what the consumer wants, and we're not putting a gun to their head to eat it. That's what they want. If we give them less, they'll buy less, and the competitor will get our market. So you're sort of trapped." (Bible would later press Kraft to reconsider its reliance on salt, sugar, and fat.)

When it came to Lunchables, they did try to add more healthful ingredients. Back at the start, Drane experimented with fresh carrots but quickly gave up on that, since fresh components didn't work within the constraints of the processed-food system, which typically required weeks or months of transport and storage before the food arrived at the grocery store. Later, a low-fat version of the trays was developed, using meats and cheese and crackers that were formulated with less fat, but it tasted inferior, sold poorly, and was quickly scrapped.

When I met with Kraft officials in 2011 to discuss their products and policies on nutrition, they had dropped the Maxed Out line and were trying to improve the nutritional profile of Lunchables through smaller, incremental changes that were less noticeable to consumers. Across the Lunchables line, they said they had reduced the salt, sugar, and fat by about 10 percent, and new versions, featuring mandarin-orange and pineapple slices, were in development. These would be promoted as more healthful versions, with "fresh fruit," but their list of ingredients—containing upward of seventy items, with sucrose, corn syrup, high-fructose corn syrup, and fruit concentrate all in the same tray—have been met with intense criticism from outside the industry.

One of the company's responses to criticism is that kids don't eat the Lunchables every day—on top of which, when it came to trying to feed them more healthful foods, kids themselves were unreliable. When their parents packed fresh carrots, apples, and water, they couldn't be trusted to eat them. Once in school, they often trashed the healthful stuff in their brown bags to get right to the sweets.

This idea—that kids are in control—would become a key concept in the evolving marketing campaigns for the trays. In what would prove to be their greatest achievement of all, the Lunchables team would delve into adolescent psychology to discover that it wasn't the food in the trays that excited the kids; it was the feeling of power it brought to their lives. As Bob Eckert, then the CEO of Kraft, put it in 1999: "Lunchables aren't about lunch. It's about kids being able to put together what they want to eat, anytime, anywhere."

Kraft's early Lunchables campaign targeted mothers. They might be too distracted by work to make a lunch, but they loved their kids enough to offer them this prepackaged gift. But as the focus swung toward kids, Saturday-morning cartoons started carrying an ad that offered a different message: "All day, you gotta do what they say," the ads said. "But lunchtime is all yours."

With this marketing strategy in place and pizza Lunchables—the crust in one compartment, the cheese, pepperoni and sauce in others—proving to be a runaway success, the entire world of fast food suddenly opened up for Kraft to pursue. They came out with a Mexican-themed Lunchables called Beef Taco Wraps; a Mini Burgers Lunchables; a Mini Hot Dog Lunchable, which also happened to provide a way for Oscar Mayer to sell its wieners. By 1999, pancakes—which included syrup, icing, Lifesavers candy, and Tang, for a whopping 76 grams of sugar—and waffles were, for a time, part of the Lunchables franchise as well.

Annual sales kept climbing, past $500 million, past $800 million; at last count, including sales in Britain, they were approaching the $1 billion mark. Lunchables was more than a hit; it was now its own category. Eventually, more than sixty varieties of Lunchables and other brands of trays would show up in the grocery stores. In 2007, Kraft even tried a Lunchables Jr. for three- to five-year-olds.

In the trove of records that document the rise of the Lunchables and the sweeping change it brought to lunchtime habits, I came across a photograph of Bob Drane's daughter, which he had slipped into the Lunchables presentation he showed to food developers. The picture was taken on Monica Drane's wedding day in 1989, and she was standing outside the family's home in Madison, a beautiful bride in a white wedding dress, holding one of the brand-new yellow trays.

During the course of reporting, I finally had a chance to ask her about it. Was she really that much of a fan? "There must have been some in the fridge," she told me. "I probably just took one out before we went to the church. My mom had joked that it was really like their fourth child, my dad invested so much time and energy on it."

Monica Drane had three of her own children by the time we spoke, ages ten, fourteen, and seventeen. "I don't think my kids have ever eaten a Lunchable," she told me. "They know they exist and that Grandpa Bob invented them. But we eat very healthfully."

Drane himself paused only briefly when I asked him if, looking back, he was proud of creating the trays. "Lots of things are trade-offs," he said. "And I do believe it's easy to rationalize anything. In the end, I wish that the nutritional profile of the thing could have been better, but I don't view the entire project as anything but a positive contribution to people's lives."

Today Bob Drane is still talking to kids about what they like to eat, but his approach has changed. He volunteers with a non-profit organization that seeks to build better communications between school kids and their parents, and right in the mix of their problems, alongside the academic struggles, is childhood obesity. Drane has also prepared a précis on the food industry that he used with medical students at the University of Wisconsin. And while he does not name his Lunchables in this document, and cites numerous causes for the obesity epidemic, he holds the entire industry accountable. "What do University of Wisconsin MBAs learn about how to succeed in marketing?" his presentation to the med students asks. "Discover what consumers want to buy and give it to them with both barrels. Sell more, keep your job! How do marketers often translate these 'rules' into action on food? Our limbic brains love sugar, fat, salt. . . . So formulate products to deliver these. Perhaps add low-cost ingredients to boost profit margins. Then 'supersize' to sell more. . . . And advertise/promote to lock in 'heavy users.' Plenty of guilt to go around here!"

III. "It's Called Vanishing Caloric Density"

At a symposium for nutrition scientists in Los Angeles on February 15, 1985, a professor of pharmacology from Helsinki named Heikki Karppanen told the remarkable story of Finland's effort to address its salt habit. In the late 1970s, the Finns were consuming huge amounts of sodium, eating on average more than two teaspoons of salt a day. As a result, the country had developed significant issues with high blood pressure, and men in the eastern part of Finland had the highest rate of fatal cardiovascular disease in the world. Research showed that this plague was not just a quirk of genetics or a result of a sedentary lifestyle—it was also owing to processed foods. So when Finnish authorities moved to address the problem, they went right after the manufacturers. (The Finnish response worked. Every grocery item that was heavy in salt would come to be marked prominently with the warning "High Salt Content." By 2007, Finland's per capita consumption of salt had dropped by a third, and this shift—along with improved medical care—was accompanied by a 75 percent to 80 percent decline in the number of deaths from strokes and heart disease.)

Karppanen's presentation was met with applause, but one man in the crowd seemed particularly intrigued by the presentation, and as Karppanen left the stage, the man intercepted him and asked if they could talk more over dinner. Their conversation later that night was not at all what Karppanen was expecting. His host did indeed have an interest in salt, but from quite a different vantage point: the man's name was Robert I-San Lin, and from 1974 to 1982, he worked as the chief scientist for Frito-Lay, the nearly $3-billion-a-year manufacturer of Lay's, Doritos, Cheetos, and Fritos.

Lin's time at Frito-Lay coincided with the first attacks by nutrition advocates on salty foods and the first calls for federal regulators to reclassify salt as a "risky" food additive, which could have subjected it to severe controls. No company took this threat more seriously—or more personally—than Frito-Lay, Lin explained to Karppanen over their dinner. Three years after he left Frito-Lay, he was still anguished over his inability to effectively change the company's recipes and practices.

By chance, I ran across a letter that Lin sent to Karppanen three weeks after that dinner, buried in some files to which I had gained access. Attached to the letter was a memo written when Lin was at Frito-Lay, which detailed some of the company's efforts in defending salt. I tracked Lin down in Irvine, Calif., where we spent several days going through the internal company memos, strategy papers, and handwritten notes he had kept. The documents were evidence of the concern that Lin had for consumers and of the company's intent on using science not to address the health concerns but to thwart them. While at Frito-Lay, Lin and other company scientists spoke openly about the country's excessive consumption of sodium and the fact that, as Lin said to me on more than one occasion, "people get addicted to salt."

Not much had changed by 1986, except Frito-Lay found itself on a rare cold streak. The company had introduced a series of high-profile products that failed miserably. Toppels, a cracker with cheese topping; Stuffers, a shell with a variety of fillings; Rumbles, a bite-size granola snack—they all came and went in a blink, and the company took a $52 million hit. Around that time, the marketing team was joined by Dwight Riskey, an expert on cravings who had been a fellow at the Monell Chemical Senses Center in Philadelphia, where he was part of a team of scientists that found that people could beat their salt habits simply by refraining from salty foods long enough for their taste buds to return to a normal level of sensitivity. He had also done work on the bliss point, showing how a product's allure is contextual, shaped partly by the other foods a person is eating, and that it changes as people age. This seemed to help explain why Frito-Lay was having so much trouble selling new snacks. The largest single block of customers, the baby boomers, had begun hitting middle age. According to the research, this suggested that their liking for salty snacks—both in the concentration of salt and how much they ate—would be tapering off. Along with the rest of the snack-food industry, Frito-Lay anticipated lower sales because of an aging population, and marketing plans were adjusted to focus even more intently on younger consumers.

Except that snack sales didn't decline as everyone had projected, Frito-Lay's doomed product launches notwithstanding. Poring over data one day in his home office, trying to understand just who was consuming all the snack food, Riskey realized that he and his colleagues had been misreading things all along. They had been measuring the snacking habits of different age groups and were seeing what they expected to see, that older consumers ate less than those in their twenties. But what they weren't measuring, Riskey realized, is how those snacking habits of the boomers compared to *themselves* when they were in their twenties. When he called up a new set of sales data and performed what's called a cohort study, following a single group over time, a far more encouraging picture—for Frito-Lay, anyway—emerged. The baby boomers were not eating fewer salty snacks as they aged. "In fact, as those people aged, their consumption of all those segments—the cookies, the crackers, the candy, the chips— was going up," Riskey said. "They were not only eating what they ate when they were younger, they were eating more of it." In fact, everyone in the country, on average, was eating more salty snacks than they used to. The rate of consumption was edging up about one-third of a pound every year, with the average intake of snacks like chips and cheese crackers pushing past twelve pounds a year.

Riskey had a theory about what caused this surge: Eating real meals had become a thing of the past. Baby boomers, especially, seemed to have greatly cut down on regular meals. They were skipping breakfast when they had early-morning meetings. They skipped lunch when they then needed to catch up on work because of those meetings. They skipped dinner when their kids stayed out late or grew up and moved out of the house. And when they skipped these meals, they replaced them with snacks. "We looked at this behavior, and said, 'Oh, my gosh, people were skipping meals right and left,'" Riskey told me. "It was amazing." This led to the next realization, that baby boomers did not represent "a category that is mature, with no growth. This is a category that has huge growth potential."

The food technicians stopped worrying about inventing new products and instead embraced the industry's most reliable method for getting consumers to buy more: the line extension. The classic Lay's potato chips were joined by Salt & Vinegar, Salt &

Pepper, and Cheddar & Sour Cream. They put out chili-cheese-flavored Fritos, and Cheetos were transformed into twenty-one varieties. Frito-Lay had a formidable research complex near Dallas, where nearly 500 chemists, psychologists, and technicians conducted research that cost up to $30 million a year, and the science corps focused intense amounts of resources on questions of crunch, mouth feel, and aroma for each of these items. Their tools included a $40,000 device that simulated a chewing mouth to test and perfect the chips, discovering things like the perfect break point: people like a chip that snaps with about four pounds of pressure per square inch.

To get a better feel for their work, I called on Steven Witherly, a food scientist who wrote a fascinating guide for industry insiders titled, "Why Humans Like Junk Food." I brought him two shopping bags filled with a variety of chips to taste. He zeroed right in on the Cheetos. "This," Witherly said, "is one of the most marvelously constructed foods on the planet, in terms of pure pleasure." He ticked off a dozen attributes of the Cheetos that make the brain say more. But the one he focused on most was the puff's uncanny ability to melt in the mouth. "It's called vanishing caloric density," Witherly said. "If something melts down quickly, your brain thinks that there's no calories in it . . . you can just keep eating it forever."

As for their marketing troubles, in a March 2010 meeting, Frito-Lay executives hastened to tell their Wall Street investors that the 1.4 billion boomers worldwide weren't being neglected; they were redoubling their efforts to understand exactly what it was that boomers most wanted in a snack chip. Which was basically everything: great taste, maximum bliss but minimal guilt about health, and more maturity than puffs. "They snack a lot," Frito-Lay's chief marketing officer, Ann Mukherjee, told the investors. "But what they're looking for is very different. They're looking for new experiences, real food experiences." Frito-Lay acquired Stacy's Pita Chip Company, which was started by a

Massachusetts couple who made food-cart sandwiches and started serving pita chips to their customers in the mid-1990s. In Frito-Lay's hands, the pita chips averaged 270 milligrams of sodium—nearly one-fifth a whole day's recommended maximum for most American adults—and were a huge hit among boomers.

The Frito-Lay executives also spoke of the company's ongoing pursuit of a "designer sodium," which they hoped, in the near future, would take their sodium loads down by 40 percent. No need to worry about lost sales there, the company's CEO, Al Carey, assured their investors. The boomers would see less salt as the green light to snack like never before.

There's a paradox at work here. On the one hand, reduction of sodium in snack foods is commendable. On the other, these changes may well result in consumers eating more. "The big thing that will happen here is removing the barriers for boomers and giving them permission to snack," Carey said. The prospects for lower-salt snacks were so amazing, he added, that the company had set its sights on using the designer salt to conquer the toughest market of all for snacks: schools. He cited, for example, the school-food initiative championed by Bill Clinton and the American Heart Association, which is seeking to improve the nutrition of school food by limiting its load of salt, sugar, and fat. "Imagine this," Carey said. "A potato chip that tastes great and qualifies for the Clinton-AHA alliance for schools. . . . We think we have ways to do all of this on a potato chip, and imagine getting that product into schools, where children can have this product and grow up with it and feel good about eating it."

Carey's quote reminded me of something I read in the early stages of my reporting, a twenty-four-page report prepared for Frito-Lay in 1957 by a psychologist named Ernest Dichter. The company's chips, he wrote, were not selling as well as they could for one simple reason: "While people like and enjoy potato chips, they feel guilty about liking them. . . . Unconsciously, people expect to be punished for 'letting themselves go' and enjoying them." Dichter listed seven "fears and resistances" to the chips: "You can't stop eating them; they're fattening; they're not good for you; they're greasy and messy to eat; they're too expensive; it's hard to store the leftovers; and they're bad for children." He spent the rest of his memo laying out his prescriptions, which in time would become widely used not just by Frito-Lay but also by the entire industry. Dichter suggested that Frito-Lay avoid using the word "fried" in referring to its chips and adopt instead the more healthful-sounding term "toasted." To counteract the "fear of letting oneself go," he suggested repacking the chips into smaller bags. "The more-anxious consumers, the ones who have the deepest fears about their capacity to control their appetite, will tend to sense the function of the new pack and select it," he said.

Dichter advised Frito-Lay to move its chips out of the realm of between-meals snacking and turn them into an ever-present item in the American diet. "The increased use of potato chips and other Lay's products as a part of the regular fare served by restaurants and sandwich bars should be encouraged in a con-centrated way," Dichter said, citing a string of examples: "potato chips with soup, with fruit or vegetable juice appetizers; potato chips served as a vegetable on the main dish; potato chips with salad; potato chips with egg dishes for breakfast; potato chips with sandwich orders."

In 2011, The New England Journal of Medicine published a study that shed new light on America's weight gain. The subjects—120,877 women and men—were all professionals in the health field, and were likely to be more conscious about nutrition, so the findings might well understate the overall trend. Using data back to 1986, the researchers monitored everything the participants ate, as well as their physical activity and smok-ing. They found that every four years, the participants exercised less, watched TV more, and gained an average of 3.35 pounds. The researchers parsed the data by the caloric content of the foods being eaten, and found the top contributors to weight gain included red meat and processed meats, sugar-sweetened beverages, and potatoes, including mashed and French fries. But the largest weight-inducing food was the potato chip. The coating of salt, the fat content that rewards the brain with instant feelings of pleasure, the sugar that exists not as an additive but in the starch of the potato itself—all of this combines to make it the perfect addictive food. "The starch is readily absorbed," Eric Rimm, an associate professor of epidemiology and nutrition at the Harvard School of Public Health and one of the study's authors, told me. "More quickly even than a similar amount of sugar. The starch, in turn, causes the glucose levels in the blood to spike"—which can result in a craving for more.

If Americans snacked only occasionally, and in small amounts, this would not present the enormous problem that it does. But because so much money and effort has been invested over decades in engineering and then relentlessly selling these products, the effects are seemingly impossible to unwind. More than thirty years have passed since Robert Lin first tangled with Frito-Lay on the imperative of the company to deal with the formulation of its snacks, but as we sat at his dining-room table, sifting through his records, the feelings of regret still played on his face. In his view, three decades had been lost, time that he and a lot of other smart scientists could have spent searching for ways to ease the addiction to salt, sugar, and fat. "I couldn't do much about it," he told me. "I feel so sorry for the public."

IV. "These People Need a Lot of Things, but They Don't Need a Coke"

The growing attention Americans are paying to what they put into their mouths has touched off a new scramble by the processed-food companies to address health concerns. Pressed by the Obama administration and consumers, Kraft, Nestlé, Pepsi, Campbell, and General Mills, among others, have begun to trim the loads of salt, sugar, and fat in many products. And with consumer advocates pushing for more government intervention, Coca-Cola made headlines in January by releasing ads that promoted its bottled water and low-calorie drinks as a way to counter obesity. Predictably, the ads drew a new volley of scorn from critics who pointed to the company's continuing drive to sell sugary Coke.

One of the other executives I spoke with at length was Jeffrey Dunn, who, in 2001, at age forty-four, was directing more than half of Coca-Cola's $20 billion in annual sales as president and chief operating officer in both North and South America. In an effort to control as much market share as possible, Coke extended its aggressive marketing to especially poor or vulnerable areas of the United States, like New Orleans—where people were drinking twice as much Coke as the national average—or Rome, Ga., where the per capita intake was nearly three Cokes a day. In Coke's headquarters in Atlanta, the biggest consumers were referred to as "heavy users." "The other model we use was called 'drinks and drinkers,'" Dunn said. "How many drinkers do I have? And how many drinks do they drink? If you lost one of those heavy users, if somebody just decided to stop drinking Coke, how many drinkers would you have to get, at low velocity, to make up for that heavy user? The answer is a lot. It's more efficient to get my existing users to drink more."

One of Dunn's lieutenants, Todd Putman, who worked at Coca-Cola from 1997 to 2001, said the goal became much larger than merely beating the rival brands; Coca-Cola strove to outsell every other thing people drank, including milk and water. The marketing division's efforts boiled down to one question, Putman said: "How can we drive more ounces into more bodies more often?" (In response to Putman's remarks, Coke said its goals have changed and that it now focuses on providing consumers with more low- or no-calorie products.)

In his capacity, Dunn was making frequent trips to Brazil, where the company had recently begun a push to increase consumption of Coke among the many Brazilians living in *favelas*. The company's strategy was to repackage Coke into smaller, more affordable 6.7-ounce bottles, just twenty cents each. Coke was not alone in seeing Brazil as a potential boon; Nestlé began deploying battalions of women to travel poor neighborhoods, hawking American-style processed foods door to door. But Coke was Dunn's concern, and on one trip, as he walked through one of the impoverished areas, he had an epiphany. "A voice in my head says, 'These people need a lot of things, but they don't need a Coke.' I almost threw up."

Dunn returned to Atlanta, determined to make some changes. He didn't want to abandon the soda business, but he did want to try to steer the company into a more healthful mode, and one of the things he pushed for was to stop marketing Coke in public schools. The independent companies that bottled Coke viewed his plans as reactionary. A director of one bottler wrote a letter to Coke's chief executive and board asking for Dunn's head. "He said what I had done was the worst thing he had seen in fifty years in the business," Dunn said. "Just to placate these crazy leftist school districts who were trying to keep people from having their Coke. He said I was an embarrassment to the company, and I should be fired." In February 2004, he was.

Dunn told me that talking about Coke's business today was by no means easy and, because he continues to work in the food business, not without risk. "You really don't want them mad at you," he said. "And I don't mean that, like, I'm going to end up at the bottom of the bay. But they don't have a sense of humor when it comes to this stuff. They're a very, very aggressive company."

When I met with Dunn, he told me not just about his years at Coke but also about his new marketing venture. In April 2010, he met with three executives from Madison Dearborn Partners, .

a private-equity firm based in Chicago with a wide-ranging portfolio of investments. They recently hired Dunn to run one of their newest acquisitions—a food producer in the San Joaquin Valley. As they sat in the hotel's meeting room, the men listened to Dunn's marketing pitch. He talked about giving the product a personality that was bold and irreverent, conveying the idea that this was the ultimate snack food. He went into detail on how he would target a special segment of the 146 million Americans who are regular snackers—mothers, children, young professionals— people, he said, who "keep their snacking ritual fresh by trying a new food product when it catches their attention."

He explained how he would deploy strategic storytelling in the ad campaign for this snack, using a key phrase that had been developed with much calculation: "Eat 'Em Like Junk Food."

After forty-five minutes, Dunn clicked off the last slide and thanked the men for coming. Madison's portfolio contained the largest Burger King franchise in the world, the Ruth's Chris Steak House chain, and a processed-food maker called AdvancePierre whose lineup includes the Jamwich, a peanut-butter-and-jelly contrivance that comes frozen, crustless, and embedded with four kinds of sugars.

The snack that Dunn was proposing to sell: carrots. Plain, fresh carrots. No added sugar. No creamy sauce or dips. No salt. Just baby carrots, washed, bagged, then sold into the deadly dull produce aisle.

"We act like a snack, not a vegetable," he told the investors. "We exploit the rules of junk food to fuel the baby-carrot conversation. We are pro-junk-food behavior but anti-junk-food establishment."

The investors were thinking only about sales. They had already bought one of the two biggest farm producers of baby carrots in the country, and they'd hired Dunn to run the whole operation. Now, after his pitch, they were relieved. Dunn had figured out that using the industry's own marketing ploys would work better than anything else. He drew from the bag of tricks that he mastered in his twenty years at Coca-Cola, where he learned one of the most critical rules in processed food: The selling of food matters as much as the food itself.

Later, describing his new line of work, Dunn told me he was doing penance for his Coca-Cola years. "I'm paying my karmic debt," he said.

Frontline

Mamas, don't let your babies grow up to be Cowboys—or members of any other NFL football team. You may have a hard time watching football after reading the transcript of *Frontline*'s account of a concerted effort by the National Football League to deny the damage done by the game to the health of its players and the league's willingness to allow players to sacrifice their bodies and brains for the lucrative franchise.

Michael Kirk, Mike
Wiser, Steve Fainaru,
and Mark Fainaru-Wada

21. League of Denial

The NFL's Concussion
Crisis

ANNOUNCER: Tonight on *Frontline,* the epic story of football's concussion crisis.

HARRY CARSON, AUTHOR, *Captain for Life*: These players come down with dementia.

ANNOUNCER: A major *Frontline* investigation of what the NFL knew and when it knew it.

STEVE FAINARU, *Frontline*/ESPN: The level of denial was just profound.

BETH WILKINSON, NFL'S ATTORNEY: We strongly deny those allegations that we withheld any information or misled the players.

DR. MICKEY COLLINS, UNIV. OF PITTSBURGH MEDICAL CTR.: We don't know who is at risk for it. We don't know if concussion in and of itself is what causes the abnormalities.

ANNOUNCER: A decades-long battle between scientists, players, and the nation's most powerful sports league.

BENNET OMALU, MD, MEDICAL EXAMINER: You can't go against the NFL. They will squash you.

ANNOUNCER: Next, "League of Denial: The NFL's Concussion Crisis."

ANN MCKEE, MD, NEUROPATHOLOGIST, BU CTE CENTER: I'm really wondering if every single football player doesn't have this.

FOOTBALL ANNOUNCERS: Erenberg touchdown! Listen to this crowd! They're on fire!

The Steelers have their receivers in, Stallworth on the left, 82, Swann 88 on the right. Franco Harris is down to thirty, big pileup.

He fumbled the ball! And let's see—Minnesota has it! Jeff Seamon on it.

Oh, yeah! It's still wild and woolly, and I love 'em that way!

You love 'em wild and woolly, and you're seeing it now.

Impressive drive by the Steelers!

Everybody loves everybody when you win.

The drive is used a lot of times. Here's a roll-out. Bradshaw fires. Stallworth touchdown!

An awesome physical team were the Steelers today, Pittsburgh, the Super Bowl champs!

NARRATOR: Pittsburgh. For seventy years, they've loved their football team, the Steelers.

STAN SAVRAN, PITTSBURGH SPORTS REPORTER: This is a tough town. The people here are tough, tough-minded. The way the Steelers played the game meshed perfectly with the people.

STEELERS FAN: Hit 'em! Hit 'em!

STAN SAVRAN: They loved that hard-hitting, punishing, brutal defense that they played.

NARRATOR: They called the defensive line the "steel curtain."

STAN SAVRAN: That just fit perfectly into the way they saw their own lives and what they had to be in order to survive.

NARRATOR: And if there was one iconic Steeler, it was number 52, "Iron Mike" Webster.

JULIAN BAILES, MD, TEAM PHYSICIAN, STEELERS, 1988–97: Well, Mike Webster exemplified what it was like to be a player in the Steel City and a player in that era that for me was the greatest team of all time.

NARRATOR: In the 1970s, Webster anchored four Super Bowl championship teams.

BOB FITZSIMMONS, WEBSTER'S ATTORNEY: Mike was a legend and a hero. He may have been "the" legend and "the" hero because here's that blue-collar worker, a center, who doesn't get any glory, doesn't catch the touchdown passes, doesn't kick the fifty-two-yard field goal to win a game. He's just in every play.

PAM WEBSTER, WIFE: I just loved watching him play. And Mike's favorite games were the ones that were cold and snowy and frigid. And he could get up there with his short sleeves. And the dirtier and muddier it got made things better.

NARRATOR: Then eleven years after he retired, the people of Pittsburgh received some bad news.

NEWSCASTER: At what price glory? The Hall of Fame center Mike Webster died at the age of fifty.

NEWSCASTER: He died on Tuesday. He was just fifty years old. He was known as "Iron Mike"—

NEWSCASTER: He had heart disease—

NARRATOR: The news that day would start a chain of events that would threaten to forever change the way Americans see the game of football.

NEWSCASTER: It is hard to find a former pro football player whose body hasn't paid a very high price.

NARRATOR: Mike Webster's body was delivered to the Allegheny County coroner's office.

MARK FAINARU-WADA, *Frontline*/ESPN: Webster ends up in the autopsy room. And the pathologist who's on call that day is this guy, Bennet Omalu.

STEVE FAINARU: Omalu parked his car and walked into the office. And he said, "What's going on?" And one of his colleagues said, "It's Mike Webster. He's—he's up in the autopsy room." And Omalu's response was, "Who's Mike Webster?"

BENNET OMALU: And everybody looked at me, like, "Where is he from? Is he from outer space? Who is this guy who doesn't know Mike Webster in Pittsburgh?"

MARK FAINARU-WADA: He's a Nigerian-born, incredibly well-educated guy. But he doesn't know anything about football.

NARRATOR: A doctor, Omalu was also a trained neuropathologist. From the beginning of the autopsy, Dr. Omalu could see the effects of seventeen years in the football wars.

DR. BENNET OMALU: Mike looked older than his age. He looked beat up. He looked—he looked worn out. He looked drained. If I had not been told his age, I would say he looked like seventy.

NARRATOR: Omalu started at the feet and worked his way up.

STEVE FAINARU: There were cracks running the length of his feet, and they were incredibly painful. And so Webster would duct tape his feet, as well, to sort of close those cracks and keep them—and keep them together.

GARRETT WEBSTER, SON: His feet and his legs were definitely—you could just tell were destroyed. You know, he had veins all over his legs, varicose veins and stuff like that.

NARRATOR: There were several herniated discs, a broken vertebra, torn rotator cuff and separated shoulder.

PAM WEBSTER: His teeth were falling out. His body—he had cellulitis. He had a heart—his heart, you know, was getting enlarged.

COLIN WEBSTER, SON: You know, he was supergluing his teeth back into his head, and he actually made that work. I mean, I think Dad's the only person who could actually, you know, have a medical problem like that and decide to fix it with superglue.

NARRATOR: Then there was the matter of Webster's forehead.

STEVE FAINARU: Webster's forehead was essentially fixed to its scalp. The skin on his forehead had built up almost a shelf of scar tissue that—from the continuous pounding of his head into other people.

NARRATOR: Webster's death certificate made Omalu suspect he may have suffered from a brain disorder.

DR. BENNET OMALU: When I opened up his skull, in my mind, I had a mental picture of what his brain would look like, based on my education. I was expecting to see a brain with Alzheimer's disease features, so a shriveled, ugly-looking brain. But upon opening his skull, Mike's brain looked normal.

JEANNE MARIE LASKAS, *GQ*, "GAME BRAIN": He didn't understand why that would be, but he became more and more curious. It became sort of like his little private mission.

NARRATOR: Dr. Omalu wanted to fix the brain, preserve it in a chemical bath for further study.

DR. BENNET OMALU: I said, "Let me fix this brain. Let me spend time with this brain. There's something—something doesn't match." And I remember the technician telling me, he said, "What are you fixing this brain for? That brain is normal."

STEVE FAINARU: And Omalu becomes very firm in that moment, and he says, "Fix the brain. I want you to fix the brain."

NARRATOR: What Omalu could not see was that hidden inside Webster's brain was evidence of a chronic disease.

STEVE FAINARU: And that decision would change the NFL because if Webster's brain had not been examined, I don't honestly think that we would be where we're at today.

NARRATOR: Steve Fainaru and his brother, Mark Fainaru-Wada, are investigative reporters. Steve has a Pulitzer Prize for reporting in Iraq. Mark broke the Barry Bonds steroids story.

For *Frontline*, ESPN, and in their own book, they've been investigating how the NFL has handled evidence that football may be destroying the brains of NFL players.

MARK FAINARU-WADA: I think in the simplest form, one major piece of our reporting just revolves around the simple question of what did the NFL know and when did it know it?

NARRATOR: The NFL would not cooperate with the Fainaru brothers, nor would it talk to *Frontline*.

MARK FAINARU-WADA: We went to New York to meet with them and say, "Look, this is what we're doing. We'd like you to participate. We'd like you to make available these various people." And the NFL's message was, "Sorry. We're not going to help you."

NARRATOR: But they continued to report the story, beginning with Mike Webster's career in the NFL.

STEVE FAINARU: There's almost a Darwinian quality about the NFL. Webster wanted to prove to the world that he was going to be the toughest, and he did anything that he possibly could to do that.

NARRATOR: Webster's Sunday afternoons were spent on the line of scrimmage, brutal territory known as "the pit."

ART ROONEY II, PITTSBURGH STEELERS PRESIDENT AND CO-OWNER: He had the violence in him. He could explode into the player. Every play was a fight.

NARRATOR: Webster's favorite weapon was his head.

FRED SMERLAS, BUFFALO BILLS, 1979–89: Well, Webby would hit you with his head first. And with that head, he'd pop you. And then he'd lift his shoulders. Now he'd get you up in the air. Once you hit full speed and you're moving backwards and he hits you, you're gone.

HARRY CARSON: When he would fire off the ball, he's coming to block me, and if I'm not ready for him, you know, he's going to pancake me. You know, he's going to hurt me.

NARRATOR: Hall of Fame linebacker for the New York Giants, Harry Carson went to war with Mike Webster.

HARRY CARSON: And so I have to meet force with force. All of my power is coming from my big rear end and my big thighs into my forearm, and I hit him in the face. I have to stun him, get my hands on him, throw him off when I see where the ball is going. And when I hit him in the face, his head is going back. He's going forward, but all of a sudden, his head is going back and his brain is hitting up against the inside of his skull.

ROBERT STERN, PH.D., NEUROPSYCHOLOGIST, BOSTON UNIVERSITY:
In football, one has to expect that almost every play of every
game and every practice, they're going to be hitting their
heads against each other. That's the nature of the game. Those
things seem to happen around 1,000 to 1,500 times a year.

Each time that happens, it's around 20G or more. That's
the equivalent of driving a car at 35 miles per hour into a
brick wall 1,000 to 1,500 times per year.

NARRATOR: For Mike Webster, the head hits just kept on coming
for seventeen years.

GEORGE ATKINSON, OAKLAND RAIDERS, 1968–77: You have to
survive, so you learn the methods to survive and be the best
at surviving in that environment. The minute you put your
pads on, you're only one play away from getting seriously
injured.

NARRATOR: For Webster and others on the field, physical injuries went with the territory.

JIM OTTO, OAKLAND RAIDERS, 1960–74: I mean, it's affected my
life. It surely has. But I'm not out there crying about it. I know
that I went to war, and I came out of the battle with what I got.
And you know, that's the way it is. That's the way Mike Webster
would say it, too. I'm sure he would. I mean, we battled in there,
and this is what—this is the result of it right here, sitting right
here looking at you.

NARRATOR: But what Otto and others do not know is whether
football has also caused injuries they cannot see, the result of
what they called getting their bell rung.

ANNOUNCERS: Oh, did they hit him that time! His helmet went
off.

I don't know how he held onto that! Sammy White, he did
a remarkable catch with Skip Thomas and Jack Tatum jack-
knifing him as he caught the ball for a first down on the Oakland forty-five-yard line.

NARRATOR: In 1991, Mike Webster left football. Soon he and his family would come to believe those hits to the head had taken a devastating toll.

PAM WEBSTER: Mike wasn't Mike. He was angrier quicker than before and didn't have the patience to have, you know, the kids on his lap or take a walk with the kids. Like, he didn't have that stamina physically.

NARRATOR: Over the years, he became increasingly confused.

COLIN WEBSTER: He would forget, you know, which way the grocery store was, which way it was to go home. He was—he actually—he broke down in tears in front of me a couple of times because he couldn't get his thoughts together and he couldn't keep them in order.

NARRATOR: At home, there were bouts of rage.

PAM WEBSTER: He took a knife and slashed all his football pictures. They were all destroyed and gone and broken glass, and they were all down, you know? And it wasn't Mike.

NARRATOR: They'd been college sweethearts. But twenty-seven years and four children later, Mike and Pam Webster's marriage ended.

PAM WEBSTER: We didn't understand what was happening. You're just trying to get by in this storm. I mean, your money's gone. Your pride's gone. Our bills are all overdue. Our house is getting foreclosed. All this security is gone. All those parameters are removed. So everything's crumbling.

NARRATOR: Once one of Pittsburgh's greatest football heroes, Webster began living out of a pickup truck.

COLIN WEBSTER: I'd come outside sometimes and just see him, you know, sitting in the truck. And it would be freezing and he'd just be sitting there, just looking miserable. He'd say, "You know, the worst thing is, is I'm actually getting to the point where sometimes, or if I don't have my medicine," he said, "I'm cold and I don't realize that I can fix it by putting a jacket on."

NARRATOR: Webster was often unable able to sleep.

SUNNY JANI, FRIEND: He had a lot of pain, and he hasn't slept for days. So he asked me, said, "Sunny, can you tase me?" I'm, like, "What does that mean?

So he pulls out this stun gun and goes "Bzz, bzz." I'm, like, "Mike, that's not healthy." He said, "But I haven't slept nothing." He said, "All you got to do is tase me right here." And I'm, like, "OK." I don't know, you know, he's my hero, I'm going to do whatever he tells me. So I tased him, and he goes— and he goes to sleep. I'm, like, "Wow!"

NEWSCASTER: A true champion who wound up homeless, depressed—

NARRATOR: The story of Webster's decline was revealed on ESPN, and then the local newspapers.

NEWSCASTER: He was arrested for forging nineteen prescriptions for Ritalin, which he used to combat the erratic behavior caused by—

PAM WEBSTER: I think he was embarrassed. He was a leader on the team. He was Mike Webster. And then to be down to a place of poverty, a place where, you know, your brain can't function to finish a sentence without some help from Ritalin or whatever you need to function for a short period of time.

NARRATOR: For Iron Mike, TV interviews became impossible.

MIKE WEBSTER: No, I'm talking about—no, I'm just trying to find—yeah, well, everybody went through trauma as a kid. I'm not saying I was different than that. I'm just saying—the things we do to one another, OK—

Hell, I don't know what I'm saying. I'm just tired and confused right now, that's why I say I can't really—I can't say it the way I want to say it. I could answer this real easy at other times, but right now, I'm just tired.

COLIN WEBSTER: Maybe the saddest I ever heard him say was when someone saw my dad and, "Aren't you Mike Webster?" And he said, "I used to be." I think that really was how he felt because he really was. He wasn't the same person. It was—it was like, you know, a picture of him that was just shattered into a million pieces.

NARRATOR: Nearly broke, homeless, and losing his mind, Webster decided football had hurt him, and the NFL was going to pay for it. In 1997, he went to see a lawyer.

BOB FITZSIMMONS, WEBSTER'S ATTORNEY: The thing that struck me the most was how intelligent Mike was, and the problem was that he just couldn't continue those thought patterns for longer than a thirty-second period, or a minute or two minutes. He would just go off on the tangents at that point. It was pretty obvious, actually, the first interview that he had some type of cognitive impairment.

NARRATOR: Attorney Bob Fitzsimmons drew up a disability claim against the NFL.

STEVE FAINARU: He began to assemble a case with Webster to basically say that Webster had suffered brain damage as a result of his seventeen-year career in the NFL.

NARRATOR: Fitzsimmons pulled together Webster's complicated medical history.

BOB FITZSIMMONS: So I took the binder of records and got four doctors together, four separate doctors, all asking them, "Does he have a permanent disability that's cognitive? And is it related to football?"

NARRATOR: Webster's final application for disability contained over one hundred pages and the definitive diagnosis of his doctors—football had caused Webster's dementia. His claim for disability was filed with the National Football League's retirement board.

STEVE FAINARU: The Disability Committee is part of the NFL. The head of the Disability Committee is the commissioner himself, so it's very much a creature of the NFL.

NARRATOR: From the beginning, the league's board was skeptical, reluctant to give Webster money.

COLIN WEBSTER: They were fighting it from the beginning, against just the common sense of, you know, here's this guy, look at him, you know? He played for nearly twenty years in a brutal and punishing sport, and you know, this is what's going on with him. Why would you fight that? What possible motive?

NARRATOR: The league had its own doctor review Webster's case.

BOB FITZSIMMONS: The NFL had not only hired an investigator to look into this, they also hired their own doctor and said, "Hey, we want to evaluate Mike Webster."

NARRATOR: Dr. Edward Westbrook examined him.

MARK FAINARU-WADA: Dr. Westbrook concurs with everything that the four other doctors have found and agrees that absolutely, there's no question that Mike Webster's injuries are football-related and that he appears to be have significant cognitive issues, brain damage, as a result of having played football.

NARRATOR: The NFL retirement board had no choice. They granted Webster monthly disability payments.

DOCUMENT: —"has determined that Mr. Webster is currently totally and permanently disabled."

NARRATOR: And buried in the documents, a stunning admission by the league's board—football can cause brain disease.

DOCUMENT: —"indicate that his disability is the result of head injuries he suffered as a football player."

BOB FITZSIMMONS: The NFL acknowledges that repetitive trauma to the head in football, football can cause a permanent disabling injury to the brain.

NARRATOR: The admission would not be made public until years later, when it was discovered by the Fainaru brothers.

MARK FAINARU-WADA: And that was a dramatic admission back in 2000. And in fact, when you talk about that later with Fitzsimmons, he describes that as the sort of proverbial smoking gun.

NARRATOR: It was now in writing. The NFL's own retirement board linked playing football and dementia. At the time, it was something the league would not admit publicly. And Webster felt he'd never received the acknowledgment that his years in the NFL had caused his problems.

PAM WEBSTER: Mike would call this his greatest battle. He'd say it was like David and Goliath, over and over, because it was. He was taking on something that was bigger than him. He took on this battle for the right reasons. He was the right person to do it. Unfortunately, it cost us everything.

NARRATOR: Just two years later, in 2002, Mike Webster died.

BROADCAST DIRECTOR: Fifteen seconds to air. Stand by all cameras. Ready with slow motion and isolated—

NARRATOR: The first broadcast of Monday Night Football in 1970 marked a turning point in the game's popularity and its revenues.

BROADCAST DIRECTOR: Take tape.

MARK FAINARU-WADA: I think the NFL has done an incredible job at marketing itself and turning itself into a spectacle, a sort of cultural part of our lives.

STAN SAVRAN: It fit the personality of a society that became more violent, that became faster, wanted instant gratification.

ANNOUNCER: [ABC Monday Night Football, 1970] O.J. Simpson gets the call. Look out!

STAN SAVRAN: Football, from the opening kickoff, it's full go.

ANNOUNCER: What a football player!

NARRATOR: The Monday night games were always among the highest-rated television broadcasts.

ANNOUNCER: Look out! Look out!

MARK FAINARU-WADA: Monday Night Football—it's not just for football fans.

ANNOUNCER: Speaking of color commentators—

LEIGH STEINBERG, SPORTS AGENT: It became an entertainment show.

ANNOUNCER: [ABC Monday Night Football, 1983]—vivid picturization of the excitement—

ANNOUNCER: They're number one in the nation.

LEIGH STEINBERG: It became a happening.

HANK WILLIAMS, JR.: [ABC Monday Night Football, 1996] [singing] Are you ready for some football, a Monday night invasion—

NARRATOR: The glory and the violence of football was beamed into tens of millions of American living rooms during prime time.

HANK WILLIAMS, JR.: *[singing]* Here come the hits, the bangs, the blocks and the spikes, because all my rowdy friends drop in on Monday nights!

STAN SAVRAN: People liked the violence of it. You watch a pro football game and, naturally, the biggest cheers are for the touchdowns, but the second biggest cheers are for a nasty hit.

STEVE YOUNG, SAN FRANCISCO 49ERS, 1987–99: And I describe it as the moment of impact, the moment when you actually have to go tackle somebody, it's really a game of will.

LEIGH STEINBERG: The actual logo of Monday Night Football showed helmets hitting together. And it became part of the popular jargon, you know, "He knocked him silly. He knocked him to the moon."

PLAYER: Set the tone! Knock him out! Knock him out! Let's go!

MARK FAINARU-WADA: There's no question the NFL marketed that violence. That's what we love about the game.

NARRATOR: The NFL's own highly crafted film productions celebrated the violence and the spectacle.

[NFL Films]

NFL NARRATOR: On this down-and-dirty dance floor, huge men perform a punishing pirouette. The meek will never inherit this turf because every play is hand-to-hand and body-to-body combat!

MIKE ORIARD, KANSAS CITY CHIEFS, 1970–73: NFL Films captures the essence of football itself, that tension between the violence and the beauty.

NFL NARRATOR: In the pit, there is more violence per square foot than anywhere else in sport!

MIKE ORIARD: The sense of football as something powerful and elemental and mythic and epic.

NFL NARRATOR: When you talk about big-hitting safeties, the Eagles Donnie Dawkins always emerges.

DONNIE DAWKINS: We're going to dominate this thing! Respect is not given—

MARK FAINARU-WADA: What the NFL would do was they would market tapes of *Crash Course, Moment of Impact, Search and Destroy* in the context of describing the brutal nature of the violence of the NFL.

NARRATOR: But away from the glamorized hits, there was a darker side. Superagent Leigh Steinberg saw it firsthand.

LEIGH STEINBERG: I watched athletes I represented play with collapsed lungs. I watched them completely fight with doctors at every time to get into the game. I watched players deceive coaches on the sidelines when they were injured and run back into a game.

NARRATOR: The inspiration for the movie sports agent Jerry Maguire, Steinberg was a powerhouse alongside the new NFL.

STEVE FAINARU: He was very much a creature of this expanding juggernaut of the NFL.

MARK FAINARU-WADA: He ends up at one point representing twenty-one quarterbacks in the—twenty-one starting quarterbacks in the NFL one year.

NARRATOR: In the early 1990s, Steinberg represented one of football's top stars, Dallas quarterback Troy Aikman.

ANNOUNCER: Second and fourteen, passing down, coming up for Aikman again—

NARRATOR: In 1994, during the NFC championship, Aikman took a knee to the head.

ANNOUNCER: Down he goes! Stubblefield was there first. Troy Aikman took a knee to the head.

ANNOUNCER: You see it right here. It's Dennis Brown coming in. You see the knee right there, knee right on his helmet.

NARRATOR: Aikman's concussion was bad enough that he could not return to the game. Aikman was taken to a local hospital.

ANNOUNCER: —back to the locker room.

LEIGH STEINBERG: I went to visit Troy, who was sitting in a darkened hospital room all alone.

STEVE FAINARU: The room is dark because Aikman can't even stand looking into the light. It's—you know, it's this sort of surreal scene where the city is celebrating and the quarterback who won the game is in the hospital with his agent.

LEIGH STEINBERG: He looked at me and he said, "Leigh, where am I?" And I said, "Well, you're in the hospital." And he said, "Well, why am I here?" And I said, "Because you suffered a concussion today." And he said, "Well, who did we play?" And I said, "The 49ers." And he said, "Did we win?" "Yes, you won." "Did I play well?" "Yes, you played well." "Did—what does that—and so what's that mean?" "It means you're going to the Super Bowl."

MARK FAINARU-WADA: Five minutes later, they're sitting there, they're continuing to hang out, and Aikman suddenly turns to Steinberg and says, "What am I doing here?" And the next thing you know, they are reliving this conversation they'd had five minutes earlier.

LEIGH STEINBERG: For a minute, I thought he was joking. And I went through the same sequence of answers again. And his face brightened and we celebrated again. Maybe ten minutes passed, and he looked at me with the same puzzled expression and asked the same sequence of questions.

It terrified me to see how tender the bond was between sentient consciousness and potential dementia and confusion was.

ANNOUNCER: Third down and nine, Young throws, and that's incomplete, and—down!

NARRATOR: 49ers quarterback Steve Young was another one of Leigh Steinberg's clients.

ANNOUNCER: —a sight that is the last thing in the world the 49ers would want to see. It looks as almost as if he's out cold.

ANNOUNCER: Al, I've been there. And there he is. He's up. That's a good sign. And what I like is he wants to get up off the ground.

ANNOUNCER: Look at this. He looks like he's out cold, and now he's walking off.

STEVE YOUNG: I remember thinking as I walked to the sidelines, "This is not good," you know? "This is just not the right thing to happen."

NARRATOR: It was Young's seventh concussion.

ANNOUNCER: Well, that's a sight we thought would be impossible. Steve Young apparently knocked cold, knocked out cold, walks off the field—

NARRATOR: He would never play again.

STEVE YOUNG: If my knee is hurt, everyone knows it and I know it, and we can go deal with it, and shoulders. And there's only one place in your body that you really don't understand. And people always say the brain is the last frontier.

NARRATOR: For Steinberg, there was a growing recognition of just how dangerous the sport was.

LEIGH STEINBERG: The damage was occurring every week. And I had people who I loved and cared for. And I intuitively knew that this was not just a football issue, that it was happening to football players in the pros, it was happening in college, it was happening in high school. It was happening to every player in every collision sport. So not only was it an issue for my clients, it was a huge societal issue.

NEWSCASTER: We have put football injuries on the "American Agenda" tonight—

NEWSCASTER: —playing with pain, increasingly the price of life in the National Football League—

NEWSCASTER: We've heard so much recently on the danger of concussions in sports—

NEWSCASTER: This year, injuries in the National Football League may be out of control—

NARRATOR: By the mid-nineties, the concussion crisis had made its way to NFL headquarters on Park Avenue in New York City.

NEWSCASTER: —escalates over the long-term effects of taking hits to head on the football field—

NARRATOR: NFL commissioner Paul Tagliabue orchestrated the league's response. Tagliabue had begun his career as a lawyer.

PETER KEATING, REPORTER, ESPN: People have suggested strongly to me that he picked up a lot of techniques about how to aggressively defend things that could turn out to be class actions. You know, the NFL has had this strategy of going nuclear every time it goes to court because the first time you ever lose, you open up the floodgates to potential billions of dollars of damage.

NARRATOR: And Tagliabue said he was skeptical about the risk from concussions, once calling the controversy the result of "pack journalism."

PAUL TAGLIABUE, NFL COMMISSIONER: *[Sports panel discussion, December 1994]* Concussions I think is, you know, one of these pack journalism issues, frankly. There's no increase in concussions. The number is relatively small. The problem is it's a journalist issue.

LEIGH STEINBERG: This is the commissioner of the NFL saying that there's no concussion issue. If it was ignorance, they should have known. They should have known because the issue is so critical.

NARRATOR: Still, Tagliabue created a scientific committee, the Mild Traumatic Brain Injury Committee, the MTBI. To lead it, he chose Elliot Pellman, the New York Jets team doctor, a firm believer that concussions were not a serious problem.

STEVE FAINARU: And so you had this—behind the scenes, you know, this dynamic going on where you had a guy, Elliot Pellman, who very clearly believed that this wasn't a problem, it just wasn't a big problem for the NFL.

NARRATOR: To outsiders, the choice of Pellman was unusual. He was not an expert in neurology and had no background in brain research.

PETER KEATING: He went to a school in Guadalajara. Dr. Pellman is not a neurosurgeon. He's not a neuro anything. He's a rheumatologist.

STEVE FAINARU: You know, putting a rheumatologist on the head of the committee that arguably was going to have more influence over brain research, you know, than any other—any particular institution in the country at the time, you know, was, I think a lot of people felt, surprising.

NARRATOR: Most of Pellman's committee was made up of NFL loyalists. Nearly half the members were team doctors.

ROBERT CANTU, M.D., NEUROSURGEON, BOSTON UNIVERSITY: If you're going to put together a blue-ribbon committee to study brain trauma, it should have as its chair somebody who has that as a background, either a neurologist, neurosurgeon, neuropathologist, preferably a clinician.

NARRATOR: For years, Pellman's committee would insist they were studying the problem, that the danger from concussions was overblown.

PETER KEATING: The way the NFL handled this was for fifteen years to do research that looks awfully like it was designed to say that the league was OK in doing what it was doing — which wasn't much —to protect players from the dangers of concussions.

NARRATOR: Pellman's committee began writing a series of scientific papers and, in 2003, got the first of them published in the medical journal *Neurosurgery.*

ROBERT STERN, PH.D., NEUROPSYCHOLOGIST, BOSTON UNIVERSITY: Those initial studies from the NFL were notorious in telling the world over and over and over again, "No, there's no relationship between hitting your head in football and later life problems. No, there's no relationship."

NARRATOR: The papers downplayed the risk of concussions—

DOCUMENT: —"Mild TBIs in professional football are not serious injuries."

NARRATOR: —insisted that players could return to the same game after suffering a concussion—

DOCUMENT: "Return to play does not involve a significant risk of a second injury."

NARRATOR: —denied players suffered any long-term problems from concussions sustained while playing football—

DOCUMENT: —"that there was no evidence of worsening injury or chronic cumulative effects of multiple MTBIs in"—

NARRATOR: —and, in one of the papers, even suggested their research might apply to younger athletes, despite the fact they had not studied high school or college players.

DOCUMENT: "It might be safe for college/high-school football players to be cleared to return to play on the same day as their injury."

DR. ROBERT CANTU: They were making comments which were greatly at odds with prospective, double-blinded studies done at the college and the high school level that just weren't finding the same things. And that just didn't make sense to anyone that's a scientist.

NARRATOR: Dr. Robert Cantu edited the journal's sports medicine section. The papers were published despite his objections.

DR. ROBERT CANTU: The papers started to make statements about multiple head injuries were not a problem in the NFL. If they went back into the same contest with a concussion, it didn't matter. If they got knocked out and went back into the same contest, it didn't matter. There were no long-term psychological problems or cognitive problems in these athletes, in essence, saying it wasn't a problem.

NARRATOR: Dr. Cantu says he took his concerns to the journal's editor-in-chief, Dr. Michael Apuzzo. Apuzzo was also a consultant for the New York Giants.

DR. ROBERT CANTU: I said that I really think this data is flawed. I really think it shouldn't be published. He's the one that made the decision to publish papers, no matter whether the reviewers felt they should be published or not, no matter whether the section editor felt they should be published or not.

NARRATOR: Mark Lovell was a member of the committee and an author on some of the studies. He now admits there were problems with the research.

MARK LOVELL, PH.D., NEUROPSYCHOLOGIST: I look back on some of the papers, yeah, I think I could have done it differently. I think the fault of the paper was, it was maybe too early to be making those statements based on a fairly small sample of players, which is the major criticism of the study which I think is a valid one.

NARRATOR: The NFL committee published sixteen papers. Neither Dr. Apuzzo, Dr. Pellman, nor Commissioner Tagliabue would speak to *Frontline* about the papers. But in those articles, the league had issued its definitive denials.

PETER KEATING: The closer you look, the less this holds up. But it did establish, you know, this kind of impressive-looking set of findings which pushed off the day of reckoning for the league.

That's really what is happening here, right? During this whole run of research that's being published, the day of reckoning, where the league has to answer to somebody about what it's doing about concussions, just keeps getting pushed off and pushed off and pushed off.

NARRATOR: In Pittsburgh at just about this time, Mike Webster's brain tissue was being examined. Dr. Bennet Omalu was studying the microscopic samples.

DR. BENNET OMALU: I put the slides in and looked. Whoa! I had to make sure the slides were Mike Webster's slides. I looked again. Ah! I looked again. I saw changes that shouldn't be in a fifty-year-old man's brains and also changes that shouldn't be in a brain that looked normal.

JULIAN BAILES, MD, TEAM NEUROSURGEON, STEELERS 1988–97: He saw collections of tau protein, collections which shouldn't be there in someone of Mike Webster's age. And this is what jumped out at him as he looked at it through the microscope.

NARRATOR: Dr. Omalu believed he saw physical evidence of the long-term damage playing football could have on the brain. It was a scientific first.

DR. BENNET OMALU: Because after I looked at it over and over and over and over, I was convinced this was something.

NARRATOR: It was a disease never previously identified in football players, chronic traumatic encephalopathy—CTE.

DR. ROBERT CANTU: Chronic traumatic encephalopathy is a disease, a progressive neurodegenerative disease, where the end stage leaves tau protein deposition in distinctive areas of the brain, in distinctive locations that separate this disease from any other, like Alzheimer's or some other dementia.

ROBERT STERN: For some reason, the repetitive brain trauma starts this cascade of events in the brain that changes the way this tau looks and behaves. It goes awry. And it starts destroying the integrity of the brain cells.

MARK FAINARU-WADA: The tau is effectively closing in around the brain cells and choking them. And it's impacting the way the brain is working and, ultimately, erupting in issues around memory, agitation, anger.

NARRATOR: Omalu shared his evidence with leading brain researchers, who confirmed his findings. Then he submitted a scientific paper on the Webster case to the one journal that seemed to be most interested in head injuries in football, *Neurosurgery*, and Dr. Apuzzo accepted it.

STEVE FAINARU: Omalu is a junior pathologist in the Allegheny County coroner's office, but the people he published with were one of the leading Alzheimer's disease experts in the country, one of the leading neuropathologists in the country, and one of the most well known coroners in the country.

NARRATOR: It was the first hard evidence that playing football could cause permanent brain damage.

JULIAN BAILES: Certainly, we knew that if you got hit on the head so many times, maybe you had a 20 percent chance of having dementia pugilistica if you were a former professional boxer. But we didn't really relate that in a modern sport like football, in a helmeted sport, that it could lead to that. And that was the big discovery, I think.

NARRATOR: Dr. Omalu believed the National Football League would want to know about his discovery.

DR. BENNET OMALU: That was what I thought, in my naive state of mind. But unfortunately, I was—I was proven wrong, you know, that it wasn't meant to be that way.

NARRATOR: In a letter to the journal *Neurosurgery*, Dr. Pellman and other members of the NFL's MTBI committee attacked Dr. Omalu's paper.

DOCUMENT: "These statements are based on a complete misunderstanding of the relevant medical literature."

NARRATOR: They even questioned whether Mike Webster was suffering from neurological problems.

DOCUMENT: —"that there is inadequate clinical evidence that the subject had a chronic neurological condition"—

PETER KEATING: The league officials, the doctors and scientists serving on the MTBI committee not only disputed those findings, they went after Dr. Omalu with a vengeance. They publicly said he should retract his findings.

NARRATOR: The NFL doctors insisted Dr. Omalu was misunderstanding the science of brain injury.

DOCUMENT: "We therefore urge the authors to retract their paper"—

STEVE FAINARU: It's an extraordinary move under any circumstances. Like, you don't try to get a paper retracted unless there's evidence of fraud or plagiarism or something like that.

DOCUMENT: "Omalu et al's description of chronic traumatic encephalopathy is completely wrong."

PETER KEATING: They went after him with missiles—I mean, like a nuclear missile strike on a guy's reputation. They basically told him to go away and never come back. And that was just for starters.

NARRATOR: In the end, Dr. Omalu's paper was not retracted. And now Omalu had another case.

NEWSCASTER: Terry Long killed himself by drinking anti-freeze.

NARRATOR: A second Steeler had died.

NEWSCASTER: Terry Long committed suicide by drinking anti-freeze.

NEWSCASTER: Terry Long was young—

NARRATOR: And Dr. Omalu received his brain.

DR. BENNET OMALU: I came to work one morning and everybody there said, "Hey, we have another case for you." I said, "What are you talking about?" They said, "Oh, Terry Long died." I'm, like, "Who's Terry Long?" Said, "Oh, he's another NFL player. He died."

NARRATOR: Long was an offensive lineman with the Steelers for eight years. He battled in the pit alongside Mike Webster.

MARK FAINARU-WADA: He—like Webster, his life had sort of fallen apart in a lot of ways. He had issues, certainly, during his career.

STEVE FAINARU: He was a steroid user. He had been involved in some serious financial problems.

MARK FAINARU-WADA: And so ultimately, he committed suicide by drinking antifreeze.

NARRATOR: As he had for Webster, Dr. Omalu sectioned part of Long's brain and again had it stained.

JEANNE MARIE LASKAS: He ran the same test, same stains, found the same splotches, CTE in his brain, too. Now two former Steelers who had gone crazy about the same time.

DR. BENNET OMALU: When I saw Terry Long's case, I became more convinced that this was not just an anomaly, a statistical anomaly.

NARRATOR: Omalu submitted another paper to *Neurosurgery*, this one about Terry Long.

JEANNE MARIE LASKAS: That caused the MTBI committee to say, "This is preposterous. This is not good science. This is still not something that we're buying into."

DR. BENNET OMALU: If you read, Pellman made statements like what I practice is not medicine, it's not science. They insinuated I was not practicing medicine, I was practicing voodoo. Voodoo!

NARRATOR: The NFL would not publicly sit down with Dr. Omalu. But one night, in a private meeting, he brought his CTE slides and finally met face to face with one of the NFL's doctors.

DR. BENNET OMALU: And the NFL doctor at some point said to me, "Bennet, do you know the implications of what you're doing?" I looked. He was on my left. I said, "Yeah, I think I do." He said, "No, you don't." *[laughs]* So we continued talking, talking. At some point, he interrupted me again, "Bennet, do you think you know the implications of what you're doing?" I said, "I think I do. I don't know." He said, "No, you don't." So we continued talking again.

Then a third time, he interrupted me, and I turned to him and I said, "OK, why don't you tell me what implications are?" He said, "OK, I'll tell you." He said, "If 10 percent of mothers in this country would begin to perceive football as a dangerous sport, that is the end of football."

JULIAN BAILES: For the most part, people didn't want to believe it's true. They didn't want to admit to themselves or anybody else that our beloved sport, probably our most popular sport, could end up with brain damage. I didn't want to admit it to myself, either. It was a hard message, a difficult message, a bad message, but it appeared to be true.

NEWSCASTER: Owners of the thirty-two teams—

NARRATOR: Then in New York, a change in the NFL's top leadership.

NEWSCASTER: The NFL will have a new commissioner—

NEWSCASTER: There's a changing of the guard at the National Football League.

NARRATOR: In September of 2006, Commissioner Paul Tagliabue stepped down.

NEWSCASTER: The right-hand man to Tagliabue is running the show.

NEWSCASTER: Tagliabue will be succeeded by Roger Goodell.

NARRATOR: His second in command and closest aide, Roger Goodell, took over. Goodell had grown up in Washington, the son of a United States senator from New York. Early in his career, he worked as former commissioner Pete Rozelle's driver.

MARK FAINARU-WADA: He basically got his job by writing to the commissioner and saying, "Please, I'd like to work in the NFL."

NARRATOR: It took Goodell twenty-four years to work his way to the top. He was chief operating officer when the league's scientific committee sent those controversial papers to the journal *Neurosurgery*.

STEVE FAINARU: Here's a guy who's spent more than half of his life in the NFL, and more than anyone should be acutely aware of the sort of dangers that are lurking in this problem.

NARRATOR: Now Goodell was fully in charge of the league's handling of the concussion crisis. He soon replaced the rheumatologist Dr. Elliot Pellman and promoted the neurologist Dr. Ira Casson.

PETER KEATING: Dr. Ira Casson, who is an expert but an abrasive person who is contemptuous of the arguments that concussion can cause damage.

NARRATOR: Casson had once joined Pellman in attacking Omalu's work. Now one of Casson's first moves, a public denial of Omalu's conclusions.

CORRESPONDENT: *[HBO Real Sports, May 14, 2007]* Ira Casson leads a team of NFL doctors who did a study of several hundred active players and reported that the concern over head injuries is overblown.

Is there any evidence, as far as you're concerned, that links multiple head injuries among pro football players with depression?

IRA CASSON, MD, COCHAIR, MTBI COMMITTEE, 2007–09: No.

MARK FAINARU-WADA: Dr. Ira Casson ends up with this sort of very famous exchange that earns him the nickname "Dr. No."

CORRESPONDENT: With dementia?

DR. IRA CASSON: No.

CORRESPONDENT: With early onset of Alzheimer's?

DR. IRA CASSON: No.

JEANNE MARIE LASKAS: And Ira Casson was asked repeatedly, "Is there any link between trauma, head trauma, and the kind of dementia we're seeing in these players?" And he says, "No. No. No. No."

CORRESPONDENT: Is there any evidence as of today that links multiple head injuries with any long-term problem like that?

DR. IRA CASSON: In NFL players?

CORRESPONDENT: Yeah.

DR. IRA CASSON: No.

NARRATOR: Then just one month later, in Chicago, a dramatic gesture from Commissioner Goodell. At an airport hotel, the league gathered the top NFL brass, team doctors, and trainers.

MARK FAINARU-WADA: The NFL convenes a summit in the summer of 2007.

STEVE FAINARU: About 200 people are gathered there, and running the show is Ira Casson. The stakes for the NFL are obvious. It's huge business. If the business is potentially lethal, then that's going to have major implications for the game.

NARRATOR: On this day, the commissioner would take a front-row seat to listen to the best medical minds in the league.

PETER KEATING: All the teams are present. All the teams had to send doctors and trainers. And the league's concussion people are there.

NARRATOR: They had even invited outside scientists who had become some of the league's biggest critics. But one person was missing.

PETER KEATING: Dr. Omalu is excluded, just underscoring how they don't want to do business with him.

DR. BENNET OMALU: I was not aware of it. Nobody ever told me. Dr. Bailes called me and said the NFL is putting together a conference on CTE, that you were not invited.

JEANNE MARIE LASKAS: He is shunned. I mean, it was a loud just, "No, not you. Yes, you're the guy with all the research, you're the guy who's published the papers, you're the guy who's got the brains. But no, you're not coming."

NARRATOR: Former Steelers team doctor and neurosurgeon Julian Bailes had become a true believer in CTE and Omalu. They were now research partners. He offered to present Omalu's work to the group.

DR. JULIAN BAILES: So I presented and showed our data, which was four or five cases at that point.

NARRATOR: Besides Mike Webster and Terry Long, Omalu also found CTE in the brains of Andre Waters and Justin Strzelczyk. Bailes delivered Omalu's message: Playing football could cause permanent brain damage.

DR. JULIAN BAILES: It wasn't met with any broad acceptance, to say the least.

STEVE FAINARU: Julian Bailes got up and talked about Omalu's work. And while he's up there, Casson is off to the side and he's rolling his eyes. He's clearly distressed by what he's hearing. And that was basically the idea that was conveyed by the NFL in that moment.

DR. JULIAN BAILES: There was skepticism. There was dismissiveness on his part. There was great doubt.

NARRATOR: As Bailes left the meeting, he ran into *New York Times* reporter Alan Schwarz.

ALAN SCHWARZ: I remember Julian being furious, absolutely furious at how they had been treated in that room. And there was clearly—among the NFL committee, there was just a very steadfast belief that this is not a problem. "You guys don't know how to do research the way we do. And thank you for coming."

DR. JULIAN BAILES: I was not the bearer of good news, probably, in many people's minds. This was not something that I made up. This was showing what the findings were.

NARRATOR: Earlier, Goodell had watched his mentor, Tagliabue, downplay the concussion controversy. Now he had heard firsthand how serious some respected scientists thought the issue was.

MARK FAINARU-WADA: Roger Goodell's on notice. The NFL has a serious issue around the question of concussions, around the issue of brain trauma, on the rising suggestion that there is a link between football and neurodegenerative disease amongst its former players, and that there is a growing body of science that clearly establishes this link.

NARRATOR: Outside the conference's closed doors, the new commissioner insisted that the NFL had the problem under control.

[June 19, 2007]

ROGER GOODELL: The evidence is that our doctors are making excellent decisions. That's proven by the six-year study that we have and the research that's been done that looks at that issue intensively.

NARRATOR: The head of Goodell's concussion committee, Dr. Ira Casson, took on the critics.

DR. IRA CASSON: Anecdotes do not make scientifically valid evidence. I'm a man of science. I believe in empirically determined, scientifically valid data. And that is not scientifically valid data.

NARRATOR: Casson insisted there was no evidence that football players were at risk for CTE.

DR. IRA CASSON: In my opinion, the only scientifically valid evidence of a chronic encephalopathy in athletes is in boxers and in some steeplechase jockeys.

NARRATOR: Dr. Casson declined to be interviewed by *Frontline*.

ANNOUNCER: This venerable stadium will be a wild scene tonight!

NARRATOR: And as the teams took the field just a few months later, in the fall of 2007, the league's definitive statement on brain injury was given to every single player in a pamphlet.

ALAN SCHWARZ: The cover says, "What is a concussion," question mark. It said, you know, "If I get a concussion, am I further at risk for long-term problems?" And the answer was, and I'm virtually quoting, "Research has not shown that there are any long-term consequences to concussions in NFL players as long as each injury is treated properly."

STEVE FAINARU: The message was that football is safe to your brain. That was the message, "Don't worry about it."

NARRATOR: The commissioner and the league had successfully held the line, denying the dangers of football.

ALAN SCHWARZ: They refused to listen to people who didn't share their opinions about the research, and it was very much, you know, putting a stake in the ground saying everybody else is wrong. And that's what they did.

NARRATOR: Shunned by the league, bruised by the struggle and looking to make a change, Dr. Omalu left Pittsburgh. He moved to Lodi, California.

MARK FAINARU: He ends up in the dust bowl of north central California, and he's working as a medical examiner there, as far removed from the NFL as anybody could be, and trying to figure out how to sort of stay in it.

DR. BENNET OMALU: I wish I never met Mike Webster. CTE has dragged me into the politics of science, the politics of the NFL. You can't go against the NFL. They'll squash you. I really, sincerely wished it didn't cross my path of life, seriously.

ANNOUNCERS: Second and three, ball on the three—

In motion, wide open, touchdown!

JANE LEAVY, JOURNALIST: The brains are precious cargo.

ANNOUNCER: Now back to the third, and he goes outside—

CHRIS NOWINSKI, AUTHOR OF THE BOOK/FILM *Head Games*: We have to get the brain usually within hours of the death.

ANNOUNCER: —scores a touchdown.

DR. ROBERT CANTU: You have a brain that's intact. It's been removed from the upper spinal cord.

ANNOUNCER: He's at the forty! He's at the forty-five! Midfield! He's going to go!

NARRATOR: It is the brain of a former football player.

JANE LEAVY: This is a process that is awe-inspiring in the old-fashioned sense of the word.

CHRIS NOWINSKI: You have the responsibility of actually possessing somebody's brain, which is probably the best representation of who they were. You know, you really treat it with the utmost respect.

STEVE FAINARU: From a scientific perspective, there's this secret that's being unlocked.

ANN MCKEE, MD, NEUROPATHOLOGIST, BU CTE CENTER: We take it out, we weigh it, we photograph it, all the external surfaces.

JANE LEAVY: The attitude is so careful about—that this is a person that's being delivered into their care.

DR. ANN MCKEE: I never forget that the brain is a human being. I feel very privileged that someone has . . . fed me with this—with this—this duty.

NARRATOR: In 2008, Dr. Ann McKee was a leading Alzheimer's researcher.

DR. ANN MCKEE: This is what I do. I look at brains. I'm fascinated by it. I can spend hours doing it. In fact, if I want to relax, that's one way I can relax.

NARRATOR: Then one day, she received a phone call from the Boston University medical school.

ROBERT STERN: I called her and said, "Are you interested in looking at the brains of former football players?" And she didn't drop a beat and said, "Are you kidding!" I had no idea that she was a super football fan.

DR. ANN MCKEE: I was born with football—my brothers, my dad. I played football when I was a kid. I mean, you know, it was part of life. It's a part of growing up. It's—you know, it's a way of life. So I get it.

NARRATOR: Now Dr. McKee was joining a team of researchers to build on Dr. Omalu's discovery.

MARK FAINARU-WADA: She's learned a little bit about the work that had previously been done in this issue by Omalu and others, and she's eager to find some brains.

NARRATOR: McKee and colleagues from Boston University were determined to examine as many brains as they could, and this man knew how to get them.

MARK FAINARU-WADA: Chris Nowinski shows up and says, "Look, I'll find the brains for you. I'll bring them to you. And they're going to be football players. Are you interested?" And she says, "Absolutely." You know, she describes it as like the greatest collision on earth for her.

NARRATOR: For Nowinski, the issue of CTE is personal. he worries he has it.

CHRIS NOWINSKI: I'd be a fool not to worry about CTE personally. And I took as much brain trauma as anybody. I think I have more than enough reasons to believe that I'm going to be fighting this myself. I am fighting it.

NARRATOR: At Harvard, Nowinski was a punishing tackler. He suffered countless head injuries. Then instead of the NFL, he became a professional wrestler..

MARK FAINARU-WADA: He ends up with the nickname Chris Harvard, the persona of this sort of snobbish wrestler who's smarter than all the fans.

CHRIS HARVARD: You people should be grateful to have someone of my intelligence in your presence!

NARRATOR: For Chris Harvard, the performance often ended with a blow to the head.

CHRIS NOWINSKI: Chris Harvard landed on his head quite a bit. You know, as much as wrestling is performance, there's a very, very small margin of error. And especially when you're learning the thing, you know, you fall on your head a lot.

NARRATOR: Nowinski began to have violent nightmares and migraine headaches.

CHRIS NOWINSKI: And I said, "There's something really wrong with me." And the headache didn't go away for five years.

NARRATOR: Brain trauma became an obsession.

CHRIS NOWINSKI: What motivated me every day was the fact that my head was killing me. And I knew that I felt awful. And I knew that I wasn't the only person, but I was a person in a position to make a difference.

NARRATOR: He would take on the task of finding brains of former football players for Dr. McKee.

STEVE FAINARU: They call him, like, the designated brain chaser, like that's his job, to go out and get the brains.

NARRATOR: Nowinski made the hard calls, asking families to donate the brain of a deceased loved one.

CHRIS NOWINSKI: At the beginning, when I first kind of got up the nerve to do it, you know, I wrote down a script and I prepared, I practiced, mentally preparing myself for wandering into someone's life like this.

NARRATOR: Almost right away, Nowinski secured a portion of the brain of a forty-five-year-old former Tampa Bay Buccaneer, Tom McHale.

ROBERT STERN: Tom McHale was a brilliant guy, went to Cornell, had been playing football since a kid. His brilliance intellectually was matched by being an incredible athlete.

NARRATOR: Tom and Lisa McHale had three sons. Once his career was over, McHale ran a successful chain of restaurants. But then, uncharacteristically, trouble.

LISA MCHALE, WIFE: Restlessness, irritability and discontent describe Tom to a T today, but no way is it anywhere near the man I had known and the man I had been married to for years.

JANE LEAVY: The change was so diabolical. He became a drug addict. He became depressed. He became—you know, had irate moments of, you know, violent temper.

NARRATOR: McHale's addictions spiraled out of control—pain killers, cocaine.

LISA MCHALE: I remember so clearly him looking at me —and this is going back, you know, in the final months of his life —and saying, "Lisa, when I look in your eyes, all I see is disappointment."

And I honestly don't know whether he was seeing my disappointment, or whether it was his own disappointment that he was seeing reflected back. But it pains me to think of how much that hurt him.

NEWSCASTER: A former Tampa Bay Buccaneer was found dead this morning—

NEWSCASTER: A former Tampa Bay Buccaneers player—

NARRATOR: He had died of an overdose. Dr. McKee had read Dr. Omalu's research, but she wanted to see for herself.

DR. ANN MCKEE: We dissect and section his brain, do a whole series of microscopic slides, look at it with all sorts of different stains for different things, and then come to a conclusion about what the diagnosis is.

NARRATOR: What she saw was that telltale protein, tau.

DR. ANN MCKEE: This is a forty-five-year-old with terrific disease. I mean, he had florid disease. He has tau in all these regions of the his brain.

NARRATOR: Dr. McKee had examined thousands of brains, but the location of the damage from CTE was different.

ROBERT STERN: I remember my feeling. I was scared. I was really scared. It really was a turning point. It was a new understanding that, "Hey, you know, this might be bigger than we think."

NARRATOR: Dr. McKee soon had three brains, all with CTE. But rather than just publish in scientific journals, Chris Nowinski was determined to get the word out.

JANE LEAVY: Nowinski, who is not a scientist, says, "There are people getting hit here. If we speak up now, we may be able to, if not save lives, at least prevent the damage that we are seeing on Ann McKee's table."

NARRATOR: Nowinski decided to take on the NFL in a very public way, at their biggest event, the 2009 Super Bowl.

FAITH HILL, ENTERTAINER: *[singing]* All right, what a night, it's finally here. Super Bowl Sunday's kicking into high gear—

NARRATOR: The glitz and glamour of the NFL production machine was in full gear, developed over decades—

FAITH HILL: *[singing]* We've been waitin' all day for a Super Bowl fight—

NARRATOR: —highly choreographed—

FAITH HILL: *[singing]* —running and hitting with all their might, yeah, everyone's ready for—

NARRATOR: —a national event with a carefully crafted story.

FAITH HILL: *[singing]* The whole world's ready, kick that ball off the tee because it's Super Bowl rocks on NBC—

NARRATOR: In Tampa, before the big game, Nowinski and McKee tried to crash the festivities by holding a press conference.

MARK FAINARU-WADA: This is the genius of Nowinski, really, I mean, right? I mean, we're going to present her findings.

DR. ANN MCKEE: This is something you would never—

MARK FAINARU-WADA: Where do we want to announce that? Oh, let's go to Tampa Bay where the Super Bowl's about to play out, where there's 4,000 media members who are there waiting to watch.

DR. ANN MCKEE: We have examined thousands of brains, and this is not a normal part of aging. This is not something you normally see in the brain.

MARK FAINARU-WADA: They were saying, "Football caused this. This is an issue." I think McKee uses the word "crisis." She says, "This is a crisis, and anybody who doesn't believe it is in denial."

NARRATOR: Also on the panel, Nowinski's other star, Lisa McHale.

LISA MCHALE: Eight months ago, I lost my best friend, my college sweetheart, and my husband of eighteen years—

NARRATOR: Lisa McHale had decided to go public with her husband's story.

LISA MCHALE: I never hesitated to be public with Tom's findings because I was so fully blown away to know that Tom could have had the kind of injury he had to his brain and that it could have been caused by football. And I said, "My God, of course. This is information that I would have like to have had."

NARRATOR: And after her husband's death, McHale decided to become an advocate for Dr. McKee's research.

LISA MCHALE: He is now the sixth confirmed case of CTE among former NFL players. And bearing in mind that only six former NFL players have been examined for CTE, I find these results to be not only incredibly significant but profoundly disturbing.

NARRATOR: But that day, there were few reporters listening.

CHRIS NOWINSKI: There were thousands of reporters across the street and probably two dozen who were willing to walk across and learn about CTE.

ROBERT STERN: That was the shocking part. You know, here we were in the midst of everything and this potentially giant story was being told, and virtually no one was there.

CHRIS NOWINSKI: Everyone, thank you so much for your time, and we're available if you want to stick around.

NARRATOR: Nowinski's press conference was no match for the show the NFL was putting on across town.

ANNOUNCER: The build-up is over, and away we go in Super Bowl 43!

NARRATOR: Then one of the most watched television broadcasts in history, a thirty-second ad sold for $3 million. It was the crowning event for a year in which the NFL earned almost $8 billion.

ANNOUNCER: Here's the run-up, and Super Bowl 43 is under way with the flashbulbs a-poppin'!

MARK FAINARU-WADA: The league is this massive force financially. The Super Bowl is a spectacle. TV is paying huge money to televise the sport.

ANNOUNCER: He gets it away quickly and finds the tight end over the middle, and it's Heath Miller!

STEVE FAINARU: The NFL is broadcast over five networks. ESPN, where we work, their new contract with the NFL is worth almost $2 billion year. So they're basically paying around $120 million per game. That's, like, the budget of a Harry Potter movie every week, week in, week out.

ANNOUNCER: And the Pittsburgh Steelers become the first franchise in history to win six Super Bowls!

STADIUM ANNOUNCER: Ladies and gentlemen, here to present the Vince Lombardi Trophy, the commissioner of the National Football League, Roger Goodell.

ROGER GOODELL: Well, some said that we could not top last year's Super Bowl, but the Steelers and Cardinals did that tonight!

NARRATOR: Presiding over it all, the most powerful man in sports.

ROGER GOODELL: —and all the Steelers fans, congratulations on your sixth world championship!

NARRATOR: He sat atop a multi-billion-dollar empire that he was determined to protect.

STEVE FAINARU: One of his mantras was to "protect the shield," the NFL shield, to protect the integrity of the game.

NARRATOR: But now the league might face huge lawsuits and a tarnished image if Dr. McKee's findings about CTE held up.

Not long after her trip to Tampa, Dr. McKee received a phone call.

DR. ANN MCKEE: I was called by Ira Casson. And I remember thinking, "Why is Ira Casson calling me?"

STEVE FAINARU: She's intimidated from the start because she knew enough about Ira Casson, she said, to know that he wasn't necessarily a friend.

DR. ANN MCKEE: And he wanted me to come to the NFL office and present the data.

NARRATOR: That May, McKee and Nowinski arrived at NFL headquarters.

CHRIS NOWINSKI: We head on up to a very, very fancy conference room, nice wood paneling, jerseys and trophies in the glass. And it was probably fifteen members of the committee.

MARK FAINARU-WADA: And one of the first things McKee notices is that there's only one other woman in the room, and it's not a doctor, it's a lawyer.

PETER KEATING: A lawyer is not there to offer medical advice. And a lawyer is not there to offer competitive athletic advice, either. A lawyer is there to figure out what the league needs to do to defend itself against a storm that may or may not come, but the league has to be ready to fight.

DR. ANN MCKEE: I'm up against a lot of doubters. I'm up against people who don't think that any of this holds any water. So, fine. I'm just going to show them what I have. And they kept interrupting.

NARRATOR: Dr. Ira Casson and others on the committee expressed their skepticism that playing football was the cause of CTE.

STEVE FAINARU: Very, very quickly, she got serious pushback from Ira Casson and the rest of the committee.

NARRATOR: Indianapolis Colt team physician Dr. Henry Feuer was one of the NFL doctors the meeting.

HENRY FEUER, MD, MTBI COMMITTEE, 1994–2010: I just have a problem. Ann McKee—she cannot tell me where it's starting.

We don't know the cause and effect. We don't know that right now. We don't know the incidence.

NARRATOR: The committee members believed Dr. McKee could not answer two important questions. Causation—did football cause CTE? And prevalence—how many players had it.

DR. HENRY FEUER: She was seeing only those that were in trouble, and we know that there are thousands roaming around that are not having problems. So again, I think that's where we had—we may have had an issue.

JOSEPH MAROON, MD, MTBI COMMITTEE, 2007–10: I think we're very early in the evolutionary understanding of CTE. A certain percentage of the individuals diagnosed with this have had steroid abuse, alcohol abuse, other substances abuses. We don't know the concussion history in many of these. And there may be other confounding factors in terms of the genetics that we simply don't understand.

DR. ANN MCKEE: They were convinced it was wrong, and I felt that they were in a very serious state of denial.

CHRIS NOWINSKI: I remember at one point, one of the NFL doctors asking, you know, "Couldn't you be misdiagnosing this? You know, these all look like they could be frontal temporal dementia." And Ann said, "Well, actually, I was on the NIH committee that defined how you diagnose that disease. So no, they're definitely different diseases." You know, like, she had the experience and they didn't.

NARRATOR: And according to Dr. McKee, there was something else, something familiar about the way the NFL committee was acting.

DR. ANN MCKEE: I don't want to get into the sexism too much, but sexism plays a big role when you're a doctor of my age who's come up in the ranks with a lot of male doctors. Sexism is part of my life. And getting in that room with a bunch of males who already thought they knew all the answers—more sexism. I mean, you know, it was, like, "Oh, the girl talked. Now we can get back into some serious business."

DR. HENRY FEUER: I—you know, I don't know why she feels that way. I thought that she presented herself, as I recall —it's been several years —that there was something—something in her manner. And—and I think she's a brilliant woman. She's done a great job. There was just something just about the way she said it. And not that everybody was looking down. You know, it was just—

NARRATOR: Dr. Feuer insists Dr. McKee is mistaken about how she was treated.

DR. HENRY FEUER: If we for some reason coming—came across as being disrespectful, then I would say that everybody else we interviewed over the fifteen years must have felt the same way. That's all I can say about that. And I feel strongly about that, too.

We would just—we would listen, and "Thank you," and that's it. Whether she wanted us to start—you know, I don't know where she's coming from on that.

NARRATOR: The meeting had changed nothing.

Just a few blocks from NFL headquarters, the commissioner had another problem. In a midtown Manhattan restaurant, an internal NFL research document was leaked to a reporter.

ALAN SCHWARZ: Documents were passed to me at Smith and Wollensky's in Manhattan, in an envelope. I mean, it was great —it was very "Deep Throat"—by somebody who shall remain nameless. But he literally slid it across the table in an envelope.

NARRATOR: It was a scientific study of former players commissioned by the National Football League itself.

ALAN SCHWARZ: At the bottom of page 32, there it was, "dementia." And they had asked players, or their representatives, their wives, "Have you been diagnosed by a physician as having Alzheimer's, dementia, or any other memory-related disease?""

ROBERT STERN: What it showed was that former NFL players seem to have memory-related disorders at a much, much higher rate than people in the regular community. And here was a study that the NFL supported, and it came out not looking too good for the NFL.

ALAN SCHWARZ: It was the people who the league hired to find out the answers to these questions giving them the answers. And that's what they were. And so you knew that this was going to be big.

NARRATOR: The study went to the heart of the prevalence question. In this case, it showed the prevalence of brain disorders was far higher among football players than the NFL anticipated.

STEVE FAINARU: So now Schwarz calls up the NFL to get a response. And what he gets from Greg Aiello, the league spokesman, is more denials. They're now denying their own study.

NARRATOR: Aiello insisted the study's design was flawed. But now the NFL's concussion crisis was again national news.

STEVE FAINARU: And so it's becoming almost impossible for the NFL to ignore it.

NARRATOR: At the same time, another force was also causing trouble for the NFL and the commissioner, the wives and widows of players with CTE.

JANE LEAVY: I don't think anyone else but the wives, sisters, mothers, daughters, and Ann McKee could have forced this issue into American consciousness.

NARRATOR: Eleanor Perfetto was one of them. Her husband, Ralph Wenzel, had played for the Pittsburgh Steelers.

ELEANOR PERFETTO: As the disease progressed, he went from being ill but fairly functional to getting to the point where he could no longer, you know, dress or feed himself. And in the last year and a half to two years before he died, he couldn't even walk anymore.

NARRATOR: She'd spent years trying to get help from the NFL and its players association. Then Perfetto took matters into her own hands. She showed up uninvited to a league meeting about caring for retired players.

MARK FAINARU-WADA: There's going to be a meeting that the commissioner is holding with former players. And you know, her husband, suffering, you know, from dementia, obviously can't be represented there by anybody but her. And she's told she's not allowed to enter the room.

NARRATOR: It was the commissioner himself who kept Perfetto out.

ELEANOR PERFETTO: And I said, "I'd like to attend this meeting." And he said, "No, you can't attend. It's only for players. It's not for anyone else." And I said, "But my player—my husband is a player who's severely disabled, and he can't be here right now."

NARRATOR: Nevertheless, the commissioner said no.

NEWSCASTER: The issue is head injuries among players, and if those injuries can lead—

NARRATOR: As the concussion story received more attention, the coverage helped spark interest in the nation's capital.

NEWSCASTER: Congress considers concussions in the NFL—

NEWSCASTER: Congress is getting into the game. They're looking into the long-term impact—

REP. JOHN CONYERS JR., (D-MICH.), JUDICIARY COMMITTEE CHAIRMAN: The meeting will come to order.

NEWSCASTER: Congress is looking into the long-term impact of concussions.

STEVE FAINARU: Congress saw it as a way to put the NFL's concussion policies on trial in the court of public opinion.

NARRATOR: The commissioner arrived like a celebrity, the star attraction at the hearing and the focus of all the cameras.

PETER KEATING: Goodell is asked point-blank if he stands by the idea that concussions don't hurt pro football players.

[October 2009]

ROGER GOODELL: Let me address your first question—

PETER KEATING: He can't answer.

ROGER GOODELL: You're obviously seeing a lot of data and a lot of information that our committees and others have presented with respect to the linkage. And the medical experts should be the one to be able to continue that debate.

REP. JOHN CONYERS: I just asked you a simple question. What's the answer?

ROGER GOODELL: The answer is the medical experts would know better than I would with respect to that, but we—

ALAN SCHWARZ: His consistent response to questions was, "I am not a scientist and any questions about the long-term effects of concussion or head trauma in NFL players are better addressed to scientists."

NARRATOR: One at a time, committee members went after Goodell.

REP. MAXINE WATERS (D-CALIF.): We have heard from the NFL time and time again. You're always studying, you're always trying, you're hopeful. I want to know, what are you doing now?

REP. LINDA SANCHEZ (D-CALIF.): The NFL sort of reminds me of the tobacco companies pre-nineties, when they kept saying, "No, there's no link between smoking and damage to your health or ill health effects."

MARK FAINARU-WADA: The last thing the league wanted to be dealing with in that moment was the analogy to big tobacco. There's nobody in America who doesn't know what that means. That means denial.

STEVE FAINARU: You have the commissioner of the NFL who's being hauled before Congress to answer why his own research arm has been denying since 1994 that football causes brain damage, when everybody from The New York Times to former

NFL players, to the respected research scientists are saying, in fact, the opposite is true.

NEWSCASTER: —talked about NFL owners as being like tobacco executives—

NEWSCASTER: —but I think it's seen as being plausible—

NEWSCASTER: —the NFL, similar to what the tobacco industry engaged in—

NARRATOR: Back in New York, with the pressure mounting, the commissioner decided to make some dramatic changes.

NEWSCASTER: The NFL changes its playbook—

NEWSCASTER: New rules for treating athletes with concussions—

NEWSCASTER: NFL commissioner Roger Goodell wants all teams to adhere to a new policy for head injuries—

STEVE FAINARU: They'd just been hauled before Congress and the commissioner was embarrassed by Linda Sanchez. They'd been compared to big tobacco. And they were trying to fight back.

NARRATOR: The commissioner initiated a series of new rules designed to protect players from concussions.

STEVE FAINARU: It was quite obvious what they were doing. They were in the middle of a major damage-control operation.

NEWSCASTER: From now on, teams should consider a concussion a game-ending injury.

NARRATOR: Dr. Casson was out.

NEWSCASTER: Dr. Casson resigned from the NFL's concussion committee.

NARRATOR: And a new concussion committee would be formed, led by two prominent neurosurgeons.

NEWSCASTER: The NFL is committed to medical and scientific research—

NARRATOR: And there was one other surprise.

ALAN SCHWARZ: I read on the wire that the NFL had given a million dollars to Boston University. What? And so I called up Chris, like, "What the hell's going on?" He didn't know what was going on. He's, like, "What are you talking about?"

CHRIS NOWINSKI: The answer was, "I don't know what you're talking about. This doesn't sound right at all."

DR. ANN MCKEE: A CBS reporter wanted to know what I thought of the gift of a million dollars. That was the first I heard of it. I was, like, floored.

NARRATOR: And Goodell offered Dr. McKee something she needed even more than money—brains.

MARK FAINARU-WADA: They get a letter from the league. It says you guys are now the NFL's "preferred" brain bank and that the league will help with efforts to direct families to donate the brains of former players to Boston so that they will be studied for CTE.

NEWSCASTER: The National Football League says it will encourage current and former players to donate their brains—

NARRATOR: As the story of the deal broke—

NEWSCASTER: The NFL is donating $1 million towards the study—

NARRATOR: —the NFL'S spokesman, Greg Aiello, received a call from reporter Alan Schwarz.

ALAN SCHWARZ: While we were talking, he said, "It's clear that there are long-term consequences to concussions in NFL players." Now, that kind of statement don't make news if anybody else says it. But this time, it was the league saying it.

STEVE FAINARU: Schwarz stops. You know, he knows that the NFL has not only been denying this for years, that they've never come close to uttering anything even remotely close to this.

ALAN SCHWARZ: And I said, "Greg, you realize that's the first time that anyone associated with the league has made that connection." And I remember, he was a little—I don't—what's the adjective? Annoyed. He was annoyed.

MARK FAINARU-WADA: The *Times* now suddenly has a huge story, that the NFL has acknowledged a link between brain damage and football. And sure enough, stripped across the top of the *Times* sports section the next day is that very story.

NARRATOR: At Dr. McKee's research lab, thanks to the NFL's endorsement, the brain bank business was booming.

DR. ANN MCKEE: There were NFL players out there that were talking to their wives and saying, "I think this might be something." You know, "I'm experiencing some problems. And I'm thinking I should donate my brain to this work."

NARRATOR: By 2010, Dr. McKee had looked at the brains of twenty NFL players. She had found CTE in nineteen of them. It was during that time that a brain arrived that would dramatically raise the stakes.

ROBERT STERN: Owen Thomas to me was a critical case. Here we have a twenty-one-year-old who was a hard-hitting lineman from the age of nine on.

CHRIS NOWINSKI: And then, seemingly out of nowhere, he decided to take his own life. Never been diagnosed with a concussion, never had a problem in the world.

NARRATOR: Owen Thomas had hanged himself in his off-campus apartment. Chris Nowinski secured his brain for Dr. McKee. without any history of diagnosed concussions, it seemed unlikely he had CTE.

DR. ANN MCKEE: I was fully prepared to see nothing. I remember late at night looking at the brain and thinking, "Just going to knock this one off." And it just floored me. It just—I just couldn't believe what I was seeing.

NARRATOR: Such an advanced case of CTE had never been found in such a young person.

DR. ANN MCKEE: In, like, twenty spots in his frontal lobe. He's twenty-one. He's so young. You know, that changes the game to me.

ANNOUNCER: —wrapped up and brought down by Owen Thomas—

NARRATOR: Because he'd never had a diagnosed concussion, Dr. McKee suspected Thomas might have gotten CTE from the everyday subconcussive hits that are an inherent part of the game.

ANNOUNCER: Another nice play by Owen Thomas—

DR. ANN MCKEE: Those subconcussive hits, those hits that don't even rise to the level of what we call a concussion, or symptoms, just playing the game can be dangerous.

ANNOUNCER: A crucial matchup in the AFC—

MARK FAINARU-WADA: McKee is saying, "Look, this is very much an issue at the core of the game, of offensive lineman and defensive linemen pounding the crud out of each other on every single play, on every single down and every single practice, and there's no getting around that."

NARRATOR: It was a controversial theory that raised fundamental questions about the way the game was played.

HARRY CARSON: The human body was not created or built to play football. When you have force against force, you're going to have injuries. And I'm not talking about the knees and— you know, all of that stuff is a given. But from a neurological standpoint, you're going to have—you're going to have some brain trauma.

NARRATOR: Harry Carson has been studying the matter since he retired twenty-five years ago.

HARRY CARSON: You know, most people are keyed in on the big hit. But the little miniconcussions are just as dangerous because you might be sustaining six to ten, maybe a dozen of these hits during the course of a game. And you know, if you're going up against top-flight players who are able to perfect those skills of hitting you upside the head, or you know, getting hit with an elbow or—it's one of those things that at some point, you're going to pay for it down the line.

STEVE YOUNG: You know, I really worry about my lineman brothers. I really worry for my running back brothers. I mean, that's the truth. We're talking about a nefarious injury, one that you never feel until it's too late. So that's the—that's just—when I look back over thirty years of—associated with football, that's the thing that's most alarming to me.

MICHAEL ORIARD: The way the game is played, I don't see how you can eliminate all of those routine hits that linemen make every play. How do you eliminate them with—and have the game still be football?

NARRATOR: Back in the lab, McKee had seen another surprising case.

DR. ANN MCKEE: We had been able to get the brain of an eighteen-year-old who had died ten days after suffering his fourth concussion playing high school sports.

NARRATOR: It was the brain of eighteen-year-old Eric Pelly. A high school senior, a straight-A student, he'd played multiple sports. His dream was to play for the Steelers.

DR. ROBERT CANTU: No one, I think, would have thought that you were going to find chronic traumatic encephalopathy in a high school athlete.

DR. ANN MCKEE: I was shocked to find that in the brain of this eighteen-year-old, there were little tiny spots, little tiny areas in the frontal lobe that looked just like this disease.

DR. ROBERT CANTU: You have an eighteen-year-old with chronic traumatic encephalopathy. That just shouldn't happen.

DR. ANN MCKEE: I had an eighteen-year-old at that time. You know that that brain is supposed to be pristine. The fact that it was there, and he was only playing high school level sports, I mean, I think that's a cause for concern.

NARRATOR: For Dr. McKee and others, it raised the obvious question. How safe is it for children to play football?

YOUTH FOOTBALL TEAM: What time is it? Game time! What time is it? Game time!

HARRY CARSON: From a physical-risk standpoint, you know what you are doing when you sign your kid up, that he can hurt his knee, OK? But what you should know now is your child could develop a brain injury as a result of playing football. It's not just on the pro level, it's on every level of football. The question is, do you want it to be your child?

NARRATOR: For Dr. McKee's colleague Dr. Cantu, the controversial answer was that no one under fourteen should play tackle football.

DR. ROBERT CANTU: With what we know about the youth brain compared with the adult brain, that it's more easily disrupted than the adult brain—the youth brain is lighter in weight, so it has less inertia to put it in motion, so you tap a youth head, and his brain moves much quicker than an adult brain that's heavier and therefore has more inertia. So I think we should be treating youths differently.

NARRATOR: And for the BU advocate Chris Nowinski, it was a danger the NFL helped to create.

CHRIS NOWINSKI: As long as the NFL dismissed this, that meant that parents were signing their kids up to go play football, believing that there was no risk. And you know, that wasn't fair to those kids or those parents, but especially those kids.

ANNOUNCER: Let's give him a big round of applause!

NARRATOR: Dr. McKee, who had grown up loving football, has struggled with her feelings about the sport.

DR. ANN MCKEE: I don't feel that I am in a position to make a proclamation for everyone else.

NEWSCASTER: If you had children who are eight, ten, and twelve, would they play football?

DR. ANN MCKEE: Eight, ten, twelve? No. They would not.

NEWSCASTER: Why?

DR. ANN MCKEE: Because the way football is being played currently that I've seen, it's dangerous. It's dangerous and it could impact their long-term mental health. You only get one brain. The thing you want your kids to do most of all is succeed in life and be everything they can be. And if there's anything that may infringe on that, that may limit that, I don't want my kids doing it.

NARRATOR: McKee's warnings about the danger of the game have made her the subject of sharp criticism.

JANE LEAVY: She's a lightening rod because people see her as the woman out to destroy football as we know it. Probably the most hurtful charge that's been leveled against her is that she's crossed a line from scientist to activist.

NARRATOR: A number of prominent scientists believe she has overstated the dangers of playing football.

PETER DAVIES, PH.D., NEUROSCIENTIST, FEINSTEIN INSTITUTE: There's a kind of polarization in that the BU group are clearly the advocates for CTE research. But it's not the only issue. You know, there are other issues that we've got to look at. And how common is this? How many brain traumas do you need to get this? Is this something that everybody will get if they have enough brain trauma? Or is it the result of steroid or drug abuse in a small number of NFL players? We don't know. These are questions, not statements of fact.

NARRATOR: Some researchers say Dr. McKee has examined only a limited sample of players and too few brains to justify her conclusions.

MARK LOVELL: There's been a sense of fear that's been put into parents that "maybe I shouldn't let my kids play sports." Having said that, I still think it's something that we need to be concerned about. We just need more information on it in terms of, you know, what exactly is the incidence and the risk. Nobody knows that at this point in time. It's still being debated. Depends on who you listen to.

KEVIN GUSKIEWICZ, PH.D., NFL HEAD, NECK, AND SPINE COMMITTEE: Those that have been conducting the autopsies are working with what they have to work with.

I think that we need to learn more about these former athletes, learn more about them during their living years so that we can better understand what their neurocognitive function is like, what their emotional status is like. We just have to be careful not to say that this causes that and be able to connect those dots without having more prospective analysis.

DR. ANN MCKEE: I'm not surprised that people don't believe me. They don't have—they don't look at—they haven't done this work. They haven't looked at brain after brain after brain. I just feel that, I guess, the more cases we get, the more we persevere, the more they hear, eventually, they'll change their mind.

NARRATOR: Still, McKee and her colleagues at BU acknowledge there are limits to her research.

ROBERT STERN: Not everyone who hits their head gets this disease. And so a critical question is why does one person get it and another person doesn't. There must be really important variables, genetics, things about the type of exposure to brain trauma people get. We need to figure those things out.

NARRATOR: Dr. McKee admits she's seeing only a small sample.

DR. ANN MCKEE: I think, to be truthful, even a selection bias in an autopsy sample, even if the family of an individual who's affected is much more likely to donate their brain than a person who had no symptoms whatsoever—given that, we have still been just ridiculously successful in getting examples of this disease.

NARRATOR: Dr. McKee has now examined the brains of forty-six former NFL players. Forty-five had CTE.

DR. ANN MCKEE: We have an enormously high hit rate. I mean, you know, that would be extraordinary with any other disease, to be able to pull in that many cases just that were suspected. So I think the incidence and prevalence has to be a lot higher than people realize.

NARRATOR: To her, it may be the beginnings of an epidemic.

DR. ANN MCKEE: I think it's going to be a shockingly high percentage. I'm really wondering where this stops. I'm really wondering, on some level, if every single football player doesn't have this.

911 OPERATOR: 911 emergency.

NARRATOR: And then another death.

MEGAN NODERER: Oh, my God! My boyfriend's been shot! My boyfriend's been shot!

NEWSCASTER: An apparent suicide by a powerful athlete—

911 OPERATOR: Your boyfriend?

MEGAN NODERER: Yes!

NEWSCASTER: A beloved NFL star apparently took his own life today—

911 OPERATOR: What is your boyfriend's name?

MEGAN NODERER: Junior Seau.

NEWSCASTER: Linebacker Junior Seau died today in an apparent suicide—

911 OPERATOR: Where did he shoot himself?

MEGAN NODERER: I can't tell, ma'am. It looks like in the heart.

NEWSCASTER: The untimely death of Junior Seau is provoking questions—

NARRATOR: As the news broke, the question emerged—did CTE play a part in Junior Seau's death?

ANNOUNCER: Here comes Seau! And he's sacked!

ANNOUNCER: All the way back at the . . .

NARRATOR: He had used his body and his head for twenty years in the NFL. Number 55 was a hard-hitting linebacker. Pain and injury were his specialty. he even bragged about it once on an NFL film.

JUNIOR SEAU: *[NFL Films]* A perfect hit is when you're faced up, coming one on one, and you hear him go, "Uh"—just a little "Uh."

NARRATOR: He talked about the price he was willing to pay.

JUNIOR SEAU: You have to sacrifice your body. You have to sacrifice years down the line. When we are fifty, forty years old, we probably won't be able to walk. That's the sacrifice that you take to play this game.

NARRATOR: And it had paid off. Seau made millions. He was a philanthropist, beloved in his community. But then a familiar story—his life fell apart.

NEWSCASTER: Junior Seau was arrested for domestic violence in Oceanside California early on Monday—

NEWSCASTER: Seau accused of hitting his twenty-five-year-old girlfriend—

NEWSCASTER: Junior Seau drove his SUV right off a cliff in California—

NEWSCASTER: The former pro football star has apparently fallen on hard times—

NARRATOR: At forty-three, his business empire had imploded.

NEWSCASTER: His behavior changed dramatically—

NARRATOR: He'd lost millions of dollars gambling.

NEWSCASTER: —including compulsive gambling, alcohol abuse—

NARRATOR: He wasted everything.

NEWSCASTER: —and violent, off-the-field incidents.

GINA SEAU, EX-WIFE: We didn't know why he was detached or forgetting, or why he would bark at us for nothing or—we didn't know.

SYDNEY SEAU, DAUGHTER: The past two years have been the roughest. And for a couple months at a time, I wouldn't hear from him at all. And that would scare me.

TYLER SEAU, SON: We got really close, and you know, I feel like it's turning around, OK, he wants to be part of my life. And then, all of a sudden, I wouldn't hear from him.

He's truly a legend, and he will be with us forever—

NARRATOR: Seau was one of the most popular players and out of the league for only two years. His brain became the most sought-after ever.

STEVE FAINARU: You've got a half dozen prominent researchers immediately began to mobilize to try to get their hands on this brain tissue.

GINA SEAU: I can understand where certain groups are saying, "Wow. This guy has played for twenty years. This would be a perfect candidate for us to study and see if he had it."

CHRIS NOWINSKI: I spent time making calls. I had, you know, a lot of—we had a lot of mutual friends, spoke to people at his foundation and just said, you know, "We would—like every other case, we would like to review this case, if you want."

NARRATOR: At the same time, far from the action, another researcher had received word of Seau's death.

DR. BENNET OMALU: So when Junior Seau died, just like every other case, people called me. I don't follow football, so I said, "Who is Junior Seau?" They said, "Oh, you don't"—just like Mike Webster, "You don't know Junior Seau?" I'm, like, "How do I?" Said, "Oh, he's even bigger than Mike Webster." They said, "Oh, he just died. He committed suicide."

NARRATOR: Dr. Omalu had been looking for a chance to get back in the game in a big way. He telephoned Seau's son, Tyler, to get consent to take his father's brain.

DR. BENNET OMALU: We did everything, spoke to the son. He gave us verbal consent. And the medical examiner requested that I come down—they've never had such a big case before, I'm an expert in this field—to help him.

STEVE FAINARU: He gets the first flight out the next morning. When he arrives at the medical examiner's office, he's telling people that he has the verbal consent from Tyler Seau to harvest the brain.

NARRATOR: And it was Omalu who actually removed Seau's brain.

DR. BENNET OMALU: I assisted at the autopsy. I took out the brain, processed the brain.

STEVE FAINARU: Just as they're finishing up the autopsy, the chaplain comes walking into the room and he says, literally, "Houston, we have a problem." And that problem is that he had just gotten off the phone with Tyler Seau, and according to Tyler, the NFL informed him that Omalu's research is bad and that his ethics are bad, that he's essentially unethical.

TYLER SEAU: People started saying things about Omalu, kind of telling me the kind of character that he has. And you know,

I got a lot of e-mail about it. But at that point, I was just kind of—you know, I don't want to hear all these things.

DR. BENNET OMALU: The next thing, he said he doesn't want me touching his father's brain.

STEVE FAINARU: At that point, there's nothing else to do except leave. I mean, he just walks out of the room, and he takes his empty brain briefcase and he gets back on the plane, and he goes back to San Francisco without having any success.

DR. BENNET OMALU: So I was very demoralized, I remember that day I was. People didn't notice. When I got into the cab I was crying. I mean, what have I done?

NARRATOR: Junior Seau's brain was sent to the National Institutes of Health, the NIH.

MARK FAINARU-WADA: The NFL very directly worked not only to get the brain to NIH, but in this case, to keep it away from Omalu's group or McKee's group by speaking badly about them.

NARRATOR: NFL doctors say the decision was made purely in the interest of science.

KEVIN GUSKIEWICZ: Getting it into the hands of good science is their—the goal there. So yes, I think that was probably what was driving the suggestion that "Let's have NIH get involved."

NARRATOR: The final diagnosis in Seau's case was national news.

NEWSCASTER: ABC News and ESPN have learned exclusively Seau's brain—

NARRATOR: He had CTE.

NEWSCASTER: —visible signs of CTE, chronic traumatic encephalopathy—

NARRATOR: In the months following Seau's death, the NFL went on the offensive. The commissioner helped to promote a youth football safety initiative, the Heads Up program. The league donated $30 million dollars to the NIH to study sports injuries, including joint disease, chronic pain, and CTE.

ROGER GOODELL: We recently committed $30 million to the National Institutes of Health—

PETER KEATING: Good PR is one part of the NFL strategy. But the other piece of it is that the NFL wants to come off as being very forward-looking. The NFL wants to keep pushing these questions into the future, keep the discoveries going, make it seem like these questions that still need to be resolved are things that the league is working with doctors and researchers on.

NARRATOR: It was a message the commissioner himself delivered, granting a rare TV news interview the morning of the Super Bowl.

BOB SCHIEFFER, CBS NEWS, *Face the Nation*: *[February 3, 2013]* I'm going to ask you this question because some widows of some NFL players have asked me to ask you. Do you now acknowledge that there is a link between the game and these concussions that people have been getting, some of these brain injuries?

ROGER GOODELL: Well, Bob, that's why we're investing in the research, so that we can answer the question, what is the link? What causes some of the injuries that our players are still dealing with? And we take those issues very seriously.

MARK FAINARU-WADA: Though the league previously, through Greg Aiello, acknowledged a link, there's no more acknowledging a link exists. There's "The science is still emerging and we're really going to try and do long-term studies on this. And we're going to figure out whether there's a link."

ROGER GOODELL: We're going to let the medical individuals make those points. We're going to give them the money, advance that science. In the meantime, we have to do everything we can to advance the game and make sure it's safe.

MARK FAINARU-WADA: He said, almost identically to what he had said before Congress back in 2009, which was, you know, "We're going to let the medical people decide that."

NARRATOR: Almost two decades after the NFL founded its first scientific committee to research the issue, the league continues to insist the evidence of a link between CTE and football is unclear.

PETER KEATING: It sure looks like it was just a relentless and endless delaying action. Year after year after year, at crisis after crisis after crisis, the concussions committee and its members assured the public that the league was looking into this.

The league actually never got around to looking at it in any kind of valid way. We're talking in the year 2013. This committee was founded in 1994. Maybe there should be better evidence by now.

NARRATOR: As the concussion crisis deepened, the commissioner faced yet another challenge, a lawsuit brought by more than 4,500 retired players.

PETER KEATING: The threat to the NFL from this litigation was existential. The threat was that the league was going to have to pay out in the billions with a B, not millions with an M.

NARRATOR: About one third of NFL veterans, including some of the biggest former stars, claimed the NFL had fraudulently concealed the danger to their brains.

THOMAS GIRARDI, PLAYERS' ATTORNEY: The main allegations here are—it's very simple. There was a very severe hazard that was present in professional football, and it was a little secret. The NFL knew it, but the players certainly didn't know it.

NARRATOR: On the other side, the NFL's lawyers.

LEGAL AIDE: OK, representing the National Football League will be Paul Clement. He'll be flanked by Anastasia Danias —she's from the National Football League—and also Beth Wilkinson from Paul Weiss—

NARRATOR: They insisted the league had done nothing wrong.

BETH WILKINSON, NFL'S ATTORNEY: Let's be clear. Let's be clear. We strong—we strongly deny those allegations that we withheld any information or misled the players. And if we have to defend this suit, as Paul was alluding to, we will do that and be able to make those factual allegations. But we absolutely deny those allegations.

NARRATOR: But away from the cameras, the two sides were engaged in tense court-ordered negotiations.

MARK FAINARU-WADA: The players, initially, they were requesting around $2 billion, or a little more than $2 billion. And what we've been told is the NFL was offering virtually nothing. They were offering "peanuts," as one person said.

NARRATOR: The players believed they had significant leverage, a threat to the NFL.

PETER KEATING: The threat was that the doctors and trainers, neuropsychologists, maybe owners, maybe commissioners and ex-commissioners, were going to have to testify under oath as to what they knew and when.

NEWSCASTER: —historic settlement today with the NFL—

NARRATOR: Then, with football season about to begin, a surprise settlement.

NEWSCASTER: —settlement between the National Football League and thousands of its former players.

NARRATOR: The league agreed to pay $765 million to resolve the lawsuit.

ALAN SCHWARZ: It appears as if it ties it up quite nicely. You know, the two sides figured out that that was fair, and they were OK with it. And so the image of the situation to most fans is that the NFL got taken to task for the concussion problem, OK?

NEWSCASTER: There is a proposed settlement in a huge concussion lawsuit—

NARRATOR: But the settlement left one big question unanswered.

MARK FAINARU-WADA: There's no admission whatsoever of guilt by the league. The league makes it very clear they're not admitting any guilt, that there's no acknowledgment of any causation between football and the possibility of long-term brain damage. And that was—you know, that was a prominent part of the settlement.

PETER KEATING: I don't think we needed a trial to know that the NFL conducted a lot of shoddy research. And it wasn't hypothetical. It wasn't a supposition. What the trial would have done was bring out that evidence. You didn't need the trial to know that there was something wrong there. But the details of how they went about it, that's what's going to stay locked away.

NARRATOR: One week later, the commissioner made the league's position clear.

ROGER GOODELL: *[CBS,* This Morning, *September 4, 2013]* There was no admission of guilt. There was no recognition that anything was caused by football.

NARRATOR: The league would not have to answer those tough questions about what they knew and when they knew it.

ROGER GOODELL: —that we've reached an agreement here that resolves these issues, and we'll move forward from there.

HARRY CARSON: I think everyone now has a better sense of what damage you can get from playing football. And I think the NFL has given everybody 765 million reasons why you don't want to play football.

ANNOUNCERS: Erenberg touchdown!

Touchdown Pittsburgh Steelers!

Listen to this crowd! They're on fire!

NARRATOR: For now, the future of the league and the game of football seem secure.

ANNOUNCER: Franco Harris is now at the thirty. Big pileup!

NARRATOR: But fundamental questions remain about how the game will be played and who will play it.

ANNOUNCER: It's still wild and woolly and I love 'em that way.

ANNOUNCER: You love 'em wild and woolly and you're seeing it now!

MARK FAINARU-WADA: You've got the most popular sport in America basically on notice. You've got the very real question being asked of whether the nature of playing the sport exposes you to brain damage and lots of science that suggests that it can.

ANNOUNCER: An awesome physical team were the Steelers today!

MARK FAINARU-WADA: And that raises all sorts of questions for guys who are playing in the league, guys who played in the league, moms, kids, all of us who love football. It's pretty scary. It's a big deal.

ANNOUNCER: And the future opponents are going to have some trouble!

Part V

Creative
Destruction

Fast Company

The pairing of the former Gap executive Mickey Drexler and the president and executive creative director Jenna Lyons, an unlikely duo, put the emphasis at J.Crew on quality and creative risk taking. Simple but effective, the new approach brought in upscale customers, including Michelle Obama, and turned the company around. Danielle Sacks goes behind the scenes for a charmingly written corporate profile.

Danielle Sacks

22. How Jenna Lyons Transformed J.Crew Into a Cult Brand

Jenna Lyons is in her corner office sucking on an iced coffee as if it were manna. The room looks like a cross between a boudoir and an artist's loft, with a peach fur draped over a white leather eames chair. The industrial windows stretch up and up, like Lyons's legs, which are punctuated by a pair of metallic, sparkled three-inch stilettos. But the coffee just isn't cutting it. "I'm so hungry. I haven't eaten in ten days," says the executive creative director and president of J.Crew, not hyperbolically. "I was like, *errrr! errrr!* with every pair of pants," she adds, making that grunting sound familiar to all women at some point in their lives. Turns out even the most fashionable manager in America can have a bad clothing day. "The inside button would pop before I even zipped it. I was like, Oh, God!" So Lyons went on an organic-juice-cleanse-plus-Isogenics bender and has consumed nothing but liquids for more than a week. "I'm a little bit mangry. Hangry mangry," she confesses, within five minutes of my arrival.

It's surprising, though comforting, to find out that Lyons is humanly imperfect. Since her coronation as creative head of J Crew in 2008, the company once known for its preppy Nantucket ancestry has become a force in fashion, with Lyons at the center of its evolution. She has created a high-low look that reflects her own boy-girl style—androgyny with some sequins and a dash of nerdy glasses. Along with annual revenue that has more than tripled to $2.2 billion since 2003, the cult of J.Crew has blossomed like a CMO's fantasy, with fashion blogs wholly devoted to the brand (from JCrewIsMyFavStore to TheJCRGirls) and a fan base that includes Michelle Obama and Anna Wintour. At Fashion Week this February (J.Crew's fourth season there, itself a symbol of the retailer's growing influence), one attendee whispered, as if Lyons were Madonna or Bono, "I am just totally obsessed with Jenna."

Her ascension seems instantaneous, but she happens to be one of the company's longest-tenured employees, having worked there her entire career. After graduating from Parsons in 1990, the then twenty-one-year-old started as an "assistant to an assistant to someone else's assistant," as she puts it, designing the company's old-world men's rugby shirts. "It's taken me years to get here, and I've cultivated it so carefully," says Lyons. "But I didn't think it was possible. I just assumed I'd plateau and that there would be no place for me to go."

She most likely would not have reached her perch if she hadn't crossed paths with Millard "Mickey" Drexler, the son of a garment district fabric buyer, the so-called Merchant Prince who transformed Gap from a $400 million enterprise into a $14 billion empire. Not since Steve Jobs and Jonathan Ive at Apple has a creative pairing been as intriguing and fruitful as that of Drexler and Lyons. Drexler became chairman and CEO at J.Crew in 2003, four months after Gap fired him following a plunge in the company's stock. His fall was both humiliating and motivational. Todd Snyder, Drexler's former head of men's wear at Gap, advised him to seek out Lyons, at the time J.Crew's vice president of women's design, likening her to Calvin Klein in the early days. "Jenna was a great designer, she looks like a model, and then she talks like the best salesperson you ever met," says Snyder.

"I think she's the most talented person he's ever worked with in design."

Their partnership would mark the end of the days when J.Crew's product design was dictated by corporate strategy. Together, they would make and sell only what they loved. The love would not be unconditional; they would adjust their product line always, trying new ideas, assessing, and quickly getting rid of anything that didn't work. Under Drexler and Lyons, J.Crew would become a company of constant and freewheeling experimentation, iteration, adaptation.

On the surface, the two are an unlikely fit—Drexler, a sixty-eight-year-old from the Bronx; Lyons, a Southern Californian who at forty-four looks like a J.Crew model before the airbrushing. Yet they share an ebullient, un-self-conscious nature, and they have set the standard for running a business focused on design. Though he is a notorious micromanager, Drexler doesn't stifle the talent, funneling his obsessiveness toward the steps that come before and after the creative process. And though she has been called a designer's designer, Lyons has instinctive business acumen. In Lyons, Drexler has found a partner to create both an ethos of mutual support for creative risk taking and a unified aesthetic that suffuses the company and is spreading through the culture at large, which is how Lyons came to have the unusual dual role of J.Crew's top creative executive and its president. "What it says," Lyons claims, "is that no financial decision weighs heavier than a creative decision. They are equal."

· · ·

J.Crew employees reveal themselves by the nakedness of their ankles. It's as if the company's uniform, ambiently dictated by Lyons, is enforced only from the knees down. Bare ankles, for men and women alike, whether with suede bucks, ballet flats, heeled ankle boots, high-top Converse, vintage Nikes, or glittery pumps, fill the company's East Village headquarters. At a review in early March for a jewelry catalogue shoot, sockless stylists, art directors, and merchants gather before Lyons as she interprets a wall mocked up with outfits paired with samples from the company's latest accessories collection. "This—not so pretty," Lyons says, her delicate hand clasping a chunky turquoise necklace hanging at the neck of a white linen suit. As she continues along the wall, her underwhelmed reaction becomes increasingly apparent. But instead of pointing fingers, she senses a deeper problem, and the jewelry review turns into a mediation session. "It seems like you guys feel you didn't have a lot to play with?" Lyons asks. The stylist agrees. Lyons starts probing to figure out how the stylists gain access to jewelry for a shoot—which is just where the problem began.

"When something hasn't been as beautiful as it can be, the reason is always bigger than the thing," Lyons tells me afterward. Here, the reason was miscommunication between the stylists and the merchandisers. "At this stage, I'm like a glorified crossing guard," says Lyons. "It's like, try to keep people motivated, keep the traffic moving, keep people from getting stumped or stopped by a problem."

She has a therapist's touch as well. "Every time I walk in her door, she reads my mind in three seconds. I think she knew I was pregnant before I did," says Ashley Sargent Price, who does art direction for J.Crew's catalogs and website. "She knows how to make you feel appreciated, even if you need to be redirected." The skill is an essential one for getting the best out of designers, who, Lyons holds, don't operate by the same rules as other people in business. "Managing creative people—not so easy," she says. "A lot of emotion, a lot of stroking. Some people need tough love. Some people need a lot of love." Above all is the challenge of managing in a subjective realm. "There's no right or wrong answer," says Lyons. "When someone creates something and puts it in front of you, that thing came from inside of them, and if you make them feel bad, it's going to be hard to fix because you've actually crushed them."

This sensitivity stems in part from a challenging childhood. Lyons was born with incontinentia pigmenti, a genetic disorder that led to scarred skin, patchy hair, and lost teeth, requiring dentures as a kid. Her gawkiness (she's now six feet tall) didn't help. As a result, she was subjected to almost constant bullying. "It's amazing how cruel kids can be and superjudgmental and really just downright mean," says Lyons. Her nonchalant manner became her defense, and she found a refuge in art. "I searched for ways to make things more beautiful and surrounded myself with beautiful things because I didn't feel that in myself," she says. Her mother, a piano teacher, encouraged Lyons to take art classes, where she discovered a passion for drawing and sketching and what might seem to be the unlikeliest of interests—fashion. "I felt a huge drive to make clothes that everybody could have because I felt ostracized by that world of beauty and fashion," says Lyons. "I never thought I would have a part in it. Never in a million years." She traces her ambition to her parents' divorce when she was in the seventh grade. "I'll never forget my mother standing in the tuna-fish aisle thinking, Are we going to get tuna fish this week?" says Lyons. "Feeling like I never wanted to rely on a man, I was like, I gotta work my ass off."

It was Lyons's candor that initially impressed Mickey Drexler. When he arrived at J.Crew in 2003, the company was in financial distress and largely seen as a bit player in the industry. Management consultants had taken over and were prescribing product designs. On Drexler's first day, recalls Lyons, "he sat down, pushed his chair back, put his foot up on the table, and he looked around and he's like, 'You're all interviewing for your jobs.'" On his second day, he asked Lyons to run through the women's collection in front of the entire team, a roomful of fifty people. She presented three pairs of skinny stretch pants. Drexler asked what she thought of them. "At that point I was like, I have to be honest," recalls Lyons. "I can't lie to him because this is sort of a do-or-die situation." She said except for one pair, she didn't think the others fit the brand. Drexler told her to throw them on the floor. Then they got to a boucle sweater, which looked like poodle fur. Lyons said she hated it, but it was a million-dollar seller. Drexler told her to drop it on the floor. Then came the cheap cashmere T-shirts, made in China. Onto the floor. "I didn't know if I was going to be fired," says Lyons. "I was so confused, and I was scared, but I was also a little bit excited, because all the things that I liked and that I thought were brand-right he was leaving up on the wall. And I was like, Is that good, is that bad? I don't know."

She kept her job. (Many of her colleagues did not.) After two days of reviewing the entire product line, Drexler told Lyons to get on a plane to Hong Kong and design new pieces to fill all the holes. He also asked her where she wanted to source the company's cashmere. A more expensive mill, she said. He told her to call them. This move marked the beginning of Drexler's turnaround strategy—a bet on quality. "You cannot copy high quality, and it takes a long time to get a reputation for quality," he says. Lyons credits this first encounter as both formative and telling of their future together. "Honestly, I think it was because I didn't bullshit him," says Lyons. "His bullshit-dar is insane."

Giving primacy to design involves more than a shift in the power structure. It means running the business in a completely different way. Before Drexler came to J.Crew, designers were ordered to develop products that would meet specific merchandising goals. "We were told we need 'this bucket' and 'this bucket' and 'this bucket,'" says the J.Crew head of women's design Tom Mora. "'I need a merino sweater that is forty-eight dollars that has a stripe.' And you are jamming your design into a bucket and that's what you got—a design in a bucket." Drexler told Lyons not only to scrap the buckets but also, she says, "'Don't tell me what you're doing, don't show any of the merchants, just go and do it and then show me.'"

In generating those designs, Lyons's style and manner give her staff implicit permission to take risks. "Jenna leads by example," says a former J.Crew employee who worked for Lyons in men's wear. "She'll be wearing an oversize men's cashmere sweater and a maxi skirt of feathers. If you described it to a famous fashion person, it would sound ridiculous. But it's liberating for everyone who works for her." Three years ago, the J.Crew designer Emily Lovecchio floated an idea for an organza jacket. The fabric was unusual for such a garment because of its delicacy, but Lyons told the team to try it anyway. The jacket ended up on the cover of the J.Crew catalog. When experiments don't work out as well, all Lyons requires is for her staff to assume responsibility. "Jenna really loves people who are themselves, flaws and all," says Lovecchio. "If you mess up or totally do the wrong thing, you have to look her in the eye and say 'I messed this up,' and she will always say, 'Okay, we'll fix it.'"

Designing distinctive clothing was only the first step in reviving J.Crew. Lyons believed that to create a coherent brand and drive the business forward, every piece of the creative organization—from retail to catalogue to web—had to be unified. She was initially frustrated that the stores and catalogue, both run by merchandising, didn't match the aesthetic of the products. "There were a lot of really talented people, but they were all doing their own thing, and it looked like it," says Lyons. "It was bifurcated and fractured. It didn't come together." While Lyons is a little coy about whose aesthetic she felt the company needed—"It's not that my vision is better. It's having one singular vision"—she ultimately did fight for it to be hers. "For me, it was like, 'I really want to get my hands on that because I want it to look more cohesive, and it's driving me crazy.' So I was asking for it," says Lyons.

In 2010, her lobbying paid off. J.Crew's president, according to the official announcement, stepped down "to spend more time with her children," and Drexler gave the title to Lyons. "It was literally a two-second conversation," says Lyons. "He pulled me into a room and said, 'So, just want to let you know you're the president.' I was like, uh, okay. Alrighty then. Then I put my head down on the table, took ten deep breaths, sat back up and was like, 'Okay, do I need to do anything different?' And he was like, 'No, just keep doing what you're doing.' I'm like, 'Okay,' and we walked out of the room. That was it."

As Lyons's domain within the company grew, the prime directive for all her teams became always to consider how the brand appears to everyone who comes into contact with it. "I don't care if it's an employee handbook or the layout of the nursing room," says Lyons, who now also oversees marketing. She started with the stores. Their design, she felt, clashed with itself—sparse interiors with clothing stacked in chockablock fashion. "It's a little bit like a modern house with tons of shit in it," says Lyons. "It really doesn't look so pretty."

Lyons set out to rehab the stores, but getting the details just the way she wanted required her to make a business case for design. "It's hard when the finance team is used to putting a light fixture in the store that costs $2,000 and I'm like, 'Well, I want an $8,000 fixture,'" says Lyons. "You have to get people to understand why having that Serge Mouille light fixture is better, because it's beautiful and people will know something's different. Maybe when you look at that $200 cashmere sweater, you'll feel like, 'Oh, yeah, look at the store, it's so beautiful. This $200 sweater is a steal.'"

More recently, Lyons worked a bold overhaul of the catalogues. With 40 million copies distributed every year, the catalogues are at the root of J.Crew's business and constitute some of the brand's most precious real estate. Yet for years, the catalogue lineup was dictated by sales from the year before. Pictures of each item ran alongside clunky color swatches and dense text; perhaps only two out of one hundred pages were devoted to material that might be called editorial. The reimagined catalogue supports the idea of J.Crew as tastemaker, with multipage stories packaged around trends, such as "The Italian Shoe Collection: Designed in New York. Made in Italy" for some fancy leather flats. Today, the J Crew Style Guide—its new name—and its website have more of the feel of a fashion magazine.

Lyons's whimsical nature can sometimes make her seem like a different species from most folks with a key to the executive floor. And she can hardly be accused of stuffy qualities like propriety or perfection. "Ask my ex-husband how perfect I am," she jokes during one of our interviews. (He might have a thing or two to say about it, too; Lyons's personal life has been tabloid fodder since 2011, when she got divorced and paired up with a woman.) "You're pretty candid," I tell her. "Maybe to a fault," she says. "I might take my teeth out." Yet her colleagues credit her with a keen business mind, and that easy oscillation between her two selves is what has brought her so much success. Libby Wadle, J.Crew's executive vice president of brand (that is, merchandising), says: "Jenna is a designer all day long, but she can have conversations about real estate and parts of the business that many designers will just tune out. She gets all the moving parts and how they connect." When I ask Lyons how going private in 2011 helped the company, she immediately cites the freedom to invest more in IT infrastructure—not the first thing you'd expect to hear from a native creative. "It's hard to make those kinds of capital expenditures when you're public," she says.

·   ·   ·

Emil Corsillo is a denim nerd. A thirty-three-year-old graphic designer, he has an affection for vintage American workwear of the sort worn up until the 1950s. In his spare time Corsillo collects samples; he even has his buddy bring him back replicas from Japan, where the style first experienced a comeback. In

2008, Corsillo became particularly fascinated with old selvedge fabric, a hallmark of the workwear movement. The selvedge mark—a heavy red stripe stitched along the fabric's edge—indicates that a piece of denim is high quality, made from an original loom. One day Corsillo was tooling around with a piece of selvedge cloth on his sewing machine and realized that it was the perfect width for a men's tie. He and his brother Sandy would use the fabric in the Hill-side, a line of ties they launched in 2009.

For the Corsillo brothers, the tie was an experiment. They wanted to start small, working out of their Bushwick, Brooklyn, apartment, and they restricted supply to three independent shops. Within two months, J.Crew somehow caught wind of it. "Somebody there found our ties at one of those stores and brought them to Frank [Muytjens, head of men's design]," recalls Emil, "and Frank got in touch with us and said they wanted to talk about carrying the collection in a couple of shops."

Bringing in products made by third parties was a new gambit for J.Crew but one that Drexler felt could raise its profile. The design team saw no point in trying to re-create, say, a beautiful handcrafted leather boot, when a Minnesota company called Red Wing had been doing it for more than a hundred years. So J.Crew cracked the door to outsiders. "We buy what other people do much better than we can ever do," explains Drexler of the outside collaborations, of which J.Crew has had more than one hundred. Playing curator was also a branding strategy. The retailer isn't making much from the twenty-five pairs of handmade Alden Revello Cordovan Longwing shoes it sells, even at $710 a pair ("You have to have a hundred perfect hides to make that many. That's why you can only have twenty-five pairs," a J.Crew store manager explains to me), but they reinforce the idea that J.Crew is carefully selecting products on the shopper's behalf. "People love scarcity," says Drexler. And scarcity brings people to the stores to buy shirts and pants.

When J.Crew approached the Corsillos about the selvedge tie, the company was an unproven partner for outside brands. While most homegrown players would view this moment as winning the lottery, the Corsillo brothers were conflicted. "To be totally honest, we were scared and uncertain," says Sandy. For one, the two didn't have the resources to make goods for a national retailer. But more important, if the Hill-side was going to establish its fashion cred, selling out to a big retailer didn't seem like the answer. "It's like not wanting your favorite punk band to sign with a major label when you're a teenager," says Emil.

The Corsillos turned down a couple of meetings with J.Crew—until they got a call at ten a.m. one morning saying that Drexler wanted to visit them at their place in Brooklyn. "I looked around our office," recalls Emil, "and saw Sandy's unmade bed and dirty clothes on the floor, and said, 'Would it be possible to come to you guys instead?'" At J.Crew headquarters, they gathered in Drexler's office, along with Muytjens and four other J.Crewers. "Very quickly Mickey said something like, 'Okay, we're going to order this stuff immediately and put it in the catalogue, right?'" says Emil. "No one had told him that we had sort of said no."

After the brothers explained their concerns, Drexler told them that J.Crew was trying its best to behave like a tiny company. And he immediately proved his point. During the meeting, as he paged through a J.Crew catalogue, he came across a sneaker from Tretorn. When Emil mentioned that he was a freelance art director for Tretorn advertising, Drexler asked if he thought J.Crew was selling the best model of the shoe. Emil said he preferred another, the men's classic. "Mickey got on the office-wide intercom," recalls Emil, referring to Drexler's most melodramatic prop, a loudspeaker system that booms through the hallways at J.Crew headquarters, "and said, 'Who's in charge of Tretorn? Come to my office!'" The person in charge of Tretorn was asked, 'Are we getting these?' Twenty minutes after leaving the J.Crew office, Emil got a call from his boss at Tretorn asking if he had just been in a meeting with Mickey Drexler. Eventually the company ended up carrying that Tretorn shoe—and the Hill-side, too, which is now on its fifteenth J.Crew collection. "I don't know if Mickey said anything specific that persuaded us, but he's very charismatic," says Emil. "Basically, any worries we had about their intentions pretty much dissolved at that meeting."

The performance was undiluted Drexler, mixing efficiency with his unique brand of persuasion. In many ways, he is the Woody Allen of retail, his New York accent still thick as garlic on his breath, a desire always to be the omniscient narrator in the world of his creation, though his neurosis is focused on cashmere instead of death. Insecurity is a shared motivator too. "Mickey has such a chip on his shoulder for being fired at the Gap and raised poor," says a former employee. "That desire and anger make him unstoppable and relentless." As with a film whose producer is also director and star, Drexler is always working his audience while telling his cast how to play the scene.

On a recent visit to J.Crew's new Ludlow Shop at 50 Hudson, Drexler's id and ego were on full display. "I wish we had a couple customers," he announces like a dinner-party host with no guests, greeting some twelve of his top staffers for a monthly store walk-through. "Just kidding. We do [have customers]," he tells me. Drexler's mouth is an engine that never stops, and his irrepressible effusiveness defeats any attempts at self-censorship. The Ludlow Shop is an outgrowth of the Ludlow suit, one of the most successful products to debut at the Liquor Store, a one-off boutique in Tribeca that has served as a petri dish for new products. "If you look at most department stores—I'm not going negative on department stores," Drexler says, then whispers, "but I am." He then shouts, so even the few customers roaming the store can hear, "I can't stand them!"

•   •   •

Lyons and Wadle are staring at a spread from the May 2013 catalogue. They decide to kill it. The two pages show models wearing thick black glasses, colorful oxfords with ties, bare ankles in heels—Lyons's signature girl-in-her-boyfriend's-clothes look. "It looks too much like the copiers," grumbles Wadle, who keeps making vague references to a *Daily Mail* article that came out the previous day and has been irking the team ever since. When I get home, I dig up the piece: "Has J.Crew finally found a rival? Gap makes big comeback." It is the worst kind of story for J. Crew, lumping it in with Drexler's ex, a name that is practically forbidden in the office. "And with a smattering of quirky spring prints (like the cat symbols on a boyfriend-style shirt), colorful outfit combos and the use of some geek-chic spectacles," the article reads, "it seems Gap's $133 million profit increase may be thanks to some strategic styling lessons from fast fashion's reigning queen bee, J.Crew."

If Drexler has taught Lyons one thing, it's that in retail you're only as good as your last suit. But in their search for the next big franchise, an important part of Lyons's job is managing Drexler. In many ways she has become both his editor and translator. At any given moment, ideas and questions machine-gun out of him. Says Wadle, who worked with Drexler at Gap, "It's a constant, and none of us can keep up because we all have to be running the business. She [Lyons] is the ultimate filter." The challenge lies in knowing which of Drexler's ever-flowing stream of proposals to act upon. "If we executed every single thing he said, we would just be spinning," says Lyons. "What he's trying to say is, Have you asked yourself every single question? He's looking for the golden nugget all the time."

Lyons is one of the few people who can rein Drexler in. She typically waits until a product is in its final form before presenting it to him. "Sometimes his head is filled with fifty other things and he has an allergic reaction to something because he looks at it crooked or he just had a bad meeting," says Lyons. "And it's like, 'Okay, hold on. Don't look at that for a second. Let's redirect. I need you to calm down.' I swear to God there are maybe three people, one of them being his wife, who can do that."

Lyons might have this power because Drexler knows he could never do alone what they can do together. "If Jenna wasn't there," says a former employee, "J.Crew would be really good, but it would not be great. Probably a healthily run company like a Banana Republic." They give each other cover, too. "Mickey wants to be so cool so bad," says the former employee. "Jenna is confident and cool and human and comfortable with herself and gives him the credibility he needs to be on fire. And he has her back in a way no one else can." I ask Lyons what everyone in the business wonders: When will she leave J.Crew to start her own line? She says it's not in the cards, at least for now. As she has said, she already is building her own collection, and she wouldn't be able to do so on her own. Her former colleague Todd Snyder argues that no designer in Lyons's shoes would ever have a reason to leave. "Mickey has given her enough runway so she can really make of it what she wants," he says. "They should just call it Jenna Crew."

And for that chance, she says that she's indebted to Drexler. "This is his last job, you know? He's probably not going to do this again," says Lyons. Whenever Drexler does decide to retire, she and Wadle are rumored to be in line to run the company. "I'll give it to Libby," laughs Lyons, feigning disinterest. "I'll sit in the corner and draw some stuff." As if Jenna Lyons has never been hungry before.

Quartz

In November 2012, the startup Envia Systems appeared poised for a breakthrough, signing a licensing deal to produce a battery for an electric car with a 200-mile range for General Motors. A year later, the deal was off, GM accused Envia of misrepresenting its technology, and the company's chief executive and its chief technology officer were at each other's throats.

Steve LeVine

23. The Mysterious Story of the Battery Startup That Promised GM a 200-Mile Electric Car

At the end of November 2012, Atul Kapadia and Sujeet Kumar hosted the staff of their startup company for a holiday lunch of Mexican food at a Palo Alto, California, restaurant. For days, the pair—the CEO and CTO, respectively, of a lithium-ion-battery company called Envia Systems—had awaited an e-mail from General Motors.

It was to contain a deal rare to an industry newcomer—a contract worth tens and possibly hundreds of millions of dollars to provide the electric central nervous system for two showcase GM models, including the next-generation Chevy Volt. Untested small suppliers almost never get in the door of the world's major automakers, which regard them as too risky to rely on. But GM was won over by what seemed to be the world's best lithium-ion battery—a cell that, if all went well, would catapult the company to a commanding position in the industry with a middle-class electric car that traveled 200 miles on a single charge and rid motorists of the "range anxiety" that disquieted them about such vehicles. GM would have the jump on the high-end Tesla S, the only other major model with that range but one that would cost much more. For Envia, the contract could lead to an IPO that would make both men rich.

But the talking had gone on so long and with such uncertainty that neither man had even told Envia's staff scientists of the impending deal. Even if they felt more confident, they could not have said anything, since such news could affect GM's share price. Word had leaked around the Envia lab anyway. An edginess hung over the lunch.

Kapadia's cell phone rang as he drove back from the holiday party. It was General Motors: Senior management had finally signed the documents. They were on their way by e-mail. Kapadia turned off the phone but tried not to let on.

Back at Envia, situated across the bay in the industrial city of Newark, company employees gathered in the conference room for a regularly scheduled office meeting. Kapadia stood before some papers. He said it was the company's first licensing deal, one involving the biggest and most prestigious possible customer of all—General Motors.

"Just to let you know this is not my achievement. This is your achievement," the CEO said. "And I am signing on behalf of you." The room erupted as Kapadia bent over and initialed the papers. Envia's three-dozen scientists and business staff sounded like 200. They cat-called and screamed. The administrative staff jumped up and down.

A year later, the deal is in tatters, GM has accused Envia of misrepresenting its technology, and a document suggests why the carmaker may be right. The startup's unraveling is a blow for GM as it transitions to a new regime next month under CEO-designate Mary Barra, setting back its ambitions in the potentially gigantic future electric-car industry. It also risks making Envia, the recipient of several small federal grants, another punching bag for critics of U.S. government funding of advanced battery companies.

Envia. meanwhile. is mired in two angry civil suits. and the two executives are at daggers drawn, with Kapadia accusing Kumar of fraud and intellectual property theft and Kumar dismissing the allegations as the rants of an ousted executive who performed badly. Envia "was an illusion," alleges Michael Pak, the plaintiff in an IP theft suit against Kumar. "While the illusion is there, you can sell the company and run away. But illusion doesn't last forever."

The Great Battery Race

Four years ago, the United States and China set in motion a race for dominance of electric vehicles. At the cusp of two crises—the collapse of Detroit and of the global financial industry—lithium-ion batteries and electric cars seemed among the likeliest chances for driving the kind of fast economic growth that the high-tech and semiconductor industries had led in the past. President Barack Obama declared that the United States would have one million electric vehicles on the road in 2015, and China vowed to accomplish the same. Both envisioned besting Japan, which had established an early lead with Toyota's Prius, along with consumer-product juggernaut South Korea.

Central to Obama's calculus was the creation of a lithium-ion-battery manufacturing industry, an aim that Congress primed with $2 billion of direct stimulus grants and an additional $400 million for Arpa-E, a funding unit for frontier innovation within the Department of Energy. First invented in 1800, batteries are an old technology, but the financial stakes should anyone crack their confounding physics have resulted in waves of unusually motivated scientists, industrial leaders, and politicians. A breakthrough in batteries could not only allow cars to go farther but smartphones and emerging wearable devices such as smart watches to last longer and solar and wind generators to better store the power they produce.

Seeming to effortlessly navigate the bewildering juncture of big science, big business and big geopolitics, Envia was a showcase success for Arpa-E. It was one of the most promising of a clutch of electric-car-battery startups that won federal grants, and the GM deal was one of the highest-level endorsements possible for its technology.

This story is the product of dozens of interviews that I conducted with Kumar, Kapadia, and their staff members over the last two years, in addition to the lawsuits filed in recent weeks.

An Immigrant's Story

Kumar, the Envia CTO, grew up in the eastern Indian city of Patna, the pampered youngest son of a civil engineer. Frequent blackouts meant that Kumar studied by kerosene lamp at night, and when he was accepted to a doctoral program in materials science at the University of Rochester, it was the first time anyone in the family had studied abroad. Kumar describes arriving penniless in New York in 1990 on his way to a full, four-year scholarship, a $1,000-a-month stipend, and a series of campus jobs.

When he graduated in 1996, Kumar's only offer was in Silicon Valley, where he became the first employee of NanoGram, an East Bay battery-and-electronics development startup. A decade, some cashed-in stock options, and a few changes of hands later, he was hired to lead a development team from scratch at NanoeXa, a lithium-ion-battery startup founded by Pak, a South Korean–born entrepreneur. Those who knew Kumar found him to have an intuitive grasp of electrochemistry. And in an industry characterized by an unusual degree of exaggeration, he was "a man of his word," according to a scientist who met him at the time. "He would do what he said."

The first task was to find potentially winning intellectual property around which to build NanoeXa. When it comes to innovation in battery development, there are three main options—you can improve the anode, the cathode, or the electrolyte. The anode and cathode are the negative and positive electrodes between which the lithium shuttles, the act that creates electricity. The electrolyte sits in the middle and facilitates this shuttling motion. The ideal battery will first hold a lot of lithium and then send as much as possible of it into the shuttling motion without causing the especially sensitive cathode to collapse. If you can do those two things, your car will go a long distance.

An additional plus for electric car batteries is the ability to draw out the lithium fast—that is the power that allows a driver to speed up immediately on depressing the accelerator. But these traits tend to work against each other—you can pack in a lot of lithium but only draw it out of the two electrodes slowly, which means that you can drive nonstop between New York and Washington but may be in trouble if you need to quickly maneuver out of someone's way. Or you can choose the alternative—you can generally accelerate fast, but go only a relatively short distance on a single charge. On top of these features, you would like your battery not to catch fire, a nonnegotiable requirement, especially when it comes to consumer batteries. That is where the electrolyte comes in—depending on the additive, it can reduce the tendency for the volatile technology to burst into flames.

NanoeXa aimed its IP search at the cathode, where the easiest performance gains are achievable since they still have far to go to catch up to the capacity of the standard graphite anode. Kumar and the company's early team perused patents and journal papers and consulted experts before settling on a promising cathode invented by Argonne National Laboratory outside Chicago. The cathode combined nickel, manganese, and cobalt into an exceptional composite that astonishingly had not attracted a single licensee. NanoeXa became the first customer for the chemistry, which is called NMC for short.

What Kumar noticed was that NMC possessed all the necessary traits. Workhorse batteries based on lithium-cobalt-oxide chemistry—the type contained in most AA and laptop batteries—deliver around 150 milliamp-hours of specific capacity per gram (a measure of how densely they can store electricity). But Argonne researchers had managed at lab scale to push an exotic formulation of NMC to 250 and even 280 milliamp hours per gram, a 66 percent jump. The composition also provided pep—the lithium could be shuttled fast. And, made with manganese, NMC is one of the safest lithium-ion formulations; lithium-cobalt-oxide is much more prone to catching fire.

When you license an invention from a national lab, what you generally receive is not a working technology but rights to a relatively raw, bench-scale patent that must be built up into a commercial product. That was what NMC was—it needed to be optimized in the lab. But, all in all, Argonne's NMC composite seemed to be a top candidate to enable an electric car that could begin to compete with the economics of incumbent gasoline-fueled vehicles.

Kumar Decides to Create His Own Startup

About a year later, Kumar resigned. As justification, Pak said in an interview, Kumar cited personal differences with him. The 2007 departure was a shock for NanoeXa, which was left "in chaos," Pak said. "Without any notice, my main engineering guy left. I was counting on him a lot." Kumar gave assurances that he would not compete with NanoeXa using NMC technology, but instead would seek employment "in another company," Pak said.

But Kumar and a NanoeXa colleague, Mike Sinkula, had in fact decided to form their own lithium-ion-battery startup. They describe holing up immediately at Palo Alto Library, where they began to make cell-phone calls, send e-mails, and put together a slide deck to raise about $3 million in venture capital to fund a team that would produce a prototype. The basis of their pitch was a fresh NMC term sheet that Kumar had negotiated with Argonne. Kumar and Sinkula would not say so publicly for awhile, but they intended to make a go using the same technology as NanoeXa and in pursuit of the same market—electric automobiles.

Kumar and Sinkula were entering the lithium-ion-battery business at the cusp of a rush of inventors and capital into renewable energy generally and energy storage in particular. At MIT, Berkeley, Stanford, the national labs, and universities around the world, attention turned to a new era when it was thought that the electric car could finally be adapted to mass use. The push coincided with an eagerness by governments and private investment funds to get behind such new inventions.

Kumar did not reply to e-mails and SMS messages requesting comment for this article. In a statement, Envia denied that Kumar wrongfully took anything from NanoeXa. After the exchange of a few e-mails, Envia's public-relations firm said in an e-mail, "Due to the highly litigious nature of this case, I have been instructed by counsel to provide no further comment."

What Pak's civil suit alleges is that, in venturing into this fresh opportunity, Kumar took with him NanoeXa's year of work on enabling NMC, in addition to its marketing strategy, downloading the information from his work computer onto an external memory device. In essence, NanoeXa was the source of the core of Kumar's product and business strategy for what was to become Envia, according to Pak.

Among Kumar's first calls was to Kapadia, whose wife had attended Rochester with the battery man. The Mumbai-born Kapadia is a bookish Stanford MBA with a steady, quiet patter who worked as an engineer at Sun Microsystems before moving to an establishment Palo Alto venture firm called Bay Partners.

According to Kapadia's account, he was so impressed with Kumar that it almost did not matter how much he wanted—he was eager to invest in him. Two hours later, he called Kumar and said he would arrange the entire $3.2 million that Kumar sought.

In the summer of 2007, Bay ended up investing alongside Redpoint Ventures, another Silicon Valley firm whose earlier investments included Juniper Networks and Netflix. They sent Kumar a check for $500,000 so he and Sinkula could get going before the rest of the money worked through the funding system. Sinkula proposed a name for the company: "En" for energy, and "via," the Spanish for "way"—the way to energy.

Over the next two years, Kumar and Sinkula worked their way into paid research work for potential licensees including Honda and GM. They announced what they said was an optimized version of the NMC, which they trademarked as a "High Capacity Manganese Rich" cathode. This was the beginning stages of the slow, years-long process of establishing a supplier relationship with one of the major auto companies.

Bay and Redpoint invested another $7 million in the company a year or so after the first tranche. But the startup was burning through the cash while potential customers were slow to commit. In 2009, while vacationing with his family in India, Kapadia received a call from Kumar: Come back and help to save Envia. As the two executives told the story in their good days, Kapadia had assured Kumar from the outset that he would always be there if he was needed. Kapadia flew back, and, pressed by both Kumar and a couple of board members, he agreed to become CEO.

About the same time, Kumar heard about a competition organized by Arpa-E, the Department of Energy's new research funding unit. It would be Arpa-E's first set of grants for ideas promising profound leaps in energy technology. They would range from $500,000 to $10 million and confer considerable prestige on the winners.

Kumar thought that his best chance to win one was to twin his in-house cathode with an anode made of a silicon composite. The combination could be the most powerful electric-car battery in the world.

Revolutionizing the Second Battery Electrode

The Obama administration's investments in the U.S. battery industry were bearing their first fruits. A123 Systems, an MIT lithium-ion-battery startup, became the biggest IPO of 2009 after winning $249 million in matching federal stimulus money for a factory in Livonia, Michigan. EnerDel won $118 million for an Indiana battery plant. But they and other battery researchers and companies were paying so much attention to the cathode that now it was time to turn to potential advances in the anode, the negative electrode.

The anode is the staging point for the lithium. When a battery is being discharged—for instance when it is propelling an electric car—the lithium moves from the anode to the cathode. When it is being charged, the lithium moves back to the anode, where it is absorbed. Anodes are judged by how much lithium they can store and the rate at which it can be extracted, delivering distance and acceleration. Now, a competition began to improve the anode, and Kumar wanted to play.

The graphite anode was invented by Bell Labs in the 1970s. One of the leading ideas was to replace it with an anode made of silicon, a metal that could absorb a much larger ratio of lithium. Next to pure lithium metal, silicon was the most powerful possible anode. Such an anode had the potential to perform an order of magnitude better than graphite, whose specific capacity was about 400 milliamp hours per gram. In practical use, the anode would not deliver ten times the capacity of graphite, but researchers thought that with work, it could produce about 1,400 milliamp hours per gram, which would more than triple the standard anode's performance.

But silicon has a problem. For practical use in an automobile, you need an anode to last for at least 1,000 charge-discharge cycles before the battery needs replacing. But as you move lithium into a silicon anode, it expands tremendously. Graphite also expands, but nowhere near as much as silicon, which blows up three or four times in size. Quickly, it pulverizes and kills the battery.

Argonne National Lab, the source of Kumar's cathode, now had an interesting concept for silicon. So Kumar applied for the Arpa-E competition in collaboration with Argonne. Their joint submission said that if you started with Envia's High Capacity Manganese Rich cathode, you would achieve energy density of about 280 watt-hours per kilogram, another measure used to evaluate batteries and their electrodes. When you coupled it with a silicon-carbon anode, you could get a 400-watt-hour-per-kilogram battery, sufficient to power a car 300 miles on a single charge at half the cost of current technology, eclipsing every model on the market. That seemed to Kumar to meet Arpa-E's requirement for a transformational breakthrough.

In all, Arpa-E received some 3,700 submissions. Thirty-seven, or 1 percent, were selected. Envia was among them. It won a $4 million Arpa-E grant for the work to be carried out jointly with Argonne.

In February 2012, the Arpa-E director Arun Majumdar spoke to a hushed audience in a large, darkened hall at the Gaylord Convention Center outside Washington. It was the third annual Arpa-E Summit, which had already heard introductory remarks by former president Bill Clinton and Microsoft cofounder Bill Gates.

Majumdar projected a slide on three gigantic screens. It was Kumar and his Envia team. Envia, he said, had just reported the achievement of "the world record in energy density of a rechargeable lithium-ion battery." It had produced a prototype car-battery cell that demonstrated energy density between 378 and 418 watt-hours per kilogram. Envia said the achievement had been validated by Crane, the Indiana-based testing facility of the U.S. Naval Surface Warfare Center, which cycled the cell twenty-two times. In testimony the next month before Congress, Majumdar said the battery is "not yet ready for prime time. But if we were to use the Envia battery today, it would cut the battery cost by half and they are trying to reduce the cost even further."

The announcement triggered a stir in the industry and the media. Such a cell—if proven in an actual electric-car battery pack—would be an enormous breakthrough that could change the market. By stuffing in more energy and reducing battery costs so significantly, cars could travel much further and high prices could come down. Kapadia, as Envia's new CEO, was deluged with calls. One reporter declared the startup "the Golden Child" of the summit. Scientific American recalled Envia's humble beginnings in the Palo Alto Library. Among those listening, including General Motors, there seemed to be much more focus on Majumdar's second sentence and not the first: The allure of a cost-competitive electric car had obscured the question of how close the battery was to commercial availability.

Breaking Into GM

One thing that makes car companies economically powerful is that they outsource virtually everything. Dollars spent on a car move through the economy into countless large and small parts and component suppliers in the United States. Quality control is therefore one of Detroit's biggest tasks. The big carmakers rely almost entirely on incumbent suppliers with long histories of reliability, so that new models are close to flawless at launch and public-relations disasters are minimized. In the case of lithium-ion batteries—volatile technologies, liable to catch fire—the carmakers contract exclusively with big Japanese and South Korean chemical companies with decades-long track records. New firms, regardless of the quality of their product, can rarely withstand the scrutiny required to win these multi-billion-dollar contracts.

GM had even greater reason for caution: In 2008, the company was forced into bankruptcy and required a $49 billion federal bailout in order to regroup. The government came to own 61 percent of the company. Two years later, GM, now out of bankruptcy, held a $20 billion IPO and began again to earn money. In 2011, it trumpeted its return to the leading edge of mainstream carmaking by launching the Volt, a plug-in hybrid that *Motor Trend* magazine named its Car of the Year. But it remained highly cautious and defensive about its continued reliance on government capital.

The Volt's battery was supplied by South Korea's LG Chemical. But in 2009, GM's research division began to take a look at Envia and asked for a sample of its cathode. The results were not perfect—the Envia battery failed to pass muster on a couple of metrics. But it performed well enough that the following year, GM's ventures unit led a $17 million fundraising round for Envia; GM itself put in $7 million, and Jon Lauckner, its ventures chief and future CTO, took a seat as an observer on the board.

GM said it would allow no employee to speak to *Quartz* for this article and direct e-mails sent to executives went unanswered. But GM employees interviewed over the last couple of years said the opinion of the engineers in such supply cases usually trumps everyone else's since they are ultimately responsible should anything go wrong with a vehicle. And GM's engineers recommended that, for the sake of reliability, the carmaker continue its supply relationship with LG for the Volt's battery, according to a source familiar with this internal debate.

That made it remarkable when, after the Arpa-E Summit, GM began to negotiate a deal to license Envia's batteries for two critically important new models. GM's R&D and venture units had prevailed over the engineers.

Under the proposed contract, Envia would provide a cathode for the next-generation Volt, to be launched in the 2015 model year, that would cut 30 percent off the cost of the current battery technology. GM loses money on each Volt it sells, and such a shift in economics could make the next-generation version profitable. Envia was also to provide the complete Arpa-E battery cells for an electric car that could go 200 miles on a single charge in 2016. (When you scale up a laboratory-size 300-mile battery into a full electric-car pack, then account for GM's usual margin of error, you end up with approximately a 200-mile car.)

Crucially for Envia, it would receive $2 million a quarter from GM, adding up to $8 million a year for at least four years. That money was sufficient to pay all of the startup's bills, representing its entire burn rate. On top of that would be royalties once the cars began to be manufactured. Depending on car sales, the contract could be worth hundreds of millions of dollars.

The November 2012 contract was a triumph not just for Envia but for Arpa-E, none of whose other investments had yet turned into commercial products. U.S. energy secretary Steven Chu remarked on the deal between GM and Envia publicly.

The draft contract went on to be quite specific: For the 200-mile car, Envia was to provide a working battery delivering around 350 watt-hours per kilogram that could endure 1,000 charge-discharge cycles. The requirement was not 400 watt-hours per kilogram—again, what you achieved in a lab could never be matched when you scaled up to the battery pack that actually went into a car. But it remained a tremendous challenge since Kumar still had to overcome the silicon expansion on the anode side, in addition to flaws in the cathode.

Kumar's deadline for the 200-mile battery was October 2013. After that, adjustments could be made to optimize the performance until August 15, 2014. But that was a full-stop deadline— Kumar could make no changes to the battery after the latter date. This point was critical to GM because once the battery was ready, all the other deadlines could follow, ending with the pure electric car's actual launch in 2016.

In August 2012, GM CEO Dan Akerson described Envia's exploits in a closed meeting with employees. Listening in was an Associated Press reporter, who was sitting alongside someone authorized to be on the conference call. "We've got better than a 50-50 chance to develop a car that will go to 200 miles on a charge," Akerson said, according to the report. That car could be in GM's fleet by 2016, he said, and if so it "would be a game changer." "These little companies come out of nowhere and they surprise you," Akerson said.

On November 30, 2012, Kapadia signed the licensing agreement. Now Kumar spoke directly to his scientists. "The business guys have delivered. Now it is our time. The onus is on us," he said. "There are no excuses. Get this done. Put the chemistry in the car."

Much precious development time had been lost. Envia had hoped for a high-profile announcement that would push one or two other carmakers with which they had been working to sign licensing contracts as well. Kumar and Kapadia had hired Goldman Sachs to parlay the contracts into a sale of the company or an IPO as A123 had done three years before. In the end, the Envia board's decision was to seek an acquisition by a large company. The value under discussion was several hundred million dollars.

But given the stringent deadline, every day counted. GM decided to delay publicly announcing the deal. Instead, the carmaker rushed a planning team to Newark three days later—on December 3—to create a quarter-by-quarter schedule of milestones that ended with delivery of the battery technology for its two signature models. As Envia hit each quarterly target, it would receive $2 million.

By the end of the following day, the two teams had agreed. The milestones were "pretty tough," Kumar said at the time. "I would say the timeline is aggressive." But he was also "very happy" with the contract. After the five years of work, Envia had arrived. The foundation stone was laid for large cash flow and a considerable fortune. The board was delighted. It awarded new stock options to twenty-five employees, about 45 percent of them to the three-man business team led by Kapadia.

"We Cannot Replicate the Arpa-E Results"

While Kumar got started on the GM contract, Kapadia moved forward on the plan to sell the company. Goldman Sachs took the acquisition proposal to Asia, sending queries to, among other potential suitors, Japan's Asahi Kasei and South Korea's LG and Samsung.

But now that Kumar had seemed on his way to what he had coveted, it all began to unravel.

At the end of February 2013, Envia's business development team received an urgent message from GM: Initial tests were complete on the 400-watt-hour-per-kilogram battery. But so far, they did not replicate the results announced at Arpa-E. Could Envia explain why?

Increasingly alarmed queries piled up from GM in phone calls and meetings. The Arpa-E results could not be reproduced—not by a long shot. Meeting a team from the carmaker on March 4, Kumar "struggled to allay GM's concerns," according to Kapadia's lawsuit. A document provides a sense of why GM was concerned.

In reporting this article, *Quartz* asked Envia for the outside evaluation that underpinned its February 2012 claims for the

Arpa-E cell—the one produced by the U.S. Navy's Crane Division. Rather than that evaluation, Envia sent a twenty-page, subsequent Crane report that both summarized the earlier, Arpa-E validation and evaluated another cell of the same type.

According to this report, dated June 28, 2012, Envia's claim was accurate—its cell demonstrated energy density of 378 to 426 watt-hours per kilogram and had been put through 409 charge-discharge cycles. But the superlative energy density registered only in the first three cycles. After that, its performance plunged: By the twenty-fifth cycle, the density was down to 290 watt-hours per kilogram. At the hundredth, it was at 266. At the 200th, it was below 250, and by the 300th, at 237.

By the last charge-discharge cycle—the 409th—the cell's energy density had fallen to 222 watt-hours per kilogram, or just 55 percent of the 400 that the startup had claimed. A chart showed that the result aligned with that found for the earlier Arpa-E cell that Crane Division had tested. And the trend suggested no flattening out ahead, but that energy density would continue falling and become less than half of the claimed 400.

Jeff Dahn, head of battery research at Dalhousie University, said in an interview for this article that technically speaking, Envia was being truthful—the cell did produce 400 watt hours per kilogram and it did cycle the 300 times it claimed at Arpa-E. But for the many who presumed that Envia had delivered the record result for all 300 cycles, the announcement's accuracy was only technical. "With battery people," Dahn said, "you have to make sure that a statement applies to all parts of the sentence."

GM was not impressed. In a March 14, 2013, letter to Envia, Matthus Joshua, head of purchasing for GM's hybrid group, formally complained that the cell provided as part of the contract failed to meet the promised Arpa-E performance and that Envia had misrepresented its technology. Joshua "(demanded) an explanation of the performance deficiency relative to the one announced exactly a year prior," Kapadia said in a lawsuit.

On March 26, the Envia and GM teams gathered for the first quarterly meeting of their new relationship. GM's team—led by Joshua and Larry Nitz, head of engineering for GM's hybrids—again raised the enormous discrepancy between the stated and actual performance of the Arpa-E cell. The Envia cell inexplicably could not match what the startup had announced.

Kumar responded with an offer—if GM were patient for another three months, he was confident he could deliver the promised result. The GM team agreed.

"Next cell—build or bust," Nitz told him.

But the performance was only the beginning of the trouble at Envia. Over the prior weeks, Kapadia had become increasingly suspicious that the Arpa-E cell was in fact not entirely the startup's intellectual property as claimed. A member of Kumar's scientific team had raised that possibility—the silicon-carbon anode material, this scientist said, was purchased outside the company and was not Envia's.

Confronted internally, Kumar denied the assertion, Kapadia said in his lawsuit. But on March 14—twelve days prior to the meeting with GM—he conceded that the scientist was right, according to the suit. The cell reported to Arpa-E and sent to GM contained anode material purchased in a confidential deal from Shin-Etsu, a Japanese supplier.

Kumar said Shin-Etsu's role was unimportant—the anode's true value emerged in the processing steps he had developed that allowed the anode to cycle hundreds of times without shattering. Shin-Etsu, he said, was providing only the basic material with which he worked, according to the lawsuit and Envia itself. But Kapadia disagreed: If Envia said that the anode material was proprietary, as it had asserted to the industry at conferences, to the media, and in the negotiation for its license with GM, it had to be so. If it was someone else's—freely available for purchase—Envia had to explicitly disclose that fact. The anode material was, plain and simple, not Envia's intellectual property, said Kapadia. And without the anode, the cell did not get to 400 watt-hours per kilogram; it didn't even near it. Envia was no better than the crowd, and a 200-mile electric car really wasn't possible.

The dispute grew into a massive internal row. Kumar and at least one board member—a small Envia investor named Purnesh Seegopaul, a partner with Vancouver-based Pangaea Ventures—were dismayed that Kapadia repeatedly committed his views to writing in messages to board members, according to the lawsuit. Any future buyer of Envia would presumably have to be given such internal correspondence during the due-diligence process. Earlier in the year, Arun Majumdar, the Arpa-E director who had touted Envia's reported breakthrough, joined the startup's board of directors. The previous year, he had left the Department of Energy and joined Google. He was drawn into the discussion over Shin-Etsu as well.

According to Kapadia, Seegopaul seemed less concerned about the anode's origins than that its discovery could upset the chances for his venture fund to cash out. Seegopaul did not respond to an e-mail from *Quartz*, and Envia declined to reply specifically to the assertion about him.

At this point, the board told Kapadia that his duties as CEO were henceforth narrowed—he was solely to attempt to sell the company and settle an outstanding lawsuit by Kumar's former employer, NanoeXa's Pak. Afterward, Kapadia's employment with Envia would terminate.

Quashing Pak's lawsuit seemed to be the easy part: Filed in 2012, it claimed that Envia's cathode was stolen from NanoeXa, but Pak would not even identify what intellectual property had been pilfered, making it seem likely that a judge would dismiss the case.

Canceling the Deal

Kumar said in an interview at the time that his team was "going crazy" attempting to replicate the Arpa-E results. He finally told GM about the purchase of Shin-Etsu's anode material. After the news settled, Joshua and Nitz said they in fact did not care who produced it—as long as Kumar delivered the promised cell performance. Kumar continued to assure them that he would.

But Kumar told me that it was not a realistic aim in the timeframe required. If GM was willing to settle for 315 watt-hours per kilogram, he could meet the mark, but not 350, not unless the carmaker could wait another six months or a year. In other words, the material would not be ready for the 200-mile car that GM wanted to launch in 2016, but possibly the following year or the year after that.

Meanwhile, Goldman Sachs returned with gloomy news—no one appeared prepared to acquire Envia. According to Kapadia's lawsuit, the word was out in the market that the startup's products did not work well. Japan's Asahi Kasei, the most likely buyer, had finally declined. So had LG and Samsung. Honda, which Envia had regarded as its second likely licensing deal after GM, declined to extend the joint-development agreement under which the two companies had collaborated until then. The talks with Honda were over.

On July 22, 2013, GM and Envia met for their second quarterly meeting. Kumar had not met the milestones promised for the Arpa-E material nor the second-generation 2015 Volt. GM's Joshua was blunt. Kumar had "made material misrepresentations during contract negotiations," he said. The Arpa-E results were not replicated and "the anode material is not Envia's." Nitz said Envia had earned "a failed grade for this quarter." Kumar apologized, but the coveted contract seemed to be in peril.

Two weeks later, Envia received a letter from Joshua, who wrote:

> Envia has failed to move the project forward or replicate the results on a timetable that could conceivably support the vehicle development process. In fact, Envia was unable even to replicate prior reported test results even when utilizing the third-party anode that had purportedly been utilized in the Arpa-E test battery.

GM, Joshua continued, was therefore "well within its rights to terminate the December 2012 agreement."

Envia's executives and board now saw no chance to salvage the contract. The deal that all hoped could lead to a substantial payoff was sure to be canceled. But the fallout could be worse if GM sued or demanded its money back.

On August 28, Kapadia and a subordinate boarded a red-eye flight to Detroit. Meeting the next day at GM's offices in the Detroit suburb of Warren, they confronted a "visibly and justifiably angry" Joshua and Nitz, according to Kapadia. Kapadia tried to appeal to their sense of decency. Envia had committed mistakes, but the two companies should try "to mitigate the employment and immigration risk on the hard-working scientists at Envia who were likely to be adversely affected" if the startup collapsed, Kapadia argued.

Remarkably, the GM men agreed, according to sources involved with the deal. The GM executives signed a waiver relieving Envia of the threat of a lawsuit, the sources say. Also, Envia would be paid for the quarter and would not have to return any money already received. But the contract was canceled. GM was relinquishing its license to the Arpa-E material.

The Fallout

On August 30, 2013, Kapadia appeared before the board and announced the good news—there would be no suit nor immediate financial ruin. Hearing this, the board fired him along with his two subordinates. Seegopaul, the Pangaea investor, assumed Kapadia's duties. In a meeting with Kapadia's team nine months to the day after the deal was signed, Seegopaul said they had "done a poor job negotiating the GM agreement," according to Kapadia's lawsuit. Seegopaul said, "The milestones in the agreement were very demanding and . . . no company in the world could achieve them."

Three months later, Kapadia and his two-man team filed their fifty-two-page civil suit in Alameda County against Envia and Kumar personally, alleging fraud, retaliation, and wrongful termination. "We were only trying to do what was right," Kapadia said.

The complaint borrowed much from the lawsuit filed last year by NanoeXa's Pak. When examined together, the suits allege that Envia, while claiming to be marketing proprietary technology, in fact relied almost entirely on IP that it either stole or appropriated without attribution from other companies. In terms of the cathode, Kapadia alleged that Kumar downloaded about one hundred files at NanoeXa, including a flurry in his last days and hours at the company. In an interview, Pak put his hand on a stack of papers that he described as the product of a private forensic investigator who examined Kumar's work computer. Pak said he has shown the files to federal and Alameda County prosecutors.

The men have different aims. Kapadia says he is seeking financial damages but that he will donate any award to an as-yet unidentified charity. Pak says he is looking for "punishment of someone who did wrong" and suggests that means a criminal penalty for Kumar.

Envia has responded with great caution. It hired Sitrick and Co., a crisis-management firm, which for a day released a series of statements and documents. Kapadia's lawsuit, Sitrick said, "is nothing more than the spurious allegations of three disgruntled former employees." A second statement attacked the rationale behind GM's cancellation of the contract. The Arpa-E cell was never intended for development into a product but "to establish proof of concept." The next step was to turn the Arpa-E cell to the "R&D cell stage and then, later, to produce the battery for commercial use." In addition, Envia bought "silicon-based raw material from multiple suppliers," and not a "fully developed anode." This was done "with full knowledge of Arpa-E." Then Sitrick said it would have no further statements.

Over Thai food with me three weeks after their fallout, Kumar blamed the mess on Kapadia. During the entire negotiation, he said, Kapadia had run "a black-box operation." Within Envia, only Kapadia and his business team were privy to the details of the GM deal. The business team had committed Envia to unrealistic milestones and Kumar to an unattainable timeline. The chances for an IPO or an acquisition were likewise squandered. "When something gets achieved, you see the CEO on CNBC. When it goes wrong, you blame the technology guys," Kumar said, his arms crossed. "They get the commission, we get the blame. It's always like that."

Key elements of Envia's and Kumar's explanations contradict the record. Internal e-mails showed that Kapadia's team checked the technological commitments and timeline with Kumar, who approved them. In Envia's announcement of the Arpa-E breakthrough on February 27, 2012, Kumar said, "Rather than just a proof-of-concept of energy density, I am pleased that our team was successful in actually delivering 400 [watt-hour per kilogram] automotive grade 45 [ampere-hour] lithium-ion rechargeable cells." The same news release spoke of "Envia's proprietary Si-C (silicon-carbon) anode." Contrary to what Sitrick claimed on behalf of Envia, Kumar was suggesting that he was ready to develop his prototype into a commercial product.

In canceling the contract, GM made it plain that it expected a product that would be put directly into the two vehicles. In an August 8, 2013, letter to the startup, GM said the contract was "predicated on a number of statements and representations made by Envia and Envia's representatives that, in retrospect and in light of more recent statements by Envia, appear to have been inaccurate and misleading."

Life After Envia

When the subject of Envia arose over the last couple of years, GM executives would express enthusiasm but add that they never bet everything on a single technology. The stakes are too high, they would say, suggesting that the company was not depending solely on Envia for the next-generation Volt and the 200-mile electric car. That is rational, and it is true that GM rapidly cut its operative ties with Envia, relinquishing the license to the Arpa-E material, which a cool head might have retained in the off chance that Kumar could later make it work. GM's Lauckner, GM's CTO and head of its ventures unit, continues to serve as an observer on Envia's board, but that could be the matter of GM's continued investment in the startup.

John Voelcker, editor of *Green Car Reports*, said it is "naïve" to conclude that GM lacks alternatives to Envia's technology. One reason for the push behind the 200-mile car had been to blunt Tesla Motors, whose CEO, Elon Musk, has boasted of plans for a $35,000, 200-mile pure-electric vehicle. About a month after the divorce with Envia, a GM executive told reporters that the carmaker has a battery to produce a 200-mile car but that it still costs too much for commercial use. "GM is a competitive company. They have no intention to let Tesla own the market for $35,000, 200-mile cars," Voelcker said.

Yet the timing could slip. Envia, in fact, was the only company at least publicly promising such exceptional performance—since Envia, other companies including BASF and Japan's Toda had licensed the Argonne material as well, but neither boasted the big performance jump promoted by the startup. Meanwhile some of the other startup competition—A123 and Ener1, the parent company of EnerDel—declared bankruptcy in 2012 and were acquired, respectively, by Chinese and Russian companies.

One would not be surprised to see the new Volt perhaps in 2016, but with less of a price difference than Envia promised. The pure 200-mile electric could launch in 2018 or later. As for Envia itself, it has suffered its first layoffs. But earlier this year it won a $3 million Department of Energy grant. Along with Stanford University and UC Berkeley, it will develop a new battery with a silicon-carbon anode.

Public attention has seized on Tesla. With his sleek, high-tech Model S, Musk has made electric vehicles a commercial and Wall Street sensation. But he has not revolutionized electrochemistry. Rather, Musk's cars are powered by thousands of off-the-shelf Panasonic nickel-cobalt-aluminum cylindrical cells—big, heavy and volatile batteries that push the base price of the 200-mile version of the Model S to $71,000. They are a design-and-engineering solution to the problem of making electrics competitive with cheaper gasoline-propelled vehicles. While sexy, their price makes it far from certain that Musk's approach will lead to large-scale consumer adoption.

Envia's collapse extinguishes what had been arguably better news for electric cars, which was a singular advance in the battery itself. Its described refinement of Argonne's NMC was superior to the incremental improvements marked by every other known cathode-anode coupling on the planet. Kumar and Kapadia persuaded GM, along with Arpa-E and many, many others, that Chevy, propelled by Envia batteries, would assume the early lead in the global electric car race. GM was perhaps not snookered, but it was credulous when it should have understood the chart in the Crane appraisal, which one must presume it demanded and was provided.

Over the last two or three years, Kapadia and Kumar themselves appeared to believe the promise for their cell, too. The electric-car age was truly here, they seemed to say. Their failure does not mean that electrochemistry cannot prevail. But the winning formulation is still nowhere in plain view.

Philadelphia

What does it look like when the Grim Reaper comes for the undertaker? Sandy Hingston tells us in this *Philadelphia* magazine story on the decline of the funeral industry and changes in how Americans dispose of their dead. The percentage of Americans choosing cremation has doubled in fifteen years to 43 percent, wringing the profit out of a rapidly consolidating industry. The United States has half the embalmers it did in 2005, and, while open-casket ceremonies are increasingly rare, funeral homes have websites that allow mourners to upload photos and video of their dearly departed. But the days of $17,950 caskets are numbered.

Sandy Hingston

24. The Death of the Funeral Business

Over the summer, my ninety-eight-year-old Aunt Elizabeth passed away, after a long, full life.

In the wake (heh) of her memorial service, I got a letter from her daughter, my cousin Stephanie. It had a chart of our family's two burial plots at Hillside Cemetery in Roslyn, showing who's interred in which graves, and . . . well, let me just quote:

> The original cemetery contract entitles one burial to be made in each grave without additional charge. . . . This is called the "first right." But if someone decides to be buried in one of the seven graves that have never yet been opened, and wants to be sure that the burial will be deep enough to allow for a second later burial in the same grave, he/she must pay a fee (currently just under $2,500) to reserve the "second right" to that grave. If the second right is not paid for at the time of the first burial, there will not be room for a second burial in the grave. It follows that if everyone who eventually uses those graves pays up front for the "second right," the two lots can accommodate 16 more burials. On the other hand, if no one who eventually uses those graves pays for the second right, the two lots will accommodate only nine more burials.

It went on from there.

Mine is a family that takes six months to decide who'll host the annual Christmas Eve party. The prospect of the dozens of us cousins jockeying for eternal occupancy of those remaining grave sites ("There are also guidelines about burials of spouses of family members") is dizzying. And frankly, the chances of any of us ponying up $2,500 at our time of death to altruistically save the space atop us are dim. When it comes to that, I love my relatives, but I'd have a hard time opting for the open slot above Aunt Phyllis, who was a wonderful woman but worried ceaselessly about my weight.

Luckily, I don't envision any grand family smackdowns over the vacant graves. I plan to be cremated. So do my siblings and husband. Forty-three percent of Americans who died last year were burned instead of buried—up from 24 percent in 1998. That's a staggering rise in the course of just fifteen years. (The figure was under 5 percent as recently as 1972.) By 2017, the Cremation Association of North America predicts, half of us will be consumed by flames. In Britain, three-quarters of the dead already are.

Much of the impetus for this is economic: A traditional American funeral costs $8,300 (not counting plot), vs. $1,400 for cremation (with urn and no service). But what we do with ourselves when we die isn't just a matter of money, and funerals aren't just about disposal of the dead. They're rituals we perform in order to adjust to the loss of a loved one and to place that loss within a larger framework that gives meaning to the life that's gone.

For Americans, religion once provided that framework. The rise in cremation dovetails neatly with the increase in those of us who have no religious affiliation—now one-fifth, the highest percentage ever, according to a recent Pew Research poll. We're not nearly as concerned with the hereafter as we used to be. The number of Americans who don't believe Christ rose from the dead jumped by 13 percent in a single year from 2012 to 2013.

A societal changeover from burial to cremation is momentous for our culture. It signals a cataclysmic shift in how we think about our bodies and ourselves. If we're no longer preserving our remains for the glorious moment when the trumpet blares the Resurrection, does it matter what we do with them? What is the meaning of life, and death, once religion goes?

·　　·　　·

When I die just show clips of me and shut the f up.
　　　　　　　　　—Tweet from comedian Albert Brooks, 2013

My mom died while I was in my early twenties; my dad, Bill, lived on for another quarter-century. But it wasn't until he died and I was going through his things that I found a photo of my mother taken for Dress-Down Day at North Penn High, where she'd taught math. She's in front of a blackboard, wearing big round glasses and a t-shirt showing the Pythagorean theorem. On the back of the photo, she wrote: "Bill doesn't like this picture but I love it. It's my favorite 'Marcie, the teacher' picture. I would like my grandchildren (?) to have copies one day."

Mom got her wish; her grandkids all have copies of that photo, and since they never knew her, it's precisely how they "remember" her. Contemporary funerals are like that picture—they're not about life after death but about how we want to be remembered or at least (since the dead can't control the living) how our loved ones want us to be.

That explains why the Verizon guy is tramping across the handsome floral carpet in the mirror-walled front lobby of the Pennsylvania Burial Co. "We're in a traditional area," says fourth-generation funeral director Peter Jacovini, by which he means South Philly, and more specifically the funeral-home-dense stretch of South Broad Street between Wharton and Oregon. The Pennsylvania Burial Co., at Broad and Reed, is built like—well, a vault. "The walls are so thick that we can't get wi-fi in our parlors," says Peter's cousin, Victor Baldi III—also a fourth-generation funeral director, at the adjacent Baldi Funeral Home. So this bastion of tradition, this crystal-and-marble temple, is putting in more routers for beaming out videos.

"Video makes it a life celebration," explains Victor, a handsome, beefy Italian guy. And who doesn't like to celebrate?

"People have so many pictures now—on their laptops, their phones," adds Peter, who's more ascetic in appearance. The home's chapels have been fitted with discreet flat-screen TVs, for showing collages and tributes; prayer cards bear photos of the deceased instead of images of Christ. Victor just had a family that wanted to livestream a funeral service overseas.

The cousins' old-school business is making other concessions to changing tastes. They're about to go, um, live with a new website that's "more interactive and friendlier," says Victor. "Families can have a memorial online. Visitors can add messages and condolences." Granted, such newfangled stuff has to be broached delicately here in traditional South Philly. "Some people don't want their pictures online," says Victor. But he and Peter recently hired their first-ever female staffer, a grief counselor. ("She's been well received," Peter says, sounding a little surprised.)

It's all part of the biggest trend in funerals: personalization. Taking a cue from Oprah, who reportedly has planned her own funeral, contemporary mourners are trying to make the worn outlines of ritual more authentic and meaningful. We're singing "My Heart Will Go On" at services and showing montages of our deceased's school days, weddings, grandkids. We're having their cremains shot into space, made into diamonds, and interred in coral reefs. The newest disposal method: dissolving the body via alkaline hydrolysis. The resultant liquid washes right down the drain.

Rituals evolve. What stays constant is our need for them, for some way to make sense of the hole in the social fabric that death creates. "While the types of services we offer are changing, our job has remained the same," say Peter. "People always told stories. We are always remembering who the people were."

For Victor and Peter's clients, remembrance is still intimately tied up, mostly, with the body; cremations sans services are still only 6 percent of their business. "We can be the nicest guys in the world," says Victor, "but if Mom or Dad doesn't look good in the casket. . . . It really helps the family if the deceased looks peaceful." This explains the pillowy satin linings of the coffins in their Casket Room, where models range from a $650 bare-bones box to a $17,950 bronze number so gorgeous that I'm tempted to climb in.

There's no sense having a coffin that nice unless people see it—and the body inside it. Almost all of Peter and Victor's funerals are open-casket. Peter says, "We have a gentleman who does the embalming"—a process in which the deceased is drenched in disinfectant and germicide, the eyes and jaw are fastened shut, blood is drained, the insides of organs are suctioned out, and makeup is used to restore a lifelike look to the corpse.

The embalming, the cosmetics, the cozy casket confines—all are meant to create a therapeutic "memory image" of the deceased that gives mourners closure. Yet even in South Philly, the business is changing. That's partly due to the recession; Peter and Victor offer more choices now at the low end of the price scale and a wall of sample urns in the Casket Room for those opting to cremate. On the second floor is a Buddhist chapel, with a special exhaust system to handle the incense monks burn at their ceremonies. "We're 80 percent Catholic, 15 percent Buddhist, and 5 percent other," Victor says as he ushers me into this exotic red-and-gold sanctuary.

Statewide, the number of licensed funeral directors dropped by almost 19 percent from 2001 to 2011. Half a dozen funeral homes in Philadelphia have closed in recent years. "Urban homes have their own challenges," says John Eirkson, executive director of the Pennsylvania Funeral Directors Association. "Parking is harder. Getting around is harder. There are tax issues. Everything is compounded when you're in the city." The funeral-home mergers-and-acquisitions consolidation that started out West is hitting the East Coast now. South Philly, once solidly white, Catholic, and Italian, today is nearly half black, Asian, and Hispanic. And Eirkson has seen dramatic changes in mortuary-school enrollment. "Classes used to be made up of men from funeral-home families," he says. "Now, women make up 60 percent or more, and the majority aren't affiliated with funeral-home families." Small family-owned homes, Eirkson says, "have to adapt—or die."

But the Pennsylvania Burial Co. is plenty lively. Besides the Verizon guy, drivers and deliverymen and clients come and go. While we talk, Peter and Victor keep an eye through the open front door on their parking lot across the street, which they're having repaved. The busyness is a reminder that at the heart of what they're selling is distraction: Do you want this casket or that? What outfit would you like your deceased to wear? In a time of intense emotional distress, they lay out choices that give us the illusion, at least, of control over something we can't control. And they do so in a setting whose grandeur—marble, mirrors, crystal, plush rugs— offers tribute to our loss in a solemn, satisfying way. We pay them, like the ferryman Charon, to row our dead from this world to the next. It's an errand too overwhelming for us to face alone.

Way back in 1970, a funeral-industry publication predicted that before long, American funeral traditions would collapse completely and services would take place without the presence of a body. This has proven prescient: Today, more and more Americans opt for corpse-free "memorial services" instead of funerals. We've gone from celebrating Christ's triumph over the grave to chuckling at poor Uncle Fred's golf game.

It's understandable. The reality is harsh. We dispose of our dead because we have no choice: Eventually they stink, and they spread disease. Down through the ages, various means of dealing with dead bodies evolved: We've covered them with stones, buried them, floated them away, engulfed them in flames, let birds pick them apart. What remains after that is picked apart by people like Janet Monge, who, unlike most of us, will miss dead bodies when they're gone.

"Most of archaeology is tombs," says Janet, between bites of a cheese steak. She's an anthropology prof at Penn and the curator and keeper of Skeletal Collections at its museum—the guardian of the bones. There's nothing grim or creepy about her, though, as we share lunch in her museum's sun-drenched cafe. A native of West Philly, she's plainspoken and wry, with deep-set eyes and a mass of wiry gray hair.

"Anthropologists use burial context to get to the identity of a people," she explains. "There are a limited number of disposal methods, but many variations. You can have the body lying straight in the grave, or in fetal position, or on its side, like Muslims. It can be sitting down, standing up, with the hands folded or extended. . . . What objects are associated with them? What are they wearing? We try to pierce through and extract the minute differences." What's useful about graves is that they're covered over, so the contents are protected. Cremation, though— "It's a glimpse," says Janet, "but it doesn't allow us to do much study."

The earliest bones in her collection are from the Middle East and were interred 25,000 years ago. "I think of them as individuals," she says of the remains she catalogs. "They have stories to tell. Not the same as a human story, but a pretty elaborate one."

Royal tombs tend to be fanciest. In ancient Egypt, that meant bigger monuments, more elaborate death scrolls, better mummification, nicer linens. Other classes emulated as much as they could afford. "We still have this attempt to mimic extravagance in burials," Janet notes. "How many flowers? How big a casket?" What has changed is our acceptance of death: "There's an expectation now that biomedicine will cure everything. We don't really think we're going to die."

Back when the first bodies went into my family plot, people died at home, in their beds. Loved ones, friends, and neighbors gathered to watch and wait for you to "pass." For Emily Dickinson, this moment was "that last Onset—when the King / Be witnessed— in the Room": the breaching of the membrane between this world and the next.

Nowadays, most deaths in the United States take place in hospitals or nursing homes. We die in cranked-up beds, tethered to machines that clinically record our last breath and heartbeat; there's no mystery, no piercing of the veil. We don't take our dead home, bathe them, dress them, and lay them out in the front parlor. Dead people, frankly, creep us out. American burial rituals—the embalming, the concrete vaults—are proof. "There's this idea that you're not going to decompose," Janet sniffs. "We're *supposed* to decompose."

One reason we're so profoundly uncomfortable with death is that it's become increasingly less familiar. In Pennsylvania in 1910, 150 out of every 1,000 children died before their first birthday. In 2010, it was less than eight. Death used to be a constant playmate; in Victorian times, a dead grandparent was mourned more than a dead child. Today, no tragedy looms larger than Sandy Hook.

My kids have been to less than a handful of funerals—and just two viewings, which totally weirded them out. I only ever go to my family's burial plot for funerals. Graveyards were once popular spots for picnics and outings, but not anymore. Not to mention that we're all increasingly mobile, likely to live hundreds or even thousands of miles from where family members are buried. A baby born today will move twelve times in her lifetime. Millennials say they hope to change jobs every three years. You can take Mom with you if she's in an urn. Eternity in the same place is becoming a tough sell.

At the corner of Twenty-Second and Market in Center City, where the Salvation Army thrift store once stood, a chain-link fence is pocked with memorials to the victims of its collapse in June: ratty stuffed animals, the remnants of a wreath, plastic wrappers surrounding desiccated bouquets. After six months, the detritus at one of the busiest intersections in town goes pretty much unnoticed; passersby don't even glance at the forlorn shrine.

Japanese Buddhists believe the dead spend three to five decades as familial ancestor spirits before losing their personal identity and joining the larger spirit world. Why three to five decades? Because that's as long as anyone who survives is likely to remember them. It's a tidy system, and it avoids the problem that plagues both cemeteries and the corner of Twenty-Second and Market: At some point, somebody will have to take down that chain-link fence and decide what to do with the clutter. Across America, graveyards demand mowing and weeding and raking and fertilizing. They're going into bankruptcy. The living no longer visit. "No one's going to take care of cemeteries," Janet Monge says mournfully.

You have to meet people where they are, though. The sociologist Peter Berger once wrote, "Every human society is, in the last resort, men banded together in the face of death." Where will we band together now that we're having our cremains packed into fireworks and made into jewels?

We're already there.

The *Daily News* columnist Ronnie Polaneczky has a video she took on her smartphone of her sister Peggy and her sister Franny. Franny is dead, and Peggy is brushing Franny's hair. Ronnie and Peggy and four other sisters were all with Franny when she died of cancer in the spring of 2011. "It was a beautiful day," says Ronnie. "You could smell the hyacinths through the window. I thought, how could this day be so beautiful and Franny be *gone*?"

Six months earlier, Ronnie's mom had died. "Mom's funeral was by the template," says Ronnie, who grew up in a large Catholic family. "We went to the funeral director. We were carried by the institutional aspect of it, and there was great comfort in that."

When the family walked into the funeral home, "Mom looked so beautiful," says Ronnie. "I don't think she ever had a manicure in her life, but her nails were done, with just a little bit of pearl at the tips." After the initial shock, everybody started laughing and joking: "The viewing was fun! Our childhood friends were there, my brothers and sisters were there, my parents' friends—it was almost like a party, a beautiful reunion. I felt bad that Mom was just lying there."

Her mom was buried the next day in the family plot after a funeral at Holy Martyrs Church. "I was baptized there. I went to grade school there," says Ronnie. "The priest adored my parents." The funeral, too, was a reunion of sorts.

Franny's services proved more problematic. She and her husband didn't belong to a church. "So we needed a place," Ronnie explains. "We thought about a catering hall. But we wanted something that felt like a place where other seekers had gathered." A pastor who knew the family asked if he could be of help, so they had a service at his church.

Franny wanted to be cremated. She had ideas about her funeral's vibe, too: "She had a fabulous sense of humor," says Ronnie. "She didn't want anyone to cry. She wanted AC/DC music. She wanted to distribute clown noses. Her funeral was very much her."

There was what Ronnie calls a "meet-and-greet" at the funeral home, with pictures and posters of Franny everywhere, and half the kids from her teenage sons' school, and her ashes in a box. Then came the service at the church (songs included "Somewhere Over the Rainbow") and then lunch, with a DJ and dancing—and clown noses. "Franny would have loved it," Ronnie says.

Ronnie has a little bag of Franny's ashes in her desk drawer at home. She also has Franny's Facebook page to look at and the brief video, taken just after Franny died, when it didn't seem right to leave her alone in her hospice bed. Ronnie and Peggy stayed until the undertaker came. Franny had always been meticulous about her appearance, so they did her hair and makeup, as a final act of love. Then Ronnie took a few last photos and the video. "I look at them all the time," she says, and touches her heart unconsciously.

Our societal switch from burial to cremation doesn't just reflect the fact we're less convinced we'll need our bodies for the Resurrection. It's our way of saying that our bodies no longer truly represent who we are or were. How could they, when, like Ronnie, we can open our phones and see our sister long after she's dead and gone?

Gary Laderman, an Emory University professor of American religious history, has written about "the uncannily appropriate fit between modern fixations on death and the fecund ritual possibilities in cyberspace." Mourners are paying to maintain their loved ones' cell-phone accounts, in order to preserve treasured voicemails. Facebook allows Timelines for the dead to stay open, so messages can be sent across that great divide. Visitors to the Pennsylvania Burial Co.'s new website will be able to sign memorial books, light candles, post photos and video clips, leave mementos and messages, all without having to look death in the eye. (And you know what? A population fixated on selfies isn't likely to trust a mortuary cosmetologist to create its last look anyway.)

The Internet will allow us to mourn in our own ways, at our own pace. We'll discover new truths about our interconnectedness; we'll touch base with long-lost family and friends. Our deaths will be woven into the twinkling reaches of the cyber-universe, spinning there forever with all the vast pictorial and textual clutter of our births, our education, our courtships, our likes and dislikes, far beyond the limitations of time and space.

And that limitlessness makes what was once the clear divide between life and death more porous. If my mom had died today instead of thirty years ago, she would have left more than a single photo for the grandkids. She would have crafted a whole online portfolio, a greatest-hits show on Twitter and Pinterest and Facebook and Vine. My kids would see her all the time. She would live in their pockets. Really, how is a grandmother who's dead any different from one who's in Seattle or Seoul? Talk about blurred lines.

So we get everlasting life without all the fuss about hell and heaven. Trust the boomers to cheat the Grim Reaper once and for all.

It makes sense, once you decide the body doesn't much matter, to have it go up in flames. Fire is spirit; it's electricity; it's energy. It's what we plug our phones and iPads into. It's the exact opposite of stasis and rot.

Not everybody is a fan of cremation, though. As I'm about to leave the Pennsylvania Burial Co., Peter and Victor introduce me to a big, burly guy in jeans and a work shirt who's striding in through the front door: "This is our embalmer, Michael."

From what I've read about the embalming process, I'm expecting Gollum, not a dead ringer for James Gandolfini. Michael clasps my hand in a grip like the grave. "Are you really the embalmer?" I ask dubiously.

"The last person to see you naked!" he booms, and grins.

Peter and Victor are appalled: "Don't say that!" But I laugh; his high spirits are contagious. If I'm going to have my body suctioned out, let it be by this cheery guy.

The Bureau of Labor Statistics says the number of U.S. embalmers has fallen by half since 2005. That makes Michael an endangered species. In the new age of everlasting online life, who's going to fork over the big bucks to be entombed?

Victor and Peter will. "We're both going to be buried," Victor says stoutly. "In the family plot. I want to be buried there with my parents and grandparents and great-grandparents. But not till a long ways off."

So will Janet Monge—"But not so I can be resurrected. I want to be dug up. I think that would be the coolest thing."

Businessweek

The profile of the executive overcoming adversity is a business-journalism staple. Typically, the adversity is something like intrigue on the board of directors or a stock that was on the ropes but is now hitting new highs. Ashlee Vance's portrait of Ramona Pierson shows an executive taking on something much more extreme. A math genius who suffered catastrophic injuries after a drunk driver ran her over three decades ago, Pierson has faced challenges that few other businesspeople have. And look where she is now.

25. Declara Co-Founder Ramona Pierson's Comeback Odyssey

As a twenty-two-year-old marine, Ramona Pierson spent most days stuck in an office at the El Toro air station near Irvine, Calif. She excelled at math and was doing top-secret work, coming up with algorithms to aid fighter attack squadrons. Pierson enjoyed the covert puzzling. She was also an exercise addict: After clocking out each day, she would head off for a thirteen-mile run. Her male counterparts were impressed enough with the workout regime to nominate her the fittest person on the base.

At about four p.m. on a weekday in April 1984, Pierson finished her work, went home, leashed her dog, Chips, and set off on her usual run through a suburban neighborhood. She stopped at an intersection, bouncing in place as she waited for the light to change. As she started across the street, a drunk driver ran the red. Chips got hit first and died instantly. The car plowed into Pierson and then ran her over as the driver kept going. Both of Pierson's legs were crushed; her throat and chest were ripped open, exposing her heart. Her aorta sprayed blood, and she sputtered as she tried to breathe. Just before everything went black, Pierson says, she felt "my life's blood emptying out of my neck and my mouth."

Passersby saved her life. One massaged her heart to keep it beating; another used pens to open her windpipe and vent her collapsed lung so she could breathe. The crude handiwork kept Pierson alive long enough to get her to a hospital.

She spent the next eighteen months in a coma, being fed through a hole in her chest. Then one day, to her doctors' surprise, she woke up. Weighing sixty-four pounds, she was bald, with a cubist face, metal bones, and a body covered in scars. And she was blind. The one part of her that wasn't ruined was her mathematical mind.

.　　　.　　　.

As a kid growing up in Waco, Tex., and Southern California, Pierson discovered she could do math in her head. Rather than pulling out pencil and paper, she'd use techniques akin to meditation and visualization to process equations. In high school in Huntington Beach, Calif., she was a standout athlete (field hockey) determined to get a free ride to college. Plan B was an academic scholarship. After flying through high school, Pierson enrolled at the University of California at Berkeley at age sixteen. She didn't get the scholarships, though, and had to pay for school on her own. Her goal was to become a cardiologist.

At Berkeley she scored so well on a standardized test that her results were flagged by on-campus military recruiters. "The marines showed up at my dorm room," says Pierson. They found a savant who could barely afford to eat and offered to pay for her two remaining years of college in exchange for enlisting. Pierson took the deal. In 1980, at eighteen, she joined the corps and was soon writing algorithms to help calculate the position of Russia's nuclear silos and guide F-18 fighter missions. Four years later, she entered that Irvine intersection at just the wrong time.

The blindness was terrifying. But it also forced Pierson to expand her ability to solve puzzles in her mind. As she listened to her doctors and other people, she began to "see" them as what she calls "glow globs," patterns of light with different properties. Then she recognized patterns within descriptions others gave her—such as how items were arranged in a grocery store or how the figures on a spreadsheet interconnected. "I learned to create a cognitive map of the world, sort of like *The Matrix*," she says. "I see the world in my head."

On September 26, Pierson, now fifty, unveiled a technology company called Declara. The year-old startup, based in Palo Alto, has essentially built a software simulation of Pierson's mind. It's a type of social network that links everyone in a company or an organization. With the help of algorithms developed by Pierson and others, including top engineers from Google and Microsoft, Declara's system learns how people interact, what types of questions they're looking to answer, and who can best answer them. The company has raised more than $5 million in funding from investors, including Peter Thiel, the billionaire who first backed Facebook.

A flurry of business-oriented social networks have appeared in recent years with a similar pitch. Microsoft, for example, spent $1.2 billion last year to acquire Yammer, which lets companies create private networks among their employees through an interface that looks almost exactly like Facebook. Box, Dropbox, and Jive Software are among the dozens of other companies that have received billions of dollars in funding to become the "collaboration platform" of choice for modern companies.

Declara does something different, say Pierson and Nelson González, the startup's cofounder. Declara's software flags people who seem to excel at certain tasks. Someone at a biotech company, for example, might want to know which enzymes seem promising for curing a particular disease. Declara will scour the company's social network to identify the people others turn to most for information about that disease and who have the most up-to-date research at hand. Pierson and González describe

Declara as a kind of automated consulting firm—except that, where the fees from a McKinsey or Bain can run into the millions, Declara charges fifteen dollars per employee per year. "We're flipping the equation so that people can become their own consultants," says González, who used to work as a consultant at Booz Allen Hamilton. "And we help people keep on learning, instead of leaving them with little more than a pretty-looking PowerPoint deck."

.   .   .

Pierson and her longtime partner, Debra Chrapaty, a technology executive, live in Menlo Park. Whenever possible, though, they head south to Carmel Valley, where they have a spread so implausibly perfect it could be the set for a Cialis commercial. There's a hot tub nestled among some trees and a pair of lounge chairs that look upon the rolling hills and rambling estates where Clint Eastwood and Arnold Schwarzenegger live. The house is part Mediterranean villa and part art museum. A George Rodrigue Blue Dog painting dominates the airy, tiled living room, and a John Lennon original drawing hangs in the hallway.

Although Pierson prefers not to talk about the accident, she's not shy about it when asked. During an interview in her kitchen, she walks over to a storage cabinet and takes out a few plastic bags. Some are filled with horrifically long screws that once held parts of her limbs together; others contain gruesome photos of her many operations. There's a black-and-silver contraption that a doctor once bolted to the outside of her leg. "They left a piece of a saw in my leg for a few years," Pierson says. "I was walking up a hill when the stupid thing snapped. The bone had become necrotic."

In the eighteen months following the accident, Pierson went from a trauma hospital to a series of VA hospitals and then National Jewish Health in Denver. None of her doctors expected her to live, and she'd been only minimally put back together. She didn't have a nose so much as an aerated mass of flesh. She'd become a "gomer," an unpleasant medical profession acronym for a hopeless case: Get out of my emergency room. When Pierson, then twenty-four, finally awoke from the coma, she couldn't begin to take care of herself, so in the fall of 1986 the doctors decided to send her to a home for senior citizens in the small ski-country town of Kremmling, Colo.

The seniors took Pierson on as a pet project. They taught her how to speak, cook, and get dressed—with results that veered between hilarious and near disastrous. For lunch one day, the men decided to educate the still-blind Pierson in the art of barbecuing. They left her alone for a few minutes only to return and find that she'd sprayed lighter fluid around the yard and singed the grass. The women, meanwhile, put Pierson in floral gowns and gave her perms and other hairstyles befitting an eighty-year-old. "It was bittersweet," she says. "They were declining every day, and I was getting better because of them."

She had few visitors. Pierson's friends from before the accident had moved on and likely had no idea where she was. Her father, an electromechanical engineer, died of a heart attack when she was twelve. Her mother, a lawyer, would sometimes run away for periods of time and "struggled with alcohol and other things and could not be a parent," Pierson says. Her two brothers had their own challenges. They fell in with the wrong crowds and bounced around, living on other people's couches. Her sister got married at eighteen "to a husband that beat the crap out of her," says Pierson, and the two no longer talked.

Without any close family or friends, Pierson lacked a confidante who could help her face up to hard questions, such as, "What do I look like?" Pierson never asked anyone about her appearance directly; she didn't need to. "I was in a grocery store with one of the ladies, and I hear this kid ask his mom, 'What happened to her?' When the mom replied, 'Shhh,' I knew I must look really f——— up."

Over time, and more than a hundred surgeries, Pierson's body improved. She had procedures to fix her eye socket, nose, and teeth. "One of my doctors did Wilt Chamberlain's nose," Pierson says. "My face seemed to come together well. Part of my butt is in my face." Her skills improved, too, and she realized it was time to try and leave the home. "I just kept moving forward," she says.

•　　•　　•

We've all met people who seem to make more of their years than the rest of us. They become experts at whatever they try and collect friends wherever they go. Driven, in part, by a maniacal fear that she had fallen behind the world, Pierson became one of those people.

The hallways of her house tell many of Pierson's stories, reflect her many tribes. Photos show her exploits as a blind rock climber and cross-country skier. At the end of one walkway are several framed newspaper clippings covering the year she spent tandem-bike racing through Russia to qualify for the Paralympics. While popping handfuls of pills a day to deal with the pain, she set some records, then joined a regular, i.e., not disabled, USA Cycling masters team, grabbed a silver at the National Championships, and was named cyclist of the year in 1995. "I never thought I'd be living that long, so I figured, 'I am going to wear this s——— out,'" she says.

The people goading Pierson into many of these adventures were the young friends she made at school during her recovery. After leaving the senior citizens home in 1989, she enrolled in a community college, hoping to figure out if she could handle going back to class. She could. Then, with the help of a guide dog, she spent two years studying psychology at Fort Lewis College in Colorado. Following her undergraduate work, she got a master's degree in education from the University of San Francisco, a Ph.D. in neuroscience from Stanford University and Palo Alto University, and attended the Danforth educational leadership program at the University of Washington.

During all this, Pierson still felt like a collection of component pieces. Her legs were different lengths. They ached. Various
bits and pieces between her heart and throat needed tending.
She volunteered for all the riskiest procedures—the latest and
greatest in cadaver bones, cow ligaments, and carbon fiber—in
her resolve to get somewhere near normal. "A lot of this stuff
failed, but they would move my life forward incrementally in a
way," she says. "Some of the surgeries were great, and I would
really take off after them." After eleven years of being blind,
Pierson regained the sight in her left eye in 1995 through another radical operation.

Determined to help people suffering from her own level of
trauma, Pierson worked for the military during the first Gulf
War. The U.S. Army discovered that desert sand was destroying
not only planes but also MRI machines. Soldiers would get shot
in the head, and the doctors trying to operate on them would
have to work off grainy images caused by malfunctioning equipment. Pierson solved the problem by developing a series of algorithms that sharpened the images. In 1997 she went to work at a
brain-research center in Palo Alto, again to aid soldiers coming
back from the Middle East.

That job set Pierson's life on a new course. She decided to
team with the Department of Veterans Affairs and study how
well returning soldiers learned skills and remembered things.
Pierson wanted to develop a solid means of assessing the soldiers
and turned to local educators to see how vets measured up against
their students. "I was shocked to walk into these classrooms and
see that they were so antiquated and similar to what our grandparents and parents would have experienced," Pierson says. She
had expected to find systems that kept track of how students
performed over time and responded to different teachers and
materials. Instead, she found a black hole. "I saw this as a data
problem," she says. Pierson got her teaching certificate and won
a fellowship funded by the Bill & Melinda Gates Foundation to

begin building data collection and analysis systems for Seattle's public schools.

From about 2003 to 2007, Pierson developed software called The Source and served in a variety of roles, including chief technology officer, within Seattle's public school system. Using The Source, parents could log on to a secure website and check their kids' performance, seeing not just grades but test scores, attendance records, and notes from teachers. The technology grew into a massive database that helped illuminate patterns in performance of both the students and the teachers, and it connected to repositories for new learning material such as videos, podcasts, and blogs. The Source remains in use today.

As the performance of Seattle's students improved, Pierson wondered if she could take the data-driven approach and turn it into a business. She formed SynapticMash, an educational startup. Three years later the British interactive learning company Promethean World acquired SynapticMash for $10 million. "All of this data was being left behind when teachers would scribble notes and put them in a binder or the students left their papers in folders," Pierson says. "The end grade would be recorded, but not the process of how people were learning. We tried to digitize that and fix it." Pierson went on to become the chief science officer and head of policy at Promethean, until she left last year to start Declara.

•   •   •

The Declara office is in an industrial part of Palo Alto, not far from an electric-motor supplier and a robot manufacturer. It's a single large, high-ceilinged room with a dozen or so desks. Pierson sits at the back of the room with Dave Matthews Band music playing and her dog, Tanqueray, sprawled on a red beanbag.

Pierson looks more normal than you might imagine. She wears her reddish-brown hair on the shorter side, parted to the left. Other than a noticeable scar on her lip, her face is surprisingly unmarred. Her nose was rebuilt with a plastic prosthesis where cartilage used to be; the only way you'd notice she's had work done is if you compare the new nose to the old one in pictures. She often wears Bono-style glasses with yellow lenses to protect her left eye. Chrapaty teases Pierson about her bushy eyebrows. ("We did a DNA test, and it came back saying she's got a lot of Neanderthal genes.") And her voice sometimes gets hoarse—her throat muscles tire easily. A crosshatched pattern of scars on her chest is visible when she wears a V-neck, and the scars on her knees and feet look like rivers with many tributaries. Pierson has the broad shoulders and build of the athlete she became again. She's a hugger, too.

The Declara team is a mix of engineers and designers who've spent the past year working in relative secrecy with governments and companies to refine the startup's technology. Chrapaty, who's worked at Cisco and Microsoft, is about to join the company. Pierson says large banks and biotech companies such as Genentech have signed on as customers. The agreements she talks most freely about, though, are with the Australian and Mexican governments.

In Australia, which has recently moved to have a single nationwide public school curriculum, educators from Sydney to Perth have digital access to the same lesson plans, tests, and all other classroom materials. Thousands of the country's teachers have been given early access to a private network built by Declara called the Scootle Community. It's a social network that will eventually link all 280,000 teachers in Australia and allow them to form groups around topics. "In one week, we saw about fifty groups set up, and the discussions amazed us," says Susan Mann, the chief executive officer of Education Services Australia, a nonprofit owned by the Australian education system. "They were all about developing curriculum, teaching new technologies, working with disadvantaged students—and on this very serious, professional level." Using Declara, teachers can pull up graphical displays that show hot topics among their colleagues, click on something like "eighth grade math," and find tests and videos that other teachers have recommended and, most important, reach out directly to their peers all over the country. "It's like having a huge staff room," says Mann. "People are getting answers to things that the other teachers in their school didn't know."

Declara's technology watches all these interactions. It learns whom people tend to turn to for, say, complex physics questions, and which teachers seem to produce high test scores quarter after quarter. The software can search and catalogue all the digital material collected during the past fifteen years by the Australian school system. So if you need to find advice on teaching gifted children, you type "gifted children" in a search box, and up pops all the available documents on the subject, along with some guesses about the experts in the area you might want to contact.

Declara makes it possible for these organizations and companies to operate in two modes—private and public. The Australian teachers, for example, can keep chats within their own network to themselves but also have an open area where companies with interesting technology or specialists in certain fields can participate. Pierson describes this as a kind of permeable membrane. "There are countries in Latin America and the Middle East that are industrializing and improving their judicial systems and moving into spaces they have never been before," Pierson says. "They need to seek experts among themselves and outsiders."

It's on this last point that Declara can challenge the big consulting firms, she says. The software studies interactions on Twitter, can see which people have frequently cited academic papers, and, with permission, scans chat sessions for verbal clues about people who know what they're talking about. (Companies such as IBM have released similar software for finding internal experts.) "In Australia, there is no McKinsey team or Harvard school telling the teachers how to develop the world's most innovative curriculum," says cofounder González. "They're doing it themselves by learning from their peers."

When Pierson turned fifty last December, she and Chrapaty threw a three-day-long celebration in Carmel Valley. The couple had been through a lot, including a series of bungled leg surgeries that left Pierson near death once again. "The doctors gave me an infected bone implant," Pierson says, adding that she's never sued. "They had to cut that out of me and start again. Debra and I almost broke up. She didn't really sign up for all this." By the time her birthday rolled around, Pierson was as healthy as she'd been in years, and it was time to party.

On the last day of the event, everyone gathered in a banquet room at the Carmel Valley Lodge, down the hill from the house. Pierson has picked up friends all over the world, and here they were spending hours chatting and reminiscing together. One of the more memorable moments came as Pierson gave a bear hug to Naomi Hoops, an octogenarian former school custodian who got to know Pierson at the community college in Colorado. "I thought she was going to squeeze the life out of me," Hoops says. "She is that same old Ramona I first met."

Another attendee that evening was Stan Chervin, a screenwriter working on a movie about Pierson. "People who dismiss *It's a Wonderful Life* as being too hokey should have been in that room," he says. "Person after person stood up and said, 'This is how Ramona Pierson changed my life.' The cliché is the triumph of the human spirit over adversity. Well, it ain't a cliché with Ramona."

Pacific Standard

The best stories often start out with the simplest questions: Like how in the heck did three-dollar-a-slice artisanal toast become a thing? The easy piece would be a snarky eye-roll at the latest hipster inanity. But in following the breadcrumbs, John Gravois ends up with an unexpectedly beautiful tale of a woman and her demons, the small business she starts up in San Francisco to combat them, and the childhood comfort food that would go on to spark a national trend.

John Gravois

26. A Toast Story

All the guy was doing was slicing inch-thick pieces of bread, putting them in a toaster, and spreading stuff on them. But what made me stare—blinking to attention in the middle of a workday morning as I waited in line at an unfamiliar café—was the way he did it. He had the solemn intensity of a Ping-Pong player who keeps his game very close to the table: knees slightly bent, wrist flicking the butter knife back and forth, eyes suggesting a kind of flow state.

The coffee shop, called the Red Door, was a spare little operation tucked into the corner of a chic industrial-style art gallery and event space (clients include Facebook, Microsoft, Evernote, Google) in downtown San Francisco. There were just three employees working behind the counter: one making coffee, one taking orders, and the soulful guy making toast. In front of him, laid out in a neat row, were a few long Pullman loaves—the boxy Wonder Bread shape, like a train car, but recognizably handmade and freshly baked. And on the brief menu, toast was a standalone item—at three dollars per slice.

It took me just a few seconds to digest what this meant: that toast, like the cupcake and the dill pickle before it, had been elevated to the artisanal plane. So I ordered some. It was pretty good. It tasted just like toast, but better.

A couple of weeks later I was at a place called Acre Coffee in Petaluma, a smallish town about an hour north of San Francisco on Highway 101. Half of the shop's food menu fell under the heading "Toast Bar." Not long after that I was with my wife and daughter on Divisadero Street in San Francisco, and we went to The Mill, a big light-filled café and bakery with exposed rafters and polished concrete floors, like a rustic Apple Store. There, between the two iPads that served as cash registers, was a small chalkboard that listed the day's toast menu. Everywhere the offerings were more or less the same: thick slices of good bread, square-shaped, topped with things like small-batch almond butter or apricot marmalade or sea salt.

Back at the Red Door one day, I asked the manager what was going on. Why all the toast? "Tip of the hipster spear," he said.

I had two reactions to this: First, of course, I rolled my eyes. How silly; how twee; how perfectly *San Francisco*, this toast. And second, despite myself, I felt a little thrill of discovery. How many weeks would it be, I wondered, before artisanal toast made it to Brooklyn, or Chicago, or Los Angeles? How long before an article appears in *Slate* telling people all across America that they're making toast all wrong? How long before the backlash sets in?

For whatever reason, I felt compelled to go looking for the origins of the fancy toast trend. How does such a thing get started? What determines how far it goes? I wanted to know. Maybe I thought it would help me understand the rise of all the seemingly trivial, evanescent things that start in San Francisco and then go supernova across the country—the kinds of products I am usually late to discover and slow to figure out. I'm not sure what kind of answer I expected to turn up. Certainly nothing too impressive or emotionally affecting. But what I found was more surprising and sublime than I could have possibly imagined.

.   .   .

If the discovery of artisanal toast had made me roll my eyes, it soon made other people in San Francisco downright indignant.

I spent the early part of my search following the footsteps of a very low-stakes mob. "$4 Toast: Why the Tech Industry Is Ruining San Francisco" ran the headline of an August article on a local technology news site called *VentureBeat.*

"Flaunting your wealth has been elevated to new lows," wrote the author, Jolie O'Dell. "We don't go to the opera; we overspend on the simplest facets of life." For a few weeks four-dollar toast became a rallying cry in the city's media—an instant parable and parody of the shallow, expensive new San Francisco—inspiring thousands of shares on Facebook, several follow-up articles, and a petition to the mayor's office demanding relief from the city's high costs of living.

The butt of all this criticism appeared to be The Mill, the rustic-modern place on Divisadero Street. The Mill was also, I learned, the bakery that supplies the Red Door with its bread. So I assumed I had found the cradle of the toast phenomenon.

I was wrong. When I called Josey Baker, the—yes—baker behind The Mill's toast, he was a little mystified by the dustup over his product while also a bit taken aback at how popular it had become. "On a busy Saturday or Sunday we'll make 350 to 400 pieces of toast," he told me. "It's ridiculous, isn't it?"

But Baker assured me that he was not the Chuck Berry of fancy toast. He was its Elvis: he had merely caught the trend on its upswing. The place I was looking for, he and others told me, was a coffee shop in the city's Outer Sunset neighborhood—a little spot called Trouble.

· · ·

The Trouble Coffee & Coconut Club (its full name) is a tiny storefront next door to a Spanish-immersion preschool, about three blocks from the Pacific Ocean in one of the city's windiest, foggiest, farthest-flung areas. As places of business go, I would call Trouble impressively odd.

Instead of a standard café patio, Trouble's outdoor seating area is dominated by a substantial section of a tree trunk, stripped of its bark, lying on its side. Around the perimeter are benches and steps and railings made of salvaged wood, but no tables and chairs. On my first visit on a chilly September afternoon, people were lounging on the trunk drinking their coffee and eating slices of toast, looking like lions draped over tree limbs in the Serengeti.

The shop itself is about the size of a single-car garage, with an L-shaped bar made of heavily varnished driftwood. One wall is decorated with a mishmash of artifacts—a walkie-talkie collection, a mannequin torso, some hand tools. A set of old speakers in the back blares a steady stream of punk and noise rock. And a glass refrigerator case beneath the cash register prominently displays a bunch of coconuts and grapefruit. Next to the cash register is a single steel toaster. Trouble's specialty is a thick slice of locally made white toast, generously covered with butter, cinnamon, and sugar: a variation on the cinnamon toast that everyone's mom, including mine, seemed to make when I was a kid in the 1980s. It is, for that nostalgic association, the first toast in San Francisco that really made sense to me.

Trouble's owner, and the apparent originator of San Francisco's toast craze, is a slight, blue-eyed, thirty-four-year-old woman with freckles tattooed on her cheeks named Giulietta Carrelli. She has a good toast story: She grew up in a rough neighborhood of Cleveland in the eighties and nineties in a big immigrant family, her father a tailor from Italy, her mother an ex-nun. The family didn't eat much standard American food. But cinnamon toast, made in a pinch, was the exception. "We never had pie," Carrelli says. "Our American comfort food was cinnamon toast."

The other main players on Trouble's menu are coffee, young Thai coconuts served with a straw and a spoon for digging out the meat, and shots of fresh-squeezed grapefruit juice called "Yoko." It's a strange lineup, but each item has specific meaning to Carrelli. Toast, she says, represents comfort. Coffee represents speed and communication. And coconuts represent survival—because it's possible, Carrelli says, to survive on coconuts provided you also have a source of vitamin C. Hence the Yoko. (Carrelli tested this theory by living mainly on coconuts and grapefruit juice for three years, "unless someone took me out to dinner.")

The menu also features a go-for-broke option called "Build Your Own Damn House," which consists of a coffee, a coconut, and a piece of cinnamon toast. Hanging in the door is a manifesto that covers a green chalkboard. "We are local people with useful skills in tangible situations," it says, among other things. "Drink a cup of Trouble. Eat a coconut. And learn to build your own damn house. We will help. We are building a network."

If Trouble's toast itself made instant sense to me, it was less clear how a willfully obscure coffee shop with barely any indoor seating in a cold, inconvenient neighborhood could have been such a successful launch pad for a food trend. In some ways, the shop seemed to make itself downright difficult to like: It serves no decaf, no nonfat milk, no large drinks, and no espressos to go. On Yelp, several reviewers report having been scolded by baristas for trying to take pictures inside the shop with their phones. ("I better not see that up on Instagram!" one reportedly shouted.)

Nevertheless, most people really seem to love Trouble. On my second visit to the shop, there was a steady line of customers out the door. After receiving their orders, they clustered outside to drink their coffees and eat their toast. With no tables and chairs to allow them to pair off, they looked more like neighbors at a block party than customers at a café. And perhaps most remarkably for San Francisco, none of them had their phones out.

Trouble has been so successful, in fact, that Carrelli recently opened a second, even tinier location in the city's Bayview neighborhood. I met her there one sunny afternoon. She warned me that she probably wouldn't have much time to talk. But we chatted for nearly three hours.

In public, Carrelli wears a remarkably consistent uniform: a crop top with ripped black jeans and brown leather lace-up boots, with her blond hair wrapped in Jack Sparrowish scarves and headbands. At her waist is a huge silver screaming-eagle belt buckle, and her torso is covered with tattoos of hand tools and designs taken from eighteenth-century wallpaper patterns. Animated and lucid—her blue eyes bright above a pair of strikingly ruddy cheeks—Carrelli interrupted our long conversation periodically to banter with pretty much every person who visited the shop.

At first, Carrelli explained Trouble as a kind of sociological experiment in engineering spontaneous communication between strangers. She even conducted field research, she says, before opening the shop. "I did a study in New York and San Francisco, standing on the street holding a sandwich, saying hello to people. No one would talk to me. But if I stayed at that same street corner and I was holding a coconut? People would engage," she said. "I wrote down exactly how many people talked to me."

The smallness of her cafés is another device to stoke interaction, on the theory that it's simply hard to avoid talking to people standing nine inches away from you. And cinnamon toast is a kind of all-purpose mollifier: something Carrelli offers her customers whenever Trouble is abrasive or loud or crowded or refuses to give them what they want. "No one can be mad at toast," she said.

Carrelli's explanations made a delightfully weird, fleeting kind of sense as I heard them. But then she told me something that made Trouble snap into focus. More than a café, the shop is a carpentered-together, ingenious mechanism—a specialized tool—designed to keep Carrelli tethered to herself.

·   ·   ·

Ever since she was in high school, Carrelli says, she has had something called schizoaffective disorder, a condition that combines symptoms of schizophrenia and bipolarity. People who have it are susceptible to both psychotic episodes and bouts of either mania or depression.

Carrelli tends toward the vivid, manic end of the mood spectrum, she says, but the onset of a psychotic episode can shut her down with little warning for hours, days, or, in the worst instances, months. Even on good days, she struggles to maintain a sense of self; for years her main means of achieving this was to write furiously in notebooks, trying to get the essentials down on paper. When an episode comes on, she describes the experience as a kind of death: Sometimes she gets stuck hallucinating, hearing voices, unable to move or see clearly; other times she has wandered the city aimlessly. "Sometimes I don't recognize myself," she says. "I get so much disorganized brain activity, I would get lost for twelve hours."

Carrelli's early years with her illness were, she says, a blind struggle. Undiagnosed, she worked her way through college—three different colleges, in different corners of the country—by booking shows for underground bands and doing stints at record stores and coffee shops. But her episodes were a kind of time bomb that occasionally leveled any structure in her life. Roommates always ended up kicking her out. Landlords evicted her. Relationships fell apart. Employers either fired her or quietly stopped scheduling her for shifts. After a while, she began anticipating the pattern and taking steps to preempt the inevitable. "I moved when people started catching on," she says. By the time she hit thirty, she had lived in nine different cities.

Like a lot of people with mental illness, Carrelli self-medicated with drugs, in her case opiates, and alcohol. And sometimes things got very bad indeed. Throughout her twenties, she was in and out of hospitals and periods of homelessness.

One day in 1999, when Carrelli was living in San Francisco and going to school at the University of California–Berkeley, she took a long walk through the city and ended up on China Beach, a small cove west of the Golden Gate. She describes the scene to me in stark detail: The sun was flickering in and out of intermittent fog. A group of Russian men in Speedos were stepping out of the frigid ocean. And an elderly man was sitting in a deck chair, sunbathing in weather that suggested anything but. Carrelli struck up a conversation with the man, whose name was Glen. In a German accent, he told her that people congregated regularly at China Beach to swim in the ocean. He had done so himself when he was younger, he said, but now he just came to the beach to sunbathe every day.

Carrelli left San Francisco shortly thereafter. ("Everything fell apart," she says.) But her encounter with the old man made such a profound impression that five years later, in 2004—after burning through stints in South Carolina, Georgia, and New York—she drove back across the country and headed for China Beach. When she arrived, she found Glen sitting in the same spot where she had left him in 1999. That day, as they parted ways, he said, "See you tomorrow." For the next three years, he said the same words to her pretty much every day. "He became this structure," Carrelli says, "a constant."

It was perhaps the safe distance between them—an elderly man and a young woman sitting on a public beach—that made Glen relatively impervious to the detonations that had wiped out every other home she'd ever had. "He couldn't kick me out," Carrelli says. She sat with her notebooks, and Glen asked her questions about her experiments with strangers and coconuts. Gradually, she began to find other constants. She started joining the swimmers every day, plunging into the Pacific with no wetsuit, even in winter. Her drinking began to taper off. She landed a job at a coffee shop called Farley's that she managed to keep for three years. And she began assiduously cultivating a network of friends she could count on for help when she was in trouble—a word she uses frequently to refer to her psychotic episodes—while being careful not to overtax any individual's generosity.

Carrelli also found safety in simply being well known—in attracting as many acquaintances as possible. That's why, she tells me, she had always worked in coffee shops. When she is feeling well, Carrelli is a swashbuckling presence, charismatic and disarmingly curious about people. "She will always make a friend wherever she is," says Noelle Olivo, a San Francisco escrow and title agent who was a regular customer at Farley's and later gave Carrelli a place to stay for a couple of months. "People are taken aback by her, but she reaches out."

This gregariousness was in part a survival mechanism, as were her tattoos and her daily uniform of headscarves, torn jeans, and crop tops. The trick was to be identifiable: The more people who recognized her, the more she stood a chance of being able to recognize herself.

But Carrelli's grip on stability was still fragile. Between apartments and evictions, she slept in her truck, in parks, at China Beach, on friends' couches. Then one day in 2006, Carrelli's boss at Farley's Coffee discovered her sleeping in the shop, and he told her it was probably time she opened up her own space. "He almost gave me permission to do something I knew I should do," she recalls. It was clear by then that Carrelli couldn't really work for anyone else—Farley's had been unusually forgiving. But she didn't know how to chart a course forward. At China Beach, she took to her notebooks, filling them with grandiose manifestoes about living with guts and honor and commitment—about, she wrote, building her own damn house.

"Giulietta, you don't have enough money to eat tonight," Glen said, bringing her down to earth. Then he asked her a question that has since appeared in her writing again and again: "What is your useful skill in a tangible situation?"

The answer was easy: she was good at making coffee and good with people. So Glen told her it was time she opened a checking account. He told her to go to city hall and ask if they had information on starting a small business. And she followed his instructions.

With $1,000 borrowed from friends, Carrelli opened Trouble in 2007 in a smelly, cramped former dog-grooming business, on a bleak commercial stretch. She renovated the space pretty much entirely with found materials and with labor and advice that was bartered for, cajoled, and requested from her community of acquaintances.

She called the shop Trouble, she says, in honor of all the people who helped her when she was in trouble. She called her drip coffee "guts" and her espresso "honor." She put coconuts on the menu because of the years she had spent relying on them for easy sustenance and because they truly did help her strike up conversations with strangers. She put toast on the menu because it reminded her of home: "I had lived so long with no comfort," she says. And she put "Build Your Own Damn House" on the menu because she felt, with Trouble, that she had finally done so.

· · ·

Glen—whose full name was Gunther Neustadt, and who had escaped Germany as a young Jewish boy with his twin sister during World War II—lived to see Trouble open. But he died later that year. In 2008, Carrelli became pregnant and had twins.

That same year, after having lived in her shop for months, Carrelli got a real apartment. She went completely clean and sober and has stayed that way. She started to hire staff she could rely on; she worked out a sustainable custody arrangement with her children's father. And Trouble started to get written up in the press. Customers began to flock there from all over town for toast and coffee and coconuts.

The demands of running the shop, caring for two children, and swimming every day allowed Carrelli to feel increasingly grounded, but her psychotic episodes hardly went away; when they came on, she just kept working somehow. "I have no idea how I ran Trouble," she says. "I kept piling through." In 2012, after a five-month episode, Carrelli was hospitalized and, for the first time, given the diagnosis of schizoaffective disorder. Under her current treatment regimen, episodes come far less frequently. But still they come.

At bottom, Carrelli says, Trouble is a tool for keeping her alive. "I'm trying to stay connected to the self," she says. Like one of her old notebooks, the shop has become an externalized set of reference points, an index of Carrelli's identity. It is her greatest source of dependable routine and her most powerful means of expanding her network of friends and acquaintances, which extends now to the shop's entire clientele. These days, during a walking episode, Carrelli says, a hello from a casual acquaintance in some unfamiliar part of the city might make the difference between whether she makes it home that night or not. "I'm wearing the same outfit every day," she says. "I take the same routes every day. I own Trouble Coffee so that people recognize my face—so they can help me."

After having struggled as an employee in so many coffee shops, she now employs fourteen people. In an almost unheard of practice for the café business, she offers them profit-sharing and dental coverage. And she plans on expanding the business even further, maybe opening up to four or five locations. With the proceeds, she hopes to one day open a halfway house for people who have psychotic episodes—a safe place where they can go when they are in trouble.

·   ·   ·

When I told friends back East about the craze for fancy toast that was sweeping across the Bay Area, they laughed and laughed. (How silly; how twee; how *San Francisco*.) But my bet is that artisanal toast is going national. I've already heard reports of sightings in the West Village.

If the spread of toast is a social contagion, then Carrelli was its perfect vector. Most of us dedicate the bulk of our attention to a handful of relationships: with a significant other, children, parents, a few close friends. Social scientists call these "strong ties." But Carrelli can't rely on such a small set of intimates. Strong ties have a history of failing her, of buckling under the weight of her illness. So she has adapted by forming as many relationships—as many weak ties—as she possibly can. And webs of weak ties are what allow ideas to spread.

In a city whose economy is increasingly built on digital social networks—but where simple eye contact is at a premium—Giulietta Carrelli's latticework of small connections is old-fashioned and analog. It is built not for self-presentation but for self-preservation. And the spread of toast is only one of the things that has arisen from it.

A few weeks ago, I went back to Trouble because I hadn't yet built my own damn house. When my coconut came, the next guy at the bar shot me a sideways glance. Sitting there with a slice of toast and a large tropical fruit, I felt momentarily self-conscious. Then the guy said to the barista, "Hey, can I get a coconut too?" and the two of us struck up a conversation.

Part VI

The Politics of Business

Boston Globe

What's Big Business to do when its interests conflict with those of high-polling organizations and issues like the Humane Society, Mothers Against Drunk Driving, and raising the minimum wage? Hire Richard Berman, a Washington public-relations man who lobs their bombs for them, provides them IRS-sanctioned anonymity, and takes the reputational damage himself. As Michael Kranish of the *Boston Globe* shows in this exposé, the cost to public discourse is high. Operating behind fronts with such legitimate-sounding names as the Employment Policies Institute and the Center for Consumer Freedom, Berman and Company smears opponents with ad campaigns while planting misinformation in the press.

Michael Kranish

27. Washington's Robust Market for Attacks, Half-Truths

Even by the contemporary standards of bare-fisted attack ads, the unlikely assault on the president of the Humane Society of the United States seems particularly brazen.

"Is Wayne Pacelle the Bernie Madoff of the Charity World?" the ad says, comparing the leader of the nation's largest animal welfare group to the swindler serving a 150-year sentence for losses of $65 billion in the world's most notorious Ponzi scheme. As a narrator speaks, an image of Pacelle is shown morphing into Madoff.

Then the attack widens. The Humane Society, the narrator says, "gives less than 1 percent of its massive donations to local pet shelters but has socked away $17 million in its own pension fund." Dollar bills are shown floating in front of Pacelle's smiling face as the narrator says donors should only continue to contribute to the Humane Society "if you want your money to support Wayne and his pension."

This one-minute ad—viewed 1.7 million times on YouTube and created by a nonprofit organization called the Center for Consumer Freedom—provides a case study of what critics say is an industry of distortion in Washington. Increasingly, groups are seeking to influence public policy not by the traditional methods of lobbying or campaign contributions but, as in this case, by hurling accusations, true or not, that are intended to destroy an influential target's credibility.

On one level, the charges can be easily refuted, according to the ad's target, Pacelle. The Humane Society president said his organization shelters more animals than any other group, mostly using its own facilities instead of contributing to others, and he said that the $17 million pension fund covers hundreds of employees, not just himself.

The ad "is comparing me to America's most notorious white-collar criminal and I have a spotless record on financial matters and we also do exactly what we say," Pacelle said, decrying what he called the ad's "lies and fabrications and misrepresentations."

But on a broader level, it is the story behind the ad that is most revealing—a story that provides a window into a world of questionable claims, powered by donations from unnamed corporations, and a Washington agenda with many millions of dollars at stake.

The group behind the ad, the Center for Consumer Freedom, is headed by a Washington-based corporate communications consultant named Richard Berman, the head of Berman and Company, a public relations and government affairs firm.

The center's funding includes large donations from corporations whose identity it does not disclose. But Berman and his associates have said in depositions and interviews that backers include food and farming corporations.

Some of those companies have been at odds with the Humane Society, which backs legislation in Congress and state legislatures to improve conditions for farm animals. An ad defending the cramped size of animal pens is, needless to say, hardly as attention-getting as one comparing the Humane Society president to Madoff.

Sarah Longwell, the vice president of Berman and Company, declined to take questions from the *Globe*, writing via e-mail that "no one here will be participating in your story." Berman did not respond to repeated requests for comment.

Washington, of course, is a city with many operatives who act for corporations seeking to shape public opinion about issues before Congress without leaving fingerprints and without having to directly associate their name and brand with the attacks made on their behalf.

Indeed, from the upper reaches of the Washington power structure on down, questionable or outright false statements have become a way of doing business.

Hyperbole and distortion are common, a carryover from the rhetorical free-for-all of political campaigns; the result is that there is much public confusion about the issues, about what is fact and what is merely an interested party's claim.

Gun-control opponents say the government plans to take away guns. Obamacare opponents say the government wants to take over health care. So-called birthers went after President Obama by suggesting he was not born in America despite indisputable evidence he was born in Hawaii. Senate Majority Leader Harry Reid last year said Republican presidential nominee Mitt Romney didn't pay federal taxes for ten years, even though Romney provided a letter from his accountant that he said refuted the charge.

Misinformation has become so widespread that a counter-industry of fact checkers has emerged at various media outlets; the *Washington Post* rates misleading statements on the number of "Pinocchios," while the Pulitzer-winning website PolitiFact gives the biggest whoppers a grade of "Pants on Fire."

In a political campaign, a candidate making questionable claims can be held accountable by voters at the ballot box. But accountability is harder to come by in the shadowy world where Berman and like operatives do their work. There, corporate backers are anonymous, funding groups that have vague but high-sounding names, such as the Center for Consumer Freedom. The work of such groups receives far less scrutiny from media fact-checking operations than that of political candidates.

In this realm of opinion molding, Berman is a pioneer. He maintains one of the longest-running and most influential enterprises in the field. His attacks typically are carefully worded so that each sentence can be defended as narrowly accurate. But his critics say many are constructed in a way that distorts the overall picture, as in the case of the ad comparing Pacelle to Madoff.

Berman boasts on his website of his influence, saying that his groups' research is cited on the floors of the House and Senate, shaping countless pieces of legislation. His op-eds run in newspapers across the country, sometimes without making clear the sources of his corporate backing. He was quoted in a 2003 book about U.S. politics as saying companies "can pay us to represent them and retain their anonymity," while he vows on his website that he will stick with an issue "as long as it takes to win."

While Berman's work has been in and out of the news over the years, his profile recently has been raised due to a confluence of events that has focused new light on his activities.

Charity Navigator, an independent group that analyzes nonprofits, recently gave five of Berman's groups its lowest rating, known as a "donor advisory," saying the nonprofits used most of their funds to pay Berman's for-profit company for management services and other costs.

Charity Navigator president Ken Berger said in an interview that such transfers were "very rare" and "raise a lot of questions." (In response, Berman's group recently posted a note on its website saying that Charity Navigator's finding is "misleading" and that there is nothing unusual about the way Berman's nonprofit groups pay into Berman's for-profit firm.)

The Humane Society, also citing transfers among Berman entities, has filed a complaint against him with the IRS, alleging that Berman's groups have engaged in "systemic abuse of their tax-exempt status." An IRS official said the agency could not comment on whether a complaint is being investigated. A Berman website says that the IRS investigated earlier complaints and "did not change the non-profit status of any of the groups they reviewed—nor was any organization sanctioned."

Melanie Sloan, the head of Citizens for Responsibility and Ethics in Washington, which filed an unsuccessful complaint with the IRS against Berman's groups in 2004, said Berman's activities have only grown since then. Corporate backers are "using Berman to say outrageous things that they themselves would never say because of the risk of alienating some of their customers," she said. Berman, in turn, has attacked Sloan's group as a "left-wing attack dog."

Berman has said he has to resort to such tactics because his adversaries—some of which also don't disclose most donors—make unsubstantiated claims and haven't been properly scrutinized. "It is a strategy," he testified before a U.S. House committee in 2002, "to reposition people who have a pristine image which is undeserved. . . . If that's shooting the messenger, then I'm guilty of it."

•   •   •

One of Berman's top vehicles for "shooting the messenger" is his Center for Consumer Freedom, which is described on a Berman website as being "supported by restaurants, food companies and thousands of individual consumers." The depth of support from consumers is unclear, but certainly the center is aggressive in going after groups that have been at odds with the food and restaurant business, including the Humane Society and organized labor.

Berman and other representatives of the center have, for example, regularly made media appearances to press the case of his corporate backers. Berman appeared on Fox News in April to castigate calls for increasing the minimum wage. A Berman employee, J. Justin Wilson, the author of a book published by the center called *An Epidemic of Obesity Myths*, appeared in February on NPR's popular *Diane Rehm Show*, presented as a counterpoint to experts who warned of the danger of addiction to high-sugar foods.

Berman and his employees have written more than one hundred op-eds and letters to the editor in newspapers this year, including a piece by Berman posted to an online forum of the *Boston Globe*, in which he was identified as the center's director and wrote that a proposed state law called the Prevention of Farm Animal Cruelty Act "is less about helping animals and more about a fringe agenda to bankrupt farmers."

Much of Berman's work is done through websites, one of which, Humane Watch, has been publicized in Times Square billboards and a Super Bowl commercial. Many are designed to counter the findings of federal health studies.

The Center for Consumer Freedom, for example, runs a highly trafficked website called Obesity Myths, which says that it is "myth" that "obesity will shorten life expectancy." The website noted—correctly—that federal officials had lowered an estimate of premature deaths from obesity. But that revised report still said that many such deaths would occur, according to federal officials.

Dr. William Dietz, who until last June was director of the CDC's division of nutrition, physical activity, and obesity, said that the Berman group's claims are "ridiculous." The evidence that obesity can shorten life is abundant, he said, even as the estimate of premature deaths has gone down. He expressed frustration that the government's reports are sometimes presented in the media on equal footing with those sponsored by groups like Berman's whose clients have a vested interest.

"Part of the problem with public debate these days is that everyone seems to have an equal voice and belief seems to have displaced science," Dietz said. "Anytime someone wants to dismiss the science they will go after the people who publish it."

•   •   •

Berman began his career working in senior executive positions for a series of corporations, including Bethlehem Steel and Pillsbury, and he served as director of labor law at the U.S. Chamber of Commerce. Then he created Berman and Company, focusing on government activity that affects corporations. He got his start with funds from tobacco giant Philip Morris, which paid at least $600,000 to fight smoking-related legislation, and millions of dollars from alcohol-related businesses.

By the mid-1990s, Berman was at the center of a fight against legislation designed to limit drunken driving fatalities. On one side was Mothers Against Drunk Driving, a group that few in Washington were anxious to take on. Berman jumped at the chance.

It was a time when many state legislatures were considering legislation to lower the blood alcohol limit from 0.10 to 0.08. In order to reach the 0.08 level, a 160-pound man must consume four drinks in an hour, while a 120-pound woman must down three drinks in two hours, according to the Food and Drug Administration. That level of intoxication makes it difficult for drivers to process in-ormation and control speed, the FDA has said. Proponents said lowering the legal level to 0.08 would let people drink in moderation while saving thousands of lives.

Berman saw it differently.

"It's feel-good, meaningless legislation that doesn't have any impact," Berman testified at a 1997 hearing. He suggested focusing instead on "the 0.14-and-above drivers [who] are at the heart of the drunk-driving problem."

U.S. senator Frank Lautenberg, a New Jersey Democrat who attended the hearing, rose from his chair to declare that "what I heard Mr. Berman say I found almost shocking," recalling how he had met with a family in which a young girl was killed by a driver whose blood alcohol content was 0.08.

Berman's efforts may have delayed efforts to lower the alcohol limit, but his argument was, in the end, unsuccessful. Spurred by federal incentives, the number of states with a 0.08 limit went from nineteen in 2000 to all fifty by 2004. As a result of that and other measures, including setting the drinking age at twenty-one, alcohol-related fatalities have dropped from 13,472 in 2002 to 9,878 in 2011, according to the National Highway Traffic Safety Administration.

But Berman, in his role as president of a trade group called the American Beverage Institute, continues to battle Mothers Against Drunk Driving. The institute says on its website that its mission is to "expose and vigorously counter the campaigns of modern-day prohibitionists."

In January, Berman associate Sarah Longwell, the managing director of the Institute, authored an op-ed in the *Milwaukee Journal Sentinel* in which she took on MADD, saying the group wants the federal government to require monitoring devices to be placed in cars of those convicted for drunken driving. Such devices prevent a car from starting until the driver has passed an in-car breathalyzer test. That's unfair, she wrote, because a person whose blood alcohol limit is at the state limit is no more impaired than someone who is "driving while talking on a hands-free cellphone."

At the same time, the American Beverage Institute runs a website called The New Prohibition, which alleges that a network of "anti-alcohol activists," including the American Medical Association and Mothers Against Drunk Driving, "seek to return the United States to the 1920s," when alcohol use was banned. The website said that if anti-alcohol activists have their way today, some people won't be able to have "a beer at a ballgame."

While MADD has advocated in-car breathalyzers for convicted drunk drivers, it supports the current 0.08 blood-alcohol limit, according to senior vice president J. T. Griffin.

"The 'new Prohibition' is an absolute lie," Griffin said. "They are trying to paint us as an extreme organization. It is shameful coming from an organization that doesn't reveal who their sponsors are."

While it is impossible to say how much impact the "new Prohibition" campaign is having, MADD officials say they are monitoring the Berman effort closely, particularly as state legislatures review their decisions to lower the drinking age and consider requiring in-car breath-test machines.

•　　　•　　　•

The Center for Consumer Freedom, as well as Berman and Company and several affiliated groups, share the address of a downtown Washington office building. The publicly available portion of the Center's 2011 tax filing shows that it is mostly funded by a handful of generous, anonymous donors. An individual identified only as "Donor No. 1" gave $300,000. "Donor No. 6" gave $520,000. All told, the nonprofit Center received $1.4 million in 2011 in contributions and grants. It spent $2.1 million, of which $1.3 million was paid to the for-profit Berman and Company for management, research, advertising, and accounting fees, according to its IRS filing.

While tax rules allow the identity of donors to nonprofits to be anonymous, the Center says on its website that its contributors must remain secret because "they are reasonably apprehensive about privacy and safety in light of the violence and other forms of aggression some activists have adopted as a 'game plan' to impose their views."

Eight blocks from the headquarters of the Center for Consumer Freedom, Wayne Pacelle sits in his office at the Humane Society and fumes over the center's attacks on him and his group. The ad comparing Pacelle to Madoff, released on April 5, is only the latest. For months, Berman's group has suggested that the Humane Society is bilking donors because it gives less than 1 percent of its money to pet shelters.

Pacelle said it is a classic Berman strategy of "false framing" of an issue. The society, he said, doesn't say it will give large amounts to independent pet shelters. Instead, Pacelle said that the Humane Society takes care of more than 100,000 animals at its own facilities, including a 1,300-animal care center near Dallas and a 1,200-acre wildlife rehabilitation center ranch near Fort Lauderdale.

Berman "doesn't give us credit for any of the animals we care for," Pacelle said. "The only metric he uses is if we give a grant to a pet shelter."

Pacelle said he has alerted Berman to "misrepresentations" many times without a response.

So why is Berman's group attacking the Humane Society and Pacelle? Pacelle believes Berman has been hired by corporate interests such as agri-business and restaurant chains that don't like the way the Humane Society has influenced food- and agri-cultural-related legislation in Congress and state legislatures. For example, the Humane Society has been fighting for years, and with some success, to force big farms to get rid of pens that prevent pigs from turning around, urging that such structures be replaced with facilities that let the animals roam a bit.

The tactics are a sign of change in Washington, Pacelle said. It used to be that a company would hire a Washington representative to oppose a particular piece of legislation. What is new, he said, is that Berman is trying to destroy the "brand" of the Humane Society, not just a pending bill.

It is hard to quantify Berman's success rate. Unlike a lobbyist who files a report declaring which legislation he is trying to influence, Berman works on behalf of unnamed backers and tries to shape public perceptions about his targets. As a result, Berman can claim success in delaying legislation or undermining an opponent. For example, in an e-mail to one of his backers—a copy of which was provided to the *Globe*—Berman wrote that the campaign against the Humane Society was "far more successful than I anticipated" in creating a negative image, asserting that he was "chilling the donation stream."

Pacelle said donations have more than doubled during the time that Berman has attacked him but added there was no way to know if more money would have come in without the assault.

Berman's group also has gone after People for the Ethical Treatment of Animals, which has angered some farm and food groups by conducting investigations into the treatment of farm animals. Berman's Center for Consumer Freedom created a website called "PETA kills animals," which says PETA killed 1,647 cats and dogs in 2012.

The strategy was a classic effort for Berman: the headline-grabbing fact is correct, and PETA says the number of killed animals is accurate. But PETA said the broader implication is misleading. PETA says it "euthanizes" only the most "broken" animals brought to its "shelter of last resort." PETA senior vice president Jeff Kerr said Berman's charges are "like complaining that a hospice has a high mortality rate. It's entirely misleading." Kerr said that the real aim of the attack is to undermine PETA because the group's promotion of a vegan diet cuts into the profits of Berman's backers.

While some groups prefer to ignore Berman's tactics, the Humane Society has filed a complaint with the IRS that alleges the Center for Consumer Freedom and other entities created by Berman have violated tax laws and may owe more than $23 million to the IRS.

"We have been the first major organization to punch back and try to expose his attacks on many of America's most respected charities," Pacelle said. "He doesn't like that and he knows that so much of it stems from my passion not to let this guy get away with his scam and I will continue to go after Rick Berman until he is completely exposed." But such steps seem to have only increased the animosity.

· · ·

It was last summer when Berman launched another hardball effort to undermine the Humane Society—an effort he may have believed would not become publicly known. He wanted one of the nation's leading charity-rating organizations—the Wise Giving

Alliance of the Better Business Bureau—to drop its accreditation of the Humane Society. If that happened, donations to the Humane Society might significantly decrease, and Berman could claim another victory.

Berman's tool was an unsubtle warning. He threatened to publicize what he called a "pay-to-play" system, in which charities that are rated by the Wise Giving Alliance have the option of paying to display the group's endorsement.

"You can protect [the Humane Society's] brand at the BBB's expense," Berman wrote in a June 27, 2012, letter to the Alliance, "or you can protect the BBB's brand."

The BBB's Wise Giving Alliance strongly denied that it engages in "pay to play," stressing that groups are not required to purchase the right to display the accreditation.

Berman then traveled in August for a meeting at the headquarters of the Wise Giving Alliance, whose officers said they received permission from him to record the conversation. The Humane Society is "as duplicitous an organization as I have ever seen," Berman said at the meeting, according to a transcript provided by the Alliance.

Berman said he was speaking for his financial supporters, calling them "big companies" who were tired of being attacked by the society. "They are very upset with the Humane Society," Berman said, according to the transcript. "We are several million dollars into going after them."

And if the Alliance wouldn't act—revoking the Humane Society's accreditation—Berman repeated his written warning that he and his backers might go after them, too. "As I try to get to the goal line, worst case scenario is, in regard to the Better Business Bureau, if you'll excuse the expression, become collateral damage," Berman said, according to the transcript.

H. Art Taylor, the chief executive of the Wise Giving Alliance, investigated Berman's allegation that the Humane Society was running a "scam." He said in an interview that he found his claim baseless and thus the society has kept its accreditation.

Taylor provided the correspondence and transcript to the *Globe* because he said he wanted the public to understand Berman's methods. "People ought to know why we are pushing back," he said.

· · ·

Berman gave one of his most revealing talks about his strategy in a locale far from his Washington office. Meeting with a group of Nebraska farmers in 2010, he told them it was more effective to "hit people in their heart rather than their head," according to a report on the talk by *Nebraska Farm Bureau News*. "Emotional understanding is very different—it stays with you. Intellectual understanding is a fact and facts trump other facts. When I understand something in my gut, you've got me in a very different way."

Berman then explained why he believes such attacks work. "People remember negative stuff," Berman said. "They don't like hearing it, but they remember it. . . . We can use fear and anger—it stays with people longer than love and sympathy."

Washington Monthly

Regulation is arcane and byzantine, and writing about it for a general audience is inherently difficult, which is why this highly readable *Washington Monthly* piece by Haley Sweetland Edwards is so impressive. Legislation gets almost all of the press, but no law can work as intended unless it's implemented well by the bureaucrats. In reporting how Wall Street gummed up the Dodd-Frank rule-making works, Edwards shows how lobbyists and lawyers outmuscle and outmaneuver regulators attempting to write the rules.

Haley Sweetland
Edwards

28. He Who
Makes the Rules

In late 2010, Bart Chilton, one of three Democratic commissioners at the U.S. Commodity Futures Trading Commission, walked into an upper-floor suite of an executive office building to meet with four top muckety-mucks at one of the biggest financial institutions in the world.

There were a handful of staff members present, but it was a pretty small gathering—one, it turns out, that Chilton would never forget.

The main topic Chilton hoped to discuss that day was the CFTC's pending rule on what are known as "position limits." If implemented properly, position limits would put a leash on speculation in the commodities market by making it harder for heavyweight traders at places like Goldman Sachs and JPMorgan Chase to corner a market, make a killing for themselves, and screw up prices for the rest of us. Position limits are also one of many ways to tamp down the amount of risk big institutions can take on, which keeps them from going belly up and minimizes the chance taxpayers will have to bail them out.

The financial institution Chilton was meeting with that day was a big commodities exchange, which is like a stock exchange except that instead of trading stocks they trade derivatives based on the value of actual products, like oil and gas. Chilton wouldn't say which major commodities exchange he was meeting with that day, but suffice it to say two of the biggest—the Chicago Mercantile Exchange and Intercontinental Exchange—have a lot to lose from federally administered position limits. To them, the more derivatives traded, the better. They've been fighting the CFTC's attempts to establish position limits for years.

The passage of the Dodd-Frank Wall Street Reform and Consumer Protection Act in July 2010 seemed to promise meaningful reform on this front. The law includes Section 737, which explicitly directs the CFTC to establish position limits and lays out detailed guidelines on how they should do so. "The Commission shall by rule, regulation or order establish limits on the amount of positions, as appropriate," it reads.

Still, even with the strength of the law behind him, Chilton waited until the end of the meeting to broach what he knew would be a tense subject. He began diplomatically. Now that the CFTC was required by law to establish position limits, his commission wanted to do so "in a fashion that made sense—one that was sensitive to, but not necessarily reflective of, the views of the exchange," he told the executives.

Chilton's gracious overture fell flat. His hosts, who had been openly discussing other topics moments before, were suddenly silent. They deferred instead to their top lawyer, who explained that the exchange's interpretation of Section 737 was that the CFTC was not required to establish position limits at all.

Chilton was blindsided. While other parts of Dodd-Frank were, admittedly, vague and ambiguous and otherwise frustrating to those, like him, who were tasked with writing the hundreds of rules associated with the act, Section 737 didn't exactly pull any punches. *The Commission shall establish limits on the amount of positions, as appropriate.*

"You gotta be kidding," Chilton told the executives. "The law is very clear here. The congressional intent is clear."

But the executives stood their ground. Their lawyer quietly referred Chilton to the end of the sentence in question: *as appropriate*. Those two little words, the lawyer said, clearly modify the verb "shall." Therefore, the statute can be interpreted as saying that the commission *shall*—but only if appropriate—establish position limits, he explained.

Anyone with a passable command of the English language should, faced with that argument, feel both dismay and a grudging sort of admiration. After all, given the context in which that sentence appears, the sheer brazenness of such a linguistic sleight of hand is, in a way, inspired. It's the kind of thing that would make Dick Cheney and John Yoo proud. Joseph Heller has written books on less.

But it's still, rather obviously, just that: a linguistic sleight of hand. The words "as appropriate" have appeared in statutes governing the CFTC's authority to implement position limits for at least forty years without challenge. In fact, the CFTC used the authority of that exact line, complete with its "as appropriate," to establish position limits on grain commodities decades ago. Even those who drafted Dodd-Frank later weighed in, saying they had intended for the language to explicitly instruct the CFTC to establish position limits *at levels that were appropriate*. The summary of Dodd-Frank, drafted by the Congressional Research Service, doesn't quibble either: "Sec. 737 Directs the CFTC to establish position limits," it reads. No ifs, ands, or "as appropriate"s.

"But this kind of thing"—manipulating the minutiae—"is how the game is played," said Bartlett Naylor, a financial policy advocate at Public Citizen, one of a handful of public interest groups tracking the rule-making process for Dodd-Frank. Since the law passed, the financial industry has been spending billions of dollars on lawyers and lobbyists, all of whom have been charged with one task: weaken the thing. One strategy has been to carve loopholes into the language of the law, Naylor said. A verb. An imprecise noun. A single sentence in an 876-page statute. "With a thousand lawyers on your payroll, that's nothing."

In the meeting that day, Chilton couldn't believe what he was hearing. He pointed out to the executives that, in Dodd-Frank, Congress had not only directed the CFTC to establish position limits, it had also imposed a deadline asking the commission to do so months before almost any other rule. It was obvious, he argued, that it was a matter of *when* position limits would be in place. Not *if*.

But the executives refused to discuss the matter further. The meeting ended abruptly, and Chilton wandered out into the hallway, dazed and reeling. One of the muckety-mucks from the meeting walked with him to the elevator. While they waited, away from the rest of the group, Chilton turned to his host. "You guys have got to be kidding about this 'as appropriate' stuff, right?" he said.

"I know," the muckety-muck replied, admitting it was a stretch. He let out a little chuckle—"but that's what we're going with."

"He *laughed*," Chilton told me recently, remembering that day. "He was laughing about how ludicrous it was."

•　　　•　　　•

A couple of months after that inauspicious meeting, the CFTC released a proposed rule establishing position limits on oil, gas, coffee, and twenty-five other commodities markets. They received about 15,000 letters during the public comment period and spent the next six months reading through all of them, incorporating the suggestions into the draft, meeting with industry and consumer groups, and revising the rule. Fearful of being sued, the CFTC held off voting on the rule several times and agreed to delay its implementation for a year to help financial institutions comply. Finally, in October 2011, the CFTC issued a final rule. It was a victory, but a short-lived one.

Two months later, two powerful industry groups, who together represent the biggest speculators in the world, hired Eugene Scalia, the son of Supreme Court Justice Antonin Scalia, as their lead counsel, and launched a lawsuit against the CFTC. The Securities Industry and Financial Markets Association and the International Swaps and Derivatives Association were suing on the same grounds that the exchange executives' lawyer had cited in that meeting with Chilton a year earlier: the CFTC had not demonstrated that establishing position limits was necessary and appropriate, they claimed. They also argued that the commission had not sufficiently studied the economic impact of the rule.

House Democrats and nineteen senators, some of whom had drafted Dodd-Frank, petitioned the court to rule in favor of the CFTC, a handful of op-eds beseeched judges to do the right thing, and financial reform advocates called foul.

None of it made a difference. In September 2012, the U.S. Court for the District of Columbia Circuit overturned the CFTC's rule. In the decision, the court wrote that the commission lacked a "clear and unambiguous mandate" to set position limits without first demonstrating that they were necessary and appropriate. And with that, more than two years after the passage of Dodd-Frank, there were still no federally administered position limits for any commodities except grain, and the CFTC was back to square one. The muckety-mucks at the exchanges rejoiced, as appropriate.

Welcome, dear readers, to the seventh circle of bureaucratic hell.

·   ·   ·

As Obama begins his second term, all the talk in Washington is about whether ongoing congressional gridlock and soul-crushing partisanship will block the administration from achieving significant legislative victories, be they immigration reform, a big fiscal deal, or an infrastructure bank. But at least as important to the future of the country and to the president's own legacy is whether that potentially game-changing legislation he signed in his first term—like the Affordable Care Act and Dodd-Frank, as well as a slew of other landmark bills—is actually implemented at all.

It may seem counterintuitive, but those big hunks of legislation, despite being technically the law of the land, filed away in the federal code, don't mean anything yet. They are, in the words of one CFTC official, "nothing but words on paper" until they're broken down into effective rules, implemented, and enforced by an agency. Rules are where the rubber of our legislation hits the road of real life. To put that another way, if a rule emerges from a regulatory agency weak or riddled with loopholes, or if it's killed entirely—like the CFTC's rule on position limits—it is, in effect, almost as if that part of the law had not passed to begin with.

As of now, there's no guarantee that either Obamacare or Dodd-Frank will be made into rules that actually do what lawmakers intended. That's partly because the rule-making process is a dangerous place for a law to go. We might imagine it as a fairly boring assembly line—a series of gray-faced bureaucrats diligently stamping laws into rules—but in reality, it's more of a treacherous, whirling-hatchet-lined gantlet. There are three main areas on this gantlet where a rule can be sliced, diced, gouged, or otherwise weakened beyond recognition.

The first is in the agency itself, where industry lobbyists enjoy outsized influence in meetings and comment letters, on rule makers' access to vital information, and on the interpretation of the law itself.

The second is in court, where industry groups can sue an agency and have a rule killed on a variety of grounds, some of which make sense and some of which most definitely do not.

The third is in Congress, where an entire law can be retro-actively gutted or poked through with loopholes, or where an agency can be quietly starved to death through appropriations bills.

And here's the really alarming part: rules run this gantlet largely behind closed doors, supervised by people we don't elect, whose names we don't know, while neither the media nor great swaths of the otherwise informed public are paying any atten-tion at all. That's not because we don't care what happens; we do. After all, millions of us spent the better part of a year closely monitoring the battles to pass Obamacare and Dodd-Frank. Re-member? It was high drama! Every detail was faithfully chroni-cled in front-page headlines and long disquisitions on *The Rachel Maddow Show*; in countless posts by wonky bloggers, who dis-sected every in and out, every committee hearing, every new study about the public option or the Volcker Rule.

That kind of stuff is the Washington journalist's bread and butter: the artful, insidious process by which a bill becomes a law. And since reporters know how the process works, how in-fluence gets wielded, and where the pressure points are, the rest of us were able to follow along closely. We knew what to root for, what to keep our eye on, and which decision makers in Wash-ington we could remind to do the right thing.

But fast-forward a couple of years, and as the fate of those very same laws is being determined in the rule-making process we've found ourselves distracted by new shiny objects, like women in combat and how Pennsylvania will allocate its electoral votes in 2016. Part of the reason for that, no doubt, is that many Wash-ington journalists, underpaid, overworked, and required to write a dozen blog posts a day, don't have time to dedicate to following the rule-making process. Others simply don't under-stand it.

Regardless, the result is that the rest of us haven't followed the progress of these landmark laws in anywhere near the same way that we followed it during the legislative process. And in our inattention we've made it infinitely easier for industry lobbyists and members of Congress who voted against the laws to begin with to destroy them by subtle, nuanced, backdoor means. By quibbling over "as appropriate"s and misplaced verbs. By crafting crafty legal arguments and drowning understaffed rule makers in industry-funded hogwash. This is the way a law ends: not with a bang but with a whimper.

For purposes of illustrating the problem, this article will focus on just one of these landmark laws, Dodd-Frank. It passed more than two and a half years ago, in July 2010, but most of its rules have yet to make it through the rule-making gantlet. While many liberals have already written it off as a total failure—some were, in fact, writing its eulogy the day it passed—it's time we had some perspective. It's true that it's not as strong as many experts on financial markets had called for. It's true that it doesn't break up the big banks, nor fundamentally change the structure of our financial system. We may have been hoping for, say, a bulletproof SUV with state-of-the-art airbags; what we got instead are a few seat belts that need to be welded into our old rig. But as of now, those jury-rigged seat belts are the only thing we've got, and given the gridlock on the Hill they're all we're likely to get. And the truth is that they're strong enough that the financial industry is willing to spend billions of dollars to keep them from being installed.

As of now, roughly two-thirds of the 400-odd rules expected to come from Dodd-Frank have yet to be finalized. That includes big, potentially game-changing rules governing inappropriate risk taking and international subsidiaries of American banks and how exactly we'll go about regulating derivatives. In the next year or so, the vast majority of these rules will be launched down the rule-making gantlet. The necessary first step in assuring that they come out the other end as strong as they should be—or that they come out the other end at all—is to understand the challenges they'll face along the way.

The Basic Rules of Rule Making

The rule-making process is governed by the Administrative Procedure Act, which became law in 1946, in response to the New Deal–era expansion of the federal bureaucracy. In the late 1930s and early 1940s, all the new agencies were dancing to their own beat; the APA established a system-wide metronome. Since then, a handful of other laws have been passed, including the Regulatory Flexibility Act, Paperwork Reduction Act, Government in the Sunshine Act, and Congressional Review Act, which also govern parts of the process, but for the most part the APA is the foundation.

Every stage in the rule-making process is guided by the APA. It begins the moment a law is passed and shunted off to the regulatory agency that will oversee its implementation. Once it's in the agency, the APA governs the activities of a team of rule makers—researchers, analysts, economists, and lawyers—who do a bunch of fact gathering, perform studies, and hold a ton of informational meetings in an attempt to get a handle on how best to abide by the intention of the law and how to apply that intention to real life. Since big laws like Obamacare and Dodd-Frank deal with complex issues, Congress often makes the statutes deliberately vague, deferring to rule makers' technical expertise and policy decisions and giving them a significant amount of authority on how to interpret a law. All of that interpretation generally happens in the very beginning of the rule-making process, which is called the Notice of Proposed Rulemaking, or, in the acronymic parlance of the federal bureaucracy, NPRM.

After spending months and months in the NPRM process, the agency eventually publishes a proposed rule, on which, the APA stipulates, the public gets an "adequate" amount of time to comment. Usually, that's about sixty days, but it can be shorter or longer, depending on how complex or controversial a rule is.

After that, the rule makers revise the rule again, taking into account concerns raised by regulated industries and the public's comment letters.

From there, executive branch agencies like the Food and Drug Administration and the Environmental Protection Agency send their rules to the White House Office of Management and Budget's Office of Information and Regulatory Affairs (OIRA), which reviews the projected costs and benefits of those agencies' major new rules, as well as the suggestions of other agencies, before the final rule is published and implemented. At independent agencies like the Securities and Exchange Commission (SEC) and the CFTC, a bipartisan panel of commissioners publicly debates and votes on the rule—a process that often results in further revisions and compromises.

Like the rest of us, rule makers use the Track Changes feature in Microsoft Word, which assigns a different color font to each contributor. By the time a complex rule has made it through this whole process, it is "lit up like a Christmas tree," said Leland Beck, who worked for various agencies for thirty years and practiced administrative law. "A rule becomes a decision on all the comments and revisions and compromises between agencies and all the individuals who got their hands on it." Eventually the agency publishes a final rule, which is implemented and enforced. *Voilà*.

Or that's how it's supposed to work. But like many things in Washington, that's just half the story. The rule-making process is actually a much messier, much more cacophonous affair, dictated to a large degree by lawmakers who voted against the law to begin with and by industry groups who would often prefer that no rules be implemented at all. In the last decade, conservative members of Congress have built ever-higher hurdles that agencies must clear, and done so while cutting their staff and budgets.

Meanwhile, since the passage of Dodd-Frank, financial industry groups have also sabotaged parts of the APA's carefully

plodding process, overwhelming rule makers with biased information and fear tactics and threatening to sue the agencies over
every perceived infraction. That's a big reason why agencies have
missed so many of their deadlines for implementing Dodd-
Frank—a subtlety reporters frequently miss.

"It's just this constant, never-ending onslaught," a former
SEC staffer told me. "You're doing battle every day."

The Gantlet, Stage 1: Asymmetric Warfare in Rule Making

Public-interest and consumer advocates tend to describe the
fight over the rules of Dodd-Frank in martial terms. "It's like
World War II," said Dennis Kelleher, the president and CEO of
the nonprofit Better Markets. "There's the Pacific theater, the Atlantic, the European, the African theater—we're fighting on all
fronts." Former senator Ted Kaufman, an outspoken advocate
for financial reform, says it's "more like guerrilla warfare." The
reformers are trying "to make it at the margins, but they're totally outgunned," he said.

The financial industry certainly has a spectacularly enormous
arsenal. Since the passage of Dodd-Frank, the industry has spent
an estimated $1.5 billion on registered lobbyists alone—a number
that most dismiss as comically low as it doesn't take into account
the industry's much more influential allies and proxies, including
a battalion of powerful trade groups, like the U.S. Chamber of
Commerce, Business Roundtable, and American Bankers Association. It also doesn't take into account the public relations firms
and think tanks, or the silos of campaign cash the industry has
dumped into lawmakers' reelection campaigns.

"The amount of money and resources they're willing to deploy
to protect the status quo is unlimited," said Kelleher. His company,
Better Markets—one of the slickest and most vocal financial
reform shops in town—has a $2 million annual budget, Kelleher

said, which is about how much the financial industry spends on its lobbying team every day and a half.

While there's no record of the total amount the industry has spent, it's clear that there's no shortage of money in its war chest. In the last quarter of 2010, just a few months after Dodd-Frank passed, the financial industry raked in nearly $58 billion in profits alone—about 30 percent of all U.S. profits that quarter. With that sort of bottom line, spending a hundred million or so to kill a single rule that could "cost" them a couple billion in profits is a pretty good return on investment.

In 2009, researchers at the University of Kansas and Washington and Lee University studied the return on corporations' investment in lobbying for the American Jobs Creation Act, which included a one-time corporate tax break, and found that it was a staggering 22,000 percent. That means that for every dollar the corporations spent lobbying, they got $220 in tax benefits. Based on the billions Wall Street has spent to weaken Dodd-Frank, it seems that they have done similar math.

One thing all that industry money buys is a well-disciplined army. According to public records, representatives from the financial industry have met with the dozen or so agencies that regulate them thousands of times in the past two and a half years. According to the Sunlight Foundation, the top twenty banks and banking associations met with just three agencies—the Treasury, the Federal Reserve, and the CFTC—an average of 12.5 times per week, for a total of 1,298 meetings over the two-year period from July 2010 to July 2012. JPMorgan Chase and Goldman Sachs alone met with those agencies 356 times. That's 114 *more* times than all the financial reform groups combined.

"For every one hundred meetings I have, only one of them is with a consumer group or citizens' organization," said Chilton. While it's good that regulated industries have a chance to express their opinions and concerns to those who regulate them, he said, "the deck is just stacked so heavily against average people."

It's not just the quantity of meetings, it's the quality, too. Kimberly Krawiec, a professor at Duke Law School, published a study last year analyzing the role of external influence during the NPRM period of Dodd-Frank's Volcker Rule. (The Volcker Rule would ban proprietary trading, which is when banks trade for their own profits, and not on behalf of their customers, making them more likely to fail.) In her study, Krawiec found that while public interest organizations met with agencies in giant group meetings on the same day, head honchos from the industry often met with the agencies' top staff alone. Former Goldman Sachs CEO Lloyd Blankfein, for instance, was not expected to share the floor.

That's not an insignificant advantage, considering that the NPRM period is when "the majority of the actual agenda setting and rule making happens," Krawiec said. Because APA stipulations require that the public get a fair shake at commenting on a rule before it is implemented, a proposed rule can't be too different from the final rule or an agency can get sued, she explained. That has the effect of pushing most of the rule making to the very beginning of the process, which is also the least transparent, since agencies don't have to publish what they're up to or who their staff is meeting with during this time. Because of increased transparency efforts surrounding Dodd-Frank, agencies have been encouraged to publish all of the meetings that occur during the NPRM period—hence Krawiec's study.

Krawiec has also found that after the Volcker Rule was proposed the vast majority of substantive public-comment letters were from the financial industry, trade groups, and their various proxies—lawyers, lobbyists, and underwritten think tanks—all of whom have the time and money to present extensive, if wildly biased, legal and economic arguments. Often, industry lawyers will simply rewrite entire paragraphs of the proposed rule, fashioning loopholes or limiting an agency's scope with a single, well-placed adjective or an ambiguous verb. Whether a rule survives that change, whether it then can be effectively implemented and enforced, really does come down to such trivialities. In the rule-making process, the minutiae aren't incidental to the rule; they *are* the rule. (Don't believe me? The U.S. Supreme Court recently heard a case on a 1934 SEC rule on fraud that centered entirely on different definitions of the verb "to make.")

Industry lobbyists are well aware that they don't need to outright kill a rule; they need only to maim it, and it's as good as dead. In fact, it's better than that: it's on the books, the newspapers cover it—it looks like a success for financial reform—but industry remains as unfettered as it was before. "That happens all the time," said a former rule maker at the CFTC, who spoke on the condition of anonymity. "The public-interest groups get the headline, but if you look at the details, the industry group has actually won. There's an order of magnitude between the public interest groups' and the industry groups' attention to detail." When I spoke to an industry lobbyist in mid-January, he put that another way. "We can't kill it, but we can try to keep it from doing any damage," he said.

Jeff Connaughton, a lobbyist turned crusader for financial reform, said that the "ubiquitous presence of Wall Street" goes beyond meetings and legalese in comment letters. In his book *The Payoff: Why Wall Street Always Wins*, he describes the tight-knit relationships between industry lobbyists and proxies and government officials as the "Blob," which, in his experience, "oozed through the halls of government and immobilized the legislative and regulatory apparatus, thereby preserving the status quo." Many in the Blob are married to one another and move fluidly from industry to government and back again, he told me. For example, CFTC Commissioner Jill Sommers, who recently announced her resignation, is married to Speaker of the House John Boehner's top aide. She used to work at the Chicago Mercantile Exchange, one of the biggest exchanges in the world, which is overseen by the CFTC; she also worked at the International Swaps and Derivatives Association, the organization that later sued the CFTC to overturn the rule on position limits.

In this light, the traditional notion of "regulatory capture" doesn't go far enough. Instead, we should think of it as "cultural capture," writes the political scientist James Kwak. There may be no bags of cash exchanging hands, but that doesn't matter when regulators, like many of the rest of us, have been steeped for so long in the idea that Wall Street produces the best and brightest our society has to offer. Regulators often look up to industry representatives or know them personally, which begets "the familiar effect of relationships," Kwak wrote in *Preventing Regulatory Capture*, a compilation of essays that will be published this year by Cambridge University Press in collaboration with the Tobin Project, a nonprofit research center. "You are more favorably disposed toward someone you have shared cookies with, or at least it is harder for you to take some action that harms her interests."

Like many reformers, Connaughton points a finger at the so-called revolving door, which sends former bureaucrats into the private sector and vice versa, blurring the line between the regulators and the regulated. From 2006 to 2010, 219 former SEC employees filed 789 statements saying that they would be representing a lobbyist or industry group in front of the SEC, according to the Project on Government Oversight. A complex law like Dodd-Frank accelerates that cycle, Connaughton said, as industry has even more incentive to hire people directly from the agencies to help them navigate the new regulations. "Put your time in at one of these regulatory agencies while they're doing the Dodd-Frank rule making and it's a license to print money when you come out," he told me.

Of course, the revolving door doesn't explain everything. A lot of the agencies are packed with ten-, fifteen-, and twenty-year veteran rule makers, who are motivated by the esprit de corps and have no interest in leaving for industry. "Money isn't everything. If you leave, there's the feeling that you're in the audience, and no longer on the public policy stage," the former CFTC rule maker told me. "That, and at the agency you're actually performing a public service. People recognize that. It's a factor."

Also, the revolving door revolves both ways. Industry leaders who are later appointed as commissioners sometimes provide a valuable asset to rule makers. In agency parlance, "they know where the bodies are buried." In many instances, these former industry officials head agencies at the end of their careers and have no intention of returning to the private sector. The CFTC Chairman Gary Gensler, for example, spent eighteen years at Goldman Sachs, eventually rising to partner, before becoming one of the most outspoken advocates in recent years for better regulation. (In 1934, President Franklin Delano Roosevelt appointed Joseph Kennedy to head the brand-new SEC for this exact reason.)

•   •   •

Another swinging mace in this stage of the rule-making gantlet is what Kelleher, the head of Better Markets, calls the "Wall Street Fog Machine." "They come at you with this jargon," he said. "They want to make you feel like it's too complicated for you to understand. You're stupid, and they're the only ones who get it—that's the end game." This is particularly true when it comes to financial products, like customized swaps, which traders on Wall Street have spent the last decade designing precisely in order to swindle their clients.

"That's how you make money. You make it so complicated the clients don't understand what it is they're buying and selling, or how much risk they're taking on," said Alexis Goldstein, who worked in cash equity and equity derivatives on Wall Street for several years, first at Merrill Lynch and then at Deutsche Bank, before joining the reform movement. The more complex the product, the higher the commission you can charge, and the less likely it is that there will be copycats driving down your profit margins with increased competition, she explained. In other words, complexity "isn't a side effect of the system—it's how the system was designed."

Partly as a result of that business model, the system really is complicated—extraordinarily so. But that doesn't mean it can't *also* be regulated in the right ways, reformers say. How exactly that should be done is often a bone of contention. Take those customized swaps, for example. Right now, they're traded in the private "over-the-counter" market, which means that they're contracted bilaterally, often between a single bank and a counterparty during a phone call, and they aren't transparent. Dodd-Frank gives the CFTC the power to regulate them, and many suggest that all trades should be conducted in clearinghouses, where customers can easily compare prices and are therefore less likely to be fleeced. Banks claim they're too complex to be traded in that way.

Kelleher says that's "just plain false." A customized swap is nothing more than a bundle of so-called two-legged swaps, he said. If you unbundle them, which the banks themselves do, for lots of reasons, like hedging, there's no reason we can't regulate them, he said. Just as Wall Street used the excuse of complexity to hoodwink their clients, they're now using the excuse of complexity to hoodwink their regulators—"it's the greatest coup they've managed to pull off," Kelleher said.

Others argue that customized swaps should be regulated but clearinghouses aren't the answer. They worry that if all such trading is moved to clearinghouses, then those institutions will balloon, leaving them vulnerable to collapse, said Peter J. Ryan, a fellow at the University of California Washington Center whose research focuses on financial-services-policy making. In other words, the clearinghouses themselves could become too big to fail.

The real problem here is not that rule makers can't understand Wall Street's complex financial products. It's that they often don't have enough information about those products or the systems that govern them to see the whole picture and therefore to choose the best possible way to regulate. As it stands, rule makers, as well as the teams of agency researchers who help them, rely to a large degree on industry to provide data about things like banks' internal trading. For proprietary reasons, only the banks have access to much of that information, and they have no incentive to share it. When regulators request data in public comment letters, industry rarely provides it; when they do, it's often incomplete, one-sided, or missing crucial variables. "If there's a datum that supports their argument, they produce it. If not, they don't—why would they?" said Naylor of Public Citizen.

This is one of the main reasons the Volcker Rule has been such a mess. It requires that regulators determine what's proprietary trading (when banks trade with their capital base for their own profit) and what's market making (the backbone of a bank's basic business model). A Credit Suisse lobbyist claimed recently that the metrics in the Volcker Rule were flawed since, in a test run, the bank found that proprietary trading and market making were indistinguishable. Credit Suisse's claim will go into the rule makers' record, which, in turn, can be used as evidence in court, should implementing agencies be sued. In that situation, rule makers and reformers are left without a card to play. "We can't dispute [their claim], because Credit Suisse owns the data and won't share it publicly," Naylor said.

While Dodd-Frank provides rule makers with access to a variety of new information sources—the new Office of Financial Research, the SEC's Consolidated Audit Trail, the CFTC's Swaps Report—none of these tools do enough yet to keep them ahead of the financial industry's constantly morphing business model, which changes every time an analyst invents a new product or a new way to trade it. "The regulators need to be able to pool all of this disparate information together into a complete picture of the financial system, which I'm not sure if they have the funding and coordination to do," said Marcus Stanley, the policy director at Americans for Financial Reform, a coalition of consumer, labor, small business, and public interest groups. If a shape shifter shows up as a mouse, building a mouse trap will only get you so far.

It is in some ways a Sisyphean task. Here you have a group of rule makers—lawyers, economists, analysts, and specialists—sitting around a table. On one side, they've got the language of Dodd-Frank, which requires them, by congressional mandate, to effectively regulate new, never-before-regulated products in never-before-regulated markets that change by the month. On the other side, they've got a pile of reports, nine out of ten of which were provided by the same industry they're trying to rein in. Meanwhile, industry lobbyists and lawyers are crowding into their conference rooms on a nearly daily basis, flooding their in-boxes with comment letters, and telling them that if they do something wrong, they'll be personally responsible for squelching financial innovation and destroying the economy. "They're scared to death," said Naylor of Public Citizen, who compares the effect the financial industry has on rule makers to Stockholm syndrome. "No one wants to be the one who writes the rule that screws up the entire financial system."

Wall Street is well aware of rule makers' human vulnerabilities. Last year, when the SEC was writing rules governing money markets, the U.S. Chamber of Commerce, one of the financial industry's staunchest allies, launched a public-relations campaign in D.C.'s Union Station, which abuts the SEC building. They papered the place with dozens of bright purple and orange posters, billboards, and backlit dioramas on the train platforms and above the fare machines, asserting that money markets are strong: "Why risk changing them now?" It is not coincidental that a good number of rule makers began and ended their daily commute beneath those very banners. "We certainly want to get the attention of those who are capable of giving us the answers," David Hirschmann, a Chamber of Commerce official, told Bloomberg at the time. One imagines him stifling a smirk.

Given the many whirling hatchets in this stage in the regulatory gantlet, it's a miracle any rules have emerged in the last couple years reasonably unscathed. But they have. When that happens, industry can appeal to the second stage in the gantlet: litigation.

The Gantlet, Stage 2: Cost-Benefit Analysis and a Conservative Court

On a sweltering summer day in 2011, the U.S. Court of Appeals for the D.C. Circuit—the de facto second most powerful court in the land, and the body that oversees the agencies—sent shock-waves through the regulatory apparatus.

In a now-infamous case, *Business Roundtable vs. SEC*, a three-judge panel decided in favor of two of the financial industry's biggest backers and overturned the SEC's so-called proxy-access rule. The rule would have made it easier for shareholders to elect their own candidates to corporate boards, allowing investors to put the brakes on out-of-control CEO pay. In the past decade, it has attempted to establish a proxy-access rule on three separate occasions, but each time it was cowed into submission by industry lobbyists claiming that the rule would destroy corporate growth. In 2011, emboldened by the language of Dodd-Frank, which explicitly authorizes the SEC to establish a proxy-access rule, the agency tried once again.

Almost immediately after the final rule was published, the Business Roundtable and the U.S. Chamber of Commerce sued the SEC on the grounds that the agency's cost-benefit analysis was inadequate. The judges agreed, marking the first time that the court had overturned a rule explicitly authorized by Dodd-Frank. But that's not the part that sent shockwaves through the regulatory apparatus. The D.C. Circuit has overturned dozens of regulations over the years, including six SEC rules in the previous seven years, for lots of reasons, including inadequate cost-benefit analyses.

What sent the shockwaves was that this case didn't seem to have anything to do with cost-benefit analysis at all. In the vitriolic decision, the panel of judges, all of whom were appointed by Republican presidents, lamented that due to "unutterably mindless" reasoning, the SEC had "failed once again" in its cost-benefit analysis. But the court never cited how exactly the agency's twenty-three-page economic-impact report could have done better. It simply appeared to *disagree* with the agency's policy choice—and that, apparently, was grounds enough to overturn the rule.

"It was a shot across the bow," said Michael Greenberger, a former regulator and professor at the University of Maryland Carey School of Law. The decision set a radical new precedent that would affect not only the SEC but all the independent agencies tasked with implementing Dodd-Frank, he said. It would also raise a powerful question: Should specific policy judgments be made by the agencies or the courts? "It upset the balance of the power," Greenberger said.

Part of the issue here is that the D.C. Circuit is packed high with conservative judges. Eight out of eleven on that bench were appointed by Republicans; despite four vacancies, Obama's nominations have been stymied consistently by Republicans in Congress. The three-judge panel that decided *Business Roundtable* included two Reagan appointees, Judge Douglas Ginsburg and Chief Judge David Sentelle, a Jesse Helms protégé. (That's the same Sentelle, by the way, who headed the panel that fired Whitewater independent counsel Robert Fiske, a moderate Republican, and replaced him with Kenneth Starr.) The third judge was George W. Bush appointee and consummate Ayn Randian Janice Rogers Brown. All three have made a bit of a name for themselves over the years as conservative activists, unafraid to mold precedent to fit their ideological ends. Their decision in *Business Roundtable* didn't break that mold.

In one section, for instance, the judges ask why the SEC would have dismissed public comments suggesting that proxy access could exact a significant economic cost to corporations. Judge Ginsburg writes, "One commenter, for example, submitted an empirical study showing that 'when dissident directors win board seats, those firms underperform peers by 19 to 40% over the two years following the proxy contest.'" But hold the phone. Or, better yet: WTF? Ginsburg fails to note here that the "one commenter" in question *is one of the plaintiffs*, the Business Roundtable. And as for that "empirical study"? It was conducted by an economic consulting group hired *by that same plaintiff*. In the rest of the decision, Ginsburg appears to ignore the precedent set by the foundational 1984 *Chevron* case, which, among other things, stressed that judges must afford "deference" to an agency's interpretation of a statute, especially when it's "evaluating scientific data within its technical expertise."

Questionable judicial behavior aside, the *Business Roundtable* decision marked "the culmination of a trend empowering regulated entities to strike down regulations almost at will," wrote Bruce Kraus, a former counsel at the SEC, in a subsequent report. For one, it established an inherent bias—reformers cannot, after all, challenge a rule in court to make it *stronger*. For another, it opened up the floodgates for future suits. If two of the industry's most powerful organizations could sue the SEC and overturn a rule on such grounds, it was suddenly feasible for industry groups to sue *any* agency and overturn *any* new Dodd-Frank rule using the same arguments.

It was a point that did not go unnoticed by industry. "I would hope the agencies are taking to heart the potential consequences for Dodd-Frank rules," said lead counsel Eugene Scalia, after the case was decided. (Scalia was also lead counsel on the case that overturned the CFTC's rule on position limits a year later.) Industry groups have since brought a half-dozen more cases against agencies on practically identical grounds.

·   ·   ·

The *Business Roundtable* decision had the immediate effect of adding a whole new lethal section to the regulatory gantlet, this time complete with flypaper and trapdoors. In the months following, the SEC's progress through the Dodd-Frank rule making is estimated to have slowed by half as they struggled to "bulletproof" their rules from future lawsuits. ("They have to be *more* than bulletproof," Chilton told me, when I asked him if that was a factor for the CFTC, too. "They have to be layered in Kevlar. We go way beyond the requirements of the law.")

The decision also had the effect of tipping the balance of power at independent agencies. By making an agency's cost-benefit analysis the centerpiece of the litigation, economic models now hold disproportionate weight. If a single economist at an agency produces a report, based on a single model, and "demonstrates" that a rule would exact steep costs from a given industry, it acts like a trump card, according to former staffers at the SEC and the CFTC. Even if the majority of that economist's colleagues disagree with him, his report will enter the public record, where it can be cited in a subsequent lawsuit and end up determining if a rule is implemented or not. And economic models are like statistics; you can always find one that supports your position.

Along those same lines, in the wake of *Business Roundtable* a single commissioner—one of five on a bipartisan panel—now has the de facto power to torpedo a rule simply by questioning its economic impact in a public forum. For example, if a Republican commissioner disagrees with a rule, he will, under normal circumstances, be required to compromise with his fellow commissioners or risk being simply outvoted. If at least three of his colleagues disagree with him, the rule will pass. The *Business*

Roundtable decision seemed to suggest that a single commissioner's verbal expression of disapproval could be used later as grounds for litigation and as evidence in court. Indeed, a year after the *Business Roundtable* decision, in the CFTC's position limits case, part of Scalia's argument rested on the fact that the former CFTC Commissioner Michael Dunn has expressed misgivings about the rule.

"When a commissioner says publicly, 'I'm concerned about the economic impact of this rule,' that's enough to lay the groundwork for a future case," said Chilton. Several former rule makers and staffers at the CFTC and the SEC told me they would "not be surprised," given the wording of these public expressions of disapproval, if these commissions were getting their language directly from industry lawyers.

The most profound weapon the *Business Roundtable* decision introduced into the regulatory gantlet is stupefying uncertainty. "It has been paralyzing for the agencies," the former CFTC rule maker told me. How extensive must their cost-benefit analyses be? What kind of costs must be measured? And costs to *whom*— the industry or the investors? What were the criteria? "It's like going into a class and not having any idea how your professor grades," he said. "Everyone is trying to figure out how to move forward without getting sued."

In the past, when an agency has been sued over a rule, that litigation has often marked the end of the rule altogether. Most are never reproposed, and those that are often emerge pitifully weak. It also has the effect of sending an agency back to the starting line, where it must run the gantlet yet again, only this time with more attention from Congress—which is often the most lethal weapon of all.

The Gantlet, Stage 3: Congress's Retroactive Attacks

Many of us think of Congress as passing a law, shunting it off to the agencies, then wiping its hands of the matter. Not the case.

Lawmakers, and particularly those who voted against Dodd-Frank to begin with, have a number of tools up their sleeves, which they've been using consistently since 2010 in an attempt to retroactively weaken the act.

One way has been to go after the regulators personally, lambasting them publicly, smearing their reputations, and wasting their time. In the wake of the *Business Roundtable* decision, for example, the House Financial Services Committee summoned the former SEC chairwoman Mary Schapiro to testify before Congress about why the SEC had failed in its cost-benefit analysis. The Senate Banking Committee, obliquely questioning her competency as a leader, also requested a series of investigations into why her agency's cost-benefit analyses were falling short. While lawmakers have a legitimate right to ask the heads of regulatory agencies to testify, in the past few years Congress has seemed to blur the line between inquiries and something more akin to the Inquisition. All told, since 2009 Schapiro has been called to testify before Congress forty-two times.

"On one hand, those attempts to create a scandal don't mean anything," said Lisa Donner, the executive director of Americans for Financial Reform, referring to Congress's harassment of Schapiro late last year. "But on the other hand, those performances waste an enormous amount of time. It plays a role. It's intimidating."

Also in the wake of *Business Roundtable*, the Alabama Republican senator Richard Shelby, as if on cue, wielded another of Congress's favorite weapons to kill a law in the regulatory process. He introduced a bill suspending all the independent agencies' major rules until they could be subjected to OIRA, the Office of Management and Budget's subsidiary, which vets the cost-benefit analyses for new executive branch rules. Had that bill passed, it would have had the effect of stopping all Dodd-Frank rule making in its tracks indefinitely. It didn't pass, but last summer a similar bill—this one bipartisan—the Independent Agency Regulatory Analysis Act, was introduced and passed in the House, before failing, in the nick of time, in the Senate.

In the two and a half years since Dodd-Frank passed, law-makers have introduced dozens of other such bills, so-called technical amendments, that purport to change or clarify certain sections of Dodd-Frank but would actually gut, defang, or kill the act entirely. Because the bills are presented as mere tweaks to an existing law, and because industry cash is the only way many of these congressmen will get reelected, the bills are often voted on quickly, sometimes even coming up for a voice vote—a procedure usually reserved for uncontroversial issues.

Take the Swap Jurisdiction Certainty Act, for example. That bipartisan bill would have prevented the CFTC and the SEC from regulating derivatives trades conducted by American companies' subsidiaries overseas. That's insanity. First, if any of those subsidiaries—much less hundreds of them at once—were to fail, they would threaten and potentially take down the U.S. market. (Indeed, during the 2008 crash, U.S. taxpayer money was used to bail out those foreign-based subsidiaries too, for precisely that reason.) And second, if you only regulate the derivatives traded by American institutions on U.S. soil, American traders will simply scoot their business over to the thousands of subsidiaries abroad, making those unregulated markets even larger and more dangerous. In other words, had this bipartisan, innocent-looking bill passed, it would have undermined all the provisions in Dodd-Frank that attempt to regulate the derivatives market at all.

While the efforts of public interest groups and financial reform advocates, like Americans for Financial Reform, have succeeded thus far in keeping any of these bills from passing, they still have an effect behind the scenes. "There are instances where regulators say, 'I know what we want to do with this, but if we go too far, Congress is just going to wipe out the whole thing, and I want what we're doing to last,'" said Stanley, the policy director at Americans for Financial Reform. "That's a calculation."

A much more common weapon congressional opponents can wield after a law has been passed is a little less dramatic. By attaching riders to appropriations bills, Congress can simply forbid an agency from using its money to enforce one specific rule or another—and, of course, an unenforced rule is a dead rule. Lawmakers can do that even if Congress has passed another law that pointedly mandates that an agency take the action in question. In 2011, for instance, the House Appropriations Committee, which is dominated by Republicans, attached a rider to its funding bill preventing the U.S. Department of Agriculture from using its funds to finalize and implement a series of specific rules helping small farmers fight back against big livestock and poultry corporations. Despite the Obama administration's attempts to get those exact rules implemented, the rider passed, tying the USDA's hands and sending small farmers adrift.

Using the same mechanism, Congress also has the power to defund or severely underfund any agency that relies on congressional appropriations, including the CFTC and the SEC—a guillotine it has successfully used for decades. Just last year, for instance, the House Appropriations Committee cut the CFTC's annual budget by $25 million, leaving it with an anemic $180 million. (For a sense of how little money this is, consider that San Bernardino, a county of about two million people in California, spends more than $180 million just on its public works department.) In 2011, congressional opponents of financial regulation blocked any increase in the SEC's budget, despite or perhaps because of the agency's massive new workload with Dodd-Frank. The Republicans' argument against funding the independent agencies is delightfully absurd: since the agencies have not written and enforced rules fast enough, Congress should "punish" them, rather than "reward" them with adequate funding.

Yet another weapon Congress uses to retroactively kill bills in the rule-making process is to block presidential appointments. In January, another three-judge panel at the D.C. Circuit, led by the same conservative crusader who voted to overturn the SEC's proxy-access rule, Judge Sentelle, ruled that Obama's recess appointments were unconstitutional. It was a radical decision that has the potential to invalidate rules and guidelines promulgated by the National Labor Relations Board and the Consumer Financial Protection Bureau for the previous year. The decision may be reconsidered (and, heaven help us, affirmed) by the Supreme Court, but in the meantime it brings the independent agencies further into Congress's orbit.

Congressional Republicans are already using the decision to strong-arm Congress into weakening the CFPB's independence. The only way Congress will allow Obama to reappoint the CFPB Director Richard Cordray, or to install another head, Republican lawmakers say, is if the agency's funding is brought under congressional appropriations controls. It's an underhanded move that would eliminate the CFPB's strongest asset—that it's *not* subject to Congress's manipulative purse strings—and may have the effect of gutting the entire agency, one of the strongest things that's come out of Dodd-Frank thus far.

Gunning for the Finish Line

It's true that Dodd-Frank started out as a compromise. "It was compromise on top of a compromise—a pile of compromises," said Kelleher of Better Markets. And that's what we can expect from the rule-making process too, he said. As it stands, how the law has fared in its journey down the regulatory gantlet has been mixed.

Some rules have been spectacularly hacked to death. Take, for example, a joint rule by the SEC and the CFTC, which was intended to force swaps dealers into maintaining more capital and to prevent horrible scenarios, like the collapse of AIG, from ever happening again. When it was first proposed, the rule required that every dealer trading more than $100 million in swaps should be subject to regulatory oversight. A bill proposed by the Illinois Republican representative Randy Hultgren raised that threshold to $3 billion, but the agencies, intimidated by lobbyists' doomsday scenarios and under the constant threat of litigation, raised it again: to $8 billion. The rule that eventually emerged now exempts about two-thirds of all swaps dealers from new capital requirements.

Scenarios like that can be deflating for reformers, but there have been wins, too. The CFPB remains a major success for consumer and investor advocates, and the SEC's rule on whistleblowers appears to have emerged fairly intact. The CFTC's brand-new Swap Data Repositories, which were designed to collect data about over-the-counter derivatives transactions, are also up and running, with the potential to shed some much-needed light on that shady industry. Whether the new repositories will be useful to regulators, or whether they will be undermined by a future lawsuit or lack of funding, is still unclear.

In some arenas, most notably the D.C. Circuit's activist bench, reformers have faced crushing defeats. Yet all is not lost. In a case this past December, the U.S. District Court for D.C., a notch below the D.C. Circuit, handed the industry its first loss in years, deciding in favor of the CFTC's rule requiring registration of mutual funds that engage in derivatives trading. It also marked the end of a five-case winning streak in lead counsel Eugene Scalia's battle against agency rules. Judge Beryl A. Howell, an Obama appointee, decided against the U.S. Chamber of Commerce and the Investment Company Institute. (Both are now appealing that case to the D.C. Circuit.)

The Dodd-Frank rules that, against all odds, have emerged relatively intact underscore an important point: those who favor strong regulations are not without shields to protect rules against the many whirling weapons along the regulatory gantlet. But in order to be effective, of course, those shields have to be used.

First and foremost, the White House has to get more involved in defending its own legislative achievements from being gutted in the rule-making process. In addition to appointing more judges to the D.C. Circuit (and that's no guarantee of success; the judge who decided against the CFTC's position-limits rule was a Democratic appointee), the administration should deploy its best Justice Department lawyers to defend against the industry's court attacks on Dodd-Frank rules. It should aggressively push to fill vacancies at the agencies with pro-regulation commissioners and other agency heads and fight harder for bigger agency budgets. And the president himself should shine a spotlight on the process, and support the work rule makers do by paying personal visits to the agencies.

Second, the administration and its allies in Congress must address as quickly as possible the asymmetry of information in the agencies. In order to do their jobs, regulators must be armed with objective information to offset the biased or incomplete reports they receive from industry. This is particularly important for a small, underfunded agency like the CFTC, which doesn't have the stable of researchers and economists employed by some of its brethren, including the Fed, the CFPB, and the FDIC.

The good news is that Dodd-Frank mandated the creation of a new office whose mission, in part, is to correct this imbalance of information. Housed in the Treasury and funded by bank fees, the new Office of Financial Research was conceived as a kind of giant weather station monitoring the financial industry in order to detect potential "storms" before they arrive. To that end, it's statutorily authorized to gather, with subpoena power if necessary, granular-level data from financial institutions, including information about banks' trading partners, positions, and transactions, and to make that data available to other regulatory agencies. The only question is whether the OFC will have the political backing it needs to fulfill those ends.

As of now, it has a very small budget and an advisory board heavily weighted with industry insiders. It's also facing extraordinary political opposition, mostly from congressional Republicans, who have called for nothing less than its immediate abolishment, arguing that it compromises data security and encroaches on the private sector. Making sure that the OFC survives and overcomes any legal challenges to its ability to share key information with regulators should be a top agenda item for congressional Democrats and the new treasury secretary, Jacob Lew.

Third, reformers and reform-minded analysts, lawyers, and academics need to do a better job of making their voices heard in the agencies. The Administrative Procedure Act, which governs the rule-making process, painstakingly enshrines public commentary, but as of now the vast majority of the substantive comments are coming from industry groups and their proxies, including bought-and-paid-for think tanks, trade groups, and consulting firms, which have the time and legal expertise to dedicate to such things. Launching a counterinsurgency in kind will obviously require a pretty chunk of change. Perhaps it's a place where foundations can make a real difference. If more individuals and groups weighed in with smart ideas and substantive research to counter industry, it could help strengthen the rule makers' hands.

Rule makers read and make note of every comment letter, and those letters have a cumulative effect of pushing policy, staff members at the SEC and the CFTC told me. That's particularly true in instances where a rule-making team believes the best public policy differs from what industry is advocating. "To the extent that there was already an argument for a given position, a public letter will give a team support. There's a sense of 'See? Other people think this too,'" a former SEC staffer told me.

Reform groups like Americans for Financial Reform, Better Markets, and Public Citizen have thus far done a heroic job writing substantive, evidence-based letters of concern and organizing public letter-writing campaigns. Groups like Occupy the SEC, which is run by people with direct experience in the financial industry, have also submitted long, well-informed reports to the agencies and engaged with rule makers personally. Those voices make a big difference. But they go only part of the way toward countering the overwhelming influence that industry has enjoyed.

Fourth, what's needed is the vigilance of the wider public. That may seem unreasonable to expect—who has the time or inclination to follow the grammatical arcana of rule making as it moves through the process? But in an age of Wikipedia, when millions of people write and edit tomes on obscure and complex issues on a daily basis, there's no reason in theory why more Americans couldn't weigh in on regulations that most of them clearly favor. Nearly 75 percent of voters, Republicans and Democrats alike, support "tougher" rules and enforcement for Wall Street financial institutions, according to a 2012 poll commissioned by a coalition of consumer, reform, and public interest groups.

Those same citizens should also prod their members of Congress. The political scientist Susan Webb Yackee has found that the attention of lawmakers is one of the primary factors that can help curb industry influence in the regulatory process. In the stew of congressional power struggles, and with the financial industry furiously underwriting lawmakers' reelection campaigns, members of Congress have a variety of reasons *not* to stick their necks out. Their constituents should insist that they do.

Finally, there's no mystery about how to stir up public attention: the press needs to do a better job of covering the regulatory process. Again, that may seem unreasonable, especially in an age when for-profit news has lost its business model. But it needs to be done. Those same editors, reporters, bloggers, and wonky producers at *The Rachel Maddow Show* who followed the passage of Dodd-Frank so closely two and a half years ago should tune in again.

As of early February, fewer than 150 of the estimated 400 rules from Dodd-Frank had been finalized, according to Davis

Polk & Wardwell, a law firm that keeps track of such things. Nearly the same number had not even been *proposed* yet. All together, almost 65 percent of the law, including potentially significant hunks, like rules on extraterritoriality and systemic risk, have yet to be finalized.

In the next year or so, the vast majority of these new rules will enter the regulatory gantlet while agencies and industry will watch carefully as those that have already been finalized are implemented and enforced. Industry and its allies in Congress will scream bloody murder and claim that Dodd-Frank rules are imposing an insurmountable burden on industry, the economy, and the American people. Meanwhile, the agencies either will attempt to hold the line or, without the glaring light of public scrutiny, they will allow industry to take the lead again. What happens in the next year or two will have a profound effect not only on Dodd-Frank, but on the future of our financial industry. "We're in the fifth inning," said Kelleher. "The only way to guarantee you'll lose is if you walk out before the end of the game."

The New Yorker

Jane Mayer's deeply reported investigation shows how public television officials scrambled to appease the multibillionaire Koch brothers after airing a documentary that displeased them. She documents in vivid detail the censorship of work that was supposed to be insulated from political pressure. It is a particularly rich narrative of how big money and powerful people can corrupt even the most independent organizations. "We live in a world where we have to be aware that people with power have power," Mayer quotes one executive telling two independent filmmakers. This piece gives a glimpse of how that works.

Jane Mayer

29. A Word from Our Sponsor

Last fall, Alex Gibney, a documentary filmmaker who won an Academy Award in 2008 for an exposé of torture at a U.S. military base in Afghanistan, completed a film called *Park Avenue: Money, Power, and the American Dream*. It was scheduled to air on PBS on November 12. The movie had been produced independently, in part with support from the Gates Foundation. *Park Avenue* is a pointed exploration of the growing economic inequality in America and a meditation on the often self-justifying mind-set of "the 1 percent." As a narrative device, Gibney focuses on one of the most expensive apartment buildings in Manhattan—740 Park Avenue—portraying it as an emblem of concentrated wealth and contrasting the lives of its inhabitants with those of poor people living at the other end of Park Avenue, in the Bronx.

Among the wealthiest residents of 740 Park is David Koch, the billionaire industrialist, who, with his brother Charles, owns Koch Industries, a huge energy-and-chemical conglomerate. The Koch brothers are known for their strongly conservative politics and for their efforts to finance a network of advocacy groups whose goal is to move the country to the right. David Koch is a major philanthropist, contributing to cultural and medical institutions that include Lincoln Center and New York–Presbyterian Hospital. In the 1980s, he began expanding his charitable contributions to the media, donating 23 million dollars to public television over the years. In 1997, he began serving as a trustee of Boston's public-broadcasting operation, WGBH, and in 2006 he joined the board of New York's public-television outlet, WNET. Recent news reports have suggested that the Koch brothers are considering buying eight daily newspapers owned by the Tribune Company, one of the country's largest media empires, raising concerns that its publications—which include the *Chicago Tribune* and the *Los Angeles Times*—might slant news coverage to serve the interests of their new owners, either through executive mandates or through self-censorship. Clarence Page, a liberal *Tribune* columnist, recently said that the Kochs appeared intent on using a media company "as a vehicle for their political voice."

Park Avenue includes a multifaceted portrait of the Koch brothers, telling the history of their family company and chronicling their many donations to universities and think tanks. It features comments from allies like Tim Phillips, the president of the Kochs' main advocacy group, Americans for Prosperity, and from activists in the Tea Party, including Representative Michele Bachmann of Minnesota, who share the Kochs' opposition to high taxes and regulation. (It also contains a few quotes from me; in 2010, I wrote an article about the Kochs for this magazine, noting that they were funding much of the opposition to President Barack Obama by quietly subsidizing an array of advocacy groups.)

A large part of the film, however, subjects the Kochs to tough scrutiny. "Nobody's money talks louder than David Koch's," the narrator, Gibney, says, describing him as a "right-wing oil tycoon" whose company had to pay what was then "the largest civil penalty in the EPA's history" for its role in more than thirty oil spills in 2000. At one point, a former doorman—his face shrouded in shadow, to preserve his anonymity—says that when he "started at 740" his assumption was that "come around to Christmastime I'm going to get a thousand from each resident. You know, because they are multibillionaires. But it's not that way." He continues, "These guys are businessmen. They know what the going rate is—they're not going to give you anything more than that. The cheapest person over all was David Koch. We would load up his trucks—two vans, usually—every weekend, for the Hamptons . . . multiple guys, in and out, in and out, heavy bags. We would never get a tip from Mr. Koch. We would never get a smile from Mr. Koch. Fifty-dollar check for Christmas, too—yeah, I mean, a check! At least you could give us cash."

For decades, federal funding for public broadcasting has been dwindling, and the government's contribution now makes up only 12 percent of PBS's funds. Affiliates such as WNET are almost entirely dependent on gifts, some of which are sizable: in 2010, WNET received 15 million dollars from James Tisch, the CEO of Loews Corporation, and his wife, Merryl. (James Tisch is now the chairman of WNET's board.) In New York City, such benefactors inevitably live in lavish buildings. Indeed, several relatives of WNET board members live at 740 Park.

In a recent phone interview, Neal Shapiro, the president of WNET, said that he grew concerned about the film, which he had not yet watched, after Ira Stoll, a conservative writer, lambasted it in the *Post*. On the Friday before the film's Monday airdate, Stoll, whose website, Future of Capitalism, has frequently defended the Kochs, wrote, "If the station has any sense, it will use the time until then to reconsider its decision to air the program." He added, "If it doesn't, its trustees and donors, some of whom live on Park Avenue, may want to consider whether they want to continue supporting an institution that insults them so viciously." The reviewer for the *Times* was more positive, writing, "There is plenty here to turn you into a Wall Street occupier," and observing, "If you were still on the fence about whether to despise the superrich, this film will almost surely make a hater out of you."

That Friday, Shapiro initially said, he called Koch at his office and told him that the Gibney film "was going to be controversial," noting, "You're going to be a big part of this thing." Shapiro offered to show him the trailer, and added that he hoped to arrange "some sort of on-air roundtable discussion of it, to provide other points of view." It could air immediately after the documentary. (Shapiro told me, "We did this after Ken Burns's film on baseball, too. We like to have a local angle.") Shapiro asked Koch, "Do you want to be involved?" He also offered Koch the opportunity to provide a written response, which the station could air after the show.

According to Shapiro, Koch, who rarely speaks in public, passed on the roundtable offer, saying, "I may just want to take it in and watch it, and form an opinion." He agreed to think about contributing a written response.

Shapiro acknowledges that his call to Koch was unusual. Although many prominent New Yorkers are portrayed in *Park Avenue*, he said that he "only just called David Koch. He's on our board. He's the biggest main character. No one else, just David Koch. Because he's a trustee. It's a courtesy." Shapiro, who joined WNET six years ago, from NBC News, added, "I can't remember doing anything like this—I can't remember another documentary centered around New York and key people in the city, and such controversial topics."

PBS has standards for "editorial integrity," and its guidelines state that "member stations are responsible for shielding the creative and editorial processes from political pressure or improper influence from funders or other sources." A PBS spokesperson, when asked if it considered WNET's actions appropriate, said, "WNET is in the best position to respond to this query," noting that member stations are autonomous.

Every so often, it becomes known that a news outlet has altered its coverage in order not to offend a sponsor. In 1998, ABC News, which is owned by Disney, canceled a report on the hiring of convicted pedophiles at Disney World. Days earlier, Michael Eisner, Disney's chairman at the time, had told NPR, "I would prefer ABC not to cover Disney." In *Brill's Content*, a report on the incident said that it validated "the viewing public's worst fears about conglomerate ownership of major news outlets."

PBS has long been a political target of conservatives. During the last presidential campaign, when Mitt Romney recommended eliminating government funding for public broadcasting, he echoed critics such as Newt Gingrich, who, in 1995, called public television elitist—a "little sandbox for the rich." Conservatives have said that the WNET host Bill Moyers exhibits a "very strident left-wing bias" and have suggested that characters on *Sesame Street* and *Arthur* indoctrinate children with left-wing values, such as acceptance of homosexuality. When Koch joined the boards of WGBH and WNET, it seemed to mark an ideological inroad, enabling him to exert influence over a network with a prominent news operation. Meanwhile, the member stations, by having Koch as a trustee, were inoculating themselves against charges of liberal bias and positioning themselves to receive substantial new donations.

In fact, according to a well-informed source, WNET was about to embark on an ambitious capital campaign, and before Gibney's film aired Koch had been planning to make a very large gift. "It was going to be a seven-figure donation—maybe more," the source said. Shapiro denies that Koch's patronage was a motive for his phone call.

· · ·

Several days after our interview, Shapiro e-mailed me to say, "I now think my timeline was off. . . . I apparently misspoke." He said that he had not called David Koch until the Monday that the Gibney documentary was to air. Shapiro added that he repeated his invitation to Koch to join the roundtable on Monday afternoon. Shapiro's timetable is puzzling, given that WNET taped the roundtable that Monday at 11 a.m. The other participants had been invited the preceding Friday. Gibney, unlike Koch, was not asked to join the roundtable, which featured Jeff Madrick, a liberal fellow at the Roosevelt Institute, and Diana Furchtgott-Roth, a conservative fellow at the Manhattan Institute; they discussed income inequality in broad terms. The moderator, who noted that Koch was a trustee, repeatedly mentioned that Koch's philanthropic contributions totaled a billion dollars.

Shortly before *Park Avenue* aired, Melissa Cohlmia, the chief spokesperson for Koch Industries, sent WNET a two-paragraph statement criticizing the film as "disappointing and divisive." Cohlmia acknowledges, however, that neither she nor Koch had watched it. WNET aired the statement, unedited, immediately after the film. Cohlmia said that she based the critique on the trailer.

The weekend before *Park Avenue* aired, Gibney said, it was clear that "something weird had happened." Shapiro called him at home. "He was very upset," Gibney said. "They were thinking of pulling the program." Gibney was told that the most pressing problem was Charles Schumer, the Democratic senator from New York. Schumer's staff had called WNET, arguing that *Park Avenue* falsely accused the senator of supporting tax loopholes for hedge-fund managers. Gibney double-checked his research and stood by his interpretation. Nevertheless, Shapiro told him that he planned to allow Schumer to add a response after the broadcast. But, Gibney noted, "Shapiro told me nothing about the Kochs."

Gibney gives credit to Shapiro and WNET for airing his film uncensored. He is disappointed, though, that the station gave Koch and Schumer the last word. "They tried to undercut the credibility of the film, and I had no opportunity to defend it," he said. Moreover, WNET replaced the introduction to *Park Avenue*, which was delivered by the actor Stanley Tucci, with one calling the film "controversial" and "provocative." Gibney noted that he had asked to interview the Kochs while making *Park Av-*

enue, but they had refused. Cohlmia initially denied this, but after Gibney's office provided me with the relevant e-mails she acknowledged that she had been contacted.

Shapiro emphasized that by showing the Gibney film, he had made "the right call." Still, spokespeople at WNET and PBS conceded that the decision to run the rebuttals was unprecedented. Indeed, it was like appending letters to the editor to a front-page article. Gibney asked me, "Why is WNET offering Mr. Koch special favors? And why did the station allow Koch to offer a critique of a film he hadn't even seen? Money. Money talks." He added that the Kochs' willingness to issue a disclaimer without seeing the film "does not give me much confidence about how they might run the Tribune's newspapers."

·　　·　　·

Despite WNET's hasty effort to mollify David Koch, *Park Avenue* apparently so offended him that he canceled his plan to make a large donation. Cohlmia refused to confirm or deny this, as did Shapiro. "We do not discuss the details of gifts made by our donors," he said, adding that he and Koch didn't discuss the film after it aired.

Shapiro said that, in the end, he was comfortable with the journalistic standards of *Park Avenue* and noted that he'd heard many positive comments from viewers, as well as negative ones. (The broadcast received high ratings for a PBS documentary.) But he said he felt blindsided by the Independent Television Service—the small arm of public television that funds and distributes independent films—for not giving him sufficient advance warning of the documentary's contents. ITVS, which is based in San Francisco and was founded some twenty years ago by independent filmmakers, prides itself on its resistance to outside pressure. Its mandate is to showcase opinionated filmmakers who "take creative risks, advance issues and represent points of view not usually seen on public or commercial television." *Park Avenue* was part of its popular series Independent Lens, which is aired by dozens of PBS member stations.

Shapiro acknowledged that in his conversations with ITVS officials about *Park Avenue*, he was so livid that he threatened not to carry its films in the future. The New York metropolitan area is the largest audience for public television, so the threat posed a potentially mortal blow to ITVS. Several months earlier, it had succeeded in holding on to a prominent slot on WNET only after a public lobbying campaign by independent filmmakers.

Five days after *Park Avenue* aired, a producer at Gibney's firm, Jigsaw Productions, was shopping in a clothing store in SoHo at the same time as two other customers: Thomas and Alice Tisch, who live at 740 Park. They are the brother and sister-in-law of James Tisch. The producer recalls that, after the Tisches heard her mention to another customer where she worked, they denounced what they called the film's incendiary rhetoric against the rich. They went on for twenty minutes, warning that such hateful attitudes could lead many wealthy New Yorkers to move to Florida, where the taxes are lower, and arguing that neighbors of theirs who spent millions of dollars on parties helped waiters and caterers.

There were reverberations on the West Coast, too, at the headquarters of ITVS. "Neal Shapiro was on a rampage against ITVS," a public-television executive said. In an effort to placate him, ITVS sent him a box of candy. "It was delicious," Shapiro told me.

A week later, Tia Lessin and Carl Deal, respected documentary filmmakers who were working on a project with ITVS, shared some good news with their funders: their film, which was about the influence of money on American politics after the Supreme Court's 2010 decision in the Citizens United case, had been accepted by the Sundance Film Festival and would compete for Best Documentary.

Lessin and Deal had provisionally called the film "Citizen Corp," but they worried that the title made it sound like a film about a corpse. After Sundance officials pressed for a final title so that they could start promoting it, Lessin and Deal told ITVS that they had settled on *Citizen Koch*.

The new title reflected the evolution of the narrative: reporting had focused increasingly on the pitched battle in Wisconsin over the efforts of Scott Walker, the Republican governor, to ban collective bargaining by public-sector-employee unions. As the *Times* reported, Koch Industries was among Walker's primary financial backers in his 2010 gubernatorial campaign.

Lessin and Deal had received widespread acclaim for their 2008 film about Hurricane Katrina, *Trouble the Water*, which won the Sundance Film Festival's Grand Jury award. They had been nominated for an Academy Award and had been producers on two films made by the progressive activist Michael Moore, *Fahrenheit 9/11* and *Bowling for Columbine*; Lessin had worked with Martin Scorsese on documentaries about Bob Dylan and George Harrison.

Lessin and Deal say that they are registered with neither political party, but an early synopsis of their proposed film reflected the liberal view that the Citizens United ruling had endangered democracy by drowning out ordinary voters' concerns in a surge of corporate cash. This stance is scarcely novel, but their narrative focus was original: working-class Republicans who felt betrayed by the party's attack on public-employee unions in Wisconsin. Virtually from the start, the Kochs had figured prominently in their proposal. On February 12, 2012, Lessin and Deal sent ITVS a six-minute preview that mentioned the Kochs multiple times as major contributors to conservative candidates and causes. At one point, the words "TWO BILLIONAIRE EXTREMISTS" appeared onscreen.

Lessin and Deal kept meticulous records of their exchanges with ITVS officials, and it seems that the collaboration was relatively smooth until Gibney's documentary aired. In April 2012, ITVS recommended that the film receive a $150,000 in funding. "Please accept this as confirmation and congratulations," the

ITVS notification said. It went on, "Everyone here at ITVS looks forward to working with you on your very exciting and promising program." A few weeks later, ITVS sent a multipage contract to the filmmakers, and negotiations seemed close to a resolution just before *Park Avenue* aired. Arash Hoda, the production manager at ITVS, sent Lessin and Deal an upbeat e-mail about the contract, saying, "This looks good . . . moving forward."

Claire Aguilar, then the vice president of programming at ITVS, was similarly encouraging after watching a two-and-a-half-hour rough cut bearing the title *Citizen Koch*. She sent the filmmakers an e-mail that said, "Great rough cut—thank you for sharing it." She said that she wasn't crazy about the new title, but she wasn't adamantly opposed to it, either.

A television producer knowledgeable about ITVS said that "there had been no concern" until the Gibney documentary aired and that few executives there had watched the rough cut. Suddenly, many ITVS officials seemed desperate to see it. Lessin and Deal were told to send a password-protected video link of the unfinished film to ITVS. Within days, the video had been played almost thirty times. "It was a real problem, because of *Park Avenue*," a public-television official aware of the situation said. "Because of the whole thing with the Koch brothers, ITVS knew WNET would never air it. Never."

According to the television producer, it seemed like ITVS executives "didn't want it to get to higher levels at PBS" that another Koch film was in the pipeline: "They were trying to hide things. They didn't want ITVS's name connected to it at Sundance. They were afraid of two things—that PBS would catch wind of it and that Lessin and Deal would go to the press and say that PBS didn't want them talking about David Koch."

Lessin and Deal took notes on their phone conversations with ITVS officials, which show that they were pushed to drop the Koch name from the title and to place less emphasis on the brothers' political influence. On December 7, the filmmakers' notes indicate, Lois Vossen, the vice president and senior series producer at ITVS, warned Lessin and Deal that the title *Citizen Koch* was "extraordinarily problematic." Vossen's job is to select films for Independent Lens and then pitch the programs to PBS. She told Lessin and Deal that the new title would make it exceedingly hard for her to champion the film at PBS, saying, "I would say I feel as though I would have both hands tied behind my back and probably duct tape over my mouth." (Vossen, reached for comment, said that she was just getting off a plane and would try to call back. She never did.)

The messages from ITVS officials grew confusing. Aguilar again praised the film as "great," and said, "I think you've preserved the anger of the film, which I love." Other officials, though, kept urging the filmmakers to change the title, add negative material about Democrats, and delete an opening sequence that showed Sarah Palin speaking at a rally sponsored by Americans for Prosperity, the Kochs' main advocacy group. Several times, Lessin and Deal asked ITVS officials if Koch's trusteeship at WNET was a factor. During the phone meeting on December 7, Vossen said, "I can absolutely assure you that ITVS does not want your film to be buried." She said of the title, "I think you understand why it's problematic. . . . We live in a world where we have to be aware that people with power have power."

During a conference call on January 14, Jim Sommers, the senior vice president of content for ITVS, acknowledged to Lessin and Deal that, after Gibney's film aired, there was "one station that gave us a lot of push-back about it." Was the station in New York? He said, "Ha, ha, ha, that might be it." According to the television producer, "They kept using words like 'balance,' but what they really meant was 'Get rid of the Koch story line.'"

Lessin said of ITVS staffers, "These are good people. Our sense was that there was something bigger than them going on. They weren't being straight with us." Deal said, "They're not supposed to be spineless bureaucrats. ITVS was set up by filmmakers to have a voice in the public-broadcasting universe. Their mission statement basically says, 'Be brave, be independent.' We never thought they'd back down."

.   .   .

Ruby Lerner, the president and the executive director of Creative Capital, which helped fund Lessin and Deal's Katrina film, said that she regards the "self-censorship" practiced by public-television officials to be "a scarier thing" than the overt kind: "They seem to be putting themselves in the Koch brothers' shoes and trying not to offend them." Even on public television, she argued, patronage buys influence. "It raises issues about what public television means," she said. "They are in the middle of so much funding pressure."

Michael Moore remembers Lessin and Deal fondly: Lessin got arrested while working with him on a documentary about labor issues at Disney World, and Deal found file footage of Paul Wolfowitz getting his hair slicked down by an aide, after Wolfowitz helpfully spat on his own comb. (The bit appeared in *Fahrenheit 9/11*.) Moore said that he's not surprised that the two ran into obstacles in public television, given Koch's trustee role, adding, "The words 'chilling effect' came immediately to mind."

In January, the film debuted at Sundance, where it was respectfully reviewed. A critic at *Variety* argued that *Citizen Koch*, still in unfinished form, had too many plot strands but concluded that it "vividly displayed" the "warping effect" of the Citizens United decision.

Lessin and Deal began to suspect that ITVS was dragging out negotiations. But they kept editing the film, following notes that ITVS had given them. Deal said, "Although we made many changes, they never looked at the new cut. They just kind of stopped." On April 15, ITVS notified Lessin and Deal that it had "decided not to move forward with the project." Lessin said, "We were in shock. We had a deal."

ITVS officials ascribe their decision to growing editorial differences. They issued a prepared statement: "ITVS commenced negotiations to fund the film 'Citizen Corp' based on a written proposal. Early cuts of the film did not reflect the proposal, however, and ITVS ceased negotiations."

Lessin and Deal said that this is untrue. Although they had changed the title, they said, in a joint statement, "The film we made is identical in premise and execution to the written and video proposals that ITVS green-lit last spring. ITVS backed out of the partnership because they came to fear the reaction our film would provoke. David Koch, whose political activities are featured in the film, happens to be a public-television funder and a trustee of both WNET and WGBH. This wasn't a failed negotiation or a divergence of visions; it was censorship, pure and simple." The filmmakers consider this an ironic turn: "It's the very thing our film is about—public servants bowing to pressures, direct or indirect, from high-dollar donors."

In the end, the various attempts to assuage David Koch were apparently insufficient. On Thursday, May 16, WNET's board of directors quietly accepted his resignation. It was the result, an insider said, of his unwillingness to back a media organization that had so unsparingly covered its sponsor.

Fortune

Amazon's creation of a $75 billion online retail Goliath is one of the great business stories of the last two decades. The building blocks were unprecedented selection, excellent customer service, a visionary CEO, and, as Peter Elkind shows, tax avoidance. In tracing the two-decade history of how Amazon cost state and local treasuries billions of dollars by exploiting tax loopholes to get a big price advantage over bricks-and-mortar rivals, Elkind presents a case study in how gaming the system can be a good business model.

Peter Elkind with
Doris Burke

30. Amazon's (Not So) Secret War on Taxes

The online retail giant has waged a lengthy and tenacious campaign against state sales taxes on Internet purchases—which Congress may finally be ready to mandate. But even when Amazon loses, it wins.

In August 2010, Cheryl Lenkowsky, an auditor for the Texas state comptroller, sent a letter to a top tax executive at Amazon.com's Seattle headquarters. At that point, Amazon had been selling a wide array of merchandise to Texans for fifteen years without collecting a penny of sales tax from them. Tax-free shopping was a delight for customers, a vital competitive edge for the company—and a hemorrhaging wound for state government.

Now, Lenkowsky informed the company, all that was about to end. Texas's audit, which had gone back four years, had resulted in an "adjustment": a bill for uncollected taxes, plus penalties and interest—$268,809,246.36 in all. Added Lenkowsky helpfully: "We have included a pre-addressed envelope for your payment convenience."

Amazon responded fiercely. It appealed the assessment. It sued the comptroller for her audit records. It lobbied Rick Perry, Texas's business-friendly governor. Most of all, Amazon insisted it had no "physical presence" in Texas—the basis for the tax claim—despite owning and operating a 630,800-square-foot distribution center (with an Amazon.com flag in front of it) in a Dallas suburb. When all that didn't work, the company shuttered the facility and threw its 119 employees out of work, vowing to abandon the Lone Star State.

"In this world," Benjamin Franklin famously wrote, "nothing can be said to be certain, except death and taxes." Since its birth, Amazon has labored mightily to defy one part of this maxim, placing itself at the forefront of an epic battle now playing out across the country. At issue is a seemingly simple question: whether Amazon—and Internet companies like it, such as Overstock and Blue Nile—should have to gather sales taxes from all their customers, just as Sears, Costco, and, say, the Peoria Camera Shop have done for decades.

There's a lot at stake. For state and local governments: an estimated $11.4 billion a year in desperately needed cash for streets, schools, police, and parks. For Amazon and archcompetitors like Wal-Mart: the struggle for retail primacy. For American consumers: what they pay and how they shop.

This story shows how the long, brutal war to force Internet retailers to collect taxes is finally being won. This saga of money, power, and commerce also provides a window into the way Amazon, which generated $61 billion in revenues last year, does business. Beneath its well-earned reputation for being customer-friendly—featuring a brilliant, affably cackling founder whom *Fortune* declared "Businessperson of the Year" in 2012—the company is a brass-knuckled battler for every penny of competitive advantage. It's no exaggeration to say you can't fully appreciate the rise of Amazon without understanding this fight.

For fifteen years the company refused to collect in most of the country, vowing to forever resist "illegal" efforts by the states. New alliances and strategies among its megarivals dramatically altered the debate, and in May the U.S. Senate passed legislation that would close the loophole for good. Its prospects for becoming law appear promising.

That's an ignominious defeat for Amazon, right? Not so fast. The longtime foe of Internet levies actually supports the Senate bill (and now insists the issue never really mattered much anyway). It's not the company's first shift in strategy. One element, however, has remained constant: Amazon has shrewdly and successfully maneuvered to turn each development, good or bad, to its own advantage.

The war over Internet sales taxes has its origins in the late 1980s, when Amazon.com was barely a twinkle in Jeff Bezos's eye. Back then it was mail-order houses that were winning business—and diverting money from government coffers—because they were allowed to sell tax-free in states where they lacked a store, sales agents, or any other sort of physical presence.

Then, as now, shoppers were legally obligated to "self-report"—to pay tax to their state on their own, even when out-of-state merchants didn't collect it from them. But as a practical matter, almost no one did. So states were eager to bring a test case that would force the out-of-state businesses to collect.

The tax men zeroed in on the Quill Corp. Although its headquarters were in Illinois, Quill was a major purveyor of office equipment in North Dakota. In 1988 the state demanded that the company begin collecting its 5 percent levy on purchases by North Dakota residents.

Quill decided to fight instead, and it prevailed in a landmark 1992 U.S. Supreme Court case. Forcing distant sellers to capture sales tax for thousands of local jurisdictions would be so burdensome that it violates the Constitution's commerce clause, the court ruled. A company is obliged to collect from shoppers only if it has a substantial physical presence in their state.

The term it used for that physical presence—"nexus"—would come to embody the entire debate even as it shifted to Amazon and online retailers. "Nexus" would loom ever larger, with states pushing hard to prove companies had it—and Amazon fighting even harder to deny it.

Among the creation fables of America's greatest enterprises, the issue of taxes doesn't usually play a central role. But it's integral to the founding of Amazon. When the company began selling books over the Internet in July 1995, three years after the Quill decision, exploiting the sales-tax loophole was very much on its founder's mind. In an interview with *Fast Company* a year later, Bezos said he'd recognized that "physical location is very important for the success of a virtual business." He based Amazon in Seattle partly to maximize the tax advantage.

"It had to be in a small state," explained Bezos, a libertarian who once donated $100,000 to defeat a proposed Washington State income tax on affluent residents. "In the mail-order business, you have to charge sales tax to customers who live in any state where you have a business presence. It made no sense for us to be in California or New York . . . I even investigated whether we could set up Amazon.com on an Indian reservation near San Francisco. This way we could have access to talent without all the tax consequences." Alas, that wasn't legally possible.

Low prices, along with convenience and huge selection, were a critical part of Amazon's appeal. Allowing customers to dodge state and local sales tax amounts to a pricing advantage of as much as 10 percent—a huge edge in the world of razor-thin retail profit margins.

From early on, Amazon fought to keep its advantage. In 1997, when Barnes & Noble also began selling books tax-free online, Amazon howled. At the time, Barnes & Noble was the industry gorilla, with 1,000 stores; it had driven scores of independent booksellers out of business and was eager to crush the online upstart. Stung by Amazon's marketing boast that it operated "Earth's Biggest Bookstore," Barnes & Noble had sued Amazon for "false and deceptive" ads.

The lawsuit was settled, but only after Amazon had countered in court that Barnes & Noble, by not collecting tax on Internet sales, was exploiting an "unfair method of competition." Barnes &

Noble got away with this by setting up its online business as an ostensibly independent enterprise, using a legal tactic known as "entity isolation."

Other traditional retailers (including Wal-Mart and Target) would also employ this approach for several years before recognizing that it wasn't legally sustainable and didn't make business sense for them. They moved instead to a "bricks-and-clicks" strategy, cross-promoting their physical sites and online business while allowing customers to pick up and return Internet orders at stores. "If you were playing the nexus game, you couldn't do that," says Warren Townsend, senior director of specialty tax for Wal-Mart. By 2003 virtually all the national chains were harvesting sales tax from online customers.

This left the competitive advantage of tax-free shopping exclusively in the hands of the online-only companies. Amazon would eagerly embrace the entity-isolation strategy just as it was expanding at an astounding pace—into electronics and toys, cameras and beauty products, jewelry and barbecue grills—and becoming a threat to every retailer on the planet.

For state tax departments, the stakes were high. Sales tax represents about a third of total revenues in the forty-five states that have such levies. But the states were too timid to act on their own. They decided to band together and form a national group called the Streamlined Sales Tax Project. The goal was to radically simplify the "burdensome" sales-tax system, then persuade Congress to pass a law allowing them to force all out-of-state businesses to collect. In 2000, the tax authorities set out to impose uniformity on the sales-tax codes of forty-five states.

But the "Streamlined" process turned out to be anything but. Work-group sessions droned on for hours over arcane details. Should pencil leads be classified as tax-exempt school supplies? Is a beverage with less than 50 percent fruit juice taxable as a soft drink? An entire five-page white paper was prepared on the definition of candy. Businesses, invited to participate in hopes of adding lobbying muscle, began larding the agreement with provisions to benefit their private interests. For its part, Amazon squabbled with eBay over which companies (based on size of revenues) would be subject to the new rules, adding yet another impediment to a consensus.

The first draft of the Streamlined agreement was completed in November 2002, but it has been amended twenty-eight times since. The document (with attached interpretive opinions) now runs to 204 pages. Yet only twenty-four states have signed on. The biggest states refused, unwilling to cede sovereignty. After more than a decade, the states were no closer to closing the Internet sales loophole than when they'd started. The effort had failed.

Throughout this time, Amazon insisted that it welcomed a "federal solution" requiring every company to collect. But it was clear that effort was going nowhere. With no consensus on Streamlined, congressional bills to overturn Quill had been repeatedly introduced and failed to make their way out of committee. By all accounts—except its own—Amazon did little in Washington to aid the federal effort. "They hid behind the skirt of this Streamlined group for fifteen years," charges Barnes & Noble CEO William Lynch. "Part of the strategy was to delay and pacify."

Indeed, as Streamlined was turning into a quagmire, Amazon was going to extreme lengths—demanding, wheedling, suing, threatening, and negotiating—to avoid collecting for as long as possible, in as many states as possible.

It wouldn't be a stretch to think of Paul Misener as Jeff Bezos's political alter ego. Both earned a degree in electrical engineering from Princeton (just one year apart), and both display a certain earnest, geeky enthusiasm. While Bezos worked on Wall Street before founding Amazon, Misener became a lawyer in Washington, D.C., where he developed an appropriately nerdy hobby, amassing some 1,500 antique books and documents. (Misener certainly differs from the shaven-pated Bezos in one respect: He's got a mane of silver—just short of a corporate mullet—with a distinctive river of white coursing left of center.)

As vice president for global public policy, Misener, fifty, is Bezos's field general in the long campaign against Internet taxes. With his cheerful demeanor and gleaming smile, Misener conveys the impression that what cynics might view as resisting taxes is in fact a noble quest to spread jobs and opportunity. Who could be against that? Indeed, Amazon says it's driven strictly by principle. "Far from an e-commerce loophole," Misener testified in Congress last August, "the constitutional limitation on states' authority to collect sales tax is at the core of our nation's founding principles." As Misener puts it in an interview with *Fortune*, "We feel very good about our position because it's a constitutional right." (Bezos declined to be interviewed.)

Misener's marching orders were clear from the outset. In 2000, the year Amazon hired him, Bezos—like many dotcom CEOs—voiced horror at the very notion of "taxing the Internet," warning that it would smother a toddler of an industry. In later years, he would argue it was "not fair" that Amazon should have to collect taxes where it lacked a physical presence because "we're not actually benefiting from any services that those states provide locally." Never mind that it was only customers who would pay the taxes (and those customers do benefit from state services)— or that startups in other industries have always had to collect on their sales.

In 2008—a point at which annual e-commerce had soared to $2.5 trillion—Bezos complained that local tax collection was so "horrendously complicated" that it imposed "an undue burden" on his company.

"Burden" doesn't seem like quite the right word. Not only was Amazon able to master the challenge by 2008—it had actually launched a service that was collecting sales tax for 2,500 merchants that used its website, including Macy's and Target.

Misener acknowledges that the "too-burdensome" premise of the Quill decision hasn't been valid for years. Yet Amazon has refused to start collecting because Quill says it doesn't have to, according to Misener. "We don't want to give up a constitutional right. There is a way to get at this collection question, which is for Congress to act."

While clinging to Quill's outdated protections, Amazon simultaneously sidestepped its dictates. Here's where the entity-isolation strategy comes in. To avoid collecting taxes, Amazon placed fulfillment centers—each as big as twenty football fields—in separate legal subsidiaries (owned by Amazon.com, needless to say). Through this arrangement, the company argues, its warehouses don't constitute a "physical presence."

By 2008, Amazon had bricks and mortar—mostly distribution centers—in seventeen sales-tax states. Yet it collected in only four: Washington, Kansas, Kentucky, and North Dakota. Among the places Amazon didn't collect: Pennsylvania, Nevada, Arizona, and Texas, all states where it had warehouses.

State tax administrators declined to lift a finger against the company. Indiana went even further. To lure an Amazon warehouse in 2007, public officials there cut a special deal to exempt the company from collecting the state's 7 percent sales tax. Amazon now has five warehouses in Indiana, where it has also received more than $11 million in economic development incentives.

Misener says his company's fulfillment centers don't constitute a physical presence because they have nothing more than a "brother-sister relationship" with Amazon's retail business. "We don't believe we have nexus," says Misener.

Tax experts view the situation differently. The University of Georgia law professor Walter Hellerstein, coauthor of a leading textbook on state taxation, calls Amazon's entity-isolation strategy "very, very aggressive." Agrees the University of Arizona tax law professor John Swain: "Amazon is trying to dress up their warehouses as if they are an independent vendor. It just doesn't pass the smell test." Contends Charles McLure, a former deputy assistant U.S. Treasury secretary and senior fellow emeritus at Stanford's Hoover Institution: Amazon is "aiding and abetting tax evasion."

The failure of Streamlined made it the bureaucratic equivalent of those notorious World War I battles in which massive, entrenched armies shed blood for months just to gain a few feet of territory. Ironically, though, it was a single state tax official whose actions eventually turned the entire conflict in a decisive new direction.

Robert Plattner, sixty-two, never had any faith in Streamlined. As an influential private tax lawyer in Albany, N.Y., he had condemned the Quill decision as "a blunder of major proportions." He dismissed prospects for a congressional solution and urged public officials to pursue a "Plan B." In 2007, Plattner became New York State's deputy commissioner for tax policy and soon hatched his own Plan B.

Amazon, of course, was the biggest target. But the company didn't have a single warehouse in the state. So Plattner targeted its New York "affiliate" network: thousands of small businesses, bloggers, and nonprofits that link to Amazon.com on their websites in return for a commission on any resulting sales. New York would define these affiliates as de facto sales agents, establishing the company's physical presence in the state. Voilà: instant nexus!

This "Amazon law," which applied to other Internet retailers as well, took effect in April 2008. (Amazon immediately sued to overturn it.) Halfway across the country, a *Dallas Morning News* reporter named Maria Halkias took note of Amazon's complaint that it didn't need to collect in New York because it didn't even have a warehouse there. Halkias recalled that she'd once received an Amazon package from a Texas address—as it turned out, a warehouse in Irving, near the Dallas/Fort Worth airport. Why, then, wasn't Amazon collecting from Texas customers?

The site was hardly a secret. Amazon had noted its Texas presence in SEC filings, and local papers had excitedly reported on the warehouse's arrival. Yet an official with the Texas comptroller's office told Halkias that the state hadn't known that Amazon had a Texas location. The agency dispatched an audit team to investigate.

As New York and Texas began bearing down, Amazon was engaging in contortions to avoid giving any opening to recession-ravaged states. "The economic outlook for many states is bleak," advised one confidential 2010 memo to the Amazon Services LLC North American Retail Group, which surfaced in unrelated litigation. "As a result, states are pursuing taxpayers more aggressively than before. Amazon's recent public experiences with New York and Texas provide timely and pertinent examples of the heightened risk. That's why our attention to nexus-related issues are [sic] more important than ever."

The company imposed an extraordinary set of rules restricting employees' travel and activities. Travel, the memo warned, "could create sales tax nexus . . . which could expose our business to significant tax costs."

The memo included a set of color-coded U.S. maps. Green and yellow states had the fewest restrictions. Travel to orange states required "preclearance" from the tax department, which tracked cumulative travel days for each state "to try to prevent the creation of a tax nexus." Travel to red states was permitted only in "very limited circumstances."

Once they arrived, employees who were allowed to attend industry meetings were instructed to avoid "soliciting or promoting the sale of products or services" as well as "speaking engagements, presentations, or other high-visibility activities" without advance approval. They were even barred from blogging while out of state.

Amazon—the company that contended that a 600,000-square-foot warehouse with more than one hundred employees didn't count as a "presence"—seemingly feared that much more tenuous links would create the dreaded nexus. Even writing promotional material for the company's website on a freelance basis from a home in Texas was too much. A well-regarded longtime contractor named Betsy Danheim was dropped, an Amazon supervisor named Paul Hart explained in a March 2008 e-mail to his work team. The reason? "Turns out," Hart wrote, "it could create a tax nexus issue."

By 2009 it had become clear to brick-and-mortar stalwarts like Sears, Walgreen, and Wal-Mart that no solution was coming from Streamlined. Some of Amazon's biggest rivals began to realize the time had come when they would need to enter the fray and take on the company.

Amazon was continuing to grab market share across more and more product lines. As a purveyor of big-ticket goods, Best Buy was among those being hurt the worst. For a customer buying a $1,800 big-screen television package, saving $180 by dodging the sales tax had considerable appeal.

Best Buy started approaching other chains and retail trade associations to build urgency. "We just saw this gridlock," says Laura Bishop, vice president for government relations at Best Buy. "We said, 'Look, we should start crafting a more aggressive approach.'"

The big retailers were impressed by New York's success in challenging Amazon. They began girding for state-by-state combat. Fresh ammunition was available from a 2009 study by three University of Tennessee professors; it projected how much each individual state was losing to the tax-free Internet. In 2010 alone, California was projected to lose $1.4 billion; Texas, $658 million. By 2012, according to the study, the total annual loss to state budgets would reach $11.4 billion.

But interviews with focus groups revealed no particular sympathy for strapped state governments. It was far better to cast the issue as a matter of fairness between traditional stores and online retail. The merchants' rallying cry became "level the playing field"—a notion even free-market conservatives could embrace. Why should a downtown shop—which paid local taxes, provided local jobs, and supported Little League baseball and the Lions Club—face a 10 percent disadvantage competing with a big out-of-state corporation?

The retailers established an advocacy group called the Alliance for Main Street Fairness, with affiliates in different states. As its frontmen, the alliance tapped sympathetic local shopkeepers—the very mom-and-pops that Wal-Mart, Best Buy, and Barnes & Noble had made an endangered species. In 2011, Main Street Fairness began pressing states to crack down.

Amazon counterattacked. In each of the five states that enacted New York–style "Amazon laws" over the next two years, the company terminated its relationship with all local affiliates, cutting off income for thousands. This erased the legal basis for forcing it to collect. Amazon blamed the states, telling the former affiliates to complain to their lawmakers.

When Colorado passed a law requiring online retailers merely to advise customers that they might owe tax (and report shopper purchases to the state), Amazon fired its affiliates there, too, and said it wouldn't bring them back until the law was repealed. That prompted Michael Mazerov, senior fellow with the Washington, D.C.–based Center on Budget and Policy Priorities, to accuse Amazon of "corporate hostage-taking."

About the same time, Amazon had begun to rethink its distribution strategy. The company had always served big states like New York with warehouses located elsewhere. But its customer base was soaring, and Bezos was moving to develop the capacity for next-day—or even same-day—delivery. This required many more distribution centers, much closer to customers. The demands of Amazon's evolving business model were encroaching on its ability to base decisions on tax avoidance.

As its political position grew less tenable, Amazon started maneuvering to combine its needs (more warehouses) with its wants (preserving tax-free shopping for as long as possible). This strategy played out first in South Carolina. In late 2010 the company struck a deal with outgoing governor Mark Sanford, who promised Amazon an exemption from gathering sales tax (along with tens of millions of dollars in traditional inducements) in return for a new distribution center with 1,250 jobs. But that agreement required approval from the state legislature.

The Alliance for Main Street Fairness rushed in to raise a stink, holding press conferences, issuing statements, and running newspaper and TV ads. Business lobbyists buttonholed legislators, demanding that Amazon start collecting sales tax immediately. Opponents wore T-shirts reading STAND WITH MAIN STREET.

Amazon finally offered a compromise: It would start capturing sales tax in January 2016—almost five years later. When the South Carolina House overwhelmingly rejected that, Amazon announced that it was taking its jobs elsewhere and abandoning its half-built warehouse. "The 1,200 jobs and nearly $100 million in capital investment that were coming to the state—aren't," Amazon's Misener declared at a press conference.

The announcement had the desired effect. Three weeks later, the legislature flip-flopped—and the retailer announced it was returning to South Carolina after all, with its exemption until 2016. Score one for Amazon.

As a dozen states, pressured by America's biggest retailers, suddenly began debating their own steps to squeeze Amazon, California and Texas loomed as the largest battlegrounds. California didn't have a single Amazon warehouse. Yet there had been efforts to make online sellers collect the state's 7.25 percent sales tax for more than a decade. They'd been led by independent booksellers, who came to see themselves as the canaries in the mineshaft in sensing the threat that Amazon posed to brick-and-mortar businesses.

To make their case that Amazon had nexus, the booksellers had focused on a half-dozen California offices the company leased for several small software businesses it had bought, as well as Lab126, the Cupertino research-and-development shop that developed the Kindle. But the state's tax-collection board rejected the idea that this represented a "physical presence," and two different governors had vetoed bills pushed by the booksellers to broaden the nexus rules in ways that would cover Amazon.

"We were trying to get Wal-Mart, Target, Best Buy, Home Depot onboard for years," says Hut Landon, executive director of the Northern California Independent Booksellers Association. "Amazon was kicking their butt. But they didn't want to get involved. We couldn't do it on our own. Politically, we just didn't have the influence and the power. We needed the big guys."

In 2011, for the first time, the booksellers found the California Retailers Association and its megacorporation members marching beside them. With fresh muscle, and California mired in deficits, a new bill to broaden the nexus rules sailed through the legislature and was signed into law by Governor Jerry Brown in June 2011. Amazon immediately terminated its 10,000 affiliates in California, urging them to besiege legislators. When that didn't work, the company put up $5 million to launch a statewide referendum to overturn the measure.

The Alliance for Main Street Fairness countered with its own campaign, which included political-style attack ads. The organization's website urged citizens to anonymously "Drop a dime on Amazon," because "Amazon.com will do and say anything to maintain an unfair advantage over Main Street businesses." The traditional retailers vowed to spend whatever it took to uphold the law. Says Lenny Goldberg, lobbyist for the booksellers: "We were looking at this as the battle of the titans."

Misener had vowed never to concede in California. But the momentum had shifted. Amazon finally relented, and the two sides hammered out a bargain. The company would start collecting sales tax in California after about a year, on September 15, 2012, and the state would get three Amazon warehouses.

As Texas state comptroller Susan Combs sees it, the states that gave Amazon extended safe harbors on sales-tax collection are "chumps." As she puts it, "It's flat-out wrong!" At six-foot-two, Combs, sixty-eight, cuts a bold figure. Raised on a West Texas cattle ranch, she was educated at Vassar and the University of Texas Law School, then worked as a prosecutor in Dallas and published a romance novel. A Republican, she's been in Texas politics for twenty years, the last seven as the state's independently elected tax collector.

Combs proudly claims bragging rights for having gotten Amazon to start corralling sales tax faster than anyone. But it required some high-dollar horse-trading.

In the fall of 2010, after Combs's auditors presented Amazon with the $269 million bill for back taxes, the company insisted it had no physical presence in Texas, citing the ownership of its local warehouse by an "independent subsidiary" called Amazon.com.kydc. Combs found this laughable. Reaching into her Amazon file, she plucks out a photo of the sprawling building and slides it toward me. "When they have a sign out front that says amazon.com, that was pretty clear," she says. "They tied everything back to Seattle. They didn't call themselves Fred's Distribution Center. They called themselves Amazon.com."

Combs pulls out a copy of a 1963 Texas law expanding tax-capturing requirements to "any retailer maintaining, occupying, or using, permanently or temporarily, directly or indirectly, or through a subsidiary, or agent by whatever name called, an office, place of distribution . . . warehouse or storage place." As Combs puts it, "When the statute is as clear as I think this one is, you need to pay up!"

Amazon certainly didn't think so. When it got Combs' $269 million tax bill, it scotched plans to build a second Texas distribution center. Then, in February 2011, Amazon announced it was pulling out of Texas altogether, shutting down the Irving warehouse and terminating all of its workers there. An Amazon executive explained that the company needed to leave because of Texas's "unfavorable regulatory climate." (*Chief Executive* magazine has named Texas as America's most business-friendly state for nine straight years.)

By this time, the Main Street Alliance had arrived on the scene, offering support for Combs and backing a bill to tighten the state's basis for forcing Amazon to collect. When the Texas Retailers Association held its annual "Retail Roundup" lobbying day in Austin, Best Buy swarmed the capitol with twenty blue-shirted store managers.

The legislature passed the Amazon bill, but Governor Perry vetoed it. As it moved forward again in a special session, Amazon offered a South Carolina–style bargain: It would build massive new warehouses in Texas, providing 6,000 jobs, in return for a sales-tax exemption until January 2016—four and a half years. Bolstered by the big-box lobbyists, the lawmakers stood their ground, tucking the measure into a veto-proof "fiscal matters" bill, before adjourning their special session in June 2011.

"We all had a nice Texas summer," says Combs. "Then we got a call eventually in the spring from some folks wanting to come talk turkey." At about two p.m. on April 13, 2012, Paul Misener arrived at the comptroller's office in Austin. Misener is a tall man. "I wore really good heels, which was smart," recalls Combs. "Because I needed to be eye to eye." The deal was struck in thirty minutes. Amazon would start collecting Texas's 8.25 percent sales tax on July 1, 2012—just two months later. The company would, of course, build distribution centers, pledging to invest $200 million and create at least 2,500 jobs in Texas over the next four years.

Combs wrote off Amazon's $269 million tax bill, reasoning that it was most crucial to get Amazon collecting quickly. Amazon did make what it later described as "an immaterial payment" to the state. "The key thing was to get certainty," Combs says. "I absolutely believe we did the right thing. We got what we think is the best deal in the country."

Amazon, as usual, got a good deal, too. Says Misener: "We're very happy to be in Texas, creating new jobs and investment."

Amazon denies that its deals in states such as Texas represent any kind of reversal. According to Misener, the company has struck tax-collection agreements merely because it wanted to expand its distribution network and was eager to avoid conflict. "We decided we wanted to go only to places that truly welcomed us," he says.

But there's no question that the past two years have represented a tipping point. This Christmas, Amazon will be collecting taxes in thirteen states; by January 2016 it will be assessing tax in seventeen states, covering about half the U.S. population. The company has now agreed to reap sales tax in every state where it operates a warehouse. In New York, it has lost its challenges to the original "Amazon law." New York officials say that since the law's passage in 2008, they have received $508 million in extra sales tax collected by thirty-five online businesses.

Even as it has reluctantly begun to yield this competitive edge, Amazon has minimized its impact, saying the company does just fine, thank you, even where it collects. Amazon has less need for the advantage than it once did; millions of consumers now treat the site as a utility, using it as a default option for a huge array of purchases. Still, academic studies suggest that the addition of sales tax drives 10 percent or more of customers to shop elsewhere. Where Amazon has begun adding tax to bills, Barnes & Noble and Best Buy both claim significant upticks in their business.

Pressure from the big-box stores has also had the desired effect in Washington. The Marketplace Fairness Act passed the U.S. Senate in May, with broad bipartisan support and the backing of President Obama. The bill would allow states to force collection, with no need to prove nexus. Advocates give it a fifty-fifty chance of passing in the House.

Among the corporate giants backing the bill: Wal-Mart, Home Depot, Best Buy—and Amazon, which is actively lobbying in

Washington after years of tepid engagement. Amazon has retained a powerhouse D.C. lobbying firm and now has two former U.S. senators, Trent Lott and John Breaux, promoting the bill's passage.

In a Senate hearing last fall, South Carolina Republican Jim DeMint (who has since left Congress) accused Amazon of backing the legislation to avoid giving online competitors the advantage it long enjoyed. "Now that you're going to have to pay taxes in all of these states where you have a physical presence," DeMint told Misener, "you want to come back and tax these other companies that don't."

Misener insisted that his company favors the measure simply to "level the playing field for all sellers"—embracing the battle cry of the company's opponents. If the Marketplace Fairness Act passes, it would supersede Amazon's negotiated agreements, moving up the dates of required collection in a few states.

The long, nasty history has been put aside as erstwhile enemies awkwardly unite. "There was bloodlust between Amazon and all the people in this coalition," says Jason Brewer, spokesman for the Retail Industry Leaders Association. "At this point, we're trying gracefully to row in the same direction."

Now it is a different online giant—eBay—that is leading the opposition, issuing its own call to arms in the name of small business (online business, that is), even though the legislation exempts any company with annual Internet sales of less than $1 million.

Meanwhile, Amazon, as promised, has been rapidly building new distribution centers across the country, including three in Texas. There, Amazon is making the most of its beefed-up presence in the state. It is, of course, happily exploiting millions in economic-development incentives.

But that isn't all. Under Texas law, the pint-size suburbs that will house new Amazon warehouses may enjoy a special windfall: They can receive a portion of the sales tax on all products shipped from that warehouse to Texas customers. In gratitude, all three municipalities have already agreed to "rebate" varying amounts—as much as 85 percent in one case—to Amazon. This bonanza would run well into the millions. After years of scorched-earth battles to avoid collecting sales tax, Amazon has managed to find a way to channel a chunk of that money—which comes out of its customers' pockets—into its own coffers.

The Atlantic

This tax-exempt nonprofit gets roughly $1 billion a year in government subsidies; its leader gets paid more than any Wall Street CEO; and for decades it actively covered up a deadly health crisis among its workers. The organization is the National Football League, and Gregg Easterbrook shows in this outraged *Atlantic* article how the league has built its multi-billion-dollar empire on the largesse of politicians and taxpayers, whom the NFL routinely extorts with threats to move beloved home teams to more generous cities.

Gregg Easterbrook

31. How the NFL Fleeces Taxpayers

L ast year was a busy one for public giveaways to the National Football League. In Virginia, Republican governor Bob McDonnell, who styles himself as a budget-slashing conservative crusader, took $4 million from taxpayers' pockets and handed the money to the Washington Redskins, for the team to upgrade a workout facility. Hoping to avoid scrutiny, McDonnell approved the gift while the state legislature was out of session. The Redskins owner, Dan Snyder, has a net worth estimated by *Forbes* at $1 billion. But even billionaires like to receive expensive gifts.

Taxpayers in Hamilton County, Ohio, which includes Cincinnati, were hit with a bill for $26 million in debt service for the stadiums where the NFL's Bengals and Major League Baseball's Reds play, plus another $7 million to cover the direct operating costs for the Bengal field. Pro-sports subsidies exceeded the $23.6 million that the county cut from health-and-human-services spending in the current two-year budget (and represent a sizable chunk of the $119 million cut from Hamilton County schools). Press materials distributed by the Bengals declare that the team gives back about $1 million annually to Ohio community groups. Sound generous? That's about 4 percent of the public subsidy the Bengals receive annually from Ohio taxpayers.

In Minnesota, the Vikings wanted a new stadium and were vaguely threatening to decamp to another state if they didn't get it. The Minnesota legislature, facing a $1.1 billion budget deficit, extracted $506 million from taxpayers as a gift to the team, covering roughly half the cost of the new facility. Some legislators argued that the Vikings should reveal their finances: privately held, the team is not required to disclose operating data, despite the public subsidies it receives. In the end, the Minnesota legislature folded, giving away public money without the Vikings' disclosing information in return. The team's principal owner, Zygmunt Wilf, had a 2011 net worth estimated at $322 million; with the new stadium deal, the Vikings' value rose about $200 million, by *Forbes*'s estimate, further enriching Wilf and his family. They will make a token annual payment of $13 million to use the stadium, keeping the lion's share of all NFL ticket, concession, parking, and, most important, television revenues.

After approving the $506 million handout, Minnesota governor Mark Dayton said, "I'm not one to defend the economics of professional sports. . . . Any deal you make in that world doesn't make sense from the way the rest of us look at it." Even by the standards of political pandering, Dayton's irresponsibility was breathtaking.

In California, the city of Santa Clara broke ground on a $1.3 billion stadium for the 49ers. Officially, the deal includes $116 million in public funding, with private capital making up the rest. At least, that's the way the deal was announced. A new government entity, the Santa Clara Stadium Authority, is borrowing $950 million, largely from a consortium led by Goldman Sachs, to provide the majority of the "private" financing. Who are the board members of the Santa Clara Stadium Authority? The members of the Santa Clara City Council. In effect, the city of Santa Clara is providing most of the "private" funding. Should something go wrong, taxpayers will likely take the hit.

The 49ers will pay Santa Clara $24.5 million annually in rent for four decades, which makes the deal, from the team's standpoint, a forty-year loan amortized at less than 1 percent interest. At the time of the agreement, thirty-year Treasury bonds were selling for 3 percent, meaning the Santa Clara contract values the NFL as a better risk than the United States government.

Although most of the capital for the new stadium is being underwritten by the public, most football revenue generated within the facility will be pocketed by Denise DeBartolo York, whose net worth is estimated at $1.1 billion, and members of her family. York took control of the team in 2000 from her brother, Edward DeBartolo Jr., after he pleaded guilty to concealing an extortion plot by a former governor of Louisiana. Brother and sister inherited their money from their father, Edward DeBartolo Sr., a shopping-mall developer who became one of the nation's richest men before *his death in 1994*. A generation ago, the DeBartolos made their money the old-fashioned way, by hard work in the free market. Today, the family's wealth rests on political influence and California tax subsidies. Nearly all NFL franchises are family-owned, converting public subsidies and tax favors into high living for a modern-day feudal elite.

·   ·   ·

Pro-football coaches talk about accountability and self-reliance, yet pro-football owners routinely binge on giveaways and handouts. A year after Hurricane Katrina hit New Orleans, the Saints resumed hosting NFL games: justifiably, a national feel-good story. The finances were another matter. Taxpayers have, in stages, provided about $1 billion to build and later renovate what is now known as the Mercedes-Benz Superdome. (All monetary figures in this article have been converted to 2013 dollars.) Saints owner Tom Benson whose net worth *Forbes* estimates at $1.2 billion, keeps nearly all revenue from ticket sales, concessions, parking, and broadcast rights. Taxpayers even footed the bill for the addition of leather stadium seats with cup holders to cradle the drinks they are charged for at concession stands. And corporate welfare for the Saints doesn't stop at stadium construction and renovation costs. Though Louisiana governor Bobby Jindal claims to be an antispending conservative, each year the state of Louisiana forcibly extracts up to $6 million from its residents' pockets and gives the cash to Benson as an "inducement payment"—the actual term used—to keep Benson from developing a wandering eye.

In NFL city after NFL city, this pattern is repeated. Century-Link Field, where the Seattle Seahawks play, opened in 2002, with Washington State taxpayers providing $390 million of the $560 million construction cost. The Seahawks, owned by Paul Allen, one of the richest people in the world, pay the state about $1 million annually in rent in return for most of the revenue from ticket sales, concessions, parking, and broadcasting (all told, perhaps $200 million a year). Average people are taxed to fund Allen's private-jet lifestyle.

The Pittsburgh Steelers, winners of six Super Bowls, the most of any franchise, play at Heinz Field, a glorious stadium that opens to a view of the serenely flowing Ohio and Allegheny Rivers. Pennsylvania taxpayers contributed about $260 million to help build Heinz Field—and to retire debt from the Steelers' previous stadium. Most game-day revenues (including television fees) go to the Rooney family, the majority owner of the team. The team's owners also kept the $75 million that Heinz paid to name the facility.

Judith Grant Long, a Harvard University professor of urban planning, calculates that league-wide, 70 percent of the capital cost of NFL stadiums has been provided by taxpayers, not NFL owners. Many cities, counties, and states also pay the stadiums' ongoing costs by providing power, sewer services, other infrastructure, and stadium improvements. When ongoing costs are added, Long's research finds, the Buffalo Bills, Cincinnati Bengals, Cleveland Browns, Houston Texans, Indianapolis Colts, Jacksonville Jaguars, Kansas City Chiefs, New Orleans Saints,

San Diego Chargers, St. Louis Rams, Tampa Bay Buccaneers, and Tennessee Titans have turned a profit on stadium subsidies alone—receiving more money from the public than they needed to build their facilities. Long's estimates show that just three NFL franchises—the New England Patriots, New York Giants, and New York Jets—have paid three-quarters or more of their stadium capital costs.

Many NFL teams have also cut sweetheart deals to avoid taxes. The futuristic new field where the Dallas Cowboys play, with its 80,000 seats, go-go dancers on upper decks, and built-in nightclubs, has been appraised at nearly $1 billion. At the basic property-tax rate of Arlington, Texas, where the stadium is located, Cowboys owner Jerry Jones would owe at least $6 million a year in property taxes. Instead he receives no property-tax bill, so Tarrant County taxes the property of average people more than it otherwise would.

·　　·　　·

In his office at 345 Park Avenue in Manhattan, NFL Commissioner Roger Goodell must smile when Texas exempts the Cowboy stadium from taxes or the governor of Minnesota bows low to kiss the feet of the NFL. The National Football League is about two things: producing high-quality sports entertainment, which it does very well, and exploiting taxpayers, which it also does very well. Goodell should know—his pay, about $30 million in 2011, flows from an organization that does not pay corporate taxes.

That's right—extremely profitable and one of the most subsidized organizations in American history, the NFL also enjoys tax-exempt status. On paper, it is the Nonprofit Football League.

This situation came into being in the 1960s, when Congress granted antitrust waivers to what were then the National Football League and the American Football League, allowing them to merge, conduct a common draft, and jointly auction television rights. The merger was good for the sport, stabilizing pro football while ensuring quality of competition. But Congress gave away the store to the NFL while getting almost nothing for the public in return.

The 1961 Sports Broadcasting Act was the first piece of gift-wrapped legislation, granting the leagues legal permission to conduct television-broadcast negotiations in a way that otherwise would have been price collusion. Then, in 1966, Congress enacted Public Law 89-800, which broadened the limited antitrust exemptions of the 1961 law. Essentially, the 1966 statute said that if the two pro-football leagues of that era merged—they would complete such a merger four years later, forming the current NFL—the new entity could act as a monopoly regarding television rights. Apple or ExxonMobil can only dream of legal permission to function as a monopoly: the 1966 law was effectively a license for NFL owners to print money. Yet this sweetheart deal was offered to the NFL in exchange only for its promise not to schedule games on Friday nights or Saturdays in autumn, when many high schools and colleges play football.

Public Law 89-800 had no name—unlike, say, the catchy USA Patriot Act or the Patient Protection and Affordable Care Act. Congress presumably wanted the bill to be low-profile, given that its effect was to increase NFL owners' wealth at the expense of average people.

While Public Law 89-800 was being negotiated with congressional leaders, NFL lobbyists tossed in the sort of obscure provision that is the essence of the lobbyist's art. The phrase *or professional football leagues* was added to Section 501(c)6 of 26 USC, the Internal Revenue Code. Previously, a sentence in Section 501(c)6 had granted not-for-profit status to "business leagues, chambers of commerce, real-estate boards, or boards of trade." Since 1966, the code has read: "business leagues, chambers of commerce, real-estate boards, boards of trade, or professional football leagues."

The insertion of *professional football leagues* into the defini-tion of not-for-profit organizations was a transparent sellout of public interest. This decision has saved the NFL uncounted mil-lions in tax obligations, which means that ordinary people must pay higher taxes, public spending must decline, or the national debt must increase to make up for the shortfall. Nonprofit status applies to the NFL's headquarters, which administers the league and its all-important television contracts. Individual teams are for-profit and presumably pay income taxes—though because all except the Green Bay Packers are privately held and do not disclose their finances, it's impossible to be sure.

For Veterans Day last year, the NFL announced that it would donate cash to military groups for each point scored in desig-nated games. During NFL telecasts that weekend, the league was praised for its grand generosity. The total donation came to about $440,000. Annualized, NFL stadium subsidies and tax favors add up to perhaps $1 billion. So the NFL took $1 billion from the public, then sought praise for giving back $440,000—less than a tenth of 1 percent.

•   •   •

In the NFL, cynicism about public money starts at the top. State laws and IRS rules generally forbid the use of nonprofit status as a subterfuge for personal enrichment. Yet according to the league's annual Form 990, in 2011, the most recent year for which num-bers are available, the NFL paid a total of almost $60 million to its leading five executives.

Roger Goodell's windfall has been justified on the grounds that the free market rewards executives whose organizations perform well, and there is no doubt that the NFL performs well as to both product quality—the games are consistently terrific—and the bottom line. But almost nothing about the league's op-erations involves the free market. Taxpayers fund most stadium costs; the league itself is tax-exempt; television images made in those publicly funded stadiums are privatized, with all gains kept by the owners; and then the entire organization is walled off behind a moat of antitrust exemptions.

The reason NFL executives' pay is known is that in 2008, the IRS moved to strengthen the requirement that 501(c)6 organizations disclose payments to top officers. The NFL asked Congress to grant pro football a waiver from the disclosure rule. During the lobbying battle, Joe Browne, then the league's vice president for public affairs, told the *New York Times*, "I finally get to the point where I'm making 150 grand, and they want to put my name and address on the [disclosure] form so the lawyer next door who makes a million dollars a year can laugh at me." Browne added that $150,000 does not buy in the New York area what it would in "Dubuque, Iowa." The waiver was denied. Left no option, the NFL revealed that at the time, Browne made about $2 million annually.

Perhaps it is spitting into the wind to ask those who run the National Football League to show a sense of decency regarding the lucrative public trust they hold. Goodell's taking some $30 million from an enterprise made more profitable because it hides behind its tax-exempt status does not seem materially different from, say, the Fannie Mae CEO's taking a gigantic bonus while taxpayers were bailing out his company.

Perhaps it is spitting into the wind to expect a son to be half what his father was. Charles Goodell, a member of the House of Representatives for New York from 1959 to 1968 and then a senator until 1971, was renowned as a man of conscience—among the first members of Congress to oppose the Vietnam War, one of the first Republicans to fight for environmental protection. My initial experience with politics was knocking on doors for Charles Goodell; a brown-and-white Senator Goodell campaign button sits in my mementos case. Were Charles Goodell around today, what would he think of his son's cupidity? Roger Goodell has become the sort of person his father once opposed—an insider who profits from his position while average people pay.

I wanted to put questions about the NFL's finances to Roger Goodell. When I was researching my book *The King of Sports*, from which this excerpt is drawn, I requested interview time with Goodell, and he agreed. When NFL headquarters learned that my questions would cover tax exemptions and health issues in the league, the interview was promptly canceled. The league spokesman Greg Aiello told me it was not in the NFL's "best interests" to discuss safety or subsidies.

.   .   .

One might suppose that with football raking in such phenomenal sums of cash, politicians could win votes by assuming populist stances regarding NFL subsidies and exemptions. Instead, in almost every instance, Congress and state legislatures have rolled over and played dead for pro football. NFL owners pressure local politicians with veiled threats of moving teams, though no franchise has moved since 1998. Public officials who back football-stadium spending, meanwhile, can make lavish (if unrealistic) promises of jobs and tourism, knowing the invoices won't come due until after they have left office.

Politicians seem more interested in receiving campaign donations and invitations to luxury boxes than in taking on the football powers that be to bargain for a fair deal for ordinary people. Arlen Specter of Pennsylvania, a moderate who served thirty years in the Senate, tried to pressure the NFL to stop picking the public's pocket but left Capitol Hill in 2011 and passed away the next year. No populist champion so far has replaced him. Specter told me in 2007, "The NFL owners are arrogant people who have abused the public trust and act like they can get away with anything."

Too often, NFL owners can, in fact, get away with anything. In financial terms, the most important way they do so is by creating game images in publicly funded stadiums, broadcasting the images over public airwaves, and then keeping all the money they receive as a result. Football fans know the warning intoned during each NFL contest: that use of the game's images "without the NFL's consent" is prohibited. Under copyright law, entertainment created in publicly funded stadiums is private property.

When, for example, Fox broadcasts a Tampa Bay Buccaneers game from Raymond James Stadium, built entirely at the public's expense, it has purchased the right to do so from the NFL. In a typical arrangement, taxpayers provide most or all of the funds to build an NFL stadium. The team pays the local stadium authority a modest rent, retaining the exclusive right to license images on game days. The team then sells the right to air the games. Finally, the NFL asserts a copyright over what is broadcast. No federal or state law prevents images generated in facilities built at public expense from being privatized in this manner.

Baseball, basketball, ice hockey, and other sports also benefit from this same process. But the fact that others take advantage of the public too is no justification. The NFL's sweetheart deal is by far the most valuable: This year, CBS, DirecTV, ESPN, Fox, NBC, and Verizon will pay the NFL about $4 billion for the rights to broadcast its games. Next year, that figure will rise to more than $6 billion. Because football is so popular, its broadcast fees would be high no matter how the financial details were structured. The fact that game images created in places built and operated at public expense can be privatized by the NFL inflates the amounts kept by NFL owners, executives, coaches, and players, while driving up the cable fees paid by people who may not even care to watch the games.

•　　　•　　　•

In too many areas of contemporary life, public subsidies are converted to private profit. Sometimes, such as with the bailout of General Motors, once the subsidies end, society is better off; sometimes, as with the bailout of AIG, subsidies are repaid. Public handouts for modern professional football never end and are never repaid. In return, the NFL creates nothing of social value—while setting bad examples, despite its protests to the contrary, regarding concussions, painkiller misuse, weight gain, and cheating, among other issues. The no. 1 sport in a nation with a childhood-obesity epidemic celebrates weight gain; that's bad enough. Worse, the sport setting the bad example is subsidized up one side and down the other.

The NFL's nonprofit status should be revoked. And lawmakers—ideally in Congress, to level the national playing field, as it were—should require that television images created in publicly funded sports facilities cannot be privatized. The devil would be in the details of any such action. But Congress regulates health care, airspace, and other far-more-complex aspects of contemporary life; it can crack the whip on the NFL.

If football images created in places funded by taxpayers became public domain, the league would respond by paying the true cost of future stadiums—while negotiating to repay construction subsidies already received. To do otherwise would mean the loss of billions in television-rights fees. Pro football would remain just as exciting and popular, but would no longer take advantage of average people.

In 2010, the National Football League moved its annual Pro Bowl away from Honolulu for the first time in thirty years. At the very time Hawaii was cutting its budget for public schools, state lawmakers voted to pay the NFL $4 million per game to bring the event back to their capital. The lawmakers' gift giving was bad enough. What was disgraceful was that the rich, subsidized owners of the NFL accepted.

Until public attitudes change, those at the top of the pro-football pyramid will keep getting away with whatever they can. This is troubling not just because ordinary people are taxed so a small number of NFL owners and officers can live as modern feudal lords and ladies. It is troubling because athletics are supposed to set an example—and the example being set by the NFL is one of selfishness.

Football is the king of sports. Should the favorite sport of the greatest nation really be one whose economic structure is based on inequality and greed?

Contributors

Writer and photographer **CHRIS ARNADE** received his Ph.D. in physics from Johns Hopkins University in 1992 and then spent twenty years working as a trader on Wall Street. His photo series "Faces of Addiction" focuses on a South Bronx neighborhood in New York City.

RUSSELL BRAND is an English comedian, actor, radio host, and author.

GREGG EASTERBROOK is a contributing editor of *The Atlantic* and *Washington Monthly* and writes the "Tuesday Morning Quarterback" column for ESPN.com. He has also been a national correspondent for *The Atlantic*, a contributing editor of *The New Republic*, a political columnist for Reuters, a columnist for NFL.com, an editor of *Washington Monthly*, a contributing editor to *Newsweek* and to *U.S. News and World Report*, a distinguished fellow of the Fulbright Foundation, a visiting fellow of the Brookings Institution, a bartender, a bus driver and a used-car salesman.

HALEY SWEETLAND EDWARDS is an editor at *Washington Monthly*. Previously, she reported from the Middle East and the South Caucasus for the *Los Angeles Times*, *The Atlantic*, *The New Republic*, *Foreign Policy*, and other publications. She began her career as a reporter at the *Seattle Times* and is a graduate of Yale University and the Columbia University Graduate School of Journalism.

JESSE EISINGER writes a regular column for the *New York Times* Dealbook. He is also a senior reporter at *ProPublica*, covering Wall Street and finance. He is the author of an e-book, *The Wall Street Money Machine*.

PETER ELKIND is an editor at large at *Fortune* magazine and an award-winning investigative reporter. Elkind is coauthor of the national bestseller *The Smartest Guys in the Room: The Amazing Rise and Scandalous Fall of Enron*, author of *The Death Shift: The True Story of Nurse Genene Jones and the Texas Baby Murders*, and author of *Client Nine: The Rise and Fall of Eliot Spitzer*. He has written for the *New York Times Magazine* and the *Washington Post*, was an associate editor at *Texas Monthly*, and is a former editor of the *Dallas Observer*.

ANDREA ELLIOTT is an investigative reporter for the *New York Times*. Her three-part series, "An Imam in America," was awarded the 2007 Pulitzer Prize.

JONAH ENGLE is a freelance reporter whose work has focused on drug policy.

Brothers **STEVE FAINARU** and **MARK FAINARU-WADA** wrote the book *The League of Denial*, on which the *Frontline* documentary was based, as ESPN reporters. Both have won awards for work done for other outlets, including Steve Fainaru's Pulitzer for International Reporting in 2008 for his coverage of the war in Iraq for the *Washington Post* and the honors Mark Fainaru-Wada won for his reporting for the *San Francisco Chronicle* on banned sports supplements and the Bay Area Laboratory Cooperative (BALCO).

SUSAN FALUDI is a contributing editor of *The Baffler* and the author of *Backlash: The Undeclared War Against American Women* and, most recently, *The Terror Dream: Myth and Misogyny in an Insecure America*.

JEFF GERTH, an investigative reporter whose honors have included the Pulitzer Prize and the George Polk Award, is a senior reporter for *ProPublica*. He is a former *New York Times* investigative reporter.

JIM GILMORE is a writer and producer for PBS *Frontline*.

JOHN GRAVOIS is deputy editor of *Pacific Standard* magazine and was previously an editor and writer at *Washington Monthly*, a magazine of politics, policy, and ideas in the nation's capital. Before that, he was a senior editor of The Review, a weekly ideas and culture supplement to *The National* newspaper in Abu Dhabi; a staff writer at *The Chronicle of Higher Education*; a researcher at the New America Foundation; and a reporter at the *Cambodia Daily*.

KIRSTEN GRIND is a financial writer for the *Wall Street Journal* and author of *The Lost Bank*, about the collapse of Washington Mutual, a savings and loan association that was the nation's largest bank failure.

SANDY HINGSTON is a senior editor at *Philadelphia* magazine.

BEN JUDAH is the author of *Fragile Empire: How Russia Fell In and Out of Love With Vladimir Putin*.

LUCY KELLAWAY is an associate editor and management columnist for the *Financial Times*. Her most recent book is *Office Hours*, a novel about workplace romance.

Award-winning documentary filmmaker **MICHAEL KIRK** has produced more than 200 national television programs. A former Nieman Fellow in Journalism at Harvard University, Kirk was the senior producer of *Frontline* from the series' inception in 1983 until the fall of 1987, when he created his own production company, the Kirk Documentary Group.

MICHAEL KRANISH is Washington Bureau deputy chief of the *Boston Globe*, author of *Flight from Monticello: Thomas Jefferson at War*, and coauthor of biographies of Mitt Romney and John Kerry.

A contributing editor of *Rolling Stone*, **DAVID KUSHNER** has written for publications including *The New Yorker*, *Vanity Fair*, *Wired*, the *New York Times Magazine*, *New York*, *GQ*, and *Playboy*. His books include *Masters of Doom*, *Jonny Magic and the Card Shark Kids*, *Levittown*, *Jacked*, and *The Bones of Marianna*.

STEVE LEVINE is *Quartz*'s Washington correspondent, focusing on the intersection of energy, technology, and geopolitics. His books include *The Oil and the Glory: The Pursuit of Empire and Fortune on the Caspian Sea*.

JANE MAYER joined *The New Yorker* as a staff writer in March 1995. Based in Washington, D.C., she writes about politics for the magazine and has been covering the war on terror. Before joining *The New Yorker*, Mayer was for twelve years a reporter at the *Wall Street Journal*. In 1984, she became the *Journal*'s first female White House correspondent. Mayer is the author of the best-selling 2008 book *The Dark Side: The Inside Story of How the War on Terror Turned Into a War on American Ideals*, *Strange Justice*, and *Landslide: The Unmaking of the President, 1984–1988*.

T. CHRISTIAN MILLER is a senior reporter for *ProPublica*. The former *Los Angeles Times* reporter and bureau chief's awards include the Selden Ring Award for Investigative Reporting and the Investigative Reporters and Editors award for online reporting.

EVGENY MOROZOV is contributing editor at *The New Republic* and the author of *The Net Delusion: The Dark Side of Internet*

Freedom and *To Save Everything, Click Here: The Folly of Technological Solutionism.*

MICHAEL MOSS is an investigative reporter for the *New York Times* who won a Pulitzer Prize for Explanatory Reporting for his work on the dangers of contaminated meat.

MATTHEW O'BRIEN is a former senior associate editor at *The Atlantic*, covering business and economics. He is the author of *Beneath the Neon: Life and Death in the Tunnels of Las Vegas*, a book about homeless people living underground.

KEVIN ROOSE covers business and technology for *New York* magazine and the Daily Intelligencer Blog. He is the author of the best-selling *Young Money*, about the world of young Wall Street bankers, and *The Unlikely Disciple*, a memoir about spending a semester undercover at Jerry Falwell's Liberty University.

DANIELLE SACKS is a senior writer at *Fast Company* who has written many profiles for the magazine. She received the New York Press Club's Nelly Bly award in 2006.

NICHOLAS SHAXSON is a British author and journalist and a part-time writer for the Tax Justice Network. He is best known for his investigative books *Poisoned Wells* (2007) and *Treasure Islands* (2011).

ROBERT SMITH is a correspondent for NPR's *Planet Money*, where he reports on how the global economy is affecting our lives.

REBECCA SOLNIT is the author of *Motion Studies: Time, Space, and Eadweard Muybridge*, about technological change in the nineteenth century.

ASHLEE VANCE a feature writer covering technology for Bloomberg *Businessweek*. He has written for the *New York Times*, *The Economist*, and *The Register*.

LIAM VAUGHAN and **GAVIN FINCH** are reporters for Bloomberg News in London. **BOB IVRY** is a reporter for Bloomberg News in New York.

MIKE WISER is a producer and writer for *Frontline*.

JIA LYNN YANG is a staff writer at the *Washington Post* who covers policy and business. Before joining the *Post*, she worked at *Fortune* magazine.

Former Heard on the Street columnist **GREGORY ZUCKERMAN** is a special writer for the *Wall Street Journal*, focusing on big financial trades, hedge funds, and private equity funds among other major business and investing issues.

Permissions